Market Dynamics and Entry

Market Dynamics and Entry

P.A. Geroski

BLACKWELL
Oxford UK & Cambridge USA

P. A. Geroski is hereby identified as author of this work in accordance with
Section 77 of the Copyright, Designs and Patents Act 1988.

First published 1991

Basil Blackwell Ltd
108 Cowley Road, Oxford, OX4 1JF, UK

Basil Blackwell, Inc.
3 Cambridge Center
Cambridge, Massachusetts 02142, USA

Library of Congress Cataloging in Publication Data

Geroski, Paul.
    Market dynamics and entry / P. A. Geroski.
       p.   cm.
    Includes bibliographical references and index.
    ISBN 0-631-15554-6 : $50.00
    1. Barriers to entry (Industrial organization) — Econometric models.
    2. Industrial organization (Economic theory) — Econometric models.
    3. Competition — Econometric models.   4. Efficiency,
    Industrial — Econometric models.   I. Title.
    HD2756.5.G474   1991
    338.6'042 — dc20   91–454
                                                              CIP

British Library Cataloguing in Publication Data

A CIP catalogue record for this book is available from the British Library.

Typeset in 10 on 12 pt Times
by Colset Pte Ltd, Singapore
Printed in Great Britain

This book is printed on acid-free paper.

For Abby, Alice and Rosa

Contents

List of Tables

List of Figures

Acknowledgements

This book effectively began with a grant from the Economic and Social Science Research Council (ESRC) that enabled me to collect some hitherto unavailable data on entry into UK manufacturing industries, and provided me with the support necessary to analyse that data. Participation in two major international comparisons studies sponsored by the Social Science Research Centre Berlin (WZB) – one on the persistence of profits organized by Dennis Mueller, and one on entry organized by Joachim Schwalbach and myself – provided enormous stimulation, and both projects affected the course that my research took in numerous important ways. Nevertheless, the book has taken more time to research and write than I like to admit, and it probably would never have been finished without the kind and very generous support of the Centre for Business Strategy and its director, John Kay.

Much of my own research on entry has gone into this work, and it is a pleasure to thank both Jim Fairburn and Saadet Toker for the very excellent research assistance that they provided over a number of years. It is also a pleasure to thank various co-authors – including Andy Murfin, Daid Encaoua, John Cubbin, Richard Gilbert, Alexis Jacquemin, Richard Pomroy, Rob Masson, Steve Davies, Saadet Toker and Tassos Vlassopoulos – for the pleasure that I had in working with them on some of the projects discussed in the book, and for what they taught me about the subject. The manuscript has undergone a number of changes over the years, and many people have sparked major revisions unknowingly. All or part of the penultimate draft was read by a number of people, and I am obliged to Dennis Mueller, Mark Roberts, John Scott, Hiro Odagiri, Steve Davies and Steve Klepper in particular for their comments, suggestions and encouragement. The many changes that have occurred over time in the manuscript have been typed and corrected by a number of people, and I am obliged to Katherine Thomas, Lisa Simpson, Tracy Mossman and, most of all, Sue Frost for their good-humoured assistance. At the end of the day, however, the usual disclaimer applies.

Last but not least, I should like to dedicate this book to my mother, my partner and my daughter. None of the three had any direct impact on its construction, but they would have been/are/will be pleased to see the finished product.

1

Introduction

Theory came to industrial organization in the middle to late 1970s, enriching some areas of the subject and revolutionizing others. In general, theorists work with fairly stylized models of the phenomena that interest them, and those working in the general area of microeconomics and industrial organization have been no different from any others in this respect. Given the rather static nature of economic theory, this means that many of their models have explored the properties of some steady state or equilibrium configuration of interest. The conceptual experiment that these models describe is a comparison between two equilibria similar but for some particular exogenous variable. Very little interest is ever evinced about the process by which a market might move from one of these equilibria to the other.

Applied economists, on the other hand, have rather less choice in how they structure their work since they are concerned with describing and explaining what they observe. The experiments that they work with are the actual, observed changes in variables of interest induced by uncontrolled changes in a range of (observed and unobserved) exogenous variables. Since what one observes about markets is the way that they respond to shocks, describing and explaining what one observes requires one to study market dynamics. Applied economists are therefore interested as much in the processes by which change occurs as they are in hypothetical steady states that would emerge were all changes to work themselves out fully.

Empirical work in industrial organization, however, has traditionally taken its lead from theory, and applied economists have often tried to make inferences about steady states by observing certain variables of interest (e.g. prices, profits and so on) in different settings (e.g. in more or less concentrated markets), usually in the name of performing hypothesis tests about the characteristics of some steady state (e.g. that prices are higher the more concentrated a market is). Interesting as these exercises are, they are as limited in scope as the theory that drives them. After all, the proposition that prices in highly concentrated markets are higher in equilibrium than they would be were the market to be more competitive does not imply that the immediate consequence of an increase in the level of concentration in any market will be an increase in price. To explore what will happen as a market concentrates, one must know something about how the process of monopolization affects prices. If, for example, monopolization occurs as the result of a predatory price war, then prices will be observed to decline (at least in the short run) as the market concentrates. Monopoly created by merger, on the other hand, may have quite a different effect on prices.

In fact, interest in testing hypotheses about the properties of various equilibria has led many applied economists away from exploring the disequilibrium dynamics that are an integral part of the process by which the data have been generated. In particular, industrial organization economists who are anxious to perform rigorous tests of theory typically use cross-section data on a group of firms or industries as the basis for their empirical analysis. Such 'experiments' are a reasonable way to mimic the comparative statics methodology of the theory that generated the testable hypotheses only if the observables differ from their long-run equilibrium values randomly. This is not an obviously appealing assumption, and a richer, better balanced methodology might start by gathering – and then analysing – the kind of data that one needs to check its usefulness (e.g. panel data). The dilemma here is that once one brings a times series dimension to the data, one necessarily introduces 'events' that are interesting but not explicable by the theory at hand. More generally, although the need to structure empirical work around carefully specified hypotheses is indispensable to the development of any subject, theory-driven empirical work can often be rather blinkered. Not only are methods of testing straitjacketed by the methodology of theorizing, but, more prosaically, the pool of testable hypotheses that provides the engine of a subject's development is limited by both the imagination and the analytical skill of theorists. If, as occasionally happens, they are cut off from the data and become inward looking, then empirical work will suffer.

It seems reasonable, therefore, to insist that some attempt be made to restore the balance between testing the properties of various equilibria and exploring the characteristics of disequilibrium dynamics. If theory cannot help to structure one's thinking about market dynamics, then it is not unreasonable to start by letting the data do some of the work. The use of inductive methods to help generate useful information on phenomena of interest is a defensible (if rather unfashionable) methodology, and recent applied work in many areas of economics has been driven by a concern to develop parsimonious statistical models that reflect the salient features of particular data sets. Such work occasionally throws up interesting tests of hypotheses that can be associated with particular theoretical models, but that is often not the major concern and the hypotheses tested are often not very fine. More commonly, such empirical work throws up puzzles which stimulate the development of theory in new directions, opening up a broad range of new hypotheses for further testing.

The subject of new entry into markets is one where economists have developed rather simple theories based on a very static view of markets. Entry is often thought of in engineering terms as an 'error correction mechanism', as part of a system of more or less automatic feedback that keeps markets in (or near) equilibrium. In some ways, the epitome of this line of thinking is 'contestability theory' (e.g. Baumol et al., 1982), which describes the conditions in which the mere threat of entry effectively disciplines incumbents. Indeed, the interest of many theorists in the role that actual or potential entry plays in markets is often incidental to a more general interest in questions about the characteristics of different long-run equilibria. The recent development of models of strategic behaviour has also stimulated interest in entry without, however, broadening this rather static conception of its role in market processes (for recent surveys, see Gilbert, 1989; Geroski et al., 1990; Tirole, 1988, and others; Jacquemin, 1987, takes a rather broader view). Models of strategic entry deterrence usually take the form of gladiatorial contests between an 'insider' and an 'outsider' to the market, two shining knights whose presence on the competitive stage is given and whose attributes mainly derive from the fact that they are either incumbents in the market or new to it. However interesting the models themselves are, the questions asked are the same, namely what are the properties of the equilibrium that results from such contests given a certain configuration of exogenous variables.

The thesis of this book is that entry can often play a more significant, more important role in the evolution of markets than the view of entry as an error correction mechanism suggests. It is a thesis that is driven less by a particular line of theory than by an intuition which has emerged after sifting through a number of case studies and regression results. My goal in writing the book is neither that of revolutionizing theory (much less of breaking the static mind set that shapes the thinking of many economists), nor that of fundamentally reorienting empirical work (much less of halting cross-section regression analysis). Rather, I hope to do no more than broaden our thinking about entry, and put the classical conception of entry as an error correction mechanism into a somewhat broader perspective about how markets function, and the role that entry plays in their evolution. Further, I hope to do this in a way that stimulates interest in – and enhances the respectability of – more inductive methods of study in economics.

My method will be that recently described as the 'consilience of induction', a strategy of co-ordinating or weaving together a wide range of disparate results from many different sources (Gould, 1989, p. 282). Although many of the individual studies that I will cite take the form of traditional hypothesis tests, weaving them together will, I hope, produce rather more than a list of theories or models with (or without) empirical certification credentials. The target that I am aiming at is the conceptions and presumptions that economists hold about entry, and the criteria to be used for evaluating these conceptions and presumptions is consilience, a term used 'to designate the confidence gained when many independent sources "conspire" to indicate a particular . . . pattern'. Aiming at this kind of target requires that some attention be paid to structuring the presentation of the argument. Since one cannot present all the evidence that one has seen, one must necessarily be selective. However, undue selectivity can undermine confidence in the generality of what one is trying to argue. Because the power of the evidence for particular arguments relies as much on quantity of studies as it does on the quality of any one of them, I have opted to mention many of the cases or econometric studies that I have found, but not to discuss most of them in any depth. Several early readers have argued that too many short citations make for a dull read, and I have tried to go some way towards meeting this objection. A second risk of adopting a policy of generous citations is that inadvertent omissions are doubly wounding, and I should like to apologize in advance for any sins of this type.

If this voyage of discovery does yield anything of value, it will be because I have been able to juxtapose simple versions of the presumptions and theories that many economists use to think about entry with the facts in a way that creates some doubt or perplexity about the subject. Of course, not all our thinking is as simple as the models that I shall use, and not all of the facts that I shall cite are as hard as one would like them to be. Further, much of what I have to say is well known and has been thoroughly digested. Nevertheless, I have some hopes that the reader will emerge with a sense that there is much that we have observed which we do not address in our models, and that some of what we do address in our models does not square very well with what we observe. If the reader emerges better informed but less satisfied than she/he once was with her/his understanding of the subject, then it will have been worth the effort.

Plan of the Book

The book consists of five main chapters that discuss various facets of the subject, followed by a sixth chapter of a more speculative character that tries to develop a broader perspective on the data discussed in the first five chapters.

The most natural place to start is with the raw data on entry into markets, and this is the subject matter of chapter 2. Entry can be measured in a number of ways – by the gross number of new firms that appear in a market each year or by the number of new firms net of exit, by market penetration in first or subsequent years post-entry, by the number or penetration of different types of entrant, and so on – and an inspection of a number of different measures of entry turns out to be rather suggestive. Entry and exit rates are very highly positively correlated, and, while most markets host a fairly large number of entrants year by year, not many of these entrants survive for very long or prosper during their short lives. It is the dynamics of turnover as much as it is the dynamics of post-entry market penetration that attract one's attention in the raw data. Entry seems to be less a process by which industry supply is expanded than it is a process by which certain types of firms come to populate the market. Further, although potential entrants are often not observable, there do seem to be systematic waves of entrant types into markets, and this pattern of entry by type can often be used to make inferences about the size and characteristics of the pool of putative competitors that surround markets.

Of course, one can only look so long at unstructured raw data without descending into the realms of pure fantasy, and the next natural step is to try to model what one observes. This is the subject of chapter 3, which contains four types of model. The first and most simple type of model that one can use to interpret the data is concerned with whether entry occurs or not; that is, with modelling the incidence of entry. Slightly more demanding and certainly more dynamic in character are models of market penetration by entrants. At their best and most elaborate, such models subsume entry into the broader picture of market share mobility that results from competition in the market. However natural and attractive they are in principle, models of incidence and models of penetration both fail in practice to come to grips with what do seem to be two interesting features of the data, namely the enormous apparently unsystematic variation in entry flows and the enormous turnover amongst firms at the bottom of the size distribution that entry induces in most markets. Taking seriously the 'noise' in entry flows inevitably leads one to think about the character of the apparently transitory shocks that affect entrants, and autoregressive models of entry – the third type of model that we shall discuss – are a natural tool to use to evaluate the effects of transitory shocks. What one needs to account for the phenomena of turnover are models of selection – models that describe the competition for places in the market that occurs amongst entrants (and smaller incumbents). Although it cannot be said that the literature has provided many of these, those that have emerged are the fourth type of model addressed in the chapter.

Interest in entry is often dominated by interest in its consequences, and these are examined in chapters 4–6. In the short run, entry often has an effect on market outcomes during the path of transition from one equilibrium to another. If, for example, entry barriers fall, then either the prospect or the actual fact of entry will affect pricing (and other) decisions made by incumbent firms, and so affect profits. Indeed, the effect that entry has on prices or profits during the transition to a new equilibrium depends in part on how incumbents react to the threat or fact of entry. That is, both the volume of entry and its effects on market performance are, in a sense, jointly determined by the strategic actions of incumbents. One way or the other, variations in industry performance will be observed over time, and the discussion in chapter 4 concentrates on measuring the size of these effects and establishing their general character.

In the long run, the effect of entry on markets depends on the height of barriers to entry. Calculating the height of entry barriers involves identifying their source and working out what would happen were they to be eliminated. Such calculations are counterfactual in nature, and their inherently conjectural character is much amplified by the fact that barriers are entrant specific and their effects can be strategically affected by incumbents. This maze of issues is the subject of the discussion in chapter 5. Taken together with the results discussed in chapter 4, one emerges with a sense that the effect of entry on profits is, in general, rather modest in both the short and long run. If entry is the primary method by which markets eliminate excess profits, then at least one reasonably natural reading of the data suggests that it is an instrument with rather modest and uncertain effects. This conclusion seems consistent with what chapter 2 reveals about the performance of most entrants in the markets that they invade, but it raises some worries about whether it is all very worthwhile.

Of course, entry may have other more subtle effects on markets. Indeed, those who emerge from chapter 2 using a natural selection metaphor to describe the raw data on entry and turnover will find themselves tempted to push that metaphor for all it is worth. In particular, the interesting feature about selection processes in natural settings is that they are an agent of change, a method by which a species searches out and discovers the best fit possible with a changing environment. Chapter 6 takes up this theme and looks at the effects that entry has on productive efficiency and innovation in markets. Here the evidence is particularly sketchy, but what little we have suggests that entry can often play a fairly important – if rather selective – role. Entrants are often directly or indirectly responsible for much innovative activity, and the modest effects that they appear to have on profits often masks a rather more profound effect that they can have on costs. More interesting (and, needless to say, more speculative), these effects often seem to vary in their intensity over the product life cycle.

One is drawn in the end to the view that entry is part and parcel of a selection process that occurs in markets. In a sense, one backs into this kind of conclusion as much as one plunges into it. The most palpable consequence of the large flow of entry that occurs in most markets is displacement and exit, and one can often observe this process occurring hand in hand with the introduction of new products, with a change in the composition of entry barriers, and with spurts of productivity growth. By contrast, one often has some difficulty in observing much in the way of systematic disequilibrium dynamics (such as the movement of margins towards their long-run equilibrium levels) associated with entry flows, and if entry does have an impact on prices in a market, much of the effect often materializes because the arrival of major entry challenges stimulates incumbent firms to improve their productivity performance and lower their costs. Entry is, then, one of several methods by which markets restructure themselves, but the evidence suggests that the role that entry plays in restructuring markets is selective. One can often see major effects associated with entry early in the evolution of markets, one frequently observes them in mature markets, and one occasionally notices the same kind of effects in microcosm during major cyclical upswings. The market dynamics associated with entry are not, it appears, so much those associated with changes in the *size of the population* of firms or products in a market as they are those associated with *changes in the population characteristics* of firms or products; that is, market dynamics are not so much a move to some specific equilibrium defined by a specific set of characteristics as they are a drift between different equilibrium configurations.

The metaphor of natural selection is one that economists frequently use, but in a way that contrasts sharply with the use made of it by ecologists. For an economist, natural selection is an equilibrating force, one that keeps a market at its steady state; for an ecologist, natural selection is the force that drives the co-evolution of a species and its environment and, indeed, that helps to encourage speciation. Pushing the metaphor of competition as a selection process in this rather unfamiliar direction leads one to think about entry and industry evolution as an interrelated process, and to ask how market structure, conduct and performance interact over time and whether they do so in a path-dependent manner. Chapter 7 concludes the book in a frankly speculative fashion by considering the role of entry in industry evolution, and the nature of the competitive selection processes that occur more widely within industries.

2

Entry Rates and Market Penetration

Introduction

The entry of new competitors into a market is an event that is generally thought likely to have a number of beneficial effects. For economists, these include bidding down prices and eliminating excess profits, reducing x-inefficiency and stimulating innovation and technical progressivity. A market subject to entry challenges is generally thought likely to be efficient, flexible and, by and large, operating in consumers' best interests. More broadly, entry and small firm formation are often associated with visions of self-reliant individuals setting up on their own and making good, visions that resonate with deeply held democratic values and ideals of individual freedom. A society where individuals are able to follow their own initiatives, where the modest are free to try their hand at challenging the mighty, is often thought to be one where individuals can realize their full potential.

Although it is possible to have too much of a good thing, many people who have thought about the subject are inclined to suspect that, if anything, too little entry occurs in most markets. There are at least three reasons, however, why evaluating this presumption is rather difficult, even if one sticks to narrow economic criteria and focuses on market performance. First, 'too little' can mean a variety of things, and, needless to say, it begs the question of what is 'too much'. Entry is occasionally thought to involve too few firms, or, more often, too few firms interested in more than establishing a small foothold in a narrow, highly specialized market niche. Complaints about a lack of entrants may reflect a concern with the lack of new broad line, high volume producers willing to present a serious challenge to market leaders. 'Too little' also frequently means 'too late' or 'too slow', the latter referring either to arrival rates, subsequent penetration speeds or both. 'Too little entry' may mean that markets adapt too sluggishly to change, and that incumbents lack the incentive to act with the alacrity that a regular flow of capable entrants might create. Finally, 'too little' is occasionally used with reference to net entry, carrying the implication that entry may cause too much turnover and exit. 'Too little' in this case may mean that too few entrants survive long enough to matter.

Second, entry itself can be defined in a variety of ways. Classical definitions of entry insist on restricting attention to new firms building new plant and installing new equipment (e.g. Bain, 1956, p. 7). However, entry by foreign-based producers through imports, entry by acquisition of an old-established firm or even entry by new managers effecting a thorough-going management shake-up in an existing firm all may have much the same effects on the competitive process as entry more narrowly defined. That is, entry might usefully be thought of in terms of new sources of supply, regardless of whether this involves new sources of production. Indeed, there is no obvious reason to think that new ideas are any less important than new firms are in creating the effects generally associated with entry. If the essence of a firm is a core of routines or operating procedures (e.g. Nelson and Winter, 1982), then a new routine in an old bottle can have substantively the same effects as a new routine in a new bottle. Further, entry through acquisition may provide most of the benefits of entry without running the risk of generating excess capacity. Thus, an apparently low rate of new firm formation may – or may not – indicate that 'too little' entry is occurring, depending on the type and level of merger activity, managerial turnover and so on that occurs in the market.

Third and perhaps most substantively, entry does not necessarily have to occur in order to have an effect on market performance. To the extent that entry is relatively easy and that entrants can commence operations quickly, then the number of actual competitors in a market is likely to substantially understate the number of effective competitors on hand. If markets are surrounded by hordes of eager potential entrants, then any tendency by incumbents to raise prices above costs or let the efficiency of their operations slide will result in instantaneous entry by other agents (if the market is contestable). Incumbents will, of course, be aware of this, and those interested in maintaining their place in the market will take steps to foreclose entry possibilities, keeping prices down to the level of best practice marginal costs. The effects on market performance will be the same as if entry occurred, and, as a bonus, they will materialize without all the noise and inconvenience (from the point of view of incumbents) of actual entry. It follows, then, that the actual flow of entry into a market may be quite small but still be more than enough. That is, actual entry flows may seriously mis-state the competitive pressures that entrants present to incumbents, and 'too little' actual entry may not matter much if potential competitors are numerous.

Thus, what can be read from the raw data on the flows of new firms into markets is distinctly limited. The sense in which 'too few' or 'too many' entrants appear cannot be established without examining the nature of the market and the kinds of structural factors which underlie the equilibria that are observed. Entry in the sense of change – of new ideas or innovations – is unlikely to be accurately reflected in figures on new firms building new plants, and, indeed, what may matter more from the point of view of market performance is potential entry. Data on the number of new firms (or on the market share that they achieve) do not reveal how many firms (actual competitors or those in the queue of potential entrants) they displace and, even more important, how long they stay in the industry. Large numbers of firms rapidly passing through a revolving door at the bottom of the industry size distribution is, in a real sense, not high entry so much as high turnover. Yet, given all of those caveats, it is important to start any examination of entry with a look at the raw data, and the question of 'is there too much entry?' is as useful a way to start the ball rolling as any. Even if 'what ought to be' cannot be directly read off 'what is', describing a phenomenon is the necessary first step in any attempt to explain and, ultimately, to evaluate it.

Our exploration of the raw data proceeds in three stages. We start by summarizing what is known about how much entry occurs in markets, about the rate of entry and about the extent of market penetration by entrants. One of the salient features of the data is the sheer variability in entry rates, net and gross, and in entry penetration that one observes over time and across industries. This poses challenges that will be discussed more extensively in chapter 3. A second salient feature of the data is the high positive correlation that exists between entry and exit, and this leads us to examine the survival rates of entrants and to track their post-entry performance over time. One emerges from inspecting these data thinking that the turnover among firms caused by entry feeds a selection process that discriminates between different types of entrant. The second stage of our examination of the data follows directly from this observation, and focuses on the characteristics and ultimate market success of different types of new competitors. The distinction between actual and potential entry plus ample case study evidence suggesting that different types of entrant arrive in markets at different times means that an understanding of the selection between entrants for a place in the market requires one to understand the process that brings entrants to a market.

This constitutes the third stage of our examination of the data. The picture that emerges is that markets develop from other markets and then from within, first drawing entrants from related industries and then generating new entrants themselves. The result can often appear as a succession of waves of entry, each wave carrying a somewhat different type of entrant to the market's shores.

The Extent of Entry in Markets

There are at least four different ways that one can measure the extent of entry into a market. Most simply, one can count the number of new firms, perhaps expressing the total as a percentage of the existing stock of incumbents to get a measure of the incidence of entry. A possibly more meaningful measure of entry might weight each entrant by its size relative to the market, producing a measure of market penetration when summed over all entrants. Entry, however, inevitably induces exit, and it can therefore be important to distinguish net from gross entry rates, or net from gross entry penetration. Finally, one might measure entry by concentrating only on those firms that survive the initial period of entry. In what follows, we shall examine the extent of entry into markets in each of these four senses.

The Incidence of Entry

At first sight, most markets appear to be absolutely deluged by entry. In the UK over the period 1974–9, an average of about 50 new firms entered each of 87 three-digit manufacturing industries per year. Table 2.1 presents some descriptive statistics on both the number of entrants and the entry rate (the number of entrants expressed as a percentage of the total number of firms) for this sample. Although the most striking feature of the data is the large number of new firms created per year, it is also interesting to note that the gradually worsening economic climate of the 1970s in the UK saw a decline in the average number of entrants per industry. It seems plain that this was due both to a steep rise in the number of industries that experienced no entry (more than a third of the total in 1979) and to a diminished flow in those industries that actually experienced entry. Much the same fall-off in entry can be observed when the data are expressed in terms of entry rates. The average entry rate over the period was about 6.5%, a figure which hides a sharp decline from the 14.5% rate recorded in 1974 to 2% in 1979. Not only do entry rates vary substantially across industries and over time, they also vary at somewhat

Table 2.1 Number of entrants and entry rates in the UK[a]
(a) Numbers of entrants (gross)

	Mean	Standard deviation	Coefficient of variation	Maximum	Zero count[b]
1974	95.73	117.89	1.23	599	7
1975	62.29	110.92	1.78	727	16
1976	58.13	108.75	1.87	877	11
1977	35.55	69.67	1.96	545	23
1978	31.09	58.96	1.90	435	26
1979	17.69	30.64	1.73	220	33
Average, 1974–9	50.08	82.81	1.70	567	193

(b) Entry rates (gross)

	Mean	Standard deviation	Maximum
1974	0.1445	0.0613	0.3609
1975	0.0771	0.0466	0.2143
1976	0.0690	0.0378	0.2008
1977	0.0430	0.0332	0.2273
1978	0.0342	0.0253	0.1227
1979	0.0205	0.0190	0.0959
Average, 1974–9	0.0647	0.0372	0.2037

[a] For a sample of 87 three-digit industries. The data were generated by comparing adjacent Censuses of Production, identifying new enterprises and those no longer in operation. The rate is defined as the ratio of entrants to the total number of enterprises.
[b] Number of industries with three or fewer entrants.

different rates over time across industries. Table 2.2 shows the cross-industry correlation in entry rates over time to be positive but fairly modest, indicating a lack of synchronization in the ebb and flow of new firm formation over time in different industries.

The same high variation over time in entry rates is evident in Canada, although it has apparently been somewhat less systematic than in the UK. Annual entry rates (at the four-digit industry level) rose from 3.39% in 1971 to a peak of 5.5% in 1974, fell to 1.84% in 1977, rose to 10.34% in 1978 and then levelled off in the 3–6% range through to 1984 (e.g. Baldwin and Gorecki, 1986). At the maximum in 1978, an average of 2048 new firms appeared per industry; at the minimum in 1977, the mean

Table 2.2   The inter-industry correlation in gross entry rates in the UK

	1974	1975	1976	1977	1978
1974	1.00000				
1975	0.48180	1.00000			
1976	0.52489	0.47404	1.00000		
1977	0.54564	0.54111	0.52191	1.00000	
1978	0.43367	0.22464	0.48925	0.26566	1.00000
1979	0.37234	0.29290	0.26442	0.33404	0.43199

The same sample was used as in table 2.1.

number of new firms was 337. Over time, these annual rates add up to impressive totals of new entrants. From 1971 to 1984, a total of 14,358 new firms appeared on average in each industry, and 33% of the firms active in 1979 entered their host industry after 1970. In the USA, average entry rates over the four five-year time periods beteen 1963 and 1982 were 41.4%, 51.6%, 51.8% and 51.7% across a sample of 387 four-digit industries (see the working paper version of Dunne et al., 1988; in the published paper, aggregate values were replaced by averages across four-digit industries). As the total population of firms was 265,599 in 1967, this translates into about 96,000 new firms, or about 250 per four-digit industry. A quarter of all such industries had entry rates less than 25% and a half had entry rates between 25% and 50%. On average, 42% of the firms in each Census industry were not producing in that industry in the previous Census. Fragments of the same picture have also been thrown up by a range of other country studies. The entry rate in Portugal over the four-year period 1983–6 was 49%, annual rates in Belgium for 1980–4 averaged 5.5–6.0%, the cumulative rate in West Germany over the three-year period 1983–5 was 11.5%, annual rates in Norway fell in the 7.5–10.3% range over the period 1980–5, three-year rates in Korea over the period 1976–81 averaged about 10% and annual rates in France ranged between 10% and 15% between 1985 and 1987 (Geroski, 1990c: see also Cable and Schwalbach, 1991, for some international comparisons).

   The observation that entry rates vary over time naturally leads one to ask whether they do so pro- or counter-cyclically. This question is difficult to answer on purely *a priori* grounds. On the one hand, most markets are bound to be more attractive during a boom, but, on the other hand, most entrants are small-scale, virtually one-person operations, and the relevant opportunity costs for most entrepreneurs is the market wage. This too moves pro-cyclically. Thus, in a boom, demand side factors encourage entry, but increasing market wages restrict the supply of players to some degree; during a recession, supply expands as unemployment becomes a real alternative to self-employment for many putative entrepreneurs. The net effect is therefore ambiguous.

Unfortunately, the evidence on this question is not wholly clear either. Certainly, small firms generally prospered at the expense of large firms during the recessions of the 1970s (e.g. Storey and Johnson, 1987). More directly, figures 2.1 and 2.2 display aggregate entry (the number of new firms) in the UK for two measures of entry (Census-based measures for manufacturing and VAT registrations covering all firms) plotted against aggregate unemployment. Both show a fairly clear negative correlation, suggesting that entry is pro-cyclical. Exit (not shown) was highly co-linear with entry, displaying the same degree of pro-cyclicality and leaving net entry largely independent of cyclical effects. Yamawaki (1991) examined the response of net entry for a panel of Japanese industries to industry-specific and aggregate demand fluctuations, finding pro-cyclical responses to both (with elasticities in the 1.2–2 range) that varied with

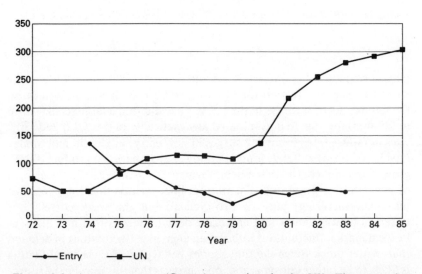

Figure 2.1 Aggregate entry (Census) over time in the UK. The entry data (divided by 100) were obtained by comparing annual Censuses of Production to identify new enterprises.

Source: Special Compilation, Business Statistics Office. The unemployment data (adult employment) are from *Economic Outlook*, Centre of Economic Forecasting, London Business School

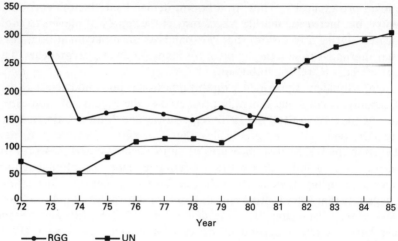

Figure 2.2   Aggregate registrations (VAT) over time in the UK. The registrations data (divided by 100) were obtained by comparing annual VAT registers to identify new firms.

Source: *British Business*, 12 August 1983. The unemployment data are as in table 2.1

market structure. In contrast, Lane and Schary (1989) found little in the way of a cyclical effect on the rate of new business incorporation or on the failure rate of business in the USA. They did find a large secular drop in failure rates, one that dominated any cyclicality in the data, and large rises in failure rates following surges in new entry. Highfield and Smiley (1987), on the other hand, found that lower gross national product (GNP) growth and higher growth in unemployment led to increases in the growth of new US incorporations. The bottom line, then, is that entry (at least into manufacturing) may be pro-cyclical, but the weak correlations observed between entry and aggregate demand means that it is likely to be local market fluctuations rather than aggregate fluctuations in demand that matter most. Since the times series behaviour of these local factors is likely to be rather idiosyncratic, one suspects that this may be the source of much of the apparent noise in the data.

Entry Penetration

Thus, in any given year, up to one in ten firms in any given industry is likely to be new, and, at the end of any five to ten year period, one is likely to observe one new face in two or, perhaps, three. Impressive as these totals are, however, there is a suspicion that they exaggerate the quantitative importance of entry flows. While average entry rates (the number of entrants divided by the total number of firms) varied between 41.4% and 51.7% per five-year period in the USA, average entry penetration (sales by entrants divided by total industry sales) ranged between 13.9% and 18.8% (in 1963–7 and 1967–72 respectively). Although the average entry rate over the four five-year periods between 1963 and 1982 was 49.1%, entry penetration averaged only 16.2%, largely because the average entrant produced ony 24.8% of the output of the average incumbent. Twenty-five per cent of all four-digit industries in the four time periods experienced less than 7% entry penetration, half experienced entry penetration between 7% and 25% and, in three-quarters of all such industries, entrants were less than 50% of the size of the average incumbent (see the working paper version of Dunne et al., 1988). Similarly, in Canada, the 33% of the 1979 population of firms not present in 1970 accounted for only 26% of total shipments in 1979, and the average size of new plants operated by new firms relative to continuing plants of continuing firms was about 60%. The percentage of employment per industry accounted for by new entrants varied between 0.62% and 5.09% over the period 1970–84 (Baldwin and Gorecki, 1986).

Table 2.3 Entry penetration in the UK

	Mean	Standard deviation	Coefficient of variation	Maximum
1974	0.0636	0.0469	0.737	0.1918
1975	0.0255	0.0212	0.831	0.0813
1976	0.0285	0.0261	0.916	0.1190
1977	0.0218	0.0217	0.995	0.1109
1978	0.0186	0.0218	1.172	0.1098
1979	0.0145	0.0170	1.172	0.0680
Average 1974–9	0.0275	0.0258	0.943	0.1135

The same sample was used as for table 2.1. Penetration is defined as the total sales of entrants (new firms identified by comparing adjacent annual Censuses) divided by total industry production plus imports less exports.

Table 2.3 shows various descriptive statistics describing the total sales of all entrants expressed as a percentage of industry sales for 87 three-digit UK industries over the period 1974–9. The overall average was a market penetration of nearly 3% (or 2% neglecting 1974) per industry per annum, a figure which declined fairly systematically throughout the period. As in the USA and Canada, the 'bark' made by the large number of entrants that appear each year far exceeds their 'bite' as measured by market penetration. More interesting is the observation that the size of this bite varies enormously over time in any given industry, as well as across industries at any given time. Certainly, the inter-industry variation in entry penetration rates in this sample was fairly high, with a standard deviation across industries roughly equal to the mean (the standard deviation of entry rates was typically rather larger than its mean). As with entry rates, there seems to be a weak tendency for the (mean-adjusted) inter-industry variation in penetration rates to have risen over time, despite the fact that the range narrowed considerably. This, in turn, suggests that there may be substantial differences across industries in the times series variation in entry. Table 2.4, which shows the correlation of entry penetration across industries over time, provides some substance for this view. As before, it is noticeable that industries do not show persistently high rates of entry over time. In the USA, market penetration showed rather more persistence than entry rates, but, as a comparison of tables 2.2 and 2.4 indicates, this is not true in the UK. The steady decline in mean entry penetration over the period suggests that inter-temporal variations in entry may exceed the cross-section variation displayed in table 2.3, an impression that is reinforced by the results of an analysis of variance on gross entry penetration, net (of exit) entry penetration, gross entry rate and net entry rates across 79 three-digit industries over the period 1975–9. This exercise revealed that the between-industry variation was only 49%, 23%, 24% and 21% respectively of the total variation in the data over time and across industries. In the USA, the corresponding amounts are 52.3%, 30.3%, 43.2% and 31.6% (see Dunne and Roberts, 1991), show-

Table 2.4   The inter-industry correlation in entry penetration across years in the UK

1974	*1975*	*1976*	*1977*	*1978*	*1979*
1974	1				
1975	0.4217	1			
1976	0.5842	0.5087	1		
1977	0.5908	0.4202	0.5923	1	
1978	0.3907	0.4579	0.5579	0.5015	1
1979	0.2922	0.2483	0.2481	0.4376	0.2377

The same sample was used as in table 2.1.

ing slightly more times series persistence, perhaps because of more stable demand conditions across the five-year intervals being compared (the UK data are annual and record a fairly dramatic decline in demand over the period). Either way, entry varies rather more over time within industries than it does across industries at any given time.

It seems natural to pursue these observations one step further and ask how systematic all of this variation is. The correlations shown in tables 2.2 and 2.4 suggest that there are some systematic (possibly moving-average) dynamics in the data, but that these are much weaker than are commonly found in other types of cross-section data. One simple way to access how systematic inter-industry variations in entry are is to examine their correlation over time using autoregressive models of entry rates or penetration on their own history, allowing for industry-specific fixed effects and time trends.[1] Table 2.5 shows four such regressions (one for each of four measures of entry). In each, 158 observations of entry (two stacked 79-industry cross-sections) are explained using 80 dummies (79 industry-specific dummies and a time trend) and four observables (four lagged dependent variables). Although it appears at first sight that a reasonable percentage of the variation in the data has been accounted for in each case, this appearance is misleading. A similar regression involving price–cost margins regularly produces R^2s in excess of 0.90 (e.g. Geroski and Toker, 1988), and this is broadly true of many standard cross-section variables such as concentration, import intensity, and so on. In the case of margins, most of the explanatory work is done by the industry-specific fixed effects, indicating that high margins persist and that there is a large permanent component in margins observed year by year corresponding (one imagines) to permanent structural features of markets (like entry barriers). This is also true in the entry equations shown in table 2.5, but much less so. The estimated fixed effects were virtually all positive, and were sufficiently large to account for the positive correlations between E_t, E_{t-1} and so on shown in tables 2.2 and 2.4 (notwithstanding the negative estimated coefficients on lagged entry shown in table 2.5). They were not able, however, to account for a substantial amount of the variation in the data. Not only is there no large permanent component in entry flows observed year by year across industries, but much of the year by year variation in the data appears to be fairly unsystematic over time. It is, of course, possible that the usual exogenous variables (to be discussed in chapter 3) will be able to account for this variation, but these regressions do suggest that entry is a fairly noisy activity.

One should not, of course, minimize the cross-section variation that does exist in the data, and, pursuant to this, table 2.6 displays entry rates and market penetration at a two-digit level for eight countries over slightly

Table 2.5 Autoregressive models of entry

Definition of entry E_t	Gross penetration	Net penetration	Gross rate	Net rate
Mean of fixed effect	0.0381	−0.0203	0.0335	−0.00057
E_{t-1}	−0.7326	−0.7367	−0.2232	−0.4354
	(6.907)	(12.70)	(4.057)	(8.208)
E_{t-2}	−0.1901	−0.6257	−0.0227	−0.2234
	(1.890)	(6.146)	(0.3996)	(4.222)
E_{t-3}	−0.1080	−0.2587	0.0164	0.0310
	(1.456)	(2.484)	(0.3938)	(0.9021)
E_{t-4}	0.0357	−0.0491	0.0657	0.0205
	(1.005)	(1.608)	(1.975)	(0.5519)
R^2	0.7374	0.7573	0.8162	0.7879
$\bar{R}^2$	0.4420	0.4850	0.6100	0.5500
$F(83, 74)$	2.503	2.781	3.959	3.312

All regressions are for a two-year pool (1979, 1978) regressed at its own history, e.g. on (1978, 1977), (1977, 1976) and so on. All equations include a time dummy and 79 industry-specific fixed effects (not shown); t statistics are given in absolute values in the parentheses.

different time periods. Concentrating first on entry rates, two features of table 2.6 are worth noting. First, the distribution of entry rates across two-digit industries is fairly symmetrical; the mean two-digit entry rate in each country is more or less exactly equal to the median entry rate. Further, in all cases, the standard deviation across industries is rather less than a third of the size of the mean. Although one must be wary about the distortions that aggregating up to two-digit-level industry classifications is likely to produce, the data seem to suggest a fairly even distribution of entry rates in each country, with a smaller number of very high and very low entry observations. Second, there seems to be at least a certain amount of clustering around similar sectors in most countries. The partial correlations between the eight columns in table 2.6 hover around the 0.4 level. Measured in terms of market share, entry is rather lower than when measured by the rate of entry. Across all industries in the eight countries in table 2.6, penetration averaged 2.8% (when all the data were expressed on an annualized basis). In general, high entry – however measured – is to be found in apparel, furniture and instruments.

A brief comparison of tables 2.1 and 2.3 and of the two columns pertaining to each country in table 2.6 suggests a further interesting feature of entry flows, namely that most entrants are extremely small. In 1974,

Table 2.6 Entry rates and penetration at two-digit level

Two-digit US SIC sectors	Belgium		Canada		West Germany		Korea		Norway		Portugal		UK		USA	
20 Food processing	5.1	2.1	30.8	21.4	6.9	5	7.2	2.5	5.2	0.6	47.0	2.8	5.4	2.1	23.9	14.8
21 Tobacco	2.5	1.7	60.6	–	5.1	–	–	–	0.0	0.0	0.0	0.0	–	2.1	20.5	2.6
22 Textiles	4.1	1.8	33.8	26.5	5.8	4.5	10.7	2.8	7.6	0.7	42.0	18	8.4	2.9	37.2	24.4
23 Apparel	5.8	2.6	26.5	27.0	18.9	11.8	15.3	4.9	10.7	1.6	63.0	47	7.4	4.7	40.3	37
24 Lumber	4.5	1.9	43.5	36.2	11.9	7.5	11.6	4.2	7.5	1.1	44.0	27	–	6.0	49.7	41.9
25 Furniture	5.6	2.1	36.4	30.4	14.3	11.9	15.4	6.8	6.5	0.9	53.0	33	6.8	6.0	47.1	36.7
26 Paper	3.3	1.4	37.1	23.6	8.5	4.9	10.0	4.7	3.7	0.3	39.0	15	–	3.0	31.4	15.9
27 Printing	7.8	1.9	27.4	29.5	17.9	7.5	5.2	2.0	9.1	1.4	36.0	19	6.9	3.0	49.0	32.9
28 Chemicals	4.1	1.5	35.9	23.8	12.2	6	10.1	3.5	7.1	0.1	46.0	14	7.4	2.4	32.5	13.2
29 Petroleum and coal	0.7	0.1	43.7	–	13.3	0.3	6.5	2.2	6.0	0.0	66.0	20	3.5	0.1	33.7	23
30 Rubber and plastics	5.7	1.6	51.4	26.4	18.5	7.5	9.0	1.8	7.2	1.3	50.0	33	–	–	43.1	18.9
31 Leather	2.7	0.9	27.3	25	7.4	7.2	4.7	4.2	5.4	0.6	48.0	21	5.7	5.1	29.4	25.2
32 Stone, clay, glass	4.9	1.6	31.7	29.4	9.1	8.5	9.2	5.2	6.7	1.0	43.0	18	6.3	2.8	34.4	18.3
33 Primary metals	3.1	0.4	39.6	13.9	11.6	5.4	11.7	3.7	3.1	0.1	50.0	14	8.9	1.4	31.9	18.2
34 Fabricated metal	5.9	2.1	41.7	35.7	11.2	10.2	12.6	6.3	9.9	2.6	52.0	22	4.9	3.5	42.9	31
35 Non-electrical machinery	3.9	0.9	63.4	32	11.1	6.8	9.8	4.9	11.9	4.1	53.0	20	8.4	10.3	46.5	25.3
36 Electrical machinery	7.6	1.3	44.3	24.5	17.4	6.8	11.7	3.7	11.1	0.9	53.0	27	9.6	2.2	46.1	21.3
37 Transportation equipment	9.3	3.4	35.9	23.8	12.3	7.6	7.3	3.8	8.2	0.9	37.0	13	5.2	1.9	46.5	27.6
38 Instruments	9.2	6.1	–	–	10.5	7.6	9.7	2.0	9.5	3.5	123.0	23	7.8	4.3	60.3	36.8

The left-hand column gives the entry rate (%) by two-digit industry for each country, while the right-hand column gives entry penetration (%). Belgium, means across years 1980–4; Canada, means across period 1971–9; West Germany, means across period 1983–5; Korea, means across two periods, 1976–8 and 1979–81; Norway, means across years 1980–5; Portugal, means across years 1980–5; UK, means across years 1974–9; USA, means across four Census periods 1963–82.

Source: Adapted from Cable and Schwalbach, 1991

roughly 96 firms entered each industry in the UK, but each captured a market share of only about 0.06%. Dividing the amount of entry penetration by the entry rate gives an estimate of the ratio of the average market share of the average entrant in each industry to the average market share of incumbent firms in each industry. Over the period 1974–9, these ratios were 0.44, 0.33, 0.414, 0.508, 0.548 and 0.704, indicating that entrants in the UK were, on average, about a third to half the size of incumbent firms (the mean incumbent is itself typically rather small given the highly skewed distribution of firm sizes in most markets). Further, the decline in both entry rates and entry penetration in the UK seems to have been accompanied by a rise in the relative size of entrants. Similar observations apply in a wide range of other countries. Belgian entrants were 25–30% of the size of incumbents over the period 1980–4, while Norwegian entrants were generally less than a tenth the size of incumbents. Looking at cumulative entry over a three-year period, relative size varies from 40% to 66% in Korea and West Germany respectively. Over four years in Portugal, entrants managed to reach a size that was 30% of that of the average incumbent; over five years, US entrants were 28–32% as large as incumbents (1975–83), while, over ten years, Canadian entrants were 87% of the size of incumbents (e.g. Geroski, 1990c). One concludes that it may take the average entrant at least ten years to reach a size comparable with that of the average incumbent.

It is possible to make a somewhat more precise assessment of the size of entrants in the UK (for the period 1983–4) using data based on registrations for value-added tax (VAT). The vast majority of the entrants observed in a sample of 95 three-digit industries based on these data fell into the size band £18,000–£2,000,000. Between 13% and 17% of entrants in 1983 and 1984 were either smaller in size than £18,000 or larger than £2,000,000. Disclosure rules made it impossible to be more precise than this for the whole sample, but it is possible to hazard some speculative inferences based on 17 non-randomly selected (and unidentified) industries in either 1983 or 1984 that were used for checking the data. In total, these industries hosted 1597 entrants, of which about 15% were less than £18,000 in size, 78% were in the interval £18,001–£500,000, 5% were in the interval £500,001–£2,000,000, and finally 2% were larger than £2,000,000 in size. Although most of the entrants who were outside the £18,000–£2,000,000 size band were very small, firms outside the £18,000–£2,000,000 size band accounted for about 88% of total gross sales by entrants in 1983, and just under 65% in 1984. Thus, the collective market share penetration recorded by the 200 or so entrants who appeared on average each year in each three-digit industry on the VAT register *may* have been largely the work of only a handful of very large firms, and, not surprisingly, entry penetration by firms outside the £18,000–£2,000,000 size band and total entry penetration were highly correlated across industries (see Geroski, 1991, from which these data were drawn).

Entry and Exit

Rather less impressive than gross entry rates are net entry rates (gross entry less gross exit as a percentage of the stock of firms). In France over the period 1985–7, exit rates were slightly larger than entry rates, and the sales accounted for by exitors exceeded that by entrants. Thus, the 6–8% market shares achieved by entrants netted out to a negative net expansion of sales less than 1% in absolute value (Asmussen, 1990). In Canada, an average annual gross entry rate of 4.76% during the period 1970–83 was offset by an average annual exit rate of 5.25%, leaving a slight net reduction in the number of firms over the period as a whole (Baldwin and Gorecki, 1986). Net entry rates did, however, fluctuate year by year. In 1978, for example, 2048 new firms entered the average Canadian four-digit industry while 875 left, leaving a net addition of 1173, or just short of 60% of the gross flow of firms. Although 33% of the 1979 population of Canadian firms accounted for 26% of shipments, they displaced the 43% of the 1970 population that did not survive until 1979, a group that accounted for about 31% of shipments in 1970. Net entry penetration over the period as a whole was therefore negative. In the USA, a gross entry rate of 36.2% over the period 1963–7 was offset by an exit rate of 43.6% and, since entrants were only 88% as large as exitors, net entry penetration was also negative. From 1967 to 1982, net entry rates were 2.7%, 9.6% and 3.1% over the five-year Census periods, all a small fraction of gross entry rates. The net market share penetration of entrants was −0.12%, −0.03% and −0.5% in the three periods. Entry and exit rates were positively correlated across industries, with correlations of the order of 0.3–0.4; entry penetration and exit penetration rates were also positively correlated (but of the order of 0.7–0.8) and correlations in net entry rates across industries were very low (Dunne et al., 1988). Across the three-, four- and five-digit industries that constitute the raw data underlying table 2.6, the correlations between entry and exit rates were as follows: 0.66 (Belgium), 0.039 (Canada), 0.342 (West Germany), 0.350 (Korea, 1979–81), 0.488 (Norway), 0.030 (Portugal), 0.318 (UK) and 0.270 (USA). For market penetration rates, these correlations were 0.161 (Belgium), 0.682 (Canada), 0.572 (West Germany), 0.219 (Norway), 0.17 (Portugal), 0.513 (UK) and 0.52 (USA) (the correlation was not available for Korea; see Cable and Schwalbach, 1991).

The typical industry in the sample of 87 UK industries shown in table

Table 2.7   Net entry penetration in the UK

	Mean	Standard deviation	Coefficient of variation	Maximum	Minimum
1974	0.0103	0.0431	4.18	0.1008	−0.2409
1975	−0.0108	0.0488	−4.52	0.0478	−0.4219
1976	0.0022	0.0208	9.45	0.0588	−0.0764
1977	−0.0119	0.0248	−2.08	0.0473	−0.0959
1978	−0.0098	0.0285	−2.91	0.0889	−0.1295
1979	−0.0053	0.0211	−3.98	0.0519	−0.0765
Average 1974–9	−0.0042	0.0312	−15.17	0.0659	−0.1735

The same sample was used as for table 2.1.

2.1 gained an average of about 50 new firms per year, lost an average of about 38 per year, and thus experienced a net entry rate of just over 1% during the period (net entry was negative from 1977 to 1979). Table 2.7 shows net entry penetration rates in the UK, and can be usefully compared with table 2.3. Net entry penetration was on average −0.42% over the period, and in absolute value it was always a modest fraction of gross entry. The variation in net entry penetration across industries was always far larger relative to its mean than the variation in gross entry, and, despite its lower mean, the standard deviation of net entry exceeded that of gross entry in five of the six years. In every year, the range of net entry was far larger than that of gross entry (which is, of course, truncated at zero) and was enormous by any standards in 1974 and 1975. Table 2.8 shows the inter-industry correlations in exit 'penetration' (exitors' sales as a percentage of industry sales) and in net entry penetration. Exit penetration seems to have much the same correlation over time across industries as gross entry penetration does (see table 2.4), but net entry rates across industries are almost wholly unrelated to each other year by year. If gross entry penetration and exit penetration are judged not to persist much over time, then one must conclude that net entry penetration rates year by year do not persist at all. Finally, table 2.9 shows the cross-industry correlations between net and gross entry penetration and exit penetration. Although they are quite unstable, one can discern generally high positive correlations between gross entry and exit across industries in each year (see also Van Herck (1984) who observed much the same across a small number of rather broadly defined Belgian industries during the period 1966–75). Net and gross entry rates are only weakly positively correlated, and net entry and exit are, in general, strongly negatively correlated.

Table 2.8   The inter-industry correlation in exit and net entry penetration across years in the UK

	1974	1975	1976	1977	1978
(a) Correlations of exit 'penetration' over time					
1974	1				
1975	0.4055	1			
1976	0.3770	0.4062	1		
1977	0.2936	0.5330	0.5762	1	
1978	0.3273	0.4162	0.3916	0.4892	1
1979	0.3267	0.2725	0.3712	0.3454	0.4972
(b) Correlations of net entry penetration over time					
1974	1				
1975	−0.813	1			
1976	−0.0473	−0.0096	1		
1977	−0.1182	−0.0482	−0.088	1	
1978	−0.0154	−0.0234	−0.0238	−0.0410	1

The same sample was used as in table 2.1.

Table 2.9   Correlations between net and gross entry penetration and exit penetration in the UK

	Net and gross entry	Gross entry and exit	Net entry and exit
1974	0.3639	0.6139	−0.5118
1975	0.2321	0.2024	−0.9056
1976	0.4121	0.6806	−0.3870
1977	0.1175	0.6061	−0.7186
1978	0.4437	0.3368	−0.6943
1979	0.4090	0.3975	−0.6447

The same sample was used as in table 2.1.

Even in this rather raw state, the data raise a number of interesting issues. First, if all entry were endogenous in the sense that entry (exit) occurred only when positive (negative) excess returns emerged in markets, then one would expect to observe either entry or exit, but not both (provided, of course, that Census industry definitions corresponded to economic markets). In fact, the data suggest that most entry occurs simultaneously with exit (often, as we shall see, leading to exit by the entrant itself within a few years of entry), contributing far more to a turnover of firms than to either a net expansion or a net contraction of industry supply (interestingly, this is not true for socialist economies; see, for example, Estrin and Petrin, 1991). Second, most entrants are, at best, of extremely modest size, and the gross (much less the net) market penetration of entrants falls far short of their contribution to industry numbers. Of course, all these penetration rates are measured as of the year of entry, and so they measure no more than the initial impact of entrants in their chosen homes. While one might hope that penetration in the long run far exceeds the modest start that most entrants appear to make in their host industries, we shall see in a moment that this may not always be true. It follows as a third observation, then, that most of the rather large number of new entrants which appear each year manage no more than a modest, fleeting presence in what one imagines is a market niche far from the centre of the competitive stage in most industries. In a very real sense, entrants are tourists, not immigrants.

Survival

A final observation to be made about the raw data concerns the survival rate of most entrants. The evidence suggests that the life cycle of the average entrant starts modestly and, in general, goes downhill from there. In the USA, the market share of each cohort of entrants declined in each Census following entry, any given cohort losing about 50% of its initial share after about ten years (e.g. Dunne et al., 1988). That is, each cohort of entrants was responsible for its largest share of industry output in its first year of entry. This decline in cohort share was almost entirely due to exit since, on average, the size of survivors increased over time (although this increase was extremely variable across entrants, industries and over time). For example, members of the 1967 cohort of entrants in the USA each produced on average about 35% of the output of an average industry member in 1967. If a member of that cohort survived until at least 1972, it produced 59.7% of the average; by 1977 it produced 91.5% and, by 1982, it produced 132%. Hence, either exits were concentrated amongst the smallest cohort members, or survivors prospered and grew. In fact, the dispersion of the success of those that grew rose sharply over time (the standard deviations around the figures quoted immediately above were 0.24, 0.486, 0.935 and 1.47 respectively). The rate of market penetration by the 1967 cohort was extremely slow, the average entrant requiring 10–15 years to reach an output similar to that of the average incumbent (Dunne et al., 1988; see also Dunne et al., 1989a, which focuses on the US chemicals industry).

Although the data are slightly less precise, a similar sort of story appears to apply in Canada and the UK. In Canada, 8.09% of the

Table 2.10 The life span of new UK firms

	Population surviving (%)				
	1 year	*2 years*	*3 years*	*4 years*	*5 years*
1974 cohort	95	81	68	57	49
1975 cohort	95	82	68	58	52
1976 cohort	95	80	67	59	52
1977 cohort	93	78	68	59	53
1978 cohort	94	82	70	63	51
1979 cohort	94	80	70	63	–
1980 cohort	94	83	73	–	–
1981 cohort	95	86	–	–	–
1982 cohort	97	–	–	–	–

The data cover all firms registered for value-added tax up to 1982; the register was first set up in 1973.

Source: Adapted from Ganguly, 1985

incumbents present in 1971 had disappeared by the end of 1972, just under 18% by the end of 1975 and just over 30% by 1980. By contrast, of entrants in the 1971 cohort, 10.6% disappeared almost immediately, nearly 35% were gone by the end of 1973, more than 46% by the end of 1975, and nearly two-thirds had expired by 1980 (Baldwin and Gorecki, 1986). In the UK, some information is available on the survival rates of firms in the VAT register in manufacturing as a whole, 1974–1982, and table 2.10 tracks these nine cohorts as far as possible over the first five years of their life. Thus, 95% of those firms first registered at any time in 1974 were still on the register in 1975, 81% in 1976, 68% in 1977, and so on. Similarly, 97% of those firms first registered in 1982 were present in 1983. In general, some 5% of these entrants had disappeared by the end of their first year post-entry, some 15–20% by the end of the second year, and some 50% by the end of five years, numbers that are rather higher than those recorded in Canada. What is particularly remarkable is the relative constancy to these survival rates across cohorts whose life spans covered years of very uneven macroeconomic performance. However pro-cyclical entry and exit rates are, it seems (surprisingly) plain that survival rates do not vary appreciably over the cycle. Table 2.10 cannot, however, be used to get an accurate reading of the ages of entrants because relatively few of them are born on the 1st of January and die on the 31st of December. Figure 2.3 remedies this defect, providing information by length of life measured in months. It appears that nearly 11% of all

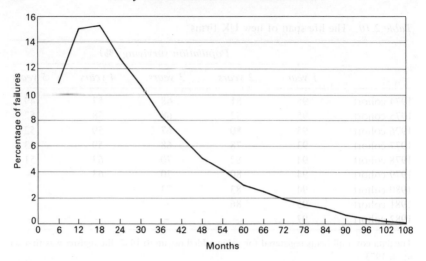

Figure 2.3 UK failure rate (VAT) by six-monthly intervals. The data cover all firms (manufacturing and non-manufacturing) for 1974–82.

Source: Ganguly, 1985

failures survive less than six months, 26% less than a year, and nearly three-quarters of all failures occur within the first three years of life. Conditional survival rates continue to rise after three years, reaching 95% for each six-month increment by four years and 99% for each six-month increment by 7.5 years.

Tables 2.11 and 2.12 track the five-year life experience of four cohorts of entrants in the UK, new firms that in this case were identified by comparing adjacent Censuses of Production at the level of *establishments*. These data are not quite the same as those on new *enterprises* (see table 2.1), not least because they will reflect the expansion of existing incumbents whenever that involves establishing a new plant. One expects entrants in the sense of new establishments to be rather more numerous, rather larger and rather more hardy than entry in the sense of new enterprises. Similarly, not only are they restricted to manufacturing (unlike the VAT data), but entry as measured by comparing adjacent Censuses may miss many of the very small, very transitory new firms recorded in other data on new firm formation (such as the VAT data). One therefore expects to (and does) see fewer Census entrants than VAT entrants, whether they be new enterprises or new establishments, but one expects that they will be longer lived than VAT entrants.

Table 2.11 The one-year life experience of new establishments in the UK

	1980	1981	1982
All establishments			
Entry rate (%)	5.7	4.6	6.8
Initial market penetration (%)	3.4	2.5	3.9
1-year survival rate (%)	88.3	86.4	93.4
1-year penetration rate (%)	3.2	2.3	3.5
Growth rate (employment) (%)	−5.1	−5.7	−0.99
Growth of all firms (%)	−11	−7.5	−5.0
Establishments with ≤ 99 employees			
Percentage of all entrants	95.6	95.9	95.5
Percentage of all entrants' initial sales	39.6	35.7	36.3
1-year survival rate (%)	88.9	87.2	93.7
Growth rate (employment) (%)	−4.6	−6.1	−3.8
Establishments with ≥ 500 employees			
Percentage of all entrants	0.81	0.95	0.77
Percentage of all entrants' initial sales	34.2	42.6	36.8
1-year survival rate (%)	88.9	90.7	77.3
Growth rate (employment) (%)	−9.6	−15.7	−8.4
All establishments			
Size of survivors relative to failures (employment) (%)	77.2	93.2	36

The calculations apply to the full sample of three-digit industries in manufacturing.

The first two rows of tables 2.11 and 2.12 show entry rates and market penetration rates that are roughly comparable with those displayed in tables 2.1 and 2.3. The third row of the two tables indicates that survival rates were in the region of 85–90% over one year post-entry and 65–70% over five years, rates that are roughly comparable with those shown for VAT entrants in table 2.10. The next three rows show that each entry cohort claimed a smaller market share in their first and fifth years post-entry, largely because of exit. The average surviving entrant shrank in size (save for the 1975 cohort), but by an amount rather less than all firms shrank. Initial and one-year market penetration rates are fairly similar on average across industries. Five-year penetration rates seem to be smaller than initial penetration rates, but the differences are not much larger than those between initial and one-year penetration rates. The second block of data in each table gives information on 'small' entrants (i.e. those initially

Table 2.12 The five-year life experience of new establishments in the UK

	1975	1976	1977	1978
All establishments				
Entry rate	9.6	9.6	5.3	6.8
Initial market penetration (%)	3.9	3.6	3.2	3.3
5-year survival rate (%)	68.6	70.4	67.6	71.7
5-year penetration rate (%)	3.1	2.5	3	2.7
Growth rate (employment) (%)	3.8	−4.2	−9.1	−8.1
Growth rate of all firms (%)	−12.7	−20.6	−26.3	−28.3
Establishments with ≤ 99 employees				
Percentage of all entrants	98.7	94.2	92.5	95.3
Percentage of all entrants' initial				
sales	33.9	39.9	26.8	32
5-year survival rate (%)	69.4	71.9	68.5	72.8
Growth rate (employment) (%)	20.1	8.4	9.8	8.2
Establishments with ≥ 500 employees				
Percentage of all entrants	0.85	0.65	1.3	0.69
Percentage of all entrants' initial				
sales	33	24.5	47.2	46.8
5-year survival rate (%)	59.8	53.2	61.8	53.2
Growth rate (employment) (%)	−11	−26	−21.1	−15.2
All establishments				
Size of survivors relative				
to failures (employment) (%)	71	43.2	78.9	80.2

The calculations apply to the full sample of three-digit industries in manufacturing.

less than 99 employees), while the third gives information on 'large' entrants (i.e. those initially larger than 500 employees). As one might imagine, the great bulk of entrants are small, and these small fry account for just over a third of all entrants' sales. Large entrants are rare, but they too account for about a third of all entrants' sales. More interestingly, smaller entrants have rather higher survival rates over five years (there is very little difference over one year). Further, while the total employment of all entrants in six of the seven cohorts decreased, small entrants shrank much less in size than large entrants over their first year of life post-entry, and, more startling, they generally expanded in size over their first five years post-entry. Large entrants, by contrast, tended to contract by between 10% and 20% over their first five years of life. These results are consistent with the observation (to be discussed below) that there are significant costs of adjustment (or expansion) that penalize over-rapid initial expansion or entry at too great a scale. This conjecture is reinforced by the data presented in the last row of the two tables, which give the ratio of the average initial size of those entrants who survived over one or five years post-entry to that of entrants who did not survive. Although there is quite a bit of variability, the basic fact seems to be that successful, surviving entrants are generally rather smaller initially than unsuccessful ones. While each individual entrant is, no doubt, tempted to make as grand an entrance into the competitive stage as possible, the data suggest that those who resist this temptation are, on average, rather more likely to survive than those who do not resist it.

Thus, entrants in the USA, Canada and the UK appear to be engaged in fighting for a place in the lower half of the industry size distribution, a struggle which results in a considerable turnover of firms but only a small accretion in market share. The pool of firms involved in this turnover over a period of five to ten years is very large relative to the number of firms active in each year, enormous relative to the net number of new firms present in any year, and simply of an entirely different order of magnitude relative to the number who survive throughout that five to ten year period.[2] The consequence of entry is a rather temporary displacement of rather small incumbents. Life at the bottom end of the industry size distribution is, no doubt, nasty, brutish and short. To reach a position remotely comparable with the mean-sized firm requires a relatively long and highly risky expansion programme that most entrants quite simply fail to achieve (particularly if they try to expand too fast). Their ability to challenge market leaders is therefore extremely easy to overrate, and it is hard to avoid the conclusion that most entrants do not possess much in the way of a competitive advantage. Even taken together as a cohort, the impact of entry on a market is, at best, modest in the short to medium run. To the extent that entry has an effect on market performance, one conjectures that the average entrant's contribution to it is likely to be pretty small and, of the large horde of firms who pass through the starting gates each year, only an extremely small number seem to have the potential of ever making a substantive contribution.

Types of Entrant

It is, of course, possible that the statistics that we have just discussed mix like with unlike, and that one ought to distinguish different types of entrant and different methods of entry.[3] There are numerous distinctions that one can make between types of entrant, but, from the point of view of survivability, the most important is likely to be between entrant firms created *de novo* and entrants created by the diversifying activities of firms established elsewhere. One expects the latter type of entrant to be somewhat larger initially, to grow somewhat faster and to survive rather longer than *de novo* entrants, largely because they can call upon the skills and the relatively deep financial pockets of their corporate parents and because this type of entry may involve lower sunk costs. This expectation must be qualified slightly, however, as different methods of diversification may have substantively different effects on size, growth and survival. Entry by acquisition can lead to a larger initial size of entrant than entry through the establishment of a greenfields site, but merger failure rates are high and that makes one suspect that the subsequent growth and survival of diversifying firms who enter markets through acquisition may not be particularly noteworthy.

These conjectures seem to be broadly consistent with US data on entry. New firms building new plants amounted to 70% of the total number of entrants, but accounted for only 54% of entrant sales (see the working paper version of Dunne et al., 1988). Diversifying firms building new plants claimed 15% of entrant sales initially, but, as their market penetration showed relatively less decline over time than that of other types of entrant using other methods of entry, their share of the total sales of their entry cohort rose over time. This seems to have occurred both because the mean exit rate of diversifying firms was lower than that of new firms, and because the size of surviving diversified entrants increased over time relative to that of other cohort members. As a consequence, new firms in the 1967 entry cohort saw an initial collective market penetration of 6.2% fall to 1.9% by 1982; diversifying firm entrants building new plants started at 2.1%, and by 1982 they still had a 1.5% share of the market. Diversifying firm entrants were also rather larger than new firm entrants. The 1967 entry cohort, for example, was initially composed of both new firms building new plants at about 27% of the size of the average industry member and diversifying firms building new plants at 141% of average incumbent size. Those new firms who had survived by 1982 were, on average, about two-thirds the size of the average industry member; diversifying firms that survived by 1982 were nearly four times the average size of incumbents. In short, although there are far more *de novo* new entrants than diversifying entrants in the USA, the latter generally enter at a larger size, grow faster over time and fail less frequently.

This also seems to be the pattern underlying what one observes in other countries. New firms in 39 Swedish industries over the period 1954–68 showed both a higher entry rate than diversified firms and a somewhat less higher penetration rate (5.8% rather than 1.7%). Although new firm formation and penetration appears to have been rather higher relative to entry by diversified firms in Sweden than in the USA, the general presumption that the latter is much less frequent but rather more substantive when it does occur appears to hold true (Hause and du Reitz, 1984). Similarly, in Canada eight times as many entrants used new plant construction rather than acquisition as a method of entry, but entrants via acquisition were about 11 times larger on average and employed 233 employees on average rather than 20 (Baldwin and Gorecki, 1986). New plants built by continuing firms were about 42% larger than those of new firms, but only slightly smaller than those of existing firms. Of all the entrants who appeared in 1971, 15% of those who entered by acquisition survived no longer than a year, while 10% of new plant builders exited after a year. Only 8% of the acquirers but 40% of the builders survived until 1982, and both factions rose fairly steadily until 1981. The average length of life for Canadian firms was estimated by Baldwin and Gorecki to be about 13–14 years, and presumably was similar for both acquirers and builders.

All these data are consistent with the view that different types of entrants have different comparative advantages, and are therefore more or less well adapted to surmount various types of entry barriers or to exploit different technologies. Since one imagines that different industries will have different types of barriers, it is not unreasonable to suppose that the incidence of different types of entry will vary across industries. In a limited sense, this seems to be true. The correlation between entry by new and by diversified firms across 39 Swedish industries was found to be a mere 0.280, and, as we shall see below, that between domestic and foreign entry in the UK is also quite low. The data also seem to suggest that entry by diversified firms is the type of entry which is most likely to have a substantive impact on market performance. Although their initial size may well be a source of advantage, one senses that the key to explaining the (relative) success of diversifying entry lies in the post-entry market penetration policies that they implement, since these policies seem to promote higher (but possibly more variable) mean growth rates and lower exit rates. It therefore seems worth a short disgression to examine the rather limited information that exists on the post-entry market penetration of diversified firm entrants.

The most substantive study of diversified entrants is that of Biggadike (1976) who looked at a sample of 40 US entrant businesses in the late 1960s to early 1970s. Virtually all their parent firms were in the *Fortune* Top 200, all were diversified and all had plenty of experience with entry; all of the entrants were survivors (at least at the time of the study). What is most startling about these entrants is that most experienced severe losses, at least through their first four years of operation. Mean and median returns on investment were −78% and −40% in the first two years of operation, the mean dropping to −43% in the second two years. Only 10% reported positive net income in their first two years of operation. Since more than 70% of the sample reported positive gross margins, their poor financial performance seems to have been largely due to high marketing and research and development (R&D) expenditures (being 41% and 51% of revenue respectively), expenditures that almost certainly constitute sunk costs of entry. The gradual improvement in financial performance over time that was generally observed appeared to stem largely from reductions in these ratios (to 25% and 23% in the second two years of operation). This reduction was due to a more rapid growth in sales revenues (87% growth on average) relative to advertising (51% growth) or R&D (33% growth) expenditures, rather than to a reduction in the absolute volume of either these types of expenditure. In fact, an analysis of the data suggested that these entrants might need as much as eight years to achieve positive returns, and 10–12 years to establish levels of returns comparable with those enjoyed by incumbents.

Biggadike worked with a non-random sample of entry into markets more narrowly defined than those typically described by the Census, and thus his observation that mean market penetration in the first two years of entry was 15% is difficult to evaluate. Even so, the mean market share of incumbents in his sample was observed to be 23%, implying that entrants only managed to achieve sales that were two-thirds of those of the average incumbent in the host market. Far more interesting is the observation that the mean market penetration by entrants after four and even eight years was also only 15%. This lack of medium-term penetration by entrants as a group hides at least one further observation of interest, and that is that the 36% of entrants who achieved at least an annual increase of share of 50% were, on the whole, those who started out with a low initial share. The 10% of entrants who actually lost share during their first four years of operation post-entry typically started with a high initial market penetration. Further, while those with a larger market share performed better financially (largely because of lower ratios of investment marketing and advertising to sales), those who experienced fast increases in share typically also experienced a lower rate of return. That is, there appear to be significant short-run costs of post-entry expansion in markets, and those entrants who tried to expand rapidly could, it appears, suffer a short-run penalty of about 35 percentage points in mean rate of return.[4] Thus, the penetration strategy choice faced by the typical entrant seems to involve a clear intertemporal trade-off in returns. Positive returns on investment appear to require capturing a significant share of the market, largely to reduce the per unit cost of advertising, R&D and other investments. However, any attempt to acquire share rapidly to reduce these unit costs is likely to carry an extremely large short-run cost penalty due to costs of adjustment. The choice, then, is between high but gradually diminishing losses, and very high but possibly more sharply declining losses.

It is possible to push somewhat further, and make some comparisons of post-entry market penetration profiles by type of entrant. Yip (1982a) studied the penetration of different types of entrants in 31 narrowly defined US markets during the period 1972–9 by obtaining data about them from incumbents. Fifty-nine entrants were observed by the incumbents he questioned in the 31 markets and, since we have seen plenty of evidence suggesting that entry rates are much higher than this, one immediately infers that the vast majority of entrants made very little impression on incumbents. Of these 59, 37 entered via internal diversification and 22 via acquisition. Since only 11 markets experienced both types of entry, one is tempted to speculate that they represent alternative methods of entry best suited to different kinds of markets. Of more interest is the intertemporal profile of post-entry market penetration displayed by these entrants. Entry via acquisition typically involved capturing a higher initial share of the market (6.8% rather than 2.3%), but then experiencing a rather lower rate of gain of share than entry by internal diversification. For a subsample of what Yip calls the 36 'most important' entrants, acquirers started with an initial market share of 7.1% and reached a plateau of about 9% after four years. After six years, those entering via internal diversification had achieved a share of 9.3% following an initial penetration of 3.9%. Thus, not only does there exist an intertemporal trade-off in the profile of post-entry market penetration, but that trade-off seems to vary by method of entry (further evidence discussed by Cooper and Smith, 1988, suggests that performance may also depend on the degree of maturity of the host market).

Distinguishing *de novo* from diversifying entry of various types is not the only breakdown between types of entrant that one might examine. Another distinction focuses on whether they produce domestically or whether the sales of entrants are sourced from production abroad – between domestic and foreign entry for short. One's interest in this comparison arises from the presumption of many that the two types of entrant are perfectly substitutable from the point of view of stimulating competition in markets, and that it is not necessarily important to encourage domestic entry if there are no barriers to trade protecting markets. More broadly, the comparison goes to the heart of recent suggestions that many markets are inherently global (see, for example, the papers in Porter,

1986). Although it is not wholly clear what 'global markets' are, the label does appear to carry the implication that firms situated in such markets ought not to distinguish rivals by country of origin. Table 2.13 shows data on the inter-industry distribution of net foreign entry for 87 three digit UK industries, where net foreign entry is defined as the change in imports divided by industry sales.[5] Comparing table 2.13 with the net (domestic) entry data shown in table 2.7 for the same sample of industries, it is clear that foreign entry is a more substantive force in the UK than domestic entry. The market penetration of the former averaged about 4.5% per industry over the period during which the latter averaged −0.4%. On the face of it, this suggests either that the barriers to entry (or, for existing importers, to expansion in the market) facing foreign entrants are lower than those facing domestic entrants, or (what amounts to pretty much the same thing) that the market niches that foreign entrants fill are larger. However, the relative size of the two flows may also indicate that foreign entrants crowd domestic entrants out. Relative to its mean, net foreign entry is rather less variable across industries than domestic entry, despite its generally much larger range.

Table 2.13   Net foreign entry penetration in the UK

	Mean	*Standard deviation*	*Coefficient of variation*	*Maximum*	*Minimum*
1974	0.0633	0.0679	1.07	0.3048	−0.0617
1975	0.0175	0.0743	4.25	0.2423	−0.2320
1976	0.0563	0.0645	1.15	0.2299	−0.2139
1977	0.0431	0.0480	1.11	0.3299	−0.0426
1978	0.0416	0.0627	1.51	0.3299	−0.0624
1979	0.0447	0.0479	1.07	0.1937	−0.0721
Average 1974–9	0.0444	0.0609	1.32	0.2718	0.1141

The same sample was used as in table 2.1.

Tables 2.8 and 2.14 show that both types of net entry penetration, domestic and foreign, are quite unstable across industries over time, although there is rather more serial correlation in the net foreign entry series than in the net domestic entry penetration series. Thus, although the 'noise' component of both series is high, foreign-based entry seems to be the more predictable of the two, a result that is surprising in view of the volatility of exchange rates. Table 2.15 shows that the correlations across industries between foreign and domestic entry are extremely weak.

Although there is a general predominance of negative correlations, their rather small size inclines one to conclude that foreign and domestic entry are basically unrelated, and that there is no obvious tendency for foreign and domestic entrants to enter the same industry, or, for that matter, to specialize in different industries. If the two types of entrant have different comparative advantages in entering different industries, then these correlations suggest that the relations between these different skills are not obvious. Domestic and foreign entrants are, apparently, neither complements nor substitutes for each other.

Table 2.14   The inter-industry correlation in net foreign entry penetration across years in the UK

	1974	1975	1976	1977	1978
1974	1.000				
1975	0.1632	1.000			
1976	0.2909	0.0845	1.000		
1977	0.5129	0.3014	0.4651	1.000	
1978	0.4235	0.3889	0.5036	0.4551	1.000
1979	0.2609	0.0785	0.5159	0.4852	0.3233

The same sample was used as in table 2.1.

Table 2.15   Correlation between domestic and foreign entry penetration in the UK

	Gross domestic entry penetration	Domestic exit penetration	Net domestic entry penetration
1974	− 0.2534	− 0.0448	− 0.2229
1975	0.0829	− 0.0938	0.1291
1976	− 0.0252	− 0.0173	− 0.0102
1977	− 0.0307	− 0.0872	− 0.1357
1978	− 0.0239	− 0.0662	− 0.0448
1979	− 0.0998	0.0231	− 0.0132

The same sample was used as in table 2.1.

A final distinction between types of entrant that is worth making is by legal type. Of the several classifications that might be made on this basis, that between worker-managed and capitalist firms has attracted a considerable amount of attention recently (see, for example, Sexton and Sexton, 1987). With the exception of Yugoslavia, the worker-owned sector of most economies is fairly modest (Ben-Ner, 1988a). In the EEC, for example, there were nearly 14,000 such firms operating in 1981, employing more than 500,000 people and generating a revenue flow of $8.4 billion. Nearly 80% of those firms operated in Italy. As many as half of them, however, were created between 1976 and 1981, and both firm and employment growth in the worker-owned sector far exceeded that in the capitalist sector post-1975. In the UK over the period 1976–81, the worker-owned firm birth rate was about 39%; for capitalist firms it was more like 12%. The great majority of these new worker-owned firms were created *de novo*, but about 4% took the form of worker buyouts of capitalist firms (mainly those in financial trouble). Birth rates reached 61% in the Netherlands over the same period, and 18–21% in France and Italy. Capitalist firm birth rates in France, by contrast, averaged 9.8%. Transformations of capitalist firms accounted for just over and just under half of the total births of worker-owned firms in the Netherlands and France respectively.

Worker-managed firms are commonly found in construction, and within manufacturing, in printing and, at a distance, glass, ceramics and furniture. They are rather smaller than capitalist-owned firms. In the UK, for example, 83% of worker-owned firms had less than 10 employees in 1980; in France and Sweden, the corresponding percentage was about 73%, 5 or 6 percentage points above that for capitalist-owned firms. In most countries, annual birth rates of worker-managed firms averaged 20% (with 10% new employment growth), but, like capitalist firms, these birth rates proved to be highly variable over time and across industries and economies. Worker-owned enterprises also seem to enjoy a rather lower risk of failure through dissolution than capitalist firms, but exit from the worker-owned sector is rather high because of a tendency for worker-owned firms to transform themselves into capitalist firms. Again, annual death rates can vary enormously, but the averages in France, Italy and the UK were below 10%, and up to a half of these deaths occurred through transfers to the capitalist-owned sector. Hazard rates seem to be much lower for UK worker-owned firms than for UK capitalist firms, although both appear to peak at about three years or so post-entry.

It seems clear from all of this that worker-owned enterprises are particularly suited to certain sectors (such as those favouring small-scale, probably high skill or craft-oriented production) and, indeed, there is a fair amount of evidence suggesting that they can be rather more efficient than their capitalist counterparts (see Defourney et al., 1985; Conte and Svejnar, 1988, and references cited therein). Further, whatever their comparative advantages are, they became much more clearly marked in the middle to late 1970s for some reason. It follows that the barriers to entry that they face probably differ from those faced by capitalist firms, and, in practice, one suspects that this is reflected in the different ports of entry that worker-owned and capitalist enterprises utilized. The two legal types tend to occupy certain types of market niches that differ in character, probably in much the same way that domestic and foreign-based firms appear to occupy different niches, and, as a consequence, neither complement nor substitute for each other. More interesting is the fact that worker-owned firms often 'die' by transforming themselves into capitalist firms. It is therefore possible that this particular legal form of enterprise is unstable and that the size of this sector in most economies will remain modest because successful worker-owned firms will sooner or later transform themselves into capitalist firms.[6] There is an analogue of this type of transformation in the distinction between domestic and foreign-based entry. Imports are often used as a way of establishing a bridge-head in new markets, and, for successful products, imports are often followed by the establishment of domestic production facilities by the foreign producer (see the discussion in Caves, 1982). Both examples of transformation suggest that the comparative advantages of different types of entrant may vary systematically over the life cycle of new firms.

Thus, there is no question that the vast numbers of entrants that one observes do not constitute a great homogeneous mass of new firms. Rather, the flow contains several streams of entrant type that intermingle, forming a mosaic whose pattern gradually changes as each cohort of entrants mature. The large number of entrants who appear each year and their extremely high mortality rate ensures that the competition for places in most markets is fierce, and the small size of most entrants probably means that the only incumbents at risk are those who are marginal, those who have only recently entered themselves. As a consequence, survival is as much the outcome of a struggle amongst entrants as it is the outcome of competition between entrants and incumbents for a place in the market.

It also seems clear that certain types of entrants join the fray with substantial advantages over others. Diversifying entrants and, less clearly, both foreign-based entrants and worker-owned enterprises all seem to outlive domestic-based *de novo* capitalist entrants who, in fact, constitute the great mass of new firms observed each year. However, too much should not be made of this observation. Both worker-owned and, perhaps, foreign-based entrants may prove to be somewhat unstable forms of entry, and in any case no entrant type seems to be terribly well adapted to life in the competitive jungle. Despite the risk of oversimplification, one is tempted to suggest that what commences as a great flow of new firms may, in the long run, end up as a more or less marginal increase in the interpenetration of each other's markets by different diversifying firms.

The Process of Entry

Although the raw data on entry flows contains much interesting information on the competitive pressures created by new entry, one must push on further than this and try to assess the volume of potential entry that could, in principle, be converted into actual entry in any market at any given time. The problem is, of course, that actual entry flows can seriously mis-state the competitive pressure that incumbents face if the threat of potential entry is perceived to be real and substantial. Indeed, given the threat of entry, the actual flow of entry that does materialize depends on how incumbents react and whether they choose to block entry or not. However, assessing the volume of potential entry is in general a rather difficult task since there is often very little in the way of observable signals that market agents transmit when they are merely holding themselves in a state of readiness prior to possible action. Nor is it very obvious how ready any one of them must be to be deemed a potential player. In some (rather long-run) sense all agents are potential steel makers, but in another, more pressing (or short-run) sense, most are not. Certainly, one can certainly do better than asserting that everyone is a potential entrant. What matters from the point of view of competitive pressure is whether incumbents believe that potential entrants can transform themselves into substantive competitors more rapidly than defences can be erected against them. This, in turn, means that potential entrants are best defined as those agents who could, in principle, mount a substantial challenge in, say, two or three years (and perhaps as many as five if the installation of new capacity or new distribution systems is particularly slow in some sector).

The simplest, most straightforward way to make some inferences about the extent of potential entry in a market is to use data on actual entry. There are (at least) two routes that one might take. Perhaps the most obvious involves a little rejigging of what one means by actual entry. If what really matters from the point of view of an incumbent is that new competitors be 'substantive', then most of the new entrants observed in the second section can hardly be described as 'actual entrants'. We have seen, for example, that an average of 50 domestic-based firms entered each of 87 three-digit industries in each year between 1974 and 1979, and that perhaps only half of them survived for more than a couple of years. If one defines 'actual entry' as the arrival of a new, substantive competitor, then these 50 new firms are only (at best) 'potential entrants'. They form the pool from which 'actual entrants' in the market are eventually selected. Actual entry (meaning survivors) into these UK industries would, in this redefinition, be rather modest, and might be difficult to determine without the benefit of five or so years hindsight.

Although it is clear that this method of identifying potential entry gets very close to merely redefining what was called 'actual entry' as 'potential entry', there is a non-trivial sense in which many observed entrants are far more concerned with the problems of getting set up than with those of challenging market leaders. It is one thing to establish a new business and quite another to commit oneself to competing in a market. Table 2.16 gives some feel for how this type of distinction might work out in practice. It lists 12 relatively recent entrants into three segments of the UK car market, defining entry as the capture of a 1% market share overall in three segments. One per cent is, of course, rather arbitrary, but in a market this size it translates into enough sales to have to take the provision of (at least) distribution and after-sales services seriously, requiring investments in infrastructure that are both substantial and (often) largely sunk. Potential entrants in the market are those likely to make such an investment, and might, in practice, be identified as firms making modest sales in the market on a 'try it and see basis'. The fourth column of table 2.16 shows what might be termed toe-hold entry, defined as the time when

Table 2.16 Entry and potential entry in the UK car industry

Firm	Small segment	Medium[a] segment	Large[a] segment	Toe-hold entry
Volkswagen	1975	1959	1970	1951
Renault	1971	1969	1970	1931
Simca	1971	1969	1971	1940
Volvo	X	1977	1971	1949
Citroen	1975	1972	1973	1931
Fiat	1974	1969	1973	1931
Peugeot	1974	1974	1974	1931
Toyota	1975	1973	1974	1960
Honda	1976	1977	X	1963
Opel	X	1976	1976	1935
Lada	1978	1978	X	1974
Mazda	X	1979	1982	1961

[a] The segments are defined by length of car: small is less than 150 inches, large is 180 inches or more, and medium lies in between.
Source: Adapted from Geroski and Murfin, 1990a

enough of the entrants' cars were sold in the UK to make it worth establishing a valuation of them for insurance purposes. The major wave of actual entry into the UK car market might be dated from, say, 1970. At that time, 11 of these 12 entrants were recognizably potential entrants, and six of them had been so since before the war. The average lag between toe-hold entry and first entry into any of the three market sequences was 26 years, ranging from 43 years (Peugeot) to four years (Lada). All but two firms took more than ten years to transform toe-hold to actual entry, and a half took more than 30 years (helped, of course, by a major war and subsequent reconstruction period). At least two further potential entrants, Daf and Wartburg, recorded toe-hold entry (in 1960 and 1972 respectively) but exited (in 1976 and 1975) without ever actually entering, and at least 14 more potential entrants (including Suzuki, Daihatsu, Hyundai, Zasaua, to name only the most recently established) had not entered by 1983. By contrast, once firms had entered some segment of the market, subsequent intra-market penetration was rapid. Of the seven who had entered all three segments by 1973, two did so instantaneously, four did so in five years or less, and the average intra-market penetration lag was 4.7 years. There seems to be such a large qualitative distinction between the activities of these firms before and after entry into one of these three market segments that it seems reasonable to apply the labels potential and actual entry respectively to the two periods.

Making inferences about the size of the pool of potential entrants by reclassifying data on actual entry flows is clearly rather hazardous, and it is worth trying other procedures. A second route that one might take is to adopt the convention that all actual entrants were once all potential entrants (however briefly), and then to use information (or hypotheses) about the process of how they transform themselves from one to the other state to make some inferences about the size of potential entry at any time from observed flows of actual entry. Consider the process by which actual entrants decide to commence operations at some time t. Two steps seem to be involved. First 'agents' at large in the economy must become actively interested in a particular market, transforming themselves into 'players', or potential entrants. Second, players attempt entry sooner or later, generating 'trials' or actual entry that transforms them from being players to being actual entrants and established competitors. What is it that transforms agents at large into players ready to attempt entry into markets? Two sets of considerations seem to be relevant. First, agents must be willing to shift into new activities (i.e. they must have a low opportunity cost) and, second, they must be aware of the possibilities which are open to them in the new market. In practice, this distinction is likely to be rather blurred, as many agents are unlikely to critically assess the worth of their current activities unless presented with an apparently golden opportunity for change. Thus, it is the arrival of new information that is likely to be the key. Those agents who do critically assess their actions on a regular basis may actively search for it in a systematic way while those who do not will encounter useful nuggets of news at random but, either way, the arrival of good news is the start of the entry process. Clearly, the more agents there are that systematically search out information and the more actively they do so, the more rapidly will actual entry eventually occur.

The kind of information that is relevant to the process of transforming agents into players is different from that which leads players to contemplate attempting entry. The second type of decision involves making detailed calculations about the probability of success and the level of profits which the entrant can expect to realize if successful, calculations which are both expensive and time consuming to make. It follows that players will not make such computations routinely but, rather, will do so only when a likely opportunity presents itself. However, the information 'sought' by an agent actively considering entry is of a broader, more conceptual nature than that sought by players or potential entrants. Agents require information on the issue of whether an opportunity exists which, in principle, might prove profitable to exploit. Players need to know when and how to exploit it; they need to decide not just whether to enter, but also when and how to do so. An analogy with labour market search behaviour may be useful. Unemployed workers search for vacancies in the first instance, posing more detailed questions about pay, conditions of work and so on only when enough vacancies exist to offer a choice. So, in a similar manner, agents search for gaps in the market where something innovative could, in principle, be done. Only when some suitable opportunity seems to be at hand would it be reasonable for a player to calculate costs, demand and the expected reaction of incumbents, and make a decision about whether, in practice, something ought to be done, and when. Needless to say, both types of decision – to become a player to attempt entry – are conjectural, but one requires imagination and the other calculation.[7]

Aside from the suggestion that such an inherently stochastic process of information transmission may help to account for the highly variable flows of entry that we observe, the principal implication of these observations would seem to be that agents are likely to become players only in markets 'close to' those that they already operate in. At least two lines of argument point in this direction. First, for an agent to act on the basis of a rumour, and to act in an economically effective fashion, that agent must understand a good deal about the market to which the rumour refers. If she/he is to indulge in her or his curiosity, she/he must know where even further, more detailed information is to be had, and how to evaluate it. Since such information can itself only be acquired at a cost, those who have already acquired it are most likely to respond. Investments in information gathering presuppose a knowledge of how to search, and those already participating in or near a market are best positioned in this respect. Second, agents who operate 'nearby' are not only better positioned than many others to act on a rumour, they are also (for much the same reasons) better positioned to hear it in the first place. That is, in the race to exploit market opportunities, those closest to a given market are likely to start first and run faster than others, becoming players more rapidly and in larger numbers than outsiders.

Thus, there seems to be a fundamental sense in which a market – or a cluster of closely related markets – creates its own entrants. 'Nearby' markets that contribute to the pool of potential entrants include those that are vertically related upstream or downstream, those that produce a similar product in a geographically different area and those following a similar technological trajectory to that followed by the host market. Agents in their guise as wage earners or as entrepreneurs elsewhere in the market (or in related markets) form the pool of potential players who, in due course, may eventually try to become and perhaps succeed in becoming entrants.

This is a pattern one encounters repeatedly in empirical work. For example, studies of 'narrow' versus 'broad spectrum' diversification (roughly, within and between two-digit industries) indicate that many diversified firms are moderately cautious in deciding how widely to spread their activities, implying that, as entrants, they often move into new industries from nearby markets.[8] Case studies reveal much the same story. Church (1976) observed that many of the early entrants supplying electrical equipment to the UK motor industry had initially been founded to supply the then developing electricity industry: 'in effect, the direction of initial development followed a process orientation, with producers of electrical equipment for marine, agricultural and domestic power turning to the needs of the emergent motor vehicle industry' (p. 230). Even where early barriers are very modest, the pattern of early entrants as those already operating close to the market in question is often clearly apparent. For example, this seems to have been the case in the UK dry cleaning industry, where two of the largest new entrants founded in the late 1950s, one by an employee who spun off from an established chain cleaning group and the other by a son whose father was in the trade, were amongst the earliest and most successful (Shaw, 1973).

Given that potential entrants follow a (possibly technological) trail from established to new markets, it is likely that those from different source markets will arrive in the host market at different times. For example, at least two generations of entrants into the early US computer industry were observed by Brock (1975). The first generation appeared in the early to middle 1950s, and largely consisted of major business machine firms like IBM, Remington, Rand, NCR and Burroughs. The second generation were technical firms interested in exploiting the new innovation rather than business machine companies interested in protecting existing markets, and they arrived in the 1958–60 period. This cohort – Philco, General Electric, CDC and DEC – also includes the first successful companies whose activities were based entirely on computers. Similarly, the US semiconductor industry was colonized by major receiving tube producers whose operations were threatened by the rise of semiconductor technology, by large diversified firms who produced electric equipment and electronics systems of various types, and by newcomers who were often formed by scientists and engineers individually (or in small groups) spinning off from established electronics or semiconductor producers. The receiving tube producers were the first to move (following AT&T's production of the original transistor – it was enjoined from selling in the commercial market), eight of the major receiving tube producers (e.g. General Electric, RCA, Sylvania and others) responding by 1954. Hughes and Motorolla, established elsewhere in the electronics sector, also entered at this stage; IBM, producing for in-house use, was a bit slower. New firms like Transitron (a 1952 spin-off from Bell Laboratories) were formed early on; others continued to enter in the 1950s and 1960s (Tilton, 1971). The expiry of patent protection in the European polyester fibres market spawned two types of entrant, established patent and licence holders diversifying geographically and new firms, including a major existing man-made fibre manufacturer (Shaw and Shaw, 1977). Finally, the newly emergent biotechnology sector is a set of technologies in search of applications, and in the USA, it is currently being developed by a range of new high technology firms (such as Genentech, founded in 1976) attempting to develop commercial products, and established companies pursuing process-oriented applications for use in pharmaceuticals, chemicals, food processing and energy. The new firms (well over a hundred formed since 1976) have been formed around core groups of university scientists (such firms are typically rather Ph.D. intensive), several getting started by placing R&D contracts with selected academics to pursue the commercial implications of laboratory discoveries. Early entrants often funded their core proprietary research by accepting contracts with large user firms or entering into joint licensing agreements, but subsequent entrants have chosen to follow a more independent route (Office of Technology Assessment, 1984).

Thus, there is a strong sense in which new markets develop first from other markets and then from within. Agents and, in due course, players in new markets often come from nearby user or producer markets, usually in a varying mixture of new and diversifying entrants, and often in successive waves loosely ordered by industry of origin. However, as new markets mature and develop, they often generate new entrants from within the ranks of existing firms. There are two major implications of these observations. First, given their origins, the identity of potential entrants ought to be fairly easy for incumbents to predict (on a case by case basis) and this, in turn, may provide useful information to use in predicting when they will strike and how. The pool of potential entrants is not some generalized faceless mass that gives rise to a diffuse – if, at times, overpowering – sense of unease amongst incumbents. Rather it is a (perhaps rather long) list of names that, for the most part, is known to alert incumbents. Second, the fact that new markets evolve from old, that entrants often come initially from industries nearby and ultimately from within, suggests that most economies are likely to be extremely slow to make major structural adjustments. If the vast majority of most firms in a market must be 'produced' by that (or another nearby) market, then major shifts in the relative importance of different sectors cannot occur overnight (unless, perhaps, they are particularly open to foreign competition). An economy that wishes to shift from specializing in electronics to biotechnology cannot simply take it for granted that displaced electronics firms are putative biotechnologists. Rather, sectoral change will evolve through a process of 'learning by doing' in which individuals gradually accumulate the skills necessary to operate in one specific sector. Since many individuals will only ever manage to do this once (if at all) successfully in their lifetimes, the pace at which sectoral shifts can occur depends (in part) on the alacrity with which one generation follows the footsteps of another.

Conclusions

The raw data on entry contain a number of interesting and unexpected features, and, taken as a whole, suggest that most markets experience a considerable amount of turbulence at the bottom end of the size distribution of firms. The clearest impression that one gets from the data is that entry is easy but that survival is not. Even apparently advantaged entrants – those that are subsidiaries of firms established elsewhere –

may require up to ten years before they are able to operate on a competitive basis with incumbents, and it may take as many as five years before their chances of survival have been raised to better than even. Part of the problem is that there appear to be significant adjustment costs to increasing market penetration, and these can severely exacerbate the (perhaps large) disadvantages of small-scale penetration. To generalize about entry using the experience of this type of entrant, however, is to paint far too rosy a picture of the entry experience. The predominant type of entrant is a very small firm created *de novo*. It is generally a traditional type of entrepreneurial firm, although there is a weak indication that from the mid-1970s on the creation of worker-owned firms may have become a great deal more common than hitherto. Whatever its legal type, this entrant is apparently rather more likely to displace a small incumbent in the host market than it is to create a new niche for itself, and it is quite likely to be displaced itself in fairly short order. The typical entrant is likely to make only a modest (if that) shift in its sectoral orientation, generally originating from the sector in question or from some nearby sector that exploits related technologies, that is geographically separate, or that is upstream to or downstream from the host sector.[9]

Thinking in terms of a 'typical' entrant trying to break into a 'typical' market that has no history is like theorizing in terms of a 'representative firm' in a macro model, a hazardous undertaking that can strip much of interest from what one actually observes. Although the clues are much too soft to support confident assertions, there does seem to be some evidence to support the view that different types of entrant can cluster in different industries, and that they tend to appear to somewhat different stages of industry development. Although its not yet clear what they are (but see below, chapter 5), it must be the case that the incentives they respond to and the barriers they face differ in subtle ways, and these differences seem to change (exogenously or endogenously) as the host market evolves. Domestic and foreign-based entrants, for example, show different patterns of net penetration across industries, as (it appears) do diversified and *de novo* entrants, and capitalist entrants and new worker-owned firms. Similarly, there is a hint in several case studies that early entrants in new markets are often those in businesses directly threatened by the new product, and that these entrants are followed by waves of *de novo* entry and entry from firms operating further along technological trajectories that pass through the host market. Either way, there is little question that entry is particularly extensive in fast growing industries (as we shall see), and it is probably the case that entry is much more common earlier than later in industry life cycles. The experience of the 1970s (particularly in the UK) also suggests that entry is probably pro-cyclical, although this may not be true for all entrant types.

Needless to say, one of the reasons why all these inferences must be hedged with so many qualifications is that the raw data on entry paint a picture of extraordinary variability. Cross-section differences in entry rates or entry penetration (gross and net, domestic and foreign) are large, but, large as they are, they are dominated by variations over time within industries. Further, within-industry variations over time appear to be somewhat poorly synchronized across industries, with the result that inter-industry differences in entry simply do not persist for very long over time. As a measure of 'competitiveness', entry stands in sharp contrast with virtually all indices of market concentration which, typically, show some between-industry variation but very little within-industry variation over periods of five to ten years. Entry also appears to vary much more over time than measures of market performance such as price–cost margins or rates of return. Although we have yet to do any serious analysis of the data on entry, one cannot escape a growing dread that much of the observed variation in the data is not very systematic, and that much of it will be rather difficult to account for. Entry may reflect the effects of a number of fundamental elements of market structure, deep exogenous determinants of industry conduct and performance, but, if it does, it is likely to be a noisy signal of them.

Although one cannot make much progress in explaining the data without delving into the exogenous determinants of entry, it is possible to say something general about the nature of the process which generated the data on the basis of what we have discovered so far. In particular, the extensive turnover of firms that is, perhaps, the most striking feature of the data suggests that the textbook account of entry as a method of overcoming artificial monopolistic restrictions on industry supply is much too simple to account for most of the interesting features of what we observe. Although there is no doubt that entry does have this effect, if this were the whole story one simply would not observe the high degree of turbulence, the extensive simultaneous entry and exit, that one does observe. To make progress, one must move away from a strictly functionalist view of entry that identifies it by what it does, and consider how the process operates. Speculating in this spirit, there are at least two characterizations of the entry process that may account for the broad features of what we observe. The first is that entry is essentially a hit-and-run process, that entrants are presented with windows of opportunity that have a strictly limited duration and that they respond to these openings with what are, by design, limited forays into the market. There are numerous reasons why market opportunities may be short lived. Costs or demand may be subject to numerous transitory shocks too small for incumbents to bother with, or to secular shifts to which incumbents are slow to react but are lethal when they finally do. Although it is not integral to this conception of entry, it is natural to describe it as a race to exploit exogenously created niches in the market that temporarily emerge as a by-product of more fundamental changes in preferences, endowments or technology. One way or the other, this view of the entry process suggests that what one observes is the consequence of deliberate choice, that entrants respond to certain kinds of limited opportunities in an apparently rational fashion.

A second, contrasting, characterization of what lies behind the data is that entry is essentially a sorting process, a form of economic selection that can only be done effectively through markets. The analogy with natural selection processes is clear. New firms – like new phenotypes – compete with others as a way of selecting amongst alternative products or production processes – alternative genotypes – in the face of scarce resources. Those that generate the largest net value to consumers survive and prosper. The process must be done through markets for much the same reason that genetic selection cannot be done in the abstract – there are many ways to achieve a fit with a given environment and the 'right one' depends on existing alternatives. Two alternative types of selection might underlie such a process. First, entrants may be genuinely uncertain about their abilities, and there may be no reasonable way to ascertain these without market experience. In this view, entry is a type of passive learning in which the market sorts the wheat from the chaff (e.g. Jovanovich (1982); see also Pakes and Ericson (1987), Evans (1987a, b) and Dunne et al. (1989b) for some indirect evidence on this view gained by looking at the aging patterns of small firms or entrants). Second, entrants may fail to invest in learning as much as they ought to prior to entry; they may be risk takers who place undue weight on very low probability, highly favourable outcomes, or they may simply make mistakes. Whether it be an instrument of passive learning or a device for identifying and correcting mistakes, the role of the entry process is to sort through this mess and select the fortunate from the unfortunate. The view of entry as a sorting process suggests that what we observe is the consequence of the rather limited abilities of decision makers to create or, at least, to match themselves with opportunities that are commensurate to their talents.

It is rather difficult to distinguish these two quite different conceptions of the entry process on the basis of the data thus far examined. The most obvious testable difference between them is likely to emerge from an inspection of post-entry returns. Hit-and-run entrants are those planning a limited foray from the start, and thus are likely (on average) to realize a positive return net of entry and exit costs. Passive learners, risk takers and other entrants who leap before they look are, on the other hand, not likely to be as well prepared for the crash as they might be. They are therefore likely to fail (on average) to cover their costs. On this basis, virtually the only evidence (outside of the odd case study) that we have to discriminate between hit-and-run entry and entry as a sorting process is the study by Biggadike on the financial performance of his sample of 40 diversifying entrants. If these most advantaged entrants cannot break even in their first four years of operation (much less in their first eight to ten years), then it is hard to see how the great majority of *de novo* entrants manage to do so in their shorter lifetimes. Of course *de novo* entrants are unlikely to indulge in advertising and R&D to the extent that Biggadike's entrants did, but this is likely to reduce their cash flow as well as reducing their fixed costs, and may not make them much better off. No one seriously disputes that many entrants suffer severe financial distress, and that at least some of those who do do so because the entrepreneurs that run them seriously underestimate the value of their time. Although not every hit-and-run entrant needs to do no worse than breaking even to make a hit-and-run conception of the entry process plausible, the suspicion that a great majority of them do not seem to do even this well counts against its plausibility. A further, much less persuasive objection to the view of entry as a hit-and-run process is the difficulty of seeing why it might result in the rather different survival rates across the entrant types that we observe. There is nothing in the logic of hit-and-run arguments to suggest that *de novo* entrants will typically exploit more finitely lived opportunities than diversifying or worker-owned entrants. Nor is it easy to see why the opportunities exploited by worker-owned firms might lead them to transform themselves into capitalist firms after some years of operation. One can, of course, think of *ad hoc* reasons why this might prove to be the case, but the fact is that these differences fit more naturally into a conception of entry as a sorting process that selects amongst entrants of different types with different characteristics.

Thus, although it is hardly above dispute, one's instincts suggest that a fruitful way to view the data is as the outcome of a sorting process in which a wide range of different more or less randomly generated possibilities are put to a market test, and most are found wanting. Rather than – or perhaps in addition to – being a mechanism by which markets generate increases in supply, entry is a mechanism by which markets make a choice between alternatives. Although these alternatives are, literally, new firms, it is perhaps rather more useful to think of them as new ideas – little insights into possible product or process innovations that may reduce costs or expand real customer choice in some valuable way.

Since individuals and firms have some imagination and some leeway to choose their characteristics (or to develop certain types of latent abilities), a concomitant of any increase in industry supply is likely to be an increase in the variety of ways that market participants choose to provide that supply. In contrast with the view that what one observes are hit-and-run entrants reacting to exogenously given transitory opportunities, the view of entry as a sorting mechanism starts from the premise that most entry is an attempt to transform the market in some way, creating or expanding demand with a new product or service, or with a lower price based on some innovation in production or distribution. The process of entry is one in which such ideas are generated and then compared with alternatives using the most direct form of market research imaginable.

Finally, read literally, the data suggest that there may, perhaps, be 'too many' entrants, that they are 'too small', that 'too few survive' and that those who do survive penetrate the market 'too slowly'. However, the fact that what we observe in the data is not so much high entry as high turnover makes one suspect that some sort of selection process is at work in most markets. Since selection requires variety for its bite to be effective, it is impossible to say whether any given selective process has been fed too much or too little variety without reference to the performance outcomes that it generates. To make more progress, then, one must push on and consider the causes and consequences of entry.

Notes

1 This type of autoregressive equation emerges from a dynamic latent factors model in which entry E_t depends on a range of unobservables e_t; e.g. $E_t = \Sigma \lambda_\tau e_{t-\tau}$. Repeated substitution transforms this into a regression of E_t on its own history, $E_t = \Sigma \beta_\tau E_{t-\tau}$. The virtue of the model is its parsimonious demand for information (i.e. observables); its weakness is the limited range of inferences that one can draw from it about the determinants of E_t. It is best thought of as a benchmark against which the structural models to be discussed in chapter 3 ought to be evaluated, and it will be discussed at greater length there.

2 These results seem broadly consistent with the results of studies of the relationship between firm size, growth and age; see Storey et al. (1987) for the UK and, for the USA, the recent work by Evans (1987a), Hall (1987) and the references cited therein. These studies seem to suggest that mean growth rates, the variability of growth rates and the probability of exit all decline with the age of a firm.

3 On the importance of distinguishing between different types of entrant, see, for example, Hines (1957); on the not entirely unrelated topic of distinguishing successful from unsuccessful innovating firms, Freeman (1982).

4 Penrose (1959) gives a classic discussion of the internal sources of costs of

adjustment encountered by firms as they attempt to grow quickly. Any such costs are, of course, likely to be exacerbated by the responses of incumbents, although these seem to have been fairly modest in the case of the firms looked at by Biggadike. Of course, one could interpret these data by arguing that entrants might be willing to buy market share by pricing low in order to grow faster, accepting a lower rate of return as a consequence. However, in as far as this strategy merely hastens an inevitable accumulation of customers, it is a form of cost of adjustment.

5 This definition of foreign entry suffers from several drawbacks in addition to being a net entry measure. The first is that imports are often shipped between subsidiaries of a multinational firm and therefore do not always represent an independently controlled increase in industry supply. Further, an expansion of imports does not necessarily reflect an increase in new firms selling in domestic markets, and much of the increase may be the result of an expansion of the existing activities of existing foreign suppliers. However, to the extent that the important feature of import competition is that foreign suppliers act independently of domestic suppliers, it is perhaps not important to distinguish the arrival of new importers from an expansion in the activities of existing ones.

6 See Miyazaki (1984) and Ben-Ner (1984). Estrin and Jones (1987, 1988) cast some doubt on these arguments using a panel of French worker-owned firms. Ben-Ner (1988b) argues that the population of worker-owned firms is likely to grow counter-cyclically, being born in recessions and transforming themselves into capitalist firms during booms.

7 It is often argued that entry is an expression of risk-taking behaviour and, to the extent that this is a useful insight, it is surely a description of the kind of mind which is willing to invest resources in exploring the possibilities hinted at in a blurred, incomplete perception. Risk taking or not, the not inconsiderable costs of gathering information to mount a trial surely suggests that most entrants will underinvest in it, an observation consistent with the high failure rates cited above.

8 See Utton (1979) for the UK, and Gort (1962) and Berry (1975) for the USA. These studies also commonly find that although diversified firms do operate in a large number of industries, their activities are far more highly concentrated than a simple count of the number of such activities suggests. Viewed as a cross-section snapshot of diversification patterns over time, these very small operations in non-primary industries may well reflect the high costs of adjustment and low penetration speeds observed by Biggadike (see the previous section).

9 Instead of distinguishing potential entrants from incumbents as is conventionally done in models of strategic competition, one might usefully distinguish 'core producers', 'fringe producers' and 'potential entrants' (see also chapter 6). From the point of view of core producers, there is not much difference between firms in the other two groups. Fringe producers are 'stuck in the middle', challenging incumbents on the one hand and fighting off potential entrants on the other. Potential entrants enter the market as fringe producers

and, by and large, seem to leave without every becoming a core producer or even challenging one. If accurate, this characterization points to a kind of hierarchy of competition between types of firms within markets, and it carries the implication that entry provides competitive discipline that affects mainly fringe rather than core producers.

3

Models of Entry

Introduction

The decision to enter a market is not a single discrete choice but the consequence of a sequence of conditional choices that gradually transform agents into actors with specific characteristics located in particular sectors at specific times. The first decision in this sequence is that which leads an agent to respond to the attractions of a particular market by beginning to contemplate the possibility of entry. The characteristic activity of agents in this state is the sinking of investments in information gathering and evaluation. As an agent becomes better informed about the specific opportunities that she/he faces, investment in information gradually gives way to investment in somewhat more tangible assets, including plant, equipment and the development of specific types of human capital. Decisions about 'whether to enter' give way to decisions on issues concerned with 'how', 'when', 'where', 'how much and fast' and 'for how long', the answer to each being conditional on those of the others. The consequence, then, is an 'entry programme', a sequential set of conditional decisions that describe the activities of an entrant both before and after its first appearance in the market.

Although it would, of course, be interesting to model each of the separate stages of a typical entry programme, this is an almost impossible task. At the simplest level, it is difficult to link each decision with an observable in a manner that might enable one to identify its occurrence accurately in space and time, not least because many of the consequences of these decisions have no effect on observable characteristics (e.g. the decision to become informed about the market often does not produce any observable difference in an agent's appearance). Further, the various decisions made by entrants typically do not separate themselves out as cleanly in practice as they do in principle. The importance of insisting on the point that what is being discussed is not so much an entry decision as an entry programme, however, is both more subtle and more important than merely asserting that entry is a complex phenomenon. There are a wide variety of ways to measure 'entry', each different measure reflecting different stages of the entry programme, and the measurement decisions that one makes determine the kind of model that one must use to explain 'entry'. The appearance of a new firm in a specific market niche at a specific time yields information on the 'when' and 'where' of entry, observing its initial size is informative on 'how much', its growth rate on 'how fast', its characteristics or entry strategy on 'how', its discount rate on 'for how long', and observing something about other potential entrants who elected not to enter enables one to say something about 'whether'. All of these observables are legitimate, defendable measures of entry, and any attempt to choose 'the measure of entry' from amongst this set and to develop 'the model of entry' to explain it is effort misplaced. To each observable manifestation of the entry programme corresponds a somewhat different model that describes the particular set of decisions which gave rise to it.

At a practical level, one can usually observe whether entry occurs (or how many entrants appear in a specific industry at a specific time), and at what scale it occurs during the first year post-entry (or how extensive the market penetration of all entrants is). The first type of observable will clearly yield information on 'when' and 'where'; the second will yield, in addition, information on 'how much' and 'how fast'. Although the two observables are not independent, one expects that a model of entry measured as the number of new firms in a market might focus on describing entry as if it were a discrete choice involving 'when' and/or 'where', while a model of entry measured as market share penetration might have more of the character of a model of investment behaviour over time. In addition, one can often observe both the gross and the net number of new firms in a market, and one can occasionally observe the activities of a specific cohort of entrants over a lengthy period of time. The new dimension that this adds to understanding entry decisions is that of 'how long', enabling one to link decisions to enter with decisions to exit (decisions that do not, of course, have to be taken by the same agent) and to develop hazard models describing the duration of a typical entrant's life.

All these different models of entry mimic parts of the whole interdependent sequence of decisions that make up the entry programme, and they are therefore bound to have much in common in the way of observable determinants of entry. More subtly, they all embody a theory which is untestable. Whatever aspect of the entry programme that one focuses upon, the basic fact of the matter is that entry depends on expected profits and these are unobservable. That entry is a sequence of decisions means that what one observes unfolding over time is guided by an evolving set of estimates of expected profits that respond to endogenous and exogenous increases in the information that entrants have at their disposal. The expected profits that guide decisions made at any time t are those expected to flow from that decision in $t + 1$, $t + 2$ and so on, and they are not observable before or, because expectations need not necessarily be realized, after t. Indeed, there are two quite different senses in which expected profits are unobservable. First, prior to making a decision, an entrant cannot observe the profit consequences of that decision and must, perforce, construct some counterfactual estimates of what it thinks is likely to happen post-entry. Second, the entrant's expectations, however constructed, cannot be observed by the econometrician. While the entrant's estimates of post-entry profits may be based on observables, these observables are structured by the entrant's 'theory' of what it thinks is likely to happen, and this is not directly observable. The bottom line, then, is that the 'theory of entry', in as far as it is a hypothesis that entry responds to expected profits, is quite untestable (at least in the absence of other maintained hypotheses).

This is not, however, the problem that it seems to be at first glance. The fact of the matter is that, as a theory to be tested, the hypothesis that entry responds to expected profits is uncontroversial and, indeed, testing it is not a particularly interesting thing to consider doing (not least because it is difficult to think of an alternative theory, although models built along more managerialist or behaviourist lines could be considered). What is far more interesting is to explore the determinants of expected profits as seen through the eyes of entrants. What is it that entrants regard as the important determinants of their future viability?, how do they evaluate the opportunities open to them?, do they take account of the likely responses of incumbents (and, perhaps, of other entrants) to their decisions?, how do they infer what these might be from past responses?, and so on. Since expected profits cannot be observed, it is impossible to examine conjectures of this type directly. However, if one can observe entry and if one assumes that entry is determined by expected post-entry profits, then one can make some indirect inferences about the effects of various observables on expected post-entry profits by looking at how they are associated with the fact of entry. In a sense, a theory of entry that runs in terms of excess profits lacks any substantive content, and it is only the addition of ancillary hypotheses about the determinants of excess profits that gives it any bite.

To account for the flows of entry that we observe, the determinants of expected profits must vary across industries and over time. It is plain that barriers to entry are a principal determinant of excess profits, but, like expected profits, barriers to entry are often uncritically used to explain everything in a way that can provide no insight whatsoever into the entry process. Considered either as obstacles in some absolute sense or as a set of adjustment costs that must be incurred during the process of market penetration, barriers are likely to loom large in the calculations of most entrants as possible indices of both the inherent long-run profitability of a market and the difficulty of obtaining access to those profits. To the extent that they are largely structural in origin, their size is liable to be fairly constant in the short to medium run, and they are likely to vary in character and importance across industries. This lack of time variation, however, means that entry barriers may only play a modest role in explaining variation in entry rates or penetration, since (as we have seen in chapter 2) both display substantial within-industry variability.

While entry barriers are stable over time, the net costs that barriers create for entrants can be significantly modified by mediating market conditions. The effect of barriers to entry may therefore vary over time in any given industry as intervening factors vary in the help or hindrance they offer to entrants trying to overcome specific obstacles. For example, the effects of economies of scale on entrant profit margins depend on the size of the market, and increases in market size are likely to encourage entry for any given degree of scale economies. Exogenous changes in market size – particularly when they are poorly anticipated – may also give rise to a variety of views about viability, providing some basis for more risk-taking agents to consider entry seriously. Further, to the extent that scale economies place no restrictions on market structure stronger than an upper limit on the number of firms that can be viable in a market, then displacement of existing incumbents and pre-emption of other possible entrants are potentially viable strategies that some entrants may pursue when some or all incumbents are particularly vulnerable. Finally, incumbents in the market may adopt more or less aggressive strategies to deter entry, strategies that make entry at any given scale more or less easy, *ceteris paribus*. In short, while an entry barrier like economies of scale may be time invariant, its effect on entry need not be.

These observations suggest that the determinants of expected profits might be classed into three broad groups: entry barriers that impose costs on entrants, variations in market conditions which modify or exaggerate these costs, and factors affecting the interaction within and between groups of entrants and incumbents. Two major distinctions help to define these three classes of putative determinants of entry in a slightly different way: barriers to entry and market conditions are likely to be exogenous to the actions of entrants (in the main), while the nature and intensity of the interactions between entrants and incumbents are likely to be endogenous, and barriers to entry are likely to be permanent structural features of markets, while mediating market conditions and interactions between firms are likely to be far more transitory. Thus, variations in expected profits across markets and over time are likely to contain three generic components, the first permanent and exogenous, the second transitory and exogenous, and the third transitory and endogenous.

We shall structure our discussion of models of entry around four basic types of model. The first two – discussed in the next two sections – focus on the 'when' and 'where', and on the 'how much' and 'how fast' of entry. Models of the incidence of entry and models of market penetration tend to have fairly similar structures, and all of them contain a collection of variables variously reflecting permanent and transitory factors, most of which are generally assumed to be exogenous. In fact, many of the most striking individual differences between these models in practice has emerged from idiosyncratic differences in the specification of expected post-entry profits. Given the plethora of possible determinants of this unobservable, the really interesting question is whether one can uncover a single, easily observable index of expected profits (such as market size, or incumbent profitability) or at least of entry barriers. Although it is possible to make quite a bit of progress on this issue, most models of entry can claim only a very modest degree of success in accounting for observed variations in entry rates or entry penetration. The inevitable conclusion – that expected profits seem to depend on a number of idiosyncratic transitory factors – challenges one to decompose entry into permanent and transitory components and to characterize some of the features of the latter more precisely. One type of model appropriate for this exercise is a latent factor model, and it is discussed in the fourth section. The other important distinction between the various putative determinants of entry separates those factors that are exogenous to the decisions of entrants from those that are endogenous. Any attempt to account for the endogeneity of expected profits requires one to focus directly on the strategic interactions between entrants and incumbents, and on the selection process which helps to determine the 'how long' of entry. Models of this type form the basis of the penultimate section, which is followed by a brief conclusion.

Modelling the Incidence of Entry

The most readily available piece of information about entry is usually the knowledge that it has occurred during the time that one observes the market in question. Given this and knowing none of the characteristics of the entrant, its strategy or its market penetration programme, one has little choice but to focus on the 'when' and 'where' decisions made by the entrant. The interesting questions to be asked, then, are what were the market conditions that facilitated entry, and how did they assist the entrant to overcome obstacles in the form of entry barriers and, possibly, adverse reactions by incumbents. The type of observation available on entry forces one to think of it as a discrete event ($P(t) = 1$ if entry occurs in the market at period t and $P(t) = 0$ otherwise) and that, in turn, dictates the general type of model that one ought to use. Letting expected (discounted post-entry) profits be denoted $\pi^e(t)$, then a very simple model of the probability of entry might take the form

$$P(t) = 1 \text{ if } \pi^e(t) > 0$$
$$P(t) = 0 \text{ otherwise} \tag{3.1}$$

and

$$\pi^e(t) = \beta_1 X_1(t) + \beta_2 X_2(t) + \beta_3 X_3(t) \tag{3.2}$$

where $X_1(t)$ are exogenous structural factors, $X_2(t)$ are exogenous transitory factors and $X_3(t)$ are endogenous transitory factors. The goal of the exercise is to learn something about the relative magnitudes of β_1, β_2 and β_3 in order to observe why a particular configuration of $X_1(t)$, $X_2(t)$ and $X_3(t)$ observed in the market at time t caused $\pi^e(t) > 0$ (or not).

The outcome of several exercises of this type have been reported in the literature. Thompson (1986) looked at successful and unsuccessful entry into the Irish provincial newspaper industry during the decade 1971–80. The determinants of $\pi^e(t)$ that he considered included industry concentration, market size (measured as area, income per head, and population), market growth and the local presence of a newspaper chain. His results suggested that market size apparently increased expected profits, growth reduced them, concentration had a weak positive effect and the local presence of a multiple operator had little effect at all. Hannan (1983) examined *de novo* entry into local banking markets in Pennsylvania over the period 1968–70 by banks located elsewhere in Pennsylvania, a set of observations on entry that enabled him to focus on whether or not a specific agent at some particular time or place chose to enter a given host market. Like Thompson, he modelled $\pi^e(t)$ as being determined by a linear combination of observables that were assumed to be exogenous to the entry decision. By and large, he found that entrants tended to open new branches in markets where their headquarters were located or where they currently operated a branch, and in markets where pre-entry 'prices' (i.e. loan rates relative to savings or deposit rates) and demand relative to existing capacity (deposits per branch) were high.

Interesting as these exercises are, the amount of information that one is able to extract from them is slightly limited by the relatively loose specification of equation (3.2), the model of expected profits, that is used (this is true for many of the models discussed below as well). It is evident that what one can learn about the variation in $P(t)$ across local markets and over time depends not only on the number and quality of measurement of the observables – $X_1(t)$, $X_2(t)$ and $X_3(t)$ – that one uses, but also on the *a priori* information that one can bring to bear on the question of how they affect $\pi^e(t)$. For example, the absence of an observed effect of the presence of an incumbent newspaper chain on entry in Thompson's regressions may be an artifact of the way in which the effect was modelled; it may not (as claimed) reflect accommodating behaviour. Further, the fact that he observed a positive effect of industry concentration on entry suggests that the concentration variable may conflate incumbent reactions with some favourable condition of entry that is a feature of highly concentrated markets. More substantively, both Thompson and Hannan observed market size to be an important determinant of the profitability of entry using an empirical model that was rather short of variables reflecting the many possible entry barriers that entrants may face. The important point here is that many of these barriers are extremely difficult to measure reliably, and it is important to know whether they all vary systematically with some specific, easily observable index like market size. In the current context, this question leads one to ask whether it is possible to measure the apparent height of barriers to entry solely in terms of the size of market necessary to support one, two or more firms.

A rather ingenious answer to this question has been proposed by Bresnahan and Reiss (1986, 1988). Suppose that one is considering a set of markets in which only one of three possible outcomes can occur: no entry, monopoly, or duopoly. Letting monopoly profits be π^M and duopoly profits be $\pi^D < \pi^M$, then the probability that $N = 0$, 1, 2 entrants are present in the market is

$$\Pr\{N = 0\} = \Pr\{\pi^M < 0\}$$
$$\Pr\{N = 1\} = \Pr\{\pi^M > 0 \text{ and } \pi^D < 0\} \qquad (3.3)$$
$$\Pr\{N = 2\} = \Pr\{\pi^D > 0\}.$$

The events $N = 0, 1, 2$, are observed, but π^M and π^D are not observable. The goal of the modelling exercise is to relate π^M and π^D to variations in some simple observable related to the incidence of entry. Suppose that marginal costs are constant and that price p depends on per capita demand q but is homogeneous of degree zero in market size z. Then profits π are given by

$$\pi = [p(q) - c]qz - F \qquad (3.4)$$

where F are fixed costs and all of the elements of (3.4) are understood to be pre-entry expectations of post-entry magnitudes. The important point to note about (3.4) is that equilibrium quantities and prices are independent of z. Thus, at some equilibrium price p^* and quantity q^* (e.g. the monopoly or the duopoly equilibrium), profits are

$$\pi^* = m^*z - F \qquad (3.5)$$

where $m^* \equiv q^*[p(q^*) - c]$. If one does not know the elasticity of demand η, then the monopoly level of prices (or the mark-up of prices over costs) is unknown; duopoly prices depend in addition on the nature of post-entry competition, the details of which may also be unknown. Despite this, it is still possible to estimate (3.3) since post-entry returns are linear in the observable z. The difference between monopoly and duopoly outcomes can therefore be observed by comparing differences in the estimated coefficient on z, while variations in fixed entry costs of various types can be estimated by including observables in addition to z in the regression. Thus, observations of the events $N = 0, 1, 2$ and z across markets enables one to estimate the relative size of m^* that is likely to prevail under monopoly and duopoly, and to work out how much entry affects profits. Further, estimates of m^* and F enable one to calculate what the critical market sizes for entry are (i.e. to compute the critical values of market size at which $\pi^* > 0$).[1]

In their first pass at the data, Bresnahan and Reiss (1986) applied the model to data on retail automobile dealerships in small well-defined local markets in the USA in 1982. Their basic result was that an entrant who converted a monopoly market into a duopoly would earn about 66% of the variable profits of the original monopolist. While this seems to imply that total duopoly profits exceed monopoly profits, the common sense of it is that entry does not substantially affect price–cost margins. Further, the apparent response by entrants to market growth appeared to be rather slow (exit appeared to be more rapid), with lags in the response to apparently profitable opportunities occasioned by market growth being typically longer than ten years. They also observed that duopolies occurred at little more than twice the breakeven market density for monopolists, and thus that the range (in terms of market size) in which monopoly predominates is rather narrow. One emerges with the impression that the retail automobile market is and is not competitive: monopoly is, in a sense, rare, but duopolists enjoy high price–cost margins.

Subsequent applications of the model (see their 1988 paper) involved looking at what amounted to a fairly wide cross-section of case studies of isolated retail and professional markets in the USA, and some of the output of this exercise is shown in table 3.1. Generally, they found the difference between monopoly and duopoly values of m^* to be fairly small and insignificant. The ratio of m^* in duopoly to that in monopoly generally exceeded 0.5 but was not always less than 1.0, suggesting that most of the difference between π^D and π^M is due to differences in fixed and entry costs rather than to differences in variable profits. The range of market sizes needed to support a duopoly in what they classified as

Table 3.1 Estimates of (3.3) for 13 US professional and retail industries

	Town size needed to support a monopoly	Town size needed to support a duopoly	Entry threshold ratio	Ratio of duopoly to monopoly margins
Physicians	552	1659	3.012	0.728
Dentists	632	1999	3.164	0.879
Veterinarians	1008	4189	4.149	0.810
Drug stores	467	1400	2.994	0.920
Opticians	1885	5447	2.890	0.595
Auto dealers	664	1538	2.315	0.631
Barbers	1003.8	2672.1	2.662	0.710
Cooking contractors	8285	20831	2.515	0.617
Electricians	1040	3242	3.114	0.626
Heating contractors	3168	5589	1.764	1.00
Plumbers	1507	3226	2.140	1.000
Movie theatres	1982	5909	2.981	0.532
Tire dealers	563	1539	2.732	1.000

The size variable used in the first two columns is population. The entry threshold ratio in the third column is the value of F/m^* at which $\pi = 0$ in duopoly expressed as a fraction of the corresponding monopoly numbers, while the fourth column shows the ratio of m^* in duopoly to m^* in monopoly. All numbers are evaluated at sample means. Bresnahan and Reiss also report the corresponding numbers evaluated at the mean values for the monopolies in each industry, and the two sets of figures are fairly similar.
Source: Bresnahan and Reiss, 1988, tables 3 and 4

professional services (shown in the first six rows of table 3.1) ranged from 2.3 times larger than monopoly market sizes for auto dealers to 4 times larger for veterinarians, while most sectors registered a ratio of duopoly to monopoly breakeven size of about 3. The corresponding figures for retail markets (shown in the last seven rows of table 3.1) were slightly lower. Electricians were the most prone to monopoly of the retail industries, while heating contractors were the least prone to monopoly of all the industries shown in table 3.1. Thus, the data seem to suggest that professional services tend slightly more toward monopoly market structures than retail markets, although it must be added that the within-group variation is substantial. The variation in entry conditions for professional services in their sample did not appear to be related to government regulation of entry, but the comparison between professional services and retail markets is consistent with the view that the former require far more sunk investments in human capital and, perhaps, in reputation formation than the latter. These, it appears, have a noticeable effect on market structure. As with automobile dealerships, one emerges with the feeling that these markets are and are not competitive.

The main difficulty with (3.3)–(3.4) as a model of entry is that of collapsing the full range of entry barriers down to a single simple index like market size.[2] This is a natural simplification to use when entrants are more or less identical and demand is homogeneous. In these circumstances, price will be equalized across all market participants, and the only barrier to entry that has to be considered is the fixed entry cost which must be covered by an entrant if it is to survive. As all firms are identical, market shares will be equal and the only thing that matters to an entrant worried about survival is therefore total market size. However, when products are differentiated, the question of how an entrant can squeeze itself into the market becomes much more interesting, and corresponding to the range of strategies open to it are a range of barriers to entry that affect the choice amongst them. It is difficult to believe that these will necessarily collapse into a single simple index like market size, not least because, when products are differentiated, market size can be rather poorly defined. That Bresnahan and Reiss (1988) observed a value of m^* in duopoly that was more than 50% of its monopoly value suggests that subsequent entrants in their sample expanded and, perhaps, segmented the monopoly markets that they entered, raising total industry profits. This, in turn, is likely to have been the result of differentiating their products (or services) in some way.

To give some feel for what an entry model with product differentiation might lead to, consider a market where product differentiation matters and, to fix ideas, focus on a market where the prices of various products

(including the entrants) are fixed (Geroski and Murfin, 1987). To understand what affects the entry decision – that is, what the entrant thinks
pre-entry that it will need to do post-entry in order to cover the costs of
entry – one needs to be explicit about how consumers make their choices
between the different products on offer in the market. Assume that the
good in question is an experience good, but that a single purchase is not,
in general, sufficient to give complete information about its characteristics. Further, assume that product characteristics change over time
more frequently than the good is purchased by the consumer, preventing
him or her from building up experience with the good. When a consumer
purchases some brand i which has quality v_i, she/he may be satisfied or
not. Since the consumer is not exactly sure of v_i, nor of any of the other
v_j, satisfaction does not necessarily guarantee a repeat purchase, and
dissatisfaction does not necessarily lead to a switch. Suppose that if
she/he is satisfied, she/he repeats the purchase in the next period t with
probability

$$p_i(t) = 1 - 1/v_i \qquad (3.6)$$

but that, if she/he is dissatisfied, the probability of a repeat purchase is
$1/v_i$.

In the event of dissatisfaction, the consumer must choose an alternative
brand, a task made difficult by lack of knowledge of the v_js. Price may,
of course, be used in this decision, but the consumer is also likely to tap
a wide range of information sources. At the end of the day, she/he is likely
to turn to an alternative brand that she or he is familiar with (in some
sense). Partly for this reason and partly because advertising may be a
signal of quality, suppose that she/he chooses an alternative to brand j
on the basis of the relative volume of advertising of the different brands.
Letting $A_i(t)$ be the advertising expended on brand i at t, we assume
that the probability of selecting brand j at t is proportional to brand j's
advertising share, $a_j(t) \equiv A_j(t)/\Sigma A_j(t)$. Thus, the probability of a
switch from i to j is

$$p_{ij}(t) = \left(1 - \frac{1}{v_i}\right) Q_{ij} + \frac{a_j(t)}{v_i} \qquad (3.7)$$

where $Q_{ij} = 1$ for $i = j$ and is zero otherwise. At a long-run equilibrium
in which all firms i have a stable level of advertising, the probability of
any one consumer selecting brand i is

$$\rho_i = v_i A_i / \Sigma v_i A_i \equiv \phi_i a_i \qquad (3.8)$$

where $\phi_i = v_i/\Sigma v_i a_i$ is an index of the relative quality of brand i. With a large number of independent buyers, ρ_i is also the market share of brand i.[3]

For an entrant brand i into a market with total revenue R and price–cost margin m, expected post-entry profits are

$$\pi_i = \phi_i Rma_i - F \qquad (3.9)$$

where F is fixed costs. The entrant's decision, then, is to enter if it thinks that it can capture an advertising share greater than $F/\phi_i Rm$ post-entry, and to stay out otherwise. As in the Bresnahan and Reiss model, entry will be easier the lower are fixed costs F, the larger is the total market R and the higher is the equilibrium price–cost margin m. Where (3.9) departs from Bresnahan and Reiss, however, is in making the entrant's market share an important endogenous determinant of expected post-entry profits. The entrant's choice is not simply when (or whether) to enter, but also how to do so, and its post-entry profitability is therefore dependent on its strategy choices and those of its rivals. In this particular model, product quality and relative advertising volume are the two weapons used by firms. Thinking in terms of (3.8), the model suggests that the effectiveness of advertising in capturing market share depends on relative product quality, and that these two competitive weapons are – at least to a limited extent – substitutes.

If R, m, f, A_i and the event of entry are observed, then (3.9) can be used to estimate ϕ_i and so to measure π_i^e. Geroski and Murfin applied (3.9) to entry into three segments of the UK car market, 1958–83, and found it to lead to surprisingly accurate predictions about when entry occurred and in what order entrants entered the three segments of the market. Expected post-entry advertising share proved to be a far more powerful predictor of entry than any of several measures of post-entry price–cost margins, and the elasticity of the probability of entry with respect to advertising was nearly 50% higher for later than for earlier entrants (the elasticities being 15.2 and 23.5 respectively). The comparison suggests that advertising may be more successful in penetrating markets than it is in defending them, and is not inconsistent with the oft expressed view that entrants into this sector produced rather higher quality products than incumbents. Although it was impossible to observe product quality directly, allowance was made for variations in quality between brands and over time using fixed effects and firm-specific time trends, and estimates of these went some way towards explaining variations in the effectiveness of advertising across firms. While advertising facilitated entry in the sense that successful entry followed the acquisition of a large advertising share, Geroski and Murfin observed that the probability of entry fell as industry-wide advertising totals rose; i.e. entry fell as the costs of achieving a given advertising share rose. They also observed that while entrants followed a well-defined route into the industry across market segments, the effect of previous experience in one segment on the probability of entry into another segment was rather modest. Across the three segments of the market, entry was related to market size (and growth) in the sense that entry typically occurred first into the largest and most fast growing of the three segments. However, as entry involved a substantial transfer of shares from incumbents to entrants, the role of market size was not, in the end, particularly important in accounting for the incidence of entry, and it appeared to have no substantive effect on the timing of entry. As one suspected, the use of market size as an index of the full range of entry barriers turns out to be much less powerful in markets where product differentiation strategies are actively pursued by entrants and incumbents.

All the models discussed thus far focus on explaining entry as if it were an infrequent event in most markets. The ability to observe discrete events like the entry of some particular firm in some particular market at some particular time is very much a matter of being able to observe well-defined and often isolated markets during fairly short intervals of time. This is not always possible and, indeed, for those anxious to make broad statements about the determinants of entry across a range of industries, this case study methodology can be somewhat exhausting. The alternative is to explain what one observes in more broadly defined national markets, using Census data on the number of firms operating in the market together with either the net or gross addition to that stock over a one to five year period. Modelling data in this form requires a change in orientation from looking at the choices of a few rather specific agents using (3.1)–(3.2) to looking at the outcome of a whole range of such decisions made simultaneously by large numbers of relatively anonymous firms. Although it is by no means necessary to do so, it is probably the case that market size will prove to play a much less central role in such markets, and it may therefore be necessary to model expected post-entry profits more extensively in terms of a wider range of observables. Certainly, one can reasonably aspire to identifying some of the major cost and demand side factors that account for variations in the incidence of entry across markets.

A natural starting point is to assume that the number of firms N that one observes in any given industry is the equilibrium number appropriate for that sector, and thus that the number N_e of new firms is such as to set expected post-entry profits to zero. Evidently, N_e will be higher the faster is market growth, the more elastic is demand, the less aggressive is the response by incumbents, and the lower is the minimum efficient scale of entry relative to market size. To express these observations more precisely, we follow Kessides (1986, 1989, 1991) and model the likely incidence of entry by establishing a relationship between post-entry prices and the (net) number of new firms, given the number of firms, market growth, technology, the elasticity of demand and incumbents' reactions. Suppose that the good in question is homogeneous and that the efficient size of entry is x. Thus, the arrival of N_e entrants results in a post-entry price of

$$p_e = p(q_o + N_e x) \tag{3.10}$$

where q_o is pre-entry output. Taking a first-order approximation to (3.10) at q_o,

$$p_e \approx p_o \left(1 - \frac{N_e s}{\eta} \right) \tag{3.11}$$

where η is the absolute value of the price elasticity of demand and $s \equiv x/q_o$ is the efficient scale of entry expressed as a market share. It follows that the change in price due to entry, $\Delta p \equiv p_e - p_o$, is

$$\Delta p = - p_o N_e s / \eta. \tag{3.12}$$

Thus far, we have assumed that market growth does not occur and that incumbents do not respond to entry. Letting exogenous market growth occur at a rate g and letting the expansion rate of incumbents be r, then (3.12) can be generalized to

$$\Delta p = \frac{- p_o [N_e s - (g - r)]}{\eta(1 + g)}. \tag{3.13}$$

Clearly a more elastic demand leads to a smaller price change, as does a smaller efficient scale of entry and a smaller number of entrants. Further, if the market grows fast enough or if incumbents cut back their output post-entry, then post-entry prices could actually exceed pre-entry prices (although this seems rather unlikely). Post-entry prices will be higher, however, the faster is the growth of residual demand in the market.[4]

Equation (3.13) forms the basis of how a rational entrant might predict post-entry prices given its knowledge of market demand (g and η), technology (s), incumbents' responses (r), and the likely number of other entrants (N_e). The present value of its expected post-entry profits is

$$\pi^e = \frac{\{p_o [1 - N_e s - (g - r)] - c\}x - F}{\eta(1 + g)} \tag{3.14}$$

where c is average costs of production and may include entry costs. Comparing (3.14) with (3.5) makes it plain that equations (3.10)–(3.13) have done no more than provide an explicit solution for m^* that is expressed in terms of a number of potentially observable determinants of entry. Clearly, any entrant considered in isolation will choose to enter the market if $\pi^e > 0$, and this will be true for all entrants. As a consequence, entry will occur until $\pi^e = 0$, and at equilibrium

$$N_e = \frac{g - r}{s} + \frac{(1 + g)\eta\,\pi_0}{s}\left(\frac{1 - K}{\pi_0}\right) \qquad (3.15)$$

where $\pi_0 \equiv (p_0 - c)/p_0$ is pre-entry price–cost margins and K reflects those elements of F that are sunk. Equation (3.15) has a natural and appealing interpretation. The first term of (3.15) gives the number of new firms that could enter the industry without causing price to fall, while the second gives that number which could squeeze in despite a fall in price post-entry because of the pre-entry elevation of price above costs. This second component of N_e is larger the larger is the pre-entry elevation of price above the entrants' costs, the more elastic is demand, the faster is market growth, the smaller is the efficient scale of entry, and the smaller are sunk costs.

Thus, using observed values of g, r, s, η, K and π_0, one can use (3.15) to predict N_e; if one cannot observe one (or more) of these five but can proxy it (them) using some observable Z and unknown parameters θ, then one can use (3.15) to measure θ and so construct an estimate of post-entry equilibrium profits π^e. Kessides applied an extension of this type of model to net entry data (the net number of new firms) for 266 four-digit US industries, 1972–7, and subsequently extended the model to the period 1977–82. Table 3.2 shows a typical equation estimated on each of the two time periods, an equation embodying the simplification that $g = r$ and the assumption that K has two components, SUM and SUB, reflecting sunk costs in materials and sunk costs in buildings respectively. The equation also omits η which never proved significant in any of his regressions. As can be seen, the results are fairly similar in the two time periods. Entry appears to increase with both market size and growth ($a_1 > 0$ and $a_2 < 0$, the latter reflecting the diminution in the effects of scale economies caused by an increase in market size), and sunk costs seem to matter in discouraging entry (a_5, $a_6 > 0$). Incumbents' profits have an encouraging effect on entry ($a_3 > 0$, and $a_7 > 0$ but small). Results reported in his 1986 paper also suggest that advertising gives rise to a sunk cost barrier to entry, and indeed that advertising is more important than physical capital in creating sunk costs which deter entry (possibly because capital equipment can be rented; for further work on sunk costs, see Mata, 1991). Further,

Table 3.2 Estimates of (3.15) for US four-digit industries

$$\ln N_e = a_0 + a_1 \ln(1 + g) + a_2 \ln s + a_3 \ln \pi_o + a_4 \ln[1 - (a_5 \text{SUM}_e + a_6 \text{SUB}_e)\pi_o^{a_7}]$$

1972-9

Parameters	a_0	a_1	a_2	a_3	a_4	a_5	a_6	a_7
Estimates	0.113	0.847	−1.021	0.830	1.663	1.520	0.384	0.837
	(0.107)	(0.096)	(0.20)	(0.044)	(0.376)	(0.052)	(0.715)	(0.060)

Number of observations 266

1977-82

Parameters	a_0	a_1	a_2	a_3	a_4	a_5	a_6	a_7
Estimates	−0.343	0.919	−0.893	0.672	0.748	0.703	−2.547	−0.613
	(0.802)	(0.242)	(0.102)	(0.326)	(0.248)	(0.165)	(1.675)	(0.206)

Number of observations 250

Standard errors are in parentheses. g is the industry growth rate, s is minimum efficient scale, π_o is pre-entry profits, and SUB and SUM are upper bound measures of sunk investments in buildings and machinery, expressed as a fraction of the typical scale of entry. *Source*: Kessides, 1991, table 1

it appears that entrants perceive a greater likelihood of success in highly advertising-intensive markets (the overall impact of advertising on entry is positive), that incumbents are more likely to respond aggressively to entry the higher is π_o and the higher is market concentration, and that $g \approx r$ on average. Finally (3.15) can be solved for the level of pre-entry 'limit' profits π^L which block entry (i.e. for which $N_e = 0$), and for the 1972-7 sample the level of limit profits appeared to be roughly 5% (the manufacturing average $\pi_o \approx 21\%$).

There are, no doubt, numerous ways in which these models of the incidence of entry can be extended. Precisely how one goes about this depends on what one wishes to observe about the expectations that entrants hold of post-entry returns. The work that has been done thus far makes it clear that market size is an important determinant of entry. Most markets are limited in the number of firms that they can support, and larger markets can support rather more firms than smaller ones, *ceteris paribus*. However, market size is by no means the sole determinant of entry rates, and it is unlikely that it can be relied upon for use as a single summary index of entry barriers. Since size is only meaningful relative to existing supply capacity, one suspects that the number, type and actions of incumbents and other potential entrants might also matter.

The evidence seems to suggest that this is true in a variety of ways that are probably industry and, to some extent, time specific. Certainly, entry into highly concentrated markets often (but not always) appears to be rather more difficult than entry into less concentrated ones, and advertising seems to have both pro- and anti-competitive effects on entry. Entry is also somewhat more likely in markets where pre-entry prices have been substantially elevated above costs.

All these factors go some way to answering the question of 'where' entry occurs, but say little about 'when'. Inter-industry differences in market size, minimum efficient scale, the elasticity of demand, industry concentration and, to a certain degree, price–cost margins are all fairly constant over time. Much of the predictive accuracy achieved by Geroski and Murfin arose from their ability to predict variations over time in industry conduct – advertising shares and rivals' advertising – and one conjectures that further work on the subject of 'when' entry occurs may need to follow this path and concentrate rather more on modelling variations in market conduct. Still, changes in market structure are always likely to affect entry, and the analogue of market size in this respect is market growth. However, what is interesting about the work discussed thus far is the positive but often rather weak effects of market growth on entry that have been observed (see also the penultimate section). Although it is somewhat speculative, one wonders whether this might indicate that it is current and not future market events that matter most to entrants, a question which begs the further question of what period of time the 'post-entry' period is, and how long a future period it is over which expectations are formed. These are interesting questions, but they are ones on which observations of the incidence of entry are unlikely to cast much light.

Models of Market Penetration by Entrants

It is not immediately apparent that one needs a different model to explain entry penetration from that which one might use to explain the incidence of entry. After all, an entrant using equation (3.14) to decide whether or not to enter is implicitly expecting to gain a market share of some size (e.g. $1/N$) should it enter. If its assessment of post-entry conditions is correct, then the explanation of the occurrence of the event $\pi^e > 0$ is, in principle, the same as the explanation of the observed degree of market penetration.[5] The major novelty involved in modelling the market penetration of entrants only emerges when one thinks seriously about how to define the 'post-entry' period – when one thinks about how and when market penetration will be achieved. Observing the cumulative market penetration of entrants over longer and longer periods of time enables one to observe the effects of decisions like 'how much', 'how fast' and 'for how long' rather more than 'when', and one naturally wonders what the determinants of these are across markets. As with all the measures of entry, there is no single optimal length over which to observe or measure entry penetration; rather, there are a variety of models that one can use, starting with those that model the 'instantaneous' (say, initial year) market penetration achieved by entrants.

The simplest – and certainly the most common – model of entry penetration has attempted to explain penetration E_t at time t in terms of expected post-entry profits π_t^e and entry costs F:

$$E_t = \gamma(\pi_t^e - F). \tag{3.16}$$

As we shall show later in this section, (3.16) can be derived from a fairly orthodox decision-theoretic model (meaning that γ can be given a fairly precise interpretation and linearity can be defended) but, for the time being, we shall take its appeal as being self-evident. Assuming for the moment that F is observable (it is usually proxied by a linear combination of factors such as market size, growth, concentration and so on) and that γ is the goal of estimation, the principal problem with (3.16) is to find an observable proxy for π_t^e. The path that most scholars have followed is to assume that entrants form their expectations on the basis of pre-entry profits π_{t-1}. Since these are observable, it is straightforward to use observed entry penetration, observed pre-entry profits and observations of F to generate estimates of γ from (3.16), estimates which one might naturally think of as measuring something about the speed of market penetration by entrants in response to excess profits. The interesting thing about the fairly large literature which has followed this route is that the estimates of γ so generated are often rather small, and occasionally they are insignificantly different from zero. One forms the impression from this work that entry responds slowly and only very sluggishly to excess profits and, since the R^2 values in these regressions are often rather low, one emerges thinking that most of the proxies for excess profits that have been used are poor and, possibly, that entry may be largely exogenous to market events.[6]

The virtue of using π_{t-1} to proxy π_t^e is that it is an easy solution to a complex latent variables problem and, for small-scale entry, it may not even be a bad one. After all, small entrants will only add a negligible amount to existing industry output, and if there is any kind of market growth they are unlikely to have much of an impact on prices. Still, one ought to be wary of a specification as simple as $\pi_t^e = \pi_{t-1}$, and there are several obvious alternatives worth consideration. For example, rather than using π_{t-1}, one might use an extrapolative predictor based on π_{t-1}, π_{t-2} and so on. Highfield and Smiley (1987) followed this course and found, *inter alia*, that such a model produced a rather higher, more statistically significant estimate of γ than a model which proxied π_t^e by π_{t-1} alone. This of course is exactly what one would expect if the use of π_{t-1} to proxy π_t^e involved a measurement error. While an extrapolative predictor is preferable to the use of π_{t-1} alone, more efficient yet is a rational expectations predictor which uses information both on the structure of the model explaining π_t^e and on exogenous variables. This type of model involves building a second equation describing profits conditional on entry. Solving the model produces a reduced form in which profits depend on all the exogenous variables in the two-equation system, and rational expectations of π_t^e can be proxied using predicted values generated from this reduced form equation. The technique is of course similar in outcome to a simultaneous equation model of entry and profitability. Geroski (1990a, 1991) and Georski and Murfin (1990b) have constructed models of this type and, like Highfield and Smiley, discovered that they generally produced larger and more statistically significant estimates of γ than did the same model using a naive predictor.

The story is rather more complex than this, however. Table 3.3 shows three net entry penetration equations estimated for the UK with data pooled over the period 1976-9 (these estimates are similar to those reported in Geroski, 1990a). F is proxied by three observables (industry growth, size and the capital–output ratio) plus a full set of industry fixed effects. Using a naive predictor yeilds an estimate of $\gamma = 0.088$ (column (i)), much lower than the estimate one gets using a rational expectations predictor ($\gamma = 1.07$ in column (ii)). This is exactly what one would expect if π_{t-1} measured π_t^e with error. The rational expectations predictor used in (ii) uses information from a reduced form equation of π_t or π_{t-1}, π_{t-2}, π_{t-3}, E_{t-1}, E_{t-2} and all the exogenous variables (including fixed effects) in (ii), and it is interesting to ask whether any particular subset of this information is particularly useful. The estimates shown in column (iii) include all the information used to produce the reduced form predictions of π_t used to proxy π_t^e in (ii), but in an unstructured form. Of the five new variables introduced instead of the proxy for π_t^e, it is the two lagged values of entry that appear to carry most of the weight. Thus, the edge that more sophisticated proxies of π_t^e have over the naive predictor π_{t-1} is (at least in this case) information on previous entry, information that somehow is not reflected in π_{t-1}, π_{t-2} and π_{t-3}. Previous entry seems to contain more useful information on π_t^e to use in predicting current entry than observed profits do, possibly because the actions of previous entrants bear more heavily on the profit expectations of current entrants than they do on the profit realizations enjoyed by current incumbents. That is, entrants may compete mainly with entrants, and it is this that (may) give more sophisticated proxies their edge. More sobering is the sense one gets in (iii) that it is rather hard to improve on purely autoregressive models of entry (see the next section), meaning that useful observable proxies for π_t^e are hard to find. One's disappointment with the implicit model of π_i^e underlying the estimates in table 3.3 is, of course, reinforced by the rather poor fit recorded by them.

Precisely what to make of estimates of γ and their sensitivity to the estimation technique used is unclear, particularly since an estimate of γ

Table 3.3 Estimates of a UK entry equation

	(i)	(ii)	(iii)
π_{it}^e	–	1.0678	–
		(3.448)	
g_{it-1}	0.0018	0.0067	0.0089
	(0.177)	(0.637)	(0.911)
z_{it-1}	0.0085	0.0184	−0.0051
	(0.496)	(1.33)	(0.332)
k_{it-1}	−0.0005	0.0033	−0.0035
	(0.097)	(0.6151)	(0.641)
π_{it-1}	0.088	–	0.0732
	(1.77)		(1.487)
π_{it-2}	–	–	0.0051
			(0.119)
π_{it-3}	–	–	0.0249
			(1.46)
E_{it-1}	–	–	−0.1864
			(3.729)
E_{it-2}	–	–	−0.1403
			(3.368)
R^2	0.050	0.087	0.118
Log likelihood	860.722	867.58	876.347

The data are pooled for 1976–9, and the i index refers to industry i. Absolute values of t statistics are given in parentheses below the estimated coefficients; all equations have a full set of fixed effects and time dummies; E_{it}, net market penetration by entrants, market size being defined as domestic sales; π_{it}^e, expected post-entry margins, proxied by using the predictions from an equation of margins in t on margins in $t-1$, $t-2$, $t-3$, entry in $t-1$, $t-2$, and g_{it-1}, z_{it-1} and k_{it-1}; g_{it-1}, lagged rate of growth of industry sales; z_{it-1}, lagged logarithm of domestic sales (= domestic production plus imports less exports); k_{it-1}, capital stock–output ratio, where output is domestic production. All estimates of standard errors are heteroscedastic consistent.

not significantly different from zero would persuade few that entry did not respond to expected profits. In fact, the absolute value of γ that one estimates is difficult to interpret on its own – it is, in some sense, a speed of adjustment – and to evaluate how large a given estimate is requires that one place (3.16) into a wider market model which describes how entry, profits and other factors mutually determine each other over time (see chapter 4). More worrying, none of the experiments discussed above (or immediately below) provide any grounds for thinking that any of the proxies of π_t^e account for much of the inter-industry and, particularly, of the intertemporal variation observed in E_t, not least because many of the measures of π_t^e used show very little within-industry variation. The measures of F that have been used in (3.16) often make a significant additional contribution to the degree of explanation achieved, but this generally also takes the form of accounting for some of the between-industry variation and rather less of the within-industry variation observed. And no amount of playing around with proxies for π_t^e or F has ever produced very high R^2 values, or a substantial improvement on the autoregressive models of entry discussed in chapter 2. No matter how one looks at it, the fact is that entry is a very noisy signal of π_t^e and F. What is worse, although it is not the case that E_{t-1} is a good predictor of E_t, it is often rather hard to find a better predictor. What this says, of course, is that the history of E_t is as good as any other observable at predicting E_t because it captures many of the inter-industry differences in market size, profitability and so on that affect entry penetration.

Despite the availability of a range of alternatives, one might still elect to use (3.16) together with the assumption that $\pi_{t-1} = \pi_t^e$ in some circumstances. However, if one were genuinely persuaded that entrants used the expectations formulation rule $\pi_{t-1} = \pi_t^e$, then one must acknowledge the possibility that incumbents will learn this and take advantage of it. Indeed, whether incumbents choose to 'limit price' or, more generally, to act strategically pre-entry to manipulate entry by affecting π_{t-1} and so π_t^e is an important question worth exploring in its own right. Masson and Shaanan (1982) have produced an interesting model with which to examine this question. Suppose that $\pi_t^e = \pi_{t-1}$, so that (3.16) becomes

$$E_t = \gamma\left(\pi_{t-1} - F\right). \tag{3.17}$$

At a long-run equilibrium, F can be interpreted as the level of profits at which entry is forestalled. While it is not directly observable, let us assume that it can be written as a simple function of a set of observable entry barriers B. Consider π°, defined as the joint industry maximum profits obtainable given entry conditions. When barriers are so high that entry is blockaded, at $B = B^*$ say, then π° reaches some maximum level, π^*

say (and, of course, $\pi^* = F$ at $B = B^*$ by the definition of a long-run equilibrium). Now, Bain argued that when barriers were high but not so high that entry was blockaded, then entry might be effectively impeded by limit pricing. Alternatively, when barriers were rather low, then it might not be worthwhile for incumbents to block entrants, and entry would be ineffectively impeded. Let $\overline{B}$ be the critical level of barriers which distinguish these two outcomes. Then one expects to observe $\pi^\circ = \pi^*$ for levels of barriers $B < \overline{B}$ (entry ineffectively impeded as incumbents enjoy short-run excess profits), but to observe $\pi^\circ = F < \pi^*$ for higher barriers $\overline{B} \leqslant B \leqslant B^*$ (entry effectively impeded at the cost of some current profits). Generalizing slightly, what Masson and Shaanan term 'stochastic dynamic limit pricing' involves trading off an increased probability of entry with increased current profits as π° rises (i.e. is chosen at levels) above F, but never so much as to foreclose entry altogether. This will be observed if π° rises with B and if $\pi^\circ > F$ for $B < B^*$. Pre-entry behaviour that ignores entry can be deduced from an outcome in which π° is independent of B.

F is an estimable function of B and, by linking π° to observed profits π, Masson and Shaanan make π° observable in this sense as well. The object of estimation, then, is to measure the unknown parameters of π° and F subject to the constraints that $\pi^\circ \leqslant F$ for $B < B^*$ and $\pi^\circ = F$ $(= \pi^*)$ at $B = B^*$. They applied this model to a single cross-section of data for 37 US industries over the period 1950-7 (taken to be $t - 1$) and 1958-63 (taken to be t). Their results suggest that π° rises with B and that $\pi^\circ > F$ for $B < B^*$, implying that entry rates are manipulated strategically by incumbents, but that entry is never entirely foreclosed by such behaviour. Their results also suggest that π° was on average about 65% larger than F (actual profits were always a little below π°), but that the amount of entry generated in the face of such a discrepancy was extremely modest and extremely slow in coming. As with other empirical models of entry, the degree of explanation that they achieved (even when restricting themselves to explaining between-industry variations in entry using cross-section data) was fairly modest. Although it is possible that applying their model to panel data might provide a more substantive explanation of what we observe than the models discussed earlier, this seems unlikely. Variations in conduct – in the extent of limit pricing – are driven by variations in B relative to $\overline{B}$ and B^* in their model, and the variables that they use to proxy B are no different (i.e. have little more within-industry variation) from those used hitherto (e.g. as proxies for F). If modelling conduct is to help explain variations in E_t over time, then conduct must be less rigidly linked to market structure.

Models of market penetration ought not to differ too much from

76   *Models of Entry*

models of the incidence of entry in their basic features, and it is also arguably the case that they ought not to differ too much from more general models of market share and market share mobility. It is a rather restrictive feature of (3.16) that it purports to describe only the actions of all entrants at some date t (or, typically in applications, in their first year of entry). To address questions of 'how fast' as well as 'how much', one would like to look more explicitly at market penetration over time and, indeed, one would like in principle to track the activities of entrants from their first appearance in the market through to their establishment as a substantial market competitor (or to their exit). Equation (3.16) focuses only on one type of competitor during one short and rather particular period in its existence, and does not appear to be able to account for the dynamics of market shares more generally. One feels that the model ought, in principle, to be applicable to any market participant, new or old; that is, that it ought to be nested into a broader model of market structure.

A model that meets this desideratum might run along the following lines (see Geroski and Murfin, 1990b, or Geroski, 1991). For simplicity, suppose that goods are homogeneous and that individual firms choose output x. Industry output is Y and demand is $p = p(Y)$. A firm making an output choice at time t has two problems to face. First, if $x_t \neq x_{t-1}$, it may incur costs of adjustment A_t that are increasing in size as $|x_t - x_{t-1}|$ increases.[7] For simplicity, we assume that marginal adjustment costs $\partial A_t/\partial x_t$ are proportional to the change in market shares implied by the choice of x_t given x_{t-1}; that is, that $\partial A_t/\partial x_t = \delta_t(S_t - S_{t-1})$ where $S_t \equiv x_t/Y_t$. If, in addition, $\delta_t/p_t = \delta$ for all t, then the real per unit adjustment cost is constant. The second problem which the firm must face is the response of rivals, and the fact that this response may occur over time. Modelling the reaction of rivals by allowing the choice of x_t to affect Y, we assume that $\partial Y_t/\partial x_t \equiv \theta_0$ and $\partial Y_{t+1}/\partial x_t \equiv \theta_1$.[8] The joint consequence of these two problems is that the choice of x_t by the firm has both current and future consequences on profits. x_t affects current profits π_t by affecting current adjustment costs A_t given x_{t-1} and by affecting current price p_t via Y_t; x_t also affects profits in $t + 1$, π_{t+1}, by affecting A_{t+1} and p_{t+1} in much the same manner. Thus, a rational firm facing one or both of these problems will need to select a penetration strategy, a sequence of x_t over time, that maximizes the expected present discounted value of its profits. In the case of an entrant, this will involve computing expected post-entry profits over its whole lifetime, and selecting an initial market penetration and subsequent penetration speed accordingly.

Letting $E_t\{\ \}$ denote expectations held in time t of the quantity in the bracket, c be marginal costs and λ be a discount factor, the expected present value of all future profits is

$$V_t = E_t \left\{ \sum_{t=0}^{\infty} \lambda^\tau \{ [p(Y_{t+\tau}) - c]x_{t+\tau} - A_{t-\tau} \} \right\} - F. \quad (3.18)$$

It is easily shown that the sequence of x_t which maximizes V_t satisfies

$$p(Y_t) - c - x_t p'(Y_t)\theta_0 - \delta_t(S_t - S_{t-1})$$
$$+ \lambda E_t \{ x_{t+1} p'(Y_{t+1})\theta_1 - \delta_{t+1}(S_{t+1} - S_t) \} = 0 \quad (3.19)$$

for all t (see, for example, Sargent (1979) for details on solving this kind of problem). Assuming that demand has constant elasticity η defined so that $\eta > 0$, then some tedious manipulations can be used to transform (3.19) into

$$\gamma_0 m_t + \gamma_1 S_{t+1}^e + \gamma_2 S_t + S_{t-1} = 0 \quad (3.20)$$

where $m_t \equiv (p_t - c)/p_t$, $S_{t+1}^e \equiv E_t \{ S_{t+1} \}$, $\gamma_0 \equiv 1/\delta$, $\gamma_1 \equiv \Omega(\theta_1/\eta - \delta)/\delta$, $\gamma_2 \equiv \theta_0/\eta - \delta + \Omega\delta$ and $\Omega \equiv \lambda p_t/p_{t+1}$, the last of which we assume to be constant over time. Solving (3.20) yields

$$S_t = \Psi_1 S_{t-1} + (\gamma_0 \Psi_1) \sum_{\tau=0}^{\infty} \left(\frac{1}{\Psi_2} \right)^\tau m_{t+\tau}^e \quad (3.21)$$

where $m_{t+1}^e \equiv E_t \{ m_{t+1} \}$ and Ψ_1 and Ψ_2 satisfy $\Psi_1 + \Psi_2 = -\gamma_2/\gamma_1$ and $\Psi_1 \Psi_2 = 1/\gamma_1$. Given that $\eta > 0$, $\delta > 0$ and $0 \leqslant \Omega \leqslant 1$ for all t, then, if $0 \leqslant \gamma_1 \leqslant 1$ and $\gamma_2 < 0$ (i.e. if θ_0 and θ_1 are not 'too large'), it follows that $0 < \Psi < 1 < \gamma_1^{-1} < \Psi_2$. Equation (3.21) can be written even more simply as

$$\Delta S_t = (1 - \Psi_1)(S_t^* - S_{t-1}) \quad (3.22)$$

where $\Delta S_t \equiv S_t - S_{t-1}$ and

$$S_t^* \equiv \frac{\gamma_0 \Psi_1}{1 - \Psi_1} \sum_{\tau=0}^{\infty} \left(\frac{1}{\Psi_2} \right)^\tau m_{t+\tau}^e.$$

As (3.20) shows, when firms face adjustment costs or when rivals do not respond initially to their actions, the choice of x_t given x_{t-1} depends, in part, on the choice that the firm expects to make in $t+1$, x_{t+1}^e. That, in turn, depends on x_{t+2}^e, and so on. Hence, the choice of x_t always involves forward-looking calculations, and in particular it depends on all future values of the price–cost margin m_t, as (3.21) makes plain. For an entrant in t, $S_{t-1} = 0$ and 'post-entry profits' are essentially the present value of the stream of all future m_t that it expects to realize over its life

as it penetrates the market. Equation (3.20) can be put into a broader
perspective by considering the special case where $\theta_1 = \delta_t = 0$. This makes
the model completely static and (3.20) reduces to

$$S_t \equiv \eta m_t / \theta_0. \qquad (3.23)$$

Equation (3.23) is exactly the model of market structure that emerges
from standard static models of price–cost margins and market structure
in which firms are able to change their market shares instantaneously
(e.g. Cowling and Waterson, 1976). At the risk of a slight abuse of
terminology, (3.23) describes a 'target' market share $\eta m_t / \theta_0$ which is
always instantly realized by the firm. When costs of adjustment exist or
when rivals do not respond instantly, then the 'target' depends on all
future m_t and the speed with which it is approached depends on S_{t-1}.
This more complex relationship is expressed in (3.22) which relates actual
shares in t, S_t, to a 'target' S_t^* and to S_{t-1}. Equation (3.22) is a familiar
looking empirical formulation. Ψ_1, the coefficient on S_{t-1} in a regression of S_t on S_{t-1} and other things, is a speed of adjustment and clearly
depends on θ_0, θ_1, δ, η and λ. In particular, it falls as adjustment costs
rise and it is lower the more severe are the adverse price consequences
of rivals' actions. Unlike familiar partial adjustment models, however,
(3.22) does not posit that adjustment is made to some permanently fixed
target. Instead, the target S_t^* changes over time as firms adjust and
update their information about market events and the actions of rivals.

Considered as a dynamic model of market structure, (3.22) includes
entry as a special case, and it establishes a linear relationship between
immediate post-entry penetration and the expected present value of all
post-entry profits which is reminiscent of (3.16). In particular, the model
suggests that entry is guided by m_t, the price–marginal cost margin of the
entrant expected at time t. In practice, however, one can only observe the
price–average cost margin of incumbents, π_t. The difference between
these expressed as a percentage of price and denoted as F is a measure of
the importance of fixed costs per unit of output and of absolute cost
differences between entrants and incumbents. Thus, written in terms of
observables, a model $\Delta S_t = E_t = \gamma m_t$ becomes $E_t = \gamma(\pi_t - F)$, which
is the form in which (3.16) typically appears. Equations (3.18)–(3.23)
suggest that one can interpret γ as a measure of η / θ_0 when adjustment
costs and future reactions by rivals are zero, and that current or
immediate post-entry values of m_t or π_t are the appropriate measures of
post-entry profits to use in this case. If $\theta_1 \neq 0$ and $\delta \neq 0$, then both γ
and π_t^e must be interpreted slightly more generally. Either way, this
argument also suggests that the use of incumbents' profits to predict
entrants' profits and thus entry is perfectly legitimate whenever entrants'

costs cannot be observed, although this empirical strategy does require one to model F with some care.

There are several ways to estimate the model (3.18)–(3.22), depending on what information one wishes to obtain from the estimates. Geroski and Murfin (1990b) applied (3.22) to market share data for 17 firms in three segments of the UK car market, 1958–83. The model was estimated using a rational expectations predictor of future values of π_t for incumbents, and included a supplementary equation explaining the difference between the margins of entrants and incumbents. The major determinants of F included advertising (also treated as endogenous), market size, tariffs, market growth and a variety of firm- and industry-specific dummies. Substituting this equation into (3.22) yielded an estimating equation which included S_{t-1}, the rational expectations proxy for π_t and the additional terms proxying F. The coefficient on S_{t-1} provided an estimate of Ψ_1 and, using that, the rest of the estimated coefficients were used to generate an estimate of S_t^*. Geroski and Murfin found that expectations were not static (S_t^* was not constant), that S_t^* (i.e. expected future returns) had a significant effect on entry and that costs of adjustment had a major effect on market dynamics. Much more interesting was the comparison between values of S_t^* estimated by the model and observed price–cost margins π_t. S_t^* was (on average across entrants) negative in the beginning of the period and only became positive in the middle to late 1960s, despite high and generally stable values of industry pre-cost margins and, indeed, industry profits throughout. This suggests that π_t had little value as a predictor of entry, both absolutely and relative to S_t^*. The important variables that accounted for the differences between observed margins π_t and S_t^* (i.e. entrants' margins) were partly structural and partly conduct related. A substantial decline in tariffs had very little effect on observed π_t, but it played a major role in encouraging entry, and, even more important, entry and the subsequent evolution of market shares were driven by the extensive variations in advertising that occurred throughout the period (for further discussion, see chapter 5). As it happened, the post-entry advertising war that developed had little effect on margins, but it did play a major role in driving changes in market shares. In fact, S_t^* proved capable of predicting the incidence of entry surprisingly accurately, and the combination of S_t^* and S_{t-1} tracked market penetration very closely. Ψ_1 was estimated to equal 0.85, implying that a new firm with a constant penetration target of $S_t^* = 10\%$ would achieve a 1.5% market penetration in its first year, 5% by five years, and only 9% after about 13 years.

Putting the various pieces together yielded the following interpretation of the data. Entry into all sectors of the UK car industry occurred late in the 1960s when the expected present value of future profits first became positive for a large number of European and Japanese firms. This seems to have occurred because of exogenous reduction in tariffs and a substantial increase in the use of non-price policies (and advertising in particular) designed to facilitate penetration into the market. This rise in the expected future returns of predominantly European and Japanese producers occurred despite relatively constant average margins enjoyed by incumbents through the period, and despite the actual fact of entry by these European and Japanese firms. Entry was 'slow' in the sense that entrant firms required a number of years to reach their initial penetration 'targets'. While entrants as a whole effected a major erosion in the market shares of incumbents, this occurred as much because of the large number of entrants that appeared as because any one of them effected a substantial penetration. The substantive form of post-entry competition involved the use of advertising and, of all the determinants of S_i^*, it was movements in advertising shares that dominated movements in the market penetration targets of firms. As a consequence, tariff reductions (and other exogenous changes in entry barriers) had a major effect on market structure not so much because they encouraged entry as because they encouraged the entry of firms who were prepared to launch aggressive advertising campaigns.

The two studies by Geroski and Murfin (1987, 1990b) tell a fairly similar tale about the role of advertising (and other factors) on entry into the UK car industry, reflecting the observation made earlier that models of the incidence of entry are bound to have numerous features in common with models of market penetration. This is also evident in Masson and Jeong (1991), for example, who regressed a range of independent variables on several different measures of entry rates and penetration over a full business cycle. They found a broad qualitative consistency in the signs of estimated coefficients, particularly that on expected profits. Similar results emerged from Lane's (1987) modelling of entry into the US automated teller machine (ATM) market. Table 3.4 shows estimated coefficients from two of her reported equations, the first explaining the incidence of entry and the second market shares and entry penetration. Both dependent variables depend on a range of characteristics of entrants which are assumed to affect their marginal costs and thence entry via a fairly tightly structured profits equation. The two regressions that are shown in table 3.4 report the estimated effects that these characteristics have on the marginal costs that emerge from her estimating equation. Consider first the incidence of entry equation shown in column (i). The coefficients on SS, COMPS and YEARS – variables reflecting previous production experience (if any) in the safes industry, in computers and in

Table 3.4 The incidence of entry and entry penetration in the US automated teller machine market

	Incidence of entry (i)	Entry penetration (ii)
IND	−2.09	−45.43
	(0.13)	(17.46)
FOR	−1.98	−54.77
	(0.17)	(21.58)
SIZE	0.00	−1.42
	(0.02)	(1.06)
SS	−0.17	08.73
	(0.01)	(3.37)
COMPS	−0.41	−7.74
	(0.02)	(3.03)
YEARS	−0.09	−9.18
	(0.01)	(3.69)

Estimated using probit and tobit methods respectively; standard errors are given in the parentheses under the estimated coefficients. IND is a dummy for being an independent firm, FOR is a dummy for being a foreign firm, SIZE is a measure of size and diversification, SS and COMPS measure production experience in 'safe and security products' and computers, and YEARS is years of production in the ATM market. The estimates are of the parameters of marginal costs in her two entry equations.
Source: Lane, 1987

ATMs – are all negative and significant (a result that is not inconsistent with that reported by Geroski and Murfin (1987) for the UK car industry). Similarly, dummies indicating whether the firm in question is independent (IND) and foreign (FOR) are also negative and significant. In all five cases, the interpretation is that a firm possessing these characteristics has lower costs and therefore a higher probability of entry. Firm size (SIZE), by contrast, has no effect on the probability of entry. Equation (ii) shows that the estimates for the corresponding model of entry penetration are qualitatively similar to those in column (i). The various characteristics that facilitate entry clearly also enable entrants to acquire relatively large market shares post-entry.

Clearly, there is a considerable overlap between models of the incidence of entry and models of entry penetration, and very little has emerged from the latter that challenges what we have learned from the former. Models of entry penetration do, however, contribute new information to our understanding of the programme followed by most entrants (and, in particular, the twin questions of 'how much' and 'how fast'). Estimates of

γ in (3.16) or Ψ_1 in (3.22) are exactly the kinds of new information that one can expect to obtain when modelling entry penetration over time, namely some sense of the time scale in which events occur. The arrival of thousands of new firms in a market says very little about the impact entry is likely to have on market performance if they are all initially small, if they all stay small and if most of them exit quickly. That entrants will have an impact sooner or later is indisputable, and the interesting questions are really 'how big' and 'how soon' that will be. Since adjustment costs tend to impose time–cost trade-offs on the expansion of firms, 'how big' and 'how soon' are, of course, not unrelated questions. Modelling penetration over time also means modelling the evolution of π_i^e, the force that attracts entry to markets. The rather limited experience that we have with models of market penetration suggests that the observed profits of incumbents are likely to be of only limited use in explaining both initial and subsequent market penetration by entrants, and this also applies to many of the standard market structure variables that one might be inclined to use as well.[9] As is made plain in Geroski and Murfin, the 'target' that drives entry varies quite a lot over time, responding to what may often be transitory changes in market structure and/or conduct. Indeed, both the importance of adjustment costs and the pattern of action and reaction in the post-entry advertising war witnessed in the UK car market suggest a kind of path dependence in the evolution of market shares, and this may need to be the focus of any future efforts that try to make sense of much of the apparent noise associated with entry flows that we observe.

Latent Factor Models of Entry

Despite their sophistication, almost all the models discussed above have yielded somewhat mixed results when applied to the data on entry. In many cases, R^2 values are rather low, and, despite a plethora of significant coefficients, many estimated models achieve no more than a modest fit. Such results are not terribly surprising given the basic features of the data (see chapter 2), and they reinforce one's inclination to describe entry as a fairly 'noisy' activity. This observation, in turn, suggests that expected profits must be fairly 'noisy', and that they must fluctuate fairly unsystematically in response to factors that are likely to be both transitory and idiosyncratic to particular sectors. The profits of incumbents or average industry price–cost margins are, by contrast, much more stable and predictable (see chapter 4), indicating that there is likely to be a range of factors that affect entrants' profit expectations much more forcefully than they affect the profit outcome realized by incumbents (as we saw above in the case of entry into the UK car sector). Much of this divergence may arise because entrants are mainly concerned with very local, very specific market niches which are both rather poorly defined and rather more short lived than the three- or four-digit national industries that encompass them. The divergence may also reflect the fighting threats made by incumbents, threats that affect profit expectations but, because they are rarely carried out, may not often affect realized profit outcomes. Whatever the cause, the consequence is that observed profits are often rather poor predictors of entry, even when they are supplemented by numerous other observables.

If expected profits are dominated by transitory and idiosyncratic factors, then modelling entry is always going to be a difficult and rather unsatisfying exercise. One can rarely hope to capture such factors fully in observable variables, and one will therefore frequently be driven to use poor proxies and plenty of imaginative *a priori* theorizing in order to link one's empirical model to questions of interest. It is possible, however, to recoup some of this lost ground by using data on entry (together with the maintained hypothesis that entry is driven by expected profits) in a very simple way to make some inferences about the nature of excess profits and, in particular, about the stochastic process driving their variation over time and across industries. The basic procedure is to imagine that expected profits can be decomposed into deterministic components (e.g. industry- or time-specific fixed effects) and non-deterministic components (e.g. a moving order process in some unobserved factor), and then use the statistical properties of (observed) entry rates or market penetration to make inferences about these (unobserved) factors. [10]

Let us suppose that entry E_t is driven by entrants' expected profits π_t^e,

$$E_t = \gamma \pi_t^e, \tag{3.24}$$

but that the latter is unobservable. Assuming that π_t^e has a time-invariant component p and a transitory component that is a moving average of some unobservable factor, c_t, then

$$E_t = \gamma \pi_t^e = p + \theta_0 c_t + \tau_1 c_{t-1} + \theta_2 c_{t-2} + \ldots \tag{3.25}$$

The operational difficulty with (3.25) is, of course, that p and the c_t are not observable. They do, however, record their effects on the observable E_t. The time-invariant component p of expected profits records the same effect on E_t as it does on E_{t-1}, E_{t-2} and so on. Each of the transitory components c_t has an effect on E_t, E_{t-1}, E_{t-2} and so on, but one that varies over time in a manner determined by θ_0, θ_1, θ_2 and so on. Put another way, E_t records the effects of p, c_t and c_{t-1}, c_{t-2}, c_{t-3} and so on, E_{t-1} the effects of p, c_{t-1}, c_{t-2}, c_{t-3}, c_{t-4} and so on. Given this invertibility between the c_t and the E_t, the unobservable factors c_t in (3.25) can be eliminated by repeated substitution to yield

$$E_t = \alpha_t + \beta_1 E_{t-1} + \beta_2 E_{t-2} + \beta_3 E_{t-3} + \ldots \tag{3.26}$$

where

$$\alpha_t \equiv p + \theta_0 c_t \tag{3.27}$$

and

$$\theta_j = \sum_{j=1}^{t} \beta_j \theta_{t-j} \qquad j = 1, \ldots, \infty. \tag{3.28}$$

If we normalize $\theta_0 \equiv 1$ and suppose that p can be written as an estimable function of industry and time dummies, then (3.26) is an estimable equation (with c_t as the residual) whose coefficients (the β_j) can be used to provide estimates of the unknown parameters of interest (the θ_j).

Table 3.5 (which reprints table 2.5 with two small additions) shows estimates of (3.26) for four measures of entry in the UK. Each equation pools data from two cross-sections (1978 and 1979), and includes a full

Table 3.5 Autoregressive models of entry

Definition of entry E_t	Gross penetration	Net penetration	Gross rate	Net rate
Mean fixed effect	0.0381	−0.0203	0.0335	−0.00057
E_{t-1}	−0.7326	−0.7367	−0.2232	−0.4354
	(6.907)	(12.70)	(4.057)	(8.208)
E_{t-2}	0.1901	−0.6257	−0.0227	−0.2234
	(1.890)	(6.146)	(0.3996)	(4.222)
E_{t-3}	−0.1080	−0.2587	0.0164	0.0310
	(1.456)	(2.484)	(0.3938)	(0.9021)
E_{t-4}	0.0357	−0.0491	0.0657	0.0205
	(1.005)	(1.608)	(1.975)	(0.5519)
R^2	0.7374	0.7573	0.8162	0.7879
$\bar{R}^2$	0.4420	0.4850	0.6100	0.5500
$F(83, 74)$	2.503	2.781	3.959	3.312
var(E_t)	0.00048	0.00045	0.00036	0.00085

All regressions are for a two-year pool (1979, 1978) regressed at its own history, as in (1978, 1977) and so on. All equations include a time dummy and 79 industry-specific fixed effects (not shown); t statistics are given in absolute values in the parentheses. var(E_t) is the variance of the dependent variable for 1979.

set of industry fixed effects and a time dummy (for 1979). In all cases, a fourth-order autoregression provided a reasonable fit to the data, and in most cases the coefficients on the third- and fourth-order terms were small and were estimated with a great deal of imprecision. Because of limitations in the length of the entry series, it was not possible to fit higher order lags in (3.26), and the fact that we have no reliable estimates of β_5, β_6 and so on makes it difficult to generate estimates of θ_6, θ_7 and so on. It is possible that omitting terms in E_{t-5}, E_{t-6} and so on will bias our estimates of the β_j, and this may have inflated the estimates of β_3 and β_4 in particular.

The first observation to be made about these regressions is that the permanent component p of π_t^e, does appear to play a role in explaining entry. The industry and time dummies cannot be simplified into a single time-invariant industry-wide constant, and they were almost always individually significant. The degree of explanation bought by using p to explain entry is fairly modest however (which is consistent with what we discovered using the more orthodox models of entry discussed in the previous two sections). Although the R^2 values are fairly high by the standards of cross-section work (and by the standards set in table 3.3 above in which entry data for four years were pooled), it requires the use of 84 independent variables to get them that high (as the much lower $\bar{R}^2$s reveal). The permanent components of the regression also affect the estimated signs on the lagged dependent variables in (3.26). Essentially, (3.26) describes adjustment to a 'target' of α_t whose short-run effect on entry is unity and whose long-run effect is $(1 - \beta_1 - \beta_2 - \ldots)^{-1}$, which is less than unity if the $\beta_j < 0$. That the estimated $\beta_j < 0$ does not imply that entry flows in t and $t - 1$ are (unconditionally) negatively correlated. Using industry-specific fixed effects means that the target towards which entry adjusts is industry specific, and its permanent industry specificity means that E_t and E_{t-1} are positively correlated, notwithstanding $\beta_1 < 0$.[11] The model (3.31)–(3.33) developed in the next section shows why $\beta_1 < 0$ is what one would expect from a model that allowed π_t^e to be endogenous.

The estimates in table 3.5 suggest that entry is largely driven by transitory factors. Since $\theta_0 \equiv 1$ and $\alpha_t = p + \theta_0 c_t$, (3.26) can be written as

$$E_t = p + \left(\sum \beta_j E_{t-j} \right) + c_t \tag{3.29}$$

The first term is the permanent component of π_t^e, the second term is a 'quasi-permanent' component created by the effects of the shocks c_t on entry over time, while the last term is the purely transitory component in π_t^e. R^2s of 0.75 or 0.80 are extremely high by the standards of entry regressions (e.g. compare table 3.3 above), but, even so, they suggest that at least a quarter of the variation in entry is due to the short-run effects of transitory components of π_i^e. If one takes the view that entry barriers are relatively fixed over time, then their effects on entry will be completely captured by the p, in which case table 3.5 suggests that entry barriers *per se* do not affect flows of entry very much. This is probably not too surprising, since the effects of entry barriers depend on market conditions – the effect of scale economies, for example, depends on market size, growth and an incumbent's reactions (see chapter 5). Interpreting the regressions discussed earlier and those shown in table 3.5 roughly, one concludes that it may be market conditions (including the behaviour of incumbents and other entrants) mediating the effects of entry barriers rather than the barriers themselves which matter most to entrants; that is, it may be market conduct as much as market structure which holds the key to explaining entry flows.

The feedthrough of the effects of c_t on entry captured by the middle term in (3.29) indicates that these mediating market conditions may have what amount to fairly permanent effects on entry. Table 3.6 shows estimates of the θ_j for each of the four measures of entry. All four equations show a fairly similar pattern. A positive (negative) shock c_t to E_t has a depressing (stimulating) effect on E_{t+1}, E_{t+2} and so on, effects that (particularly in the case of gross penetration) can have noticeable effects over an (apparently) almost indefinite period of time. One way to appreciate what this means is to think of E_t as a filtered version of c_t and ask just how variable the shocks c_t are, and how much filtering occurs. Since

$$\operatorname{var}(E_t) = \operatorname{var}(c_t) \left[\sum_{j=0}^{\infty} \theta_j^2 \right], \tag{3.30}$$

Table 3.6   Estimates of the θ_j using (3.26) and (3.28)

Definition of entry E_t	Gross penetration	Net penetration	Gross rate	Net rate
θ_0	1	1	1	1
θ_1	−0.7326	−0.7367	−0.2232	−0.4354
θ_2	−0.5933	−0.2757	−0.2181	−0.3381
θ_3	−0.5292	−0.2043	−0.2217	−0.3486
θ_4	−0.5480	−0.1943	−0.2363	−0.3415
θ_5	−0.5480	−0.1743	−0.2363	−0.3415
$\sum_{j=0}^{5} \theta_j^2$	2.448	1.7286	1.2582	1.6585

then the information in the last row of table 3.6 suggests that the effects of variation in the c_t are magnified by at least 1.5 times when they are transmitted to the E_t (and by 2.5 times in the case of gross penetration). Upper bound estimates of the variance of c_t for the four measures of entry are (using estimates of the variance of E_t given in the last row of table 3.5) 0.00019, 0.00026, 0.00029 and 0.00051 respectively. The corresponding standard deviations of c_t are not much different from the mean values of E_t for each of the four entry measures. Thus, the data suggest that a highly variable stream of shocks affects expected profits and therefore entry over time, and that much of the noise in this series is magnified when transmitted to entry, not least because each individual shock registers an effect for a fairly long period of time. The estimates of the θ_j shown in table 3.6 indicate that penetration measures of entry are affected slightly more strongly by this amplification than entry rates, while the estimates of the variance of c_t suggest that the variability of the shocks affecting entry penetration are slightly lower than those affecting entry rates. The broad similarity in the variance of c_t and in $\Sigma \theta_j^2$, however, indicates that both types of measures of entry have fairly similar determinants. Somewhat more interesting is the observation that net and gross measures of entry also have fairly similar statistical properties.

The estimates in table 3.6 enable one to trace the effects of a single period shock c_t on entry over time. In all cases, a 1% rise in c_t initially raises entry and then reduces it in subsequent periods. In a sense, a single unsustained current-period shock reallocates entry away from the future to the present, and, indeed, does so to such an extent that the total cumulative flow of entry is reduced (relative to what would have happened without the shock, a counterfactual flow of entry that is measured by the fixed effects). A substantial rise in c_t will therefore have a much larger effect on entry in the short run than in the long run (and similarly with p). Using the estimates in table 3.5, the long-run effect of a 1% sustained rise in c_t (or p) is 0.5%, 0.39%, 0.86% and 0.62% respectively. The ratio of short- to long-run effects is rather higher for entry rates than for entry penetration, reflecting the weaker offset of the initial effects of shocks in the case of entry rates. In all cases, however, much of the amplification of the effect of the shocks c_t on entry (via π_j^c) arises from the fact that initial responses are offset by subsequent responses. However variable c_t is, this almost certainly means that E_t will be even more so.

The pattern of effects associated with the shocks c_t seem at first sight to be slightly bizarre. They are consistent, however, with a situation in which some favourable event encourages an increase in entry in the short run, but in which that surge of entry adversely alters the conditions facing later entrants. That is, it corresponds to a situation in which (current) entrants crowd out (future) entrants, presumably because their response to mediating market conditions worsens those faced by later entrants. One way in which this kind of effect may emerge occurs when a surge in current entry by some particular type of entrants alters the population characteristics of incumbents that subsequent types of entrant have to face (see chapter 2). Another occurs when the actions taken by entrants at some time (e.g. their advertising activities) increase barriers to subsequent entry (see chapter 5). Either way, this apparent link between the activities of earlier and later entrants suggests that models of entry ought to focus more directly on interactions between cohorts of entrants, and consider how the actions of early entrants affect subsequent market conditions. That is, to explain entry flows accurately, it seems likely that one must allow for the possibility that the market conditions which seem to be so important in explaining entry are endogenous to the entry process itself (see the next section).

While latent variables models do have some uses (as we shall see below), they are inherently difficult to interpret (our discussion, in particular, has been extremely speculative!). Sooner or later, one simply must try to model expected profits π_t^e in terms of observables if one is to understand what drives entry. Autoregressive models like (3.26) are useful, however, as a benchmark against which to judge more elaborate models. If an estimating equation that embodies some observable information on π_t^e cannot improve on an autoregressive equation (that does not), one is entitled to conclude that the gain to using that observable is modest (relative to what is already known from the history of entry). Put another way, one can only claim to have made serious progress in modelling entry if there is some value added attributable to the new observables; that is, if they contain information on π_t^e not already contained in E_t. As we saw in table 3.3 above, it can often be difficult to attribute much value added to many of the standard variables that have traditionally been used to explain entry.

Modelling Interactions and Selection between Entrants

If, as it appears, standard structural variables provide only limited assistance in accounting for the extensive variation in entry across industries and, more important, over time that we observed in chapter 2, then one is likely to be thrown back on the expedient of looking at structural change (like growth and technological disruption) or at variations in market conduct over time as major determinants of entry. This second modelling strategy raises two interesting issues: the first is whose conduct it is that matters from the point of view of entrants; and the second is how such conduct can be observed and quantified. Anticipating evidence to be discussed in chapter 4 and recalling the sheer number of new firms that attempt entry in each year, one is tempted to suggest that what matters from the point of view of any given entrant are the actions taken by other entrants. Quite what these actions are is not clear, but it is clear that they are liable to be highly time and industry specific. As we have seen, one not unattractive modelling strategy to follow is to treat those actions as latent variables and to model around them, and it is worth pursuing one particular extension of this kind of modelling.

In most markets, there seems to be only a limited amount of room for new entrants. The emergence of new profitable opportunities, it seems, opens up only a finite window of opportunity for new firms. The consequence is that entry into a market can often take the form of a race, and this means that faster, more able entrants may 'crowd out' less able ones.[12] The basic channel through which different types of entrant affect each other is via the effect that they have on post-entry profits. Entrants form expectations pre-entry about market outcomes likely to prevail after entry, outcomes that depend, *inter alia*, on the number and types of entrants that eventually materialize. If, say, one type of entrant suffers a competitive disadvantage *vis-à-vis* a second, then the former will find the possibility of entry by the latter inhibiting, and one will observe the second type crowding out the first type. If neither type of entrant enjoys a competitive advantage relative to the other, then both will find the total volume of entry inhibiting, but neither will be particularly concerned with the composition of that total between the two types. Finally, if the two types of entrants are basically non-competing, then neither will be concerned with total entry, or, more accurately, with that component of it associated with the other. Thus, to explore how different types of entrant interact, one needs a model that describes the behaviour of each and the consequences that each type of entrant has on market outcomes, and thus on the other.

The simplest type of interaction between entrants is that between early and late entrants. Given the opening of a window of opportunity at some time t, those who arrive first pre-empt those who come later. One way of capturing this interaction is to extend (3.16) by adding an equation that tracks the effects of early entry on the market prospects facing later entrants. Thus, suppose that

$$E_t = \gamma \left(\pi_t^e - F \right) \tag{3.31}$$

describes the behaviour of entrants, and

$$\pi_t = A - \beta \sum_{\tau=1}^{\infty} E_{t-\tau} \tag{3.32}$$

the (cumulative) effect of entry on profits. Then, supposing that the expected profits π_t^e of concern to entrants is π_{t+1}, (3.32) can be used together with (3.31) and the assumption of rational expectations to yield

$$E_t = \phi(A - F) + \lambda \sum E_{t-\tau} \tag{3.33}$$

where $\phi \equiv \gamma/(1 + \gamma\beta) > 0$ and $\lambda \equiv -\gamma\beta/(1 + \gamma\beta) < 0$. Equation (3.33), the reduced form of the system (3.31)–(3.32), is, in fact, a familiar, textbook-like characterization of market dynamics.[13] Starting from an initial level of A at time $t = 0$, profits are eroded by entry over time until they reach a level given by F, at which point all entry ceases. The volume of entry at any time t is proportional to the difference between π_t and F. That is, $E_1 = \phi(A - F)$. Thereafter, entry is positive but is smaller and smaller in each period. The sense in which early entry forecloses late entry is the sense in which entry at t removes the need for entry at time $t + 1$, and this depends on how fast entry responds to profits in excess of F and on how fast entrants bid profits away; that is, on the combined effects of γ and β, as summarized by λ.[14]

When there are two different types of entrants, then an additional layer of interaction is imposed on that displayed in (3.31)–(3.33). Following Geroski (1988b), consider a model with two types of entrant, domestic and foreign based. Using superscripts d and f for the two types of entrants, (3.31) can be generalized to

$$E_t^d = \gamma^d(\pi_t^e - F^d)$$
$$E_t^f = \gamma^f(\pi_t^e - F^f) \tag{3.34}$$

and (3.32) to

$$\pi_t = A - \beta^d \sum E_{t-\tau}^d - \beta^f \sum E_{t-\tau}^f \tag{3.35}$$

Using (3.35), the two equations (3.34) can be rearranged to produce an analogue to (3.33), namely

$$E_t^d = \phi^d(A - F^d) + \lambda \sum E_{t-\tau}^d + \theta \sum E_{t-\tau}^f$$
$$E_t^f = \phi^f(A - F^f) + \eta \sum E_{t-\tau}^d + \alpha \sum E_{t-\tau}^f \tag{3.36}$$

where λ, θ, η, α, ϕ^d and ϕ^f are defined in the same way that ϕ and λ were in (3.33).

Clearly, increasing F^f (lowering F^d) lowers the total flow of foreign entry in each period, so raising domestic entry (*ceteris paribus*). Increasing γ^d not only increases the extent to which early domestic entrants pre-empt later ones, but also raises E_t^d in each period t at the cost of E_t^f (*ceteris paribus*). Lowering γ^f, by contrast, eases entry conditions for late arriving foreign entrants and, more important, facilitates entry by domestic-based firms in every period. Finally, raising β^d increases the impact that domestic entry has on profits, enabling early domestic entrants to pre-empt later domestic entrants and all foreign entrants. All this information is embodied in (3.36), and a very simple testing procedure using estimates of (3.36) readily suggests itself. If the coefficient of E_{t-1}^d and higher lags in E_t^d exceed those on E_{t-1}^f and higher lags in E_t^f in *both* equations (3.36), then one concludes that domestic entry has an impact on profits much larger than that associated with foreign entry, and therefore that it crowds the latter out. Conversely, if the effect of E_{t-1}^f, E_{t-2}^f and so on exceeds that of E_{t-1}^d, E_{t-2}^d and so on in *both* equations (3.36), then one concludes that the impact of foreign entry is so strong as to crowd out domestic entry. That is, domestic entry crowds out foreign entry if $\lambda > \theta$ *and* $\eta > \alpha$, while foreign entry crowds out domestic entry if $\theta > \lambda$ *and* $\alpha > \eta$.

What alternative hypotheses can be set against this composite null? The first springs from the observation that it is possible that the effects of E_{t-1}^d, E_{t-2}^d and so on are the same as those of E_{t-1}^f, E_{t-2}^f and so on in *each* equation (i.e. $\lambda = \eta$, $\theta = \alpha$). This parameter configuration corresponds to a situation in which the product of the speed of response and the size of the effect on profits is broadly similar between types of entrants and therefore to a state of affairs in which neither crowds the other out. Thus, while the total volume of entry crowds both types of entrant out, its composition between types does not affect either type of entrant. A second possible form of interaction between the two types of entrant arises if the effect of E_{t-1}^d etc. on E_t^d dominates that of E_{t-1}^f etc. on E_t^d, *but* the effect of E_{t-1}^f etc. on E_t^f dominates that of E_{t-1}^d etc. on E_t^f; that is, if $\lambda > \theta$ *but* $\alpha > \eta$. In the limit, if $\theta = \eta = 0$, domestic and foreign entrants do not compete at all in the same market, and hence entry by one does not preclude entry by the other. If θ and η are non-zero but if $\lambda > \theta$ and $\alpha > \eta$, then no crowding out occurs, either because the presence of one enhances opportunities for the other, or because the two enter relatively distinct non-competing market segments.

Using a slight generalization of (3.36) and data on a net foreign and domestic-based market penetration into 87 three-digit UK industries in 1974–9, Geroski (1988b) found clear evidence that crowding out occurs in the sense that previous domestic entry pre-empts current domestic entry

92 *Models of Entry*

and previous foreign entry pre-empts current foreign entry.[15] However, there was no tangible evidence to suggest that foreign entry crowds out domestic entry, or that domestic entry crowds out foreign entry; that is, the two types of entrant appear to be non-competing. Table 3.7 sets out the basic regressions used in the test. Columns (i) and (iii) are the full models that allow foreign entry to affect domestic entry and domestic entry to affect foreign entry. Columns (ii) and (iv) are simplifications that correspond to the hypothesis that $\theta = \eta = 0$; that is, that foreign and domestic entrants are non-competing. It is clear at a glance that this restriction is data acceptable. Both (ii) and (iv) show a pattern of coefficient sizes not inconsistent with those displayed in table 3.5 (although the coefficients in (ii) are a little smaller than the corresponding figures in the second column of table 3.5), implying the same intertemporal reallocation of entry in response to current shocks that was noted in the previous section. This pattern is, of course, consistent with the crowding out of future by current entrants outlined in (3.31)–(3.33). Finally, shocks seem to have a somewhat more permanent effect on foreign entry, a series which, in addition, is rather more variable than domestic entry.[16]

Table 3.7 Estimates of (3.35) for the UK, 1974–1979

Dependent variable	E_t^d		E_t^f	
	(i)	(ii)	(iii)	(iv)
E_{it-1}^d	0.4153	0.4183	0.1024	–
	(5.22)	(5.23)	(0.960)	–
E_{it-1}^f	−0.0264	–	−0.6580	−0.6732
	(0.748)	–	(4.88)	(5.06)
E_{it-2}^d	−0.3074	−0.2961	0.0969	–
	(5.11)	(4.83)	(1.16)	–
E_{it-2}^f	−0.0382	–	−0.3215	−0.2978
	(0.947)	–	(2.73)	(2.43)
E_{it-3}^d	−0.1516	−0.1399	−0.0585	–
	(4.33)	(4.23)	(0.794)	–
E_{it-3}^f	0.0311	–	−0.3145	−0.3036
	(1.21)	–	(2.63)	(2.53)
Log likelihood	684.418	682.361	533.562	531.394
R^2	0.234	0.234	0.214	0.214
SSR	0.08063	0.08191	0.2561	0.2605

The dependent variable in (i) and (ii) is net domestic entry penetration, while that in (iii) and (iv) is the change in import shares. All equations include a full set of fixed effects; t statistics in absolute value are given in parentheses below the estimated coefficients. The variances of E^d and E^f in 1979 were 0.00045 and 0.0027.
Source: Adapted from Geroski, 1988b

The conclusion that domestic and foreign entrants are non-competing groups is not wholly inconsistent with what is known (or conjectured) much more widely about the effects of entry, and two types of phenomenon may account for it. First, it is often the case that foreign entrants tend to occupy the low price, highly standardized mass market positions, while domestic firms occupy more up-market custom niches, a pattern of market segmentation that suggests the existence of an evolutionary process in which foreign firms chase domestic firms up the quality ladder in markets. This segmentation of the market and its associated allocation of different types of firm to different parts of it is likely to result in an outcome in which different types of firms form non-competing groups. Second, the two types of firm may form non-competing groups even in markets for homogeneous goods. For example, one might hazard the supposition that small domestic entrants have effects only on local markets, effects which do not spread widely in the national markets our data describe. By contrast, it is often the case that imports are controlled by large firms, and have no real competitive effects on markets in the large or the small. The combination of local (and perhaps very small) effects on the one hand and no systematic competitive effects on the other may produce a pattern of interaction similar to that which was observed.

That some entrants may crowd out other entrants is, of course, quite likely to give rise to a certain amount of turnover amongst firms. As we have seen, one of the interesting features of the raw data on entry is the high degree of turbulence that occurs in the small firm end of the size distribution of firms, and it is a phenomenon that has, as yet, been poorly explored. Modelling this turnover requires working with a model that integrates the interdependent entry and exit decisions made by different members of the population, and the goal of such an exercise would include answering questions such as 'when', 'where' and, most novel and most interesting, for 'how long'. One might use such a model to ask whether most entry is, in fact, hit-and-run entry, or whether, by contrast, it is predominantly a learning or a selection process. And, needless to say, one would like to know what particular features of markets create finite windows of opportunity for entrants, or give rise to certain types of learning experiences or selection pressures.

One further attractive feature of such a model is that it might integrate the entry and exit of firms into a broader picture of industry dynamics, making clear the kind of role that turnover plays as part of the market response to shocks. Although it has not, as yet, been made operational and estimated, Chetty and Heckman (1986) have sketched out the broad features of one such model. The starting point of the argument is that firms are heterogeneous, each using a fixed coefficients production technology. As output and factor prices vary over time, some of these technologies will prove to be more efficient than others, and some may actually turn out to be non-viable. Responses to changes in factor prices are driven by the same interaction between entrants observed earlier – namely, more adept entrants better suited to current market conditions driving less adept ones out of the limited space available. The willingness of firms to enter depends (in the model) on current and expected future market conditions, since entrants will wish to amortize their entry costs during their stay in the market. That is, their expected return to investment must take account of the possibility that they may shut down during unfavourable periods. The members of the total pool of firms at any time are in any of three states: investing and producing output, producing but not investing, and neither producing nor investing. As output and factor prices change, one will observe transit between these three states, and hence entry and exit.

Entry and exit are not symmetrical, however, in this model since investments in capacity are sunk, and this gives rise both to asymmetric and lagged market responses to shocks as well as to a less than full utilization of capacity. Further, adjustment costs ensure that an increasing proportion of new output is supplied by entrants in response to favourable industry shocks, rather than through the expansion of existing firms. And, as product prices increase, an increasing share of industry output is produced by firms whose technology is not perfectly suited to the environment. The obverse of under-utilization of capital in response to downward shocks, then, is what looks like increasing allocative inefficiency in response to upward ones. Turnover will be higher in markets where output and factor prices are more turbulent, and the life cycle of any firm will depend on how well its production technology is suited to 'average conditions' and, in a more extended model, on how flexible that technology is.[17] Although one does not observe substitution between factors of production in response to changing factor prices at the level of firms in Chetty and Heckman's model, one does observe it at market level. Entry and exit are, in effect, both the mechanism and the visible manifestation of movements along the industry isoquant.

The forces driving entry and exit in the Chetty and Heckman model are exogenous fluctuations in output and factor prices. This is not, of course, the only kind of turbulence that might affect entry and exit. One might, for example, imagine that technical progress will have much the same effects. Further, in as far as early entrants provide useful information for later entrants about the opportunities that technological advance uncovers, then the response of entry to such turbulence might be a flow of entry in response to major innovations that increases logistically over time. Gort and Kanakayama (1982), for example, have argued that the probability of entry depends, *inter alia*, on the perception of profit opportunities and their risks by entrants, perceptions that depend at least partly on the previous experience of others in the market. To this, one might add the notion that technical change – to the extent that new knowledge is not the patented property of incumbents – may give rise to entry possibilities if it is not fully exploited by incumbents, or if it is insufficiently diffused throughout the industry. Both arguments appear to be consistent with data derived from 46 product histories that they constructed over the postwar period in the USA. Entry was perceived by Gort and Kanakayama to rise logistically and, at any given point, to be larger the faster the rate of technical advance.

Whatever its source, turbulence is likely to manifest itself in fluctuations in demand. The aspect of this observation that has caught the most attention (as we have already seen) is the association between industry growth and entry. Hause and du Reitz (1984) have produced a model of how this relationship might arise that has a number of similarities with the model of Chetty and Heckman. The basic argument is that incumbents face convex adjustment costs, making it less than optimal to respond immediately to rapid growth. The population of entrants can be ranked according to those that are more or less able to enter and produce efficiently, and, as growth outstrips the ability of incumbents to respond, the inability of the most advantaged entrants to fill the gap in the market allows more and more entrants of lesser and lesser ability into the market. Hence, one expects industries with faster growth to experience more and more entry. Their results, obtained using a sample of 39 Swedish industries for three four-year periods, are broadly consistent with this view. Also of interest is their result that the variance of entry over time in any industry is likely to rise in mean entry rates, and therefore in industry growth, *ceteris paribus*. Similar correlations between entry and growth have also been noted elsewhere by simple inspection of the raw data on entry. Baldwin and Gorecki (1986), for example, observed entry rates (over 1970–9) of 46.5% in 'fast' growing industries and 26.6% in 'declining' areas in Canada (the average across all industries was 36.1%). Exit rates were 47.1% and 42.3% respectively. More spectacular was gross entry penetration, averaging 62% in fast growing industries and 25.8% in declining areas; net penetration rates were 33.4% and 14.9% respectively (see also table 3.8 below).

Neither Gort and Kanakayama nor Hause and du Reitz extend their arguments from explaining entry to explaining turnover, largely because neither focus seriously on heterogeneities between firms. In a more general model of the effects of technology or fluctuations in market demand, one would expect to discover that the opportunities opened up to some firms are created, in part, by the shortcomings of others, and that some selection amongst both entrants and incumbents would occur. If learning by firms occurs as part of this process, then mortality rates are likely to decrease in the age of firms and may also, depending on the details of the learning process, affect the size distribution of firms (Pakes and Ericson, 1987). Putting these various observations together, Dunne et al. (1989b) have regressed various measures of entry on a collection of industry and time dummies, industry growth and growth squared and a set of categorical age variables. The age variables were observed to have a negative effect on the market shares of entrants, indicating that each cohort of entrants tends to lose market share over time post-entry. This is a phenomenon that appears to be particularly true of single-plant firms and new firms. Growth of the market had little effect on market shares or on the relative size of new entrants. The decrease in market share with age seems to be largely due to exit, since the relative size of entrants increased over time (particularly that of multi-plant diversifying entrants) and the proportion of an industry's producers that belong to a particular entry cohort decreased sharply with age (and was not much affected by growth). Heterogeneities amongst firms stand out as a major feature of the process isolated by Dunne et al. Most numerous and smallest amongst any given cohort of entrants are *de novo* single-plant firms. Although some of these firms survive and grow, most fail and exit. Multi-plant firms, less frequent but rather larger, survive rather more often, particularly those diversifying from other industries. It is hard to believe that their success is not achieved (at least in part) at the expense of new single-plant firms who are increasingly cut out of the market. One way or the other, the consequence is that the characteristics of any given cohort of entrants are liable to change systematically over time, a process that seems discernible up to 20 years post-entry but that does not – surprisingly – seem to be very strongly or systematically related to market growth or contraction, at least in the US chemical industries (see Dunne et al., 1989a).

One can also see this selection process at work and observe the interaction between different types of entrants that it induces in a variety of settings.[18] To take just one example (for others, see chapter 2), Lane (1987) focused explicitly on the role of previous production experience in explaining the incidence of entry and survival in the US ATM market. As we saw above, her data appear to be consistent with the view that firms with greater production experience in related areas were more likely to enter the market, and that the probability of survival increased the longer the firm was present and operating in the market. Advantages to early entry were observed, but early entrants generally failed to match the competitiveness of later diversifying entrants whose production experience in the market did not reduce the incidence of entry by other less advantaged firms so much as it restricted their post-entry penetration and, occasionally, induced them to exit. As a consequence of the competitive strength that they enjoyed from their experience, such later but more able entrants – generally diversified firms with experience in safes and computers – usually commanded a larger market share than earlier, faster moving entrants.

These observations lead one, finally, to the question of the relationship between entry and exit. We have already observed that the two are, in general, highly positively correlated (see chapter 2), and this leads one to suspect that they will share many common determinants. Dunne and Roberts (1991), for example, regressed entry and exit (rates and penetration) on a range of industry characteristics, discerning that (in the main) those characteristics which were positively correlated with entry were negatively correlated with exit (and vice versa). However, the fixed effects from both equations were highly positively correlated (suggesting that entry and exit barriers are highly interrelated), and this positive correlation (presumably) accounted for the high positive correlations between entry and exit that they observed. Table 3.8 reproduces some of their

Table 3.8 Entry and exit equations for the USA

Entry measured as	Entry rate	Entry share	Exit rate	Exit share
Growth	0.483	1.208	−0.280	−0.246
	(0.047)	(0.031)	(0.023)	(0.021)
Growth^2	2.682	6.392	1.322	1.222
	(0.434)	(0.245)	(0.189)	(0.151)
Price–cost margin	0.313	0.043	0.114	0.065
	(0.080)	(0.046)	(0.038)	(0.026)
Capital–output ratio	−0.012	−0.006	0.014	0.010
	(0.005)	(0.006)	(0.005)	(0.001)
Number of firms	−0.054	0.008	0.008	0.008
	(0.015)	(0.006)	(0.005)	(0.005)
Average firm size	0.057	0.028	0.001	−0.009
	(0.044)	(0.020)	(0.018)	(0.008)

Standard errors are included in parentheses beneath the estimated coefficients. All equations result from pooling 386 four-digit US industries over four Census periods from 1963 to 1982. Each of them have a full set of industry effects and a time dummy.
Source: Dunne and Roberts, 1991

Models of Entry

results, and shows that industry growth was a positive determinant of
entry and a negative determinant of exit. Price–cost margins were a
positive determinant of both entry and exit rates (which may induce a
positive correlation between the two), but the capital–output ratio dis-
couraged entry rates and stimulated exit rates. The number of firms and
average firm size had no discernible impact on either. Khemani and
Shapiro (1987) performed a not dissimilar exercise on Canadian data
and found that a number of industry characteristics had the same sign in
both entry and exit equations. Thus, whether one observes it through
fixed effects or through same signed coefficients on observable independent variables, the fact is that entry and exit equations can often look
rather similar.

The bottom line is that most industries experience either high entry *and*
exit rates (or penetration) or low entry *and* exit rates (or penetration).
Since the two – entry and exit – appear to share common determinants
(e.g. industry growth) and since entry and exit barriers appear to be
similar (see also chapter 5), one concludes that entry causes displacement
and therefore exit. This causal channel from entry to exit implies that the
reduced form of any two-equation entry–exit model will contain the structural determinants of entry and, if displacement is the sole cause of exit,
the two-equation system will not be identified. In fact, this is probably too
strong. Khemani and Shapiro (1987) estimated a recursive two-equation
system (entry causes exit but not the reverse) and discovered coefficients
on (the log of) entry of 0.8 and higher in the exit equation, suggesting that
displacement may well be the major cause of exit. Notwithstanding this,
however, they observed advertising to have a positive effect and average
firm size to have a negative effect on exit, holding constant the effect of
entry on exit via displacement. One suspects that this independent effect
of industry characteristics on exit over above the effect that they have on
entry is discernible in table 3.8 for those variables (growth in particular)
whose impact on entry is different in absolute size from their effect on
exit. One way or the other, it is clear that entry causes displacement and
therefore that models of entry and exit are likely to share rather a large
number of common features.

Thus, there seems to be little doubt that much of the turnover of firms
that one observes in markets is bound up with a selection process that
selects between different types of firm. This process is very much one of
fitting types of firms embodying certain technological and marketing
choices to the environment of a specific market at any given time. What
we observe in the way of industry responses to shocks often emerges,
it seems, from the blood and thunder of early entry displacing small
incumbents (leading to exit) and crowding out later entry. It follows that

one expects turnover to increase as market turbulence – price and output shocks, growth, technological change, and so on – increases, and the data are at least broadly consistent with this view. Certainly rapid market growth and technological change appear to be at least loosely associated with increased entry and, in all likelihood, with increased exit. More interestingly, there is very little doubt that this selection process makes the competition between entrants for a place in the market rather more severe than that between entrants and incumbents, at least initially. Early entrants often pre-empt potential entrants and are, in turn, often displaced by later entrants embodying characteristics better suited to the environment. Many entrants need little help in stumbling towards the exit door, and they are often so pre-occupied with survival that they do not (or, given costs of adjustment, cannot) expand rapidly. Under the circumstances, it is hard to see why incumbents should pay much attention to most entrants, at least initially. The fact that competition amongst entrant types occurs over time – that some types of entrants respond faster to market opportunities than others – means that responses to industry shocks by entrants may take some time to be fully realized, and this provides one possible reason why entry data are hard to explain using traditional market structure variables.

Selection amongst entrants is a competitive pressure that is felt most strongly by young *de novo* firms, and it is a force which continues to provide intensive pressures on them for, perhaps, between 5 and 15 years post-entry. It seems unlikely that this is merely a matter of older wiser heads being more adept at survival. If, as may be the case, a typical response to structural change is a series of waves of entry by different entrant types, then it seems clear that selection criteria will change in response to the different ecological pressures that successive waves of entry create. Survivors are unlikely to be firms that were well adapted to the environment that prevailed when they entered, much less firms that needed time to acquire information about that environment. Rather, survivors are likely to be those who were initially well suited to the environment that they initially encountered in the market *and* who were then able to adapt to subsequent changes in the market environment that their own entry – and that of subsequent entrants – caused. It may not be so much a question of the wisdom of older heads as it is the flexibility in operations that their experience enables them to deploy.

Conclusions

To sum up, then, there are a wide range of decisions that define a typical entry programme, and a correspondingly wide range of observables that affect these decisions. Net entry rates, gross market penetration, post-entry growth rates, entry hazard rates and so on are all legitimate measures of 'entry', and all reflect (at least some of) the decisions that entrants make as they progress through their programme. To each set of decisions that results in an observable measure of entry corresponds an unobservable – expected profits – which reflects the net effects of taking that decision (or not). The major challenges of modelling entry are to discern the (observable) determinants of the (unobservable) expected profits corresponding to the (observable) measure of entry that one is examining.

The work discussed in this chapter has gone some way towards identifying some of the major determinants of post-entry profits. There seems little doubt that large markets attract more entrants than small ones, and that market growth has a positive (if often rather imprecisely estimated) effect on entry. Variations in the realized profits of incumbents are, by contrast, often rather poorly correlated with variations in entry, although more reasonable proxies for expected profits seem to go a little way towards explaining 'where' entry is likely to occur and 'how much' of it there is likely to be. However, latent variable models that obviate the need for measuring expected profits suggest that the latter contain a good deal of noise, and that whatever systematic time variation expected profits have may, in large part, be induced by the activities of previous entrants. Questions about 'when' entry occurs also seem to rely on information about variations over time in industry conduct (such as advertising), suggesting that at least some (but definitely not all) of the considerable within-industry variation in entry that we observe follows a systematic path-dependent evolution over time. Such factors also seem likely to play a role in answering questions about 'how long', although the age and the actions of other entrants are also strongly associated with survival rates. Of course, any allocation of specific independent variables to specific stages of the entry programme is bound to be misleading at some level, and almost no work has been done on integrating these decisions in a way that enables information generated from one stage to affect another stage. At best, we have some hints that entry may come in waves, with some entrants following a quick-response, opportunistic strategy (one that may be explicitly hit-and-run) that crowds out later entrants of the same type. Early opportunistic entrants, however, can be displaced by more substantial competitors who, one imagines, are less sensitive to transitory fluctuations in market conditions and are interested in making a serious long-term commitment to the market.

Perhaps the most striking feature of the work discussed in this chapter is the relatively poor degree of explanation that most models of entry have managed to achieve (including autoregressive models that are estimated on a number of pooled cross-sections). Such poor fits persist even when fixed effects are used to eliminate all the between-variation in the data, meaning that, although cross-section variation poses a number of challenges, the times series variation in the data is both substantial and poorly understood. This is, in some ways, a rather puzzling outcome. If, as one might suppose, barriers to entry were the major determinant of entry, then virtually any sensible model of entry would uncover major effects on entry flowing from permanent, exogenous variables like market size, growth, profitability and so on. However, although these factors do appear to play a role in conditioning entry flows, it is apparent that they do not explain much of what we observe. Instead, it appears that variations in entry across industries and over time reflect the influence of mediating market conditions, a set of transitory factors that are, in part, endogenous to the entry process as it unfolds over time. The next step in modelling entry might be to regard entry as a process rather than as a discrete event, focusing more on the stochastic properties of the stream of new firms that appear over time in a market and less on the actions of any particular one of them. It may also prove to be the case that modelling this process requires one to focus more on the market environment in which entry occurs, perhaps distinguishing new markets from mature ones and isolating the events affecting particular market niches more carefully than hitherto.

There are several ways that one can interpret the empirical results discussed in this chapter. One obvious explanation is that most markets are generally in a state of long-run equilibrium. At such an equilibrium, net entry will be a mere fraction of gross entry because there is no need for a major expansion in – or contraction of – industry supply. Most entry will therefore involve displacement as new firms embodying incremental innovations supplant older, less well adapted incumbents. Turnover will occur as market pressures encourage market participants to improve the fit that they have achieved with the environment, and what one will observe in these circumstances is a certain jostling amongst players of the fringes at the market, not an error correction process responding to restrictions in supply. At first sight, this seems to be pretty much what we actually do observe. Further, because entry flows are not, on the whole, driven by disequilibrium pressures (in this view), then, expected profits just equal entry costs on average. As a consequence, entry costs and the structural barriers that underlie them will not be strongly related to entry; one will only observe noise around a long-run equilibrium rather than systematic responses to movements towards equilibrium over time. Only changes in barriers that are not fully mirrored in changes in expected profits will give rise to systematic movements in entry flows. What one observes are data generated mainly from long-run equilibrium configurations, and these are, perforce, noisy data.

Although this view has a lot to commend it, there are a number of reasons why one must treat it with some caution. Perhaps the most important of these is the notion that it is only in disequilibrium situations that structural factors matter, and thus that the absence of an effect of market structure on entry reflects the establishment of equilibrium. This presumption ought to be questioned. While permanent exogenous structural factors probably do affect entry a lot in the long run, their effect in the short run is likely to depend on a range of endogenous and exogenous transitory factors that transmit the effects of market structure to entrants' expected profits. It is not, after all, economies of scale *per se* that matter, but rather the fact that incumbents can use the existence of economies to squeeze entrants strategically by producing large quantities of output themselves post-entry. Further, the effect of scale economies upon entrant profits is necessarily less in growing markets than it is in shrinking ones. In a sense, then, what is likely to matter most to entrants is patterns of conduct in the market (including the responses by incumbents to entry), patterns that may, in the long run, be determined by structure but which, in the short run, are likely to vary rather more idiosyncratically, following a logic of their own over time. This alternative view, then, suggests that what we observe is not noise generated in the neighbourhood of a long-run equilibrium but, rather, subtle and local changes in entry provoked by a range of mediating market conditions, including the conduct of rivals.

There are several ways in which one can think that 'conduct matters', the most obvious being that entrants act and incumbents react. More subtly, conduct may refer to the mix of types of competitors that entrants face. Even if individual firms never change their strategies and even if all innovations are produced by new firms, it is nevertheless the case that the high influx of new firms in most markets effectively changes the parameters of the environment that each individual firm faces, a change that occurs continuously and endogenously. The effect is to change the immediate market environment in which different types of entrants must compete, not so much changing market structure as changing what structure means for the expected profits of entrants. The alternative view, then, is that the data reveal a pattern of activity in which very short-run effects matter, effects that are strictly local in impact, transitory in nature and, in part, endogenous. These effects are likely to change over time in sufficiently systematic ways to enable one to get a rough fix on predicting entry flows (e.g. through autoregressive models or through models that allow for variations in conduct), but the effects themselves are probably too subtle and too local to make this fix a very sure one (which is, roughly, what our experience with these models has suggested). As a consequence, autoregressive models of entry and models in which conduct varies over time in a systematic (and even endogenous) manner work, and they may even work better than structural models without, however, necessarily working terribly well in an absolute sense. The role of market structure, as reflected in the permanent exogenous variables that have been used to account for entry, is, in this view, restricted to that of providing a broad backdrop within which variations in conduct occur as the market evolves (largely but not entirely) in a path-dependent manner through a series of temporary equilibria.

Thus, at the end of the day, one is left knowing that, in practice, market structure (as conventionally measured by market size, by various proxies for entry barriers and so on) matters, but that it does not matter much in affecting entry. This may either reflect data generated from some long-run equilibrium determined by these structural factors or reflect the fact that it is mediating market conditions which really matter. Either way, it seems clear that there are no simple associations between entry and market events that correspond to the textbook conception of entry as an automatic error corrective mechanism. Entry seems far too noisy, idiosyncratic and, perhaps, insubstantial to play such a role efficiently, and one naturally wonders whether that means that it plays some other role in market processes as well.

Notes

1 As Bresnahan and Reiss note, probit (or logit) estimates of (3.3) only estimate m^* up to a scale factor. This leads them to focus on what they call an 'entry threshold ratio', which is the ratio of F/m^* at which $\pi = 0$ in duopoly to that in monopoly. This measure conflates 'the fraction by which variable profits fall between monopoly and duopoly and the ratio of fixed costs between the first and second firm' (1988, p. 839). Another ratio of interest is the ratio of m^* in duopoly to that in monopoly. This measures the decrease in (variable) profits caused by an increase in competition.

2 The model in (3.3) is slightly profligate in its use of information, focusing on no entry ($N = 0$), monopoly ($N = 1$) and 'duopoly' ($N > 2$) outcomes, and thus throwing away information on how m^* and F vary as N increases beyond $N = 2$ (this has been relaxed in subsequent work by Bresnahan and Reiss). Concentrating on outcomes in which $N = 0$, 1 or 2 is a cause and consequence of looking at isolated markets, and this sample selection criterion undoubtedly limits the generalizations that one can make from the markets they looked at, not least because it rules out any kind of niche entry. In a

broader, national market perspective, of course, all of the Bresnahan–Reiss entrants are niche entrants.

3   For further details of this model of consumer behaviour, see Smallwood and Conlisk (1979) and Schmalensee (1978a). Cross (1983) discusses a range of similar models, and Ehrenberg (1988) looks at models of brand loyalty.

4   Note that, if $g = r = 0$, then (3.13) describes the fall in prices due to entry when the 'Sylos postulate' is an accurate description of incumbent behaviour (Modigliani, 1958). If $g = 0$ but incumbents react by increasing output, then the fall in price will exceed that given by the Sylos postulate; if $g > 0$ but $r = 0$, then incumbents behaving according to the Sylos postulate will experience more entry than if $g = 0$ (i.e. the post-entry price fall for a given N_e will be less).

5   A similar point is made by Carlton (1983) who shows that the location and employment choices of a new firm are linked. The first decision requires that profits at the chosen location exceed those available elsewhere, while the second decision depends on the derivative of the profit function with respect to wages. Evidently similar sets of factors affect both decisions, and this opens up the possibility of realizing efficiency gains by estimating both jointly.

6   This model was first introduced by Orr (1974b) who was mainly interested in explaining the determinants of F. Surveys of subsequent work using the model to make inferences about F can be found in Geroski and Masson (1987) and Cable and Schwalbach (1991); see also chapter 5.

7   There are several sources of such adjustment costs; see Nickell (1978) for a discussion in the context of investment models. For a classic discussion of managerial limitations creating costs of adjustment, see Penrose (1959) and, for a formalization, Slater (1980).

8   We restrict attention to the effects of x_t on Y_t and Y_{t+1} for simplicity. Both θ_0 and θ_1 are termed conjectural variations; for surveys of the literature devoted to estimating θ_0, see Geroski (1988a) or Bresnahan (1989). The problem with conjectural variations in static simultaneous choice models is that the notion of a reaction makes no conceptual sense unless the game is played more than once (see Shapiro, 1989, for a clear exposition of this point). Hence, θ_1 is the parameter of major interest. Notice also that increases in x_t lower prices in $t + 1$ and raise costs of adjustment, and thus that the effects captured by θ_1 and δ will in practice be rather difficult to distinguish empirically.

9   At least some of the problem arises because different types of entrants appear to respond to these variables in different ways; e.g. see Gorecki (1975, 1976) and Morch van der Fehr (1991) on new and diversifying and domestic and foreign entry; Acs and Audretsch (1987) look at large and small entrants, as does Mata (1991). Both Baldwin and Gorecki (1987) and Geroski (1991) noted differences in the response of domestic and foreign-based entrants to profits (positive but weak and statistically insignificant respectively), although Geroski found that the overall height of barriers facing the two types of entrant were fairly similar. For a survey of not unrelated work on

the determinants of direct investment, see Caves (1982); Caves and Mehra (1985) examine the methods and determinants of the entry by foreign multinational firms into US manufacturing industries.

10 If expected profits are a stationary process (not an unreasonable assumption), then Wold's decomposition theorem establishes that it can be written as the sum of two mutually uncorrelated processes, one of which is linearly deterministic and the other of which is MA(∞); e.g. Granger and Newbold (1986). On the use of factor analysis and latent variables models more generally, see Judge et al. (1980, ch. 13) and Aigner et al. (1984).

11 An estimate of the net penetration equation (for example) without fixed effects is

$$E_t = -0.0053 + 0.0929E_{t-1} - 0.1688E_{t-2} + 0.1758E_{t-3} - 0.0299E_{t-4}$$
$$(1.74) \quad (1.23) \quad\quad (1.61) \quad\quad (1.41) \quad\quad (1.41)$$

where t statistics are in parentheses, $R^2 = 0.0041$ and $\bar{R}^2 = -0.0219$. The $\chi^2(78)$ statistic testing the restrictions that simplify the equation shown in table 3.3 to that above is 232.942, several times larger than its 1% critical value. The comparison between this estimated equation and that shown in table 3.5 shows clearly how the fixed effects affect estimates of the β_j.

12 For theoretical work on the slightly more subtle proposition that potential entrants deter entry, see Sherman and Willett (1967). James (1986) critically examines the subsequent literature, identifying a mixed strategy Nash equilibrium in which the probability of entry falls as the number of potential entrants rises.

13 A comparison between (3.26) and (3.33) shows the two to be observationally equivalent, as indeed they must be since the model (3.31)–(3.32) differs from (3.24)–(3.25) only in being slightly more explicit about the determinants of π_t^e. That is, (3.31)–(3.32) makes plain why π_t^e may have an MA representation in (3.25). Notice also that (3.33) shows that the negative coefficients on the lagged dependent variables shown in tables 3.3 and 3.4 are not uninterpretable.

14 This argument does not distinguish between the number of entrants and their average size. However, given the large number of very small entrants that appear in most markets and given that numbers and average size have occasionally been observed to be negatively correlated across industries, there is also a sense in which entrants may crowd other entrants out by restricting their market penetration. For more entrants in a market to translate into a lower market share for each, it must be the case that the total market open to entrants is strictly limited, as, for example, might occur if entrants were competing for places in a narrow well-defined market niche.

15 Masson and Shaanan (1987) have pursued a slightly simpler route, looking at the interaction between imports and domestic entry rates by including each as a determinant of the other in addition to other determinants like π_t^e and F. They observed a negative but only weakly significant correlation between import intensity and the incidence of entry. Khemani and Shapiro (1987) found entry to be a significant determinant of exit in the same type of model,

suggesting that much entry may involve little more than displacement of earlier entrants by later ones.

16 Note that as one pools more and more data – two years in table 3.5, three years in table 3.7 and four years in table 3.3 – the fit of one's model of entry falls off noticeably. This reflects the high within-variance of entry (meaning that the fixed effects do less and less work), but may also indicate some structural instability in estimated coefficients over time.

17 For some theoretical work explaining the relationship between demand fluctuations and market structure – the number of firms, their technological flexibility and their size – see Sheshinski and Dreze (1976), Mills and Schumann (1985), Mills (1986) and others.

18 Relatively few formal models exist which explicitly model entrants' strategy choices and the dependence of entry on such choices. Rather more work has been done on the issue of how types of strategies affect market penetration. Biggadike (1976) found that 'incremental innovators' performed worse than 'me too' entrants during the first two years post-entry, but that performance rankings reversed over the next two years. For case studies and further descriptive work along these lines, see Romanelli (1987), Willard and Savara (1988) and others.

4

Entry and the Short-run Dynamics of Prices and Margins

Introduction

One of the more important questions that can be asked about the performance of markets is whether competition amongst incumbent firms is sufficiently vigorous to bring prices down to the level of marginal costs. While it is clearly in the interests of incumbents to co-operate with each other and elevate prices above marginal costs, such agreements, overt or tacit, can be difficult to sustain in the face of incentives to cheat. Secretly cutting prices while other industry members maintain theirs at agreed levels is essentially a myopic act designed to take advantage of the existing structure of prices, and if it is detected it can have serious adverse effects on industry pricing discipline in the medium and long run. Firms that keep track of the future consequences of their current actions will balance the costs of a cheating-induced price war and the future non-cooperation of rivals against the current gains from undercutting rivals, and may therefore resist the temptation to upset pricing patterns for what may turn out to be no more than transitory profits. In particular, if cheating is relatively easy to detect and if rivals are quick to respond to secret price cuts, then competitors need not be terribly long sighted to realize that cheating may not pay. Although it does not follow from this that prices will typically be nearer to joint profit-maximizing levels than to marginal costs, it does seem likely that prices will often exceed marginal costs in stable, highly concentrated, well-established markets.[1]

That competition amongst existing incumbent firms may not, in general, be vigorous enough to drive prices down to competitive levels is not a major cause for concern if there exists a sufficiently large supply of potential entrants capable of breaking up established pricing policies. In particular, the threat of entry can have one of three types of effect on pricing behaviour. First, the threat of entry may actually materialize as a flow of new entrants whenever prices exceed competitive levels. The short-run effect of this is likely to be some sort of price war as entrants attempt to undercut incumbents in order to penetrate the market and as incumbents respond by defending their market positions. The size of this first effect of entry on prices depends on how extensive the supply of potential entrants is, how much penetration entrants actually achieve, the nature of competition between entrant and incumbent, and so on. Second, entry may affect prices indirectly if the fact of entry provokes a non-price response by incumbents (an advertising war, say, or a pre-emptive expansion in capacity) that feeds through to prices. Active non-price competition between firms generally leads each to make investments in various types of assets that alter the cost and demand curves of all competitors in the market, changes that are likely to lead firms to revise their prices away from the levels that would have been considered to be profit maximizing in their absence. There is no necessary reason to think that all such revisions will be downwards, and it is therefore possible that entry-induced non-price competition may lead to higher prices post-entry than those that prevailed pre-entry.

The third type of effect that the threat of entry may have on prices can materialize even if entry does not actually occur. The mere anticipation of entry by incumbents may lead them to cut prices in advance of entry in order to deter entrants. For this kind of effect to materialize, incumbents must anticipate the arrival of entrants, choose to block them and prefer price to most other instruments of deterrence. For the strategy to be effective, entrants must either treat pre-entry prices as a signal containing information on the profitability of entry, or they must believe that the low pre-entry prices that they observe will persist post-entry. One way or the other, the result of this third effect is that prices are likely to approach long-run levels without any change in market structure when there are plenty of potential entrants to a market, and competition amongst existing incumbents will appear to be roughly competitive to an unwary observer. Indeed, in the limit, potential competition may be so effective that prices never diverge much from marginal costs. In this case, actual entry will have no effect on prices or margins (although it will affect market structure) and, what is more, actual market structure (the number and size distribution of existing incumbents) will also have no effect on market performance. Markets surrounded by a great buzzing swarm of able, active and alert potential competitors will in general yield competitive outcomes regardless of whether they are monopolies or atomistic. Potential competitors are in this case a perfect substitute for actual competitors.[2]

The notion that competition among existing firms may not be an important determinant of price – that potential entrants are a perfect substitute for actual competitors – is rather an extreme one, and it provokes one to ask whether the mere threat of entry does substitute for active price competition between incumbents. More fundamentally, it is worth asking whether entry, actual or potential, plays a major role in affecting price competition, and how big an affect it has on pricing behaviour. Our goal in this chapter is to explore the evidence which exists on this question, and we shall do this by looking directly at the effect that entry has on prices or price–cost margins and, somewhat less directly, by looking at the methods and instruments – including price – that incumbents typically use when (and if) they choose to deter entry.

The problems involved in assessing the effects of entry, however, are slightly more subtle than they appear at first sight. In trying to empirically evaluate the extent to which actual or potential entry substitutes for competition amongst existing incumbents, one must distinguish the size of the *long-run* effect of entry on price from that which materializes in the *short run*. In the long run, the only thing that matters from the point of view of market performance is the height of entry barriers. If barriers are high, incumbents will feel able to behave as they like, secure in the knowledge that they are free from the predatory challenge of entrants. In a sense, high entry barriers mean that there are few entrants in the total population of potential entrants who are sufficiently advantaged to compete on a par with incumbents. If, by contrast, barriers are low, then any attempt by incumbents to restrict output will flounder on their inability to control the total potential supply of goods to the market. In effect, low barriers mean that there is no real limit to the supply of capable entrants to the market, and in these circumstances it is unlikely that prices can be maintained above marginal cost for very long.

Although apparently prosaic, these arguments do not necessarily hold in the short run. The arrival of the one advantaged entrant ever likely to enter an industry protected by high entry barriers may provoke a major price war, while, in contrast, entry into an industry with low entry barriers may be so slow in incidence and so gentle in impact as to enable prices to remain fairly high for very long periods of time. Further, an industry protected by high barriers promises golden rewards to those few firms able to enter successfully, and one expects that the response to the opening up of such an opportunity, however small, will be prompt. The long-run future of anyone entering an industry with low barriers is, at best, modest, and it is not unreasonable to think that the response of potential competitors in that sector may be commensurate with their expected rewards. Thus, it is not wholly inconceivable that the moderate potential long-run effects of entry in an industry protected by high barriers to entry may be realized rather more rapidly than the more substantial effects in an industry protected by low barriers.

While one would not wish to push the distinction too hard, it is nevertheless the case that the effect of entry in the long run depends primarily on entry barriers, while the short-run effect of entry depends much more on the arrival rate of entrants, on their planned penetration rate into the market and, probably most of all, on the reactions of incumbents to their arrival (reactions which, as we shall see, may depend on the height of barriers). Indeed, these two sets of determinants are sufficiently different that it is difficult *a priori* to accept the proposition that high prices will in general converge smoothly and monotonically to their long-run levels under the influence of entry. It seems more than reasonable to argue that the short-run price effects of entry may exceed those experienced in the long run, particularly when the response to early entrants is expected to affect the decisions of later entrants. In this case, the initial appearance of entry in response to high prices is likely to be punctuated by a price war driving prices down to, and perhaps below, long-run levels, followed by a return to prices no higher than they were initially and perhaps rather lower. In other situations, positions of market power may erode more steadily, with price falling gradually from monopoly levels as entrants slowly eat into the sales of incumbents at a rate which the latter are willing to tolerate. The height of entry barriers may, of course, be one of the factors which helps to determine which of these two rather different short-run outcomes prevails. Others include industry growth and the behaviour of anti-trust or regulatory bodies. High growth enables entrants to encroach on incumbents' market shares without leading to a diminution in their revenue, and capacity limitations may prevent incumbents from responding. Anti-trust and regulatory policy can substantially affect 'the rules of the game' and, indeed, major discrete changes like deregulation can have effects on the behaviour of both entrants and incumbents that differ substantially from what one might observe when barriers to entry fall more gradually.

Thus, our goal in this chapter is to explore the effects of entry, actual and potential, on price and price–cost margins. In doing so, we shall focus on the short-run effects of entry, leaving the subject of entry barriers to the next chapter. We proceed in three steps. The natural place to start is with the behaviour of incumbents in the face of entry, and the next section examines the theory of entry deterrence. Our goals in this section are two: first, to explore the observable effects that the use of deterrence strategies are likely to have on price and price–cost margins over time, and second, to ascertain whether there is any systematic ordering in the likely use of various instruments of deterrence by incumbents. The next two sections apply the insights gained from these arguments to the data. First, we examine the dynamics of margins, developing econometric models to measure the effects of both actual and potential entry and examining the results that have emerged from their use. Then we examine the available (mainly case study) evidence on the use of particular instruments of deterrence and, more broadly, on whether (or when) incumbents find it optimal to respond to entry. A few conclusions are discussed in the final section.

Strategic Entry Deterrence

It is natural to begin by examining the kinds of price responses to entry that incumbents might use, assuming for the moment that it is optimal for them to respond at all. There are, in principle, two types of pricing strategies that one might expect to observe: 'limit pricing' and 'entry regulation' (entry may also be accommodated if the incumbent maintains high prices by reducing output in the face of entry). Limit pricing is a pre-emptive, pre-entry strategy designed to block entry, while entry regulation is a post-entry strategy designed to limit the market penetration of entrants, a strategy whose predatory extreme aims to induce the entrant to exit. The two strategies have quite different implications for price dynamics. When observed over time, a market in which limit pricing occurs will display no entry, and prices will be below joint profit-maximizing levels to an extent determined by the height of entry barriers. By contrast, entry regulation will manifest itself in systematic (but not necessarily monotonic) movements in price, in some amount of entry and in systematic movements in market structure. The contrast between these two responses to entry is, perhaps, rather stronger than is the contrast between entry regulation and a strategy of no response to entry. A policy which makes no attempt to regulate entry rates will also exhibit price dynamics, actual entry and movements in market structure, but the scale of entry will be larger and the convergence of prices to long-run levels will be more rapid than would have been the case had entry regulation been attempted. When incumbents do not respond to either potential or actual entry, the effects of entry on price occur only through induced changes in market structure. Entry regulation involves some pre-emptive pricing and some accommodation of entry, leading both to price effects that occur without any change in market structure and to price effects induced by changes in structure. Limit pricing, a pre-entry strategy designed to block entry, causes no change in market structure, and any price dynamics associated with limit pricing are caused by (largely unobservable) changes in the threat of entry posed by potential competitors.

The mechanism by which limit pricing is thought to work is easily described. The essential problem faced by an entrant is to calculate the price that it expects to prevail post-entry – a calculation which requires it to form a view about what it thinks the likely response of incumbents will be to its entry attempt. This, in turn, requires that it know something about the incumbents cost and demand functions, and about incumbents expectations regarding its likely behaviour. One of the many potentially useful pieces of information available to the entrant to use in making these inferences is the price prevailing in the market pre-entry. There is, of course, no one unique inference that it can make from observing pre-entry prices, but a 'low' price (together with other reinforcing scraps of information) might suggest that the incumbent is particularly efficient, and thus that the low price observed pre-entry is, at best, the maximum that the entrant can expect to prevail post-entry. If, at this price, the entrant cannot cover its expected average costs, then it is likely to desist from entering. Of course, a sophisticated entrant will recognize that the mere possibility that such inferences can be made makes it reasonable to expect that the incumbent will attempt to manipulate pre-entry prices strategically, and this is bound to undermine the effect that observed pre-entry prices have on the entrants' calculations. Indeed, an even more sophisticated entrant will question whether an incumbent willing to set sub-monopoly level prices in order to deter entry will also be willing to maintain such low prices if the attempt to block entry fails. That is, given the fact of entry and, for the sake of argument, supposing that no further entry were possible, the optimal strategy of an incumbent faced with the fact of entry is likely to involve trying to accommodate and, indeed, co-operate with the entrant to raise prices.[3] In these circumstances, low pre-entry prices designed to convey the threat of low post-entry prices will carry little credence with a sophisticated entrant, and therefore a limit pricing strategy is unlikely to be used.[4]

The essential idea behind entry regulation is that price can affect the penetration speed of entrants, with high prices generating higher entry rates and faster penetration by entrants. This creates an intertemporal trade-off in the profits of incumbents, high price trajectories leading to higher but more rapidly declining profit streams than a trajectory of lower prices. Quite why high prices ought to lead to faster entry penetration is slightly unclear, however. At the simplest level, entrants may adopt the fairly myopic view that current prices will prevail indefinitely, that their actions are either too insignificant to affect market outcomes or that incumbents will good-naturedly accommodate their presence by restricting output *pari passu*. Perhaps more compelling is the argument that many entrants rely on current profit flows to finance their expansion either directly or indirectly via the effect that such flows have on the willingness of putative lenders to provide finance on reasonable terms. Hence, a policy of holding down prices may restrict the ability of entrants to finance their expansion, and so will slow their market penetration. One way or the other, the link between current prices and the rate of expansion of entry opens up the possibility that price can be used strategically by incumbents to affect the evolution of market structure and prices over time in preferred ways.[5]

As a strategy, entry regulation produces a picture of market dynamics which is often thought to describe the fate of large market leaders, or 'dominant firms' (e.g. Worcester, 1957). In the conventional model, a dominant firm is assumed to be able to manipulate entry penetration rates using prices in the manner discussed above, but is otherwise unable to affect the behaviour of entrants. That is, it is unable to persuade them to restrict output levels and assist in keeping prices high, and so it effectively maximizes profits defined on residual market demand; that is, on the difference between total market demand and the total supply by all current and past entrants ('the fringe' hereafter) at each price. The consequence is that the entire burden of output restriction is shifted onto the shoulders of the dominant firm and, what is more, the weight of this burden increases over time as prices are kept high. The dominant firm enjoys some market power, but it is power that evaporates with use, for the very act of exploiting it (i.e. raising prices) provokes a reaction (i.e. the expansion of the fringe) which leads to its erosion. The consequence is that price declines, the market share of the dominant firm declines, and entry occurs at a rate depending, *inter alia*, on the price trajectory chosen by the dominant firm, a choice that depends on the elasticity of demand, on its rate of time preference and on the elasticity of supply of the fringe. Price falls because of the fact that actual entry erodes residual demand and thus the power of the dominant firm to keep prices high, and because prices are used to regulate the flow of entry (at least partially), keeping it lower than it would otherwise have been.

Both of these price strategies seem to be fairly tepid responses to entry, and the likely effects of either on entry seem to be most uncertain. Limit pricing as a strategy seems uncompelling because it conveys little credible force. The circumstances in which a low pre-entry price forcefully suggest a post-entry price too low to allow profitable entry to occur seem somewhat contrived, not least because price is only a small part of the information set that entrants will use in making their decisions. Entry regulation, on the other hand, seems to be a rather passive response to entry. The dominant firm seems unable to do more than temporarily restrict the fringe's erosion of its market power, and this transitory gain is bought at the cost of a reduced ability to exploit whatever market power it does have. Despite its apparent market power, the dominant firm does very little to try to alter the behaviour of the fringe or to raise the entry and mobility barriers that fringe firms face. Indeed, its whole strategy is more akin to learning to live with a disability than trying to overcome it.

A far more reasonable strategy for an incumbent concerned about entry to follow might be to try to target entry with a strategic weapon which has more permanent effects on the fringe, freeing price to be used to exploit market power. Indeed, although limit pricing and entry regulation have been presented as alternatives – the one a pre-entry and the other a post-entry choice – it may be more natural to see price as a weapon of the last resort, to be used when all else has failed and the only remaining issue to be resolved is 'how fast will entry occur?'[6] Following the spirit of this observation, a more general view of the hierarchy of entry deterrence weapons might go as follows. In the first instance, an incumbent may try to block entry through the use of various bluffs, threats and pre-commitments undertaken pre-entry, hoping to discourage the entrant from making any irrevocable commitment to entering the market. Then, if this posturing fails, the incumbent can at least try to recover some of its lost ground by manipulating price post-entry to slow the initial investment or subsequent market penetration of entrants, maintaining the flow of at least some supernormal profits for a while. Thinking of entry-deterring price strategies in this way suggests that incumbents are likely to prefer using non-price to price entry-deterring strategies (at least in the first instance), if, indeed, they choose to respond to entry at all.

The first step to take in pursuing the argument that there is a hierarchy of entry deterrence instruments is to explore the circumstances in which an incumbent might find it optimal to respond to entry. This depends, in the first instance, on the costs of doing so; that is, on the height of barriers in the market and on current market conditions such as growth and the elasticity of demand. If barriers are very high, entry is unlikely to be successful, and there will be little need for incumbents to respond. Entry will be blocked 'innocently' (as it were), and the incumbent can act as if it were alone in the market. If, by contrast, barriers are low, then blocking entry may require major expenditures by the incumbent, expenditures far in excess of the likely benefits to blocking entry. Entry is more or less inevitable in these circumstances, and entry-deterring expenditures sufficiently large to protect the incumbent are unlikely to be justified by the subsequent flow of monopoly profits that they generate. Levels of barriers in between make the decision to respond more difficult, and this has led scholars to make a distinction between 'effectively impeded' and 'ineffectively impeded' entry (Bain, 1956). This captures the notion that when barriers are high but not high enough to block entry, then it may be worth responding to entry; by contrast, low barriers that only slightly impede entrants may not be worth building upon. In the former case, entry will be blocked by a combination of 'innocent' and 'strategic' factors, and entry deterrence – incurring current costs in exchange for a longer stream of near monopoly profits over time – will be attractive for all but the most myopic incumbents. When entry is ineffectively impeded, barriers are so low that the current costs of blocking entry are higher than the discounted present value of the longer run profit stream that the incumbent will enjoy as a result, and all but the most long-sighted incumbents are likely to find this unattractive.

Two further arguments suggest that entry deterrence is often likely to be optimal except when entry barriers are low. First, it is the case that entry can be irreversible, and thus even if it appears initially to be in the incumbent's interest to accommodate entry, the possibility that this may not always be so might lead the incumbent to choose to block the entrant nevertheless. To see this argument, suppose that marginal costs are v and fixed costs are F. If the entrant produces x post-entry, its costs are $C(x) = vx + F$. Prior to entry, the entrant has not yet sunk its fixed costs F, and thus it will enter if it expects a price p which will cover its average costs, $p > v + F/x$. Once it has entered, however, F is sunk and irretrievable and, provided that $p > v$, the option of exiting (and thus sacrificing F) is less attractive than that of soldiering on when $p < v + F/x$. Hence, *to block entry*, the incumbent must set $p \leqslant v + F/x$, but, *to induce exit given that entry has occurred*, price must be set even lower, at a level of $p \leqslant v$ (for a fuller discussion concentrating on how uncertainty affects these limits, see Dixit, 1989a). More generally, any kind of learning or other type of capital accumulation that reduces v relative to F makes it increasingly expensive to induce the exit of a rival and more attractive to strangle it at birth. In short, blocking a rival when it attempts entry may prove to be the most efficient time to do so, and it may therefore be an optimal strategy even when it appears to conflict with the short-run interest of the incumbent.[7]

The second argument that leads one to suspect that it may often be optimal to block an entrant focuses on the incentives that incumbent firms have to act against entrants, and emerges most clearly when one puts the deterrence problem into an explicitly sequential context. Imagine that one firm (hereafter, the incumbent) discovers an innovation that creates an entirely new market, and suppose that initially there is room for only one producer in the market. As a. consequence, the market becomes monopolized and price is set at monopoly levels. Suppose further that, in due course, some event occurs which makes it possible for entry to occur – the market grows, a new and complementary innovation becomes feasible, or whatever – and let us refer to this increment uf space as 'the new market' to distinguish it from 'the old market' which the incumbent initially monopolized. The proposition in question asserts that the new market is always more valuable to the incumbent than it is to the entrant. If the incumbent monopolizes both markets, it can maximize returns jointly over both markets and earn, say, π_1. If the entrant enters, then they will share both markets in some fashion or another, the entrant earning, say, π_2 and the incumbent π_3. Now, unless entrant and incumbent collude perfectly, $\pi_1 > \pi_2 + \pi_3$, in which case the gain to the incumbent from pre-empting the entrant in the new market, $\pi_1 - \pi_3$, exceeds the entrant's gain from entering, π_2. Thus, the incumbent will always be willing to pay more than the entrant to acquire the new market and, if it can force the entrant to incur entry costs in excess of π_2 at a cost of no more than $\pi_1 - \pi_3$ to itself, it has an incentive to block entry.[8]

Accepting the presumption that it will frequently be in the interests of incumbents to block entry, the next question to be faced is how this might be done. Basically, the incumbent's problem is that, to block entry, it needs credibly to commit itself to satisfying a sufficiently large percentage of total market demand that the entrant cannot cover its costs on the residual demand remaining to it. That is, the incumbent must credibly commit itself to producing some output y such that post-entry price $p = p(x, y)$ is less than the entrant's average costs $v + F/x$, where the entrant's variable costs are v, its fixed costs are F and x is the entrant's best output choice given y. Suppose that the output that the incumbent needs to produce in order to block entry is y^*. For the entrant to be persuaded that entry is not worthwhile, it must be sure that the incumbent will in fact produce y^* post-entry should it enter. If the incumbent's best output given the fact of entry is some $\bar{y} \geqslant y^*$, then clearly entry will not be profitable for the entrant.[9] The incumbent need take no special precautions as entry will be blocked 'innocently'. If , however, $\bar{y} < y^*$, then it will be in the incumbent's interests to threaten to produce y^* in the event of entry. If the entrant believes the threat, then no entry will occur; if, however, it disregards the threat, then the incumbent will produce $\bar{y}$ rather than y^* post-entry and, as a consequence, the post-entry price will exceed $v + F/x$. Thus, if $\bar{y}$ is the incumbent's best response to entry and if the entrant knows that, then the threat to produce $y^* \geqslant \bar{y}$ is empty and entry will occur. To have an effect on the entrant's behaviour, the threat to produce y^* post-entry must be made credible; the incumbent must, in some sense, ensure that it 'has no choice' but to produce y^*.

To make the pre-emptive threat of producing y^* post-entry credible when some $\bar{y} < y^*$ would be optimal, the incumbent must limit the options open to it in such a way as to preclude the possibility of choosing $\bar{y}$ or, indeed, of choosing anything aside from y^* (see Encaoua et al. (1987), Geroski and Jacquemin (1984), Salop (1979), Gilbert (1989), Dixit (1982) and Geroski et al. (1990) for surveys of what follows in the next six paragraphs). There are two ways to do this. The first (and intuitively more natural) is to alter the entrant's costs or demand in such a way as to make it unable to operate profitably if the incumbent produces $\bar{y}$. It is clear that anything which raises v or F or shrinks $p(x, y)$ for a given x and y will reduce the profits earned by the entrant and, as a consequence, makes blocking that entrant possible at output rates less than y^*. Somewhat less intuitive is a second strategy that the incumbent can follow. If it is impossible to inflate its rival's costs or diminish the demand for its goods, then the incumbent may find it attractive to affect its own costs or demand. Instead of trying to lower y^* to $\bar{y}$, it may seek to raise $\bar{y}$ towards y^*. This will involve making investments to raise its demand or lower its costs in a manner which, in the short run without entry, appear to be unprofitable. This pre-entry diminution in profits, however, may be more than compensated for over the longer run if it makes the threat to produce y^* credible when it otherwise would not have been. These investments are, in a sense, self-crippling since they involve a cost and restrict the actions of the incumbent post-entry (it can now no longer sensibly choose $\bar{y}$). Nevertheless, by reducing its range of choice post-entry, the incumbent may, paradoxically, be able to gain the considerable competitive advantage of persuading the entrant that, come what may, it will produce y^* (see Schelling, 1960, for a general discussion of this type of strategy).

What are the characteristics of the types of strategy which can credibly commit an incumbent to producing y^* post-entry? There are, perhaps, three of importance. First, the effects of any strategic investment made by the incumbent must be *observable* so that the implicit threat to produce y^* is communicated to the entrant.[10] Second, the effects of the strategy must be *durable*; they must last from the 'pre-entry' period when they are made well into the 'post-entry' period when they are meant to be working and deterring entry. Third, and most important, the strategies must be *irreversible*. To make the threat of producing y^* post-entry credible, the incumbent must make it plain that the choice of y^* is out of its hands, that it cannot choose $\bar{y}$ even if it wanted to. This effectively ensures that the threat to produce y^* given entry will be carried out if provoked, and removes from consideration any likelihood that it is no more than a bluff. Of course, irreversibility, like durability, is a relative concept and what matters is that the strategy is 'too costly' to reverse, that its effects do not depreciate 'too fast'. In essence, this amounts to saying that the expenditures that create the pre-commitment to y^* are sunk into an asset whose effective life is not only long, but also exogenous to the actions of the incumbent.

The simplest way to implement this type of pre-emption strategy is through accepting binding long-term contracts with third parties (e.g. Williamson, 1968; Salop and Scheffman, 1983; Aghion and Bolton, 1987). If, for example, labour intensity falls markedly with scale, then large incumbents may be able to raise the costs of small-scale entrants by agreeing to high wages with a monopoly supplier of labour. Although this policy raises incumbent's costs, it affects smaller-scale entrants more seriously and makes it easier to block them. Similarly, an incumbent may concede generous terms to a major retailer in exchange for practices which deny entrants good shelf space or, indeed, any shelf space at all. Aside from any question of legality, the principal difficulty with such strategies is that contracts must be binding to be credible, and for this to be the case the third party involved must be proof to any counter-offers proposed by the entrant. Although there are circumstances where long-standing relations between the incumbent and various suppliers or retailers may make the latter extremely wary of supporting a new entrant, this is unlikely to be the case in all situations. Retailers or trade unions may benefit from some limited competition between those who seek their services, and thus may well find it optimal to encourage entry, or at least the threat of it. This, in turn, suggests that incumbents may have to resort to more complex strategies of various types in many circumstances.

There are a wide range of assets that incumbents can create through strategic investments, assets whose effect is to shift post-entry outcomes permanently in favour of the incumbent. On the demand side, advertising appears at first sight to be an attractive type of strategic investment. To the extent that a massive advertising campaign generates buyer loyalty or reinforces purchasing habits which favour the incumbent, or to the extent that it raises the cost to the entrant of announcing its wares and attracting the attention of buyers, then it is likely to make entry more difficult. And, to the extent that scale economies make the per unit costs of large-scale advertising lower, then an entry-induced advertising war is likely to raise entrant's costs far more than those of the incumbent. Although it seems reasonable to believe that advertising will often be necessary for entrants seeking to enter at large scale or to penetrate quickly into the market, the effect of advertising on consumer's behaviour may be of rather short duration and this will reduce the attractions of using advertising to deter entry.[11]

Investments in product quality or product specification are often thought of in terms similar to investments in specific geographical locations. In both cases, commitments to a particular product type or to a specific geographical niche can be made credible by the fact of costly relocation. The immobility of incumbents causes congestion in the relevant market space, and this restricts the market open to entrants. As with advertising, the source of the problem for entrants has its roots in buyer behaviour. The fact that consumers are physically distributed over geographical space or that their preferences over the characteristics of different goods are diverse tends to localize competition. Adjacent products compete with each other for consumers lying between them, but do not compete with firms several niches removed. The implications of this are that the demand an entrant can expect to encounter at any particular location is limited, and can be made more or less so the closer incumbents are located to each other. If serious fixed costs or economies of scale exist, then there is a minimum market penetration that the entrant needs to achieve if it is to break even. Consequently, a systematic strategy of crowding the relevant economic space by brand proliferation or the flooding of particular geographical markets may deter entry (or limit the penetration of entrants), and, if such actions are costly to reverse, may do so credibly.[12]

On the cost side, the most commonly discussed type of strategic investment is capacity choice. The effect of this is to alter the incumbent's marginal cost curve. Roughly speaking, the existence of excess capacity pre-entry means that the expansion of the incumbent's output post-entry will be less costly than it would otherwise have been had it been forced to install capacity as it expanded output. A threat to respond to entry by increasing output to y^* is then correspondingly more credible. Suppose that it costs αk to install capacity sufficient to produce k units of output and that, prior to entry, the incumbent installs $\bar{k}$. As long as these expenditures are sunk, there is no opportunity cost to using the capacity, and the incumbent's per unit costs of production are, say, v for any output produced up to $\bar{k}$. However, to produce any output level, the entrant must first install capacity costing α per unit. Its per unit costs, then, are the sum of production plus installation costs, $v + \alpha$. Hence, the choice of $\bar{k}$ prior to entry gives the incumbent something that looks like an absolute cost advantage post-entry. If the incumbent installs a sufficiently large capacity base, it may persuade the entrant that producing an output close to y^* post-entry is in its interests despite the fact that it would choose $\bar{y} < y^*$ if it had to install capacity at the same time that it chose output;

that is, if its per unit cost were $v + \alpha$. Similar arguments may also apply to holding inventories. Holding an inventory of $y^* - \bar{y}$ means that production post-entry can remain at $\bar{y}$ while sales increase to the level of y^*, and the fact that $y^* - \bar{y}$ has already been produced pre-entry is likely to make it easy to believe that y^* will be sold post-entry. Of course, what makes such investments in capacity or in inventories credible is the extent to which they are sunk, and this depends on their product specificity, maintenance costs and so on.[13] Other cost side strategies include research and development, exploiting learning effects, and other investments which create an absolute cost advantage for the incumbent relative to the entrant. While every firm has an incentive to lower its costs, this is true only up to the point where the marginal costs of doing so equal the marginal benefits. Compared with a monopolist protected by impossibly high entry barriers, a monopolist incumbent facing an entry threat is likely to be willing to incur extra costs in the short run if this will help to preserve the flow of monopoly profits in the longer run. This increment in investment expenditures is the strategic component of its cost-reducing activities.

The basic argument, then, is that there is a hierarchy of entry-deterring policy choices that are likely to be used whenever incumbents elect to impede entry. In general, one expects to see non-price strategies dominating price strategies, with the latter often implemented to cushion a blow that cannot otherwise be avoided (Schmalensee, 1978b, for example, has argued that space crowding will always dominate limit pricing as an entry deterrence strategy). This presumption follows from observing the easy reversibility of price and the somewhat contrived circumstances in which its effects on entrants' expectations can be expected to materialize. Somewhat less strongly, one might argue that entry deterrence strategies will typically involve a judicious mix of several types of strategic investment used with an appropriate pricing strategy. Thus, for example, price cuts may be used in conjunction with a strategic denial of input supplies that raises rivals' costs, while product proliferation may squeeze demand from one side at the same time that an advertising war inflates entrants' fixed costs on the other side. Indeed, the right mix of policies clearly will depend on the specific circumstances of the market. Omori and Yarrow (1982), for example, have argued that brand proliferation strategies are likely to be optimal when substitutability in demand between goods is low, or at higher levels of substitutability when fixed set-up costs are low. Both are situations in which price is an expensive tool to use, in the one case because price has little effect on rivals' brands and in the other because small fixed costs imply that breakeven penetration levels for the entrant are low and so the size of price cuts needed to block entry will be large.

All of this said, however, one senses that price is a less effective and long-lasting investment than other non-price weapons, and that using price to extract rents and assigning other weapons to block entry is likely to be an optimal assignment of tools to targets in many circumstances.

One final observation is in order. All the arguments made thus far have been expressed in terms of 'the incumbent', as if it were possible for a number of incumbents to collude perfectly to block entry. In fact, the existence of several incumbents complicates the problem of entry deterrence in several interesting ways (see Gilbert and Vives, 1986, for a simple model and Caves and Porter, 1977, more generally). In the first place, entry deterrence is a public good from which all members of the industry benefit, and this gives rise to incentives for each to free-ride on the strategic investments of others. Although this observation suggests that too little investment in entry deterrence is likely to occur, two further considerations cut against this presumption. In very simple terms, the object is to persuade the entrant that $y*$ will be produced post-entry rather than $\bar{y}$, the preferred monopoly output. If, however, incumbents do not collude perfectly over price, their rivalry will ensure that an aggregate output in excess of $\bar{y}$ will be produced in the absence of any strategic actions. Indeed, if their rivalry is intense, they may end up producing more than $y*$ regardless of the threat of entry. Further, strategic investments (such as capacity expansion, advertising and so on) not only pre-empt entrants, they also can pre-empt rivals and, to the extent that they are sunk and irreversible, the effects that they can have on the balance of power amongst existing incumbents can be long lasting. In these circumstances, pre-empting rivals may actually bring more benefits than pre-empting entrants. What is more, the competitive drive by each incumbent to gain an advantage over the others may lead to 'too much' strategic investment, and may end up blocking entry as a more or less innocent by-product. The bottom line, then, is that one imagines that entry is (probably) more likely to be blocked and (almost certainly) for that to occur more efficiently the more concentrated is the industry in question. If, as has often been alleged, such highly concentrated markets also have a marked propensity to indulge in non-price rather than price competition, then this will reinforce one's expectation that price is unlikely to be used strategically against entrants in these markets.

Entry and the Dynamics of Margins

The principal difficulty in tracing the effects of entry on the dynamics of prices or price–cost margins arises from the fact that the mere threat of entry may have an effect on prices – that entry need not actually occur to have an effect on market performance. Indeed, the extent to which entry actually does occur in a market depends in part on how incumbents respond to the threat of entry. If, on the one hand, incumbents choose to ignore entrants, then entry will occur and prices will fall, probably at a rate related to the rate of entry penetration. On the other hand, a policy of blocking entry will lead to lower prices and increased expenditures on non-price activities whenever the threat of entry looms, and one will observe, in consequence, a narrowing of price–cost margins but no entry. In general, one expects to see a combination of both policies in operation. Incumbents are likely to allow some entry to occur (willingly or not), but will attempt to pre-empt other entrants by lowering prices and indulging in various forms of non-price competition.

The effect of a strategy of partial accommodation is to induce two different systematic dynamics in price–cost margins, one associated with actual flows of entry and the other not. To the extent that entry is accommodated by incumbents, the rate of convergence of prices to their long-run levels will be associated with changes in market structure caused by actual flows of entry. Attempts to pre-empt and block entrants will induce a similar dynamic in prices without, however, leading to any changes in market structure. It follows, then, that one ought to be able to make some inferences about the relative importance of actual and potential entry on prices by looking at the extent to which movements in prices are correlated to changes in market structure caused by actual entry. If, on the one hand, prices tend to fall systematically to their long-run levels without any entry or observable change in market structure, then that convergence is likely to reflect the competitive effects of potential entry. On the other hand, if all systematic price movements are highly correlated to entry flows, then it seems reasonable to think that potential entry does not have much effect on prices. Although one should be cautious about translating predictions made about prices and entry into predictions about margins and entry, it is generally far easier to collect data on margins (or profitability more generally) than on prices. It is also the case that profit maximization implies that there is a direct link between prices and margins, given marginal costs and the elasticity of demand. Further, the fact that non-price activities can have unexpected effects on prices suggests that it may be easier (it may not, of course) to detect the effects of competition in margins rather than on prices. Accordingly (and with some trepidation), we shall look for two types of dynamics in industry price–cost margins, associating one with the effects of actual entry and the other with those of potential entrants whose arrival in the market is pre-empted by incumbents.

Simple Structural Models of Entry

It is simplest to start with observables, and to focus on the effect that observed entry flows have on margins. Simple textbook stories of market dynamics generally tell the following kind of story. Highly concentrated, imperfectly competitive markets generate supernormal profits which, in turn, attract entrants who bid away profits by undercutting incumbents and reducing market concentration. Adopting the not unreasonable assumption that this entire process does not occur instantaneously, one might describe it using the following three-equation model. Profits at time t, π_t, are assumed to depend on market structure S_t, and on other things which we neglect for simplicity. Thus,

$$\pi_t = \beta S_t \tag{4.1}$$

where $\beta > 0$. Entry E_t is assumed to be attracted with a one-period lag whenever profits exceed their long-run levels π^*, which we assume to be constant for simplicity. Neglecting other factors which affect entry,

$$E_t = \gamma(\pi_{t-1} - \pi^*) \tag{4.2}$$

where $\gamma > 0$. Finally, market structure (say, for concreteness, the level of market concentration) changes whenever entry occurs, and, although other things may also affect market structure independently of entry, we shall neglect them here. This third equation we shall write as

$$S_t = \phi E_t \tag{4.3}$$

where $\phi < 0$. If $\beta > 0$, $\gamma > 0$ and $\phi < 0$. The system (4.1)–(4.3) exhibits the error correcting feedback characteristic of textbook stories about the competitive process. High profits attract entry through (4.2) and entrants, in turn, reduce profits by altering conditions of supply through (4.3), the new supply conditions leading to a new, lower profit outcome via (4.1).

The dynamics of margins implicit in (4.1)–(4.3) is extremely simple, largely because of the linearity of the model and the very simple temporal relations between profits and entry (a one-period lag) and between entry and profits (no lag). The long-run equilibrium level of π_t is π^* in the system (4.1)–(4.3), and, in the short run, π_t is given by substituting (4.2) into (4.3) and thence into (4.1), yielding

$$\pi_t = -\beta\phi\gamma\pi^* + (1 + \phi\gamma\beta)\pi_{t-1}. \tag{4.4}$$

If $|\phi\gamma\beta| < 1$, then π_t monotonically approaches π^* from above (if $\pi_0 > \pi^*$) or below (if $\pi_0 < \pi^*$), while if $|\phi\gamma\beta| > 1$, the system oscillates around π^*, overshooting but eventually converging if $|\phi\gamma\beta| < 2$. If $\phi\gamma\beta = -1$, then $\pi_t = \pi^*$ for all t. Thus, if entry is strongly attracted by profits and, in turn, has a big effect on profits via its effect on S_t, then π_t will converge quickly to π^*, but may display a tendency to overshoot. If, on the other hand, entry is only weakly attracted by excess returns or only has a small effect on market structure, then π_t will converge directly towards π^* at a speed which is slower the more weak and gradual is the entry mechanism.

Models of this type have appeared in several guises in the literature. Gabel (1979), for example, produced a five-equation model of the US petroleum refining industry, the core of which can be expressed in reduced form as

$$N_t = \alpha_1 N_{t-1} + \alpha_2 \pi_t + C_1 \qquad (4.5)$$

$$H_t = \alpha_3 N_t + C_2 \qquad (4.6)$$

$$\pi_t = \alpha_4 H_t + \alpha_5 N_t + \alpha_6 \Delta N_t + C_3. \qquad (4.7)$$

N_t is the number of refineries at time t, modelled in (4.5) as a partial adjustment to an equilibrium stock of refineries that is determined by minimum efficient scale (suppressed here into C_1), with an added flow arising when profits π_t are high. Industry concentration, measured by the Herfindahl index H_t, depends in (4.6) on the number of refineries and on minimum efficient scale and a dummy variable (both suppressed into C_2). Profits have three sources of dynamics, one arising from industry concentration, a second from movements in refinery capacity utilization and a third arising from divergences between the growth of sales and the growth of refining capacity. The first force is captured in equation (4.7) by α_4, the second is the product of the effect of entry on capacity utilization and the effect of the latter on profits and is captured by α_5, and the third reflects the effect of changes in the number of firms, ΔN_t, on refining capacity multiplied by the latter's effect on profits and is captured by α_6. In addition, vertical integration and minimum efficient scale affect profits (suppressed here into C_3).

Solving (4.5)–(4.7) and collecting the three constants into one (denoted as C) produces an equation which implies that profits follow the time path

$$\pi_t = C + \phi\alpha_2\pi_{t-1} + \phi\alpha_2\alpha_1\pi_{t-2} + \phi\alpha_2\alpha_1^2\pi_{t-3} + \ldots \qquad (4.8)$$

where $\phi \equiv [(\alpha_3\alpha_4 + \alpha_5 + \alpha_6)\alpha_1 - \alpha_6]/[1 - (\alpha_3\alpha_4 + \alpha_5 + \alpha_6)\alpha_2]$. Gabel's estimates of the unknown parameters $\alpha_1, \ldots, \alpha_6$ all appear to be fairly plausible when looked at equation by equation, but when they are combined together into (4.8), they carry the extremely strong implication that observed entry has little effect on profits. Using his ordinary least squares (OLS) estimates, $\alpha_1 = 0.9$, $\alpha_2 = 0.98$, $\alpha_3 = 0.0001$, $\alpha_4 = 0.8$, $\alpha_5 = -0.0005$ and $\alpha_6 \approx -0.0001$, and substituting them into (4.8) produces a simulation model of profits

$$\pi_t = C - 0.0652\pi_{t-1} - 0.00059\pi_{t-2} - \ldots \quad (4.9)$$

Equation (9) describes a process in which profits start from some initial level determined by C (which depends on entry barriers and other permanent features of industry structure) and then fall to a long-run level of $C/(1 - \phi\alpha_2 - \phi\alpha_2\alpha_1 - \phi\alpha_2\alpha_1^2 - \ldots)$, displaying a very slight tendency to oscillate around the long-run equilibrium. The interesting feature of the parameter estimates produced by Gabel is that they suggest that the long-run level of π_t is about 94% of the size of its initial level. One concludes that the long-run effect of observed entry on profits is extremely modest in this sector and, given that it induces movements in profits only within the interval $[C, 0.94C]$, that its effects on short-run profits dynamics are also quite modest.

Very much the same story emerges from some work by Geroski and Murfin (1990b). They developed a three-equation reduced form model of the UK car industry describing the dynamics of margins, advertising and market share for all the major producers in the market. The entry equation took a form very similar to (4.2) except that entry was assumed to be driven not by π_{t-1} but by the expectations held in $t - 1$ of π_t. These depended on all the exogenous variables of the system plus lagged advertising and market shares. Advertising also entered the entry equation, and it too was allowed to be endogenous. The advertising and margins equations included a range of lagged terms designed to capture as rich a picture of industry dynamics as possible, and, being estimates of reduced forms, they were used to provide instruments for the entry equation. The basic mechanics of the estimated model hinged on the interrelationships that were observed between entry, advertising and margins over time. High margins induced entry and both, in turn, stimulated advertising. Entry reduced margins while advertising raised them, and advertising first stimulated and then depressed entry. The result was an escalation in advertising over time (from the starting point of 1958), a positive flow of entry for a finite period of time and, as it turned out, a slight net rise in margins post-entry!

It is worth exploring these estimates somewhat more fully. Simplified versions of the reduced forms of the estimated advertising shares and price–cost margins equations produced by Geroski and Murfin are

$$a_t = B_1 + 0.8022a_{t-1} + 0.1639S_{t-1} + 0.0078\pi_{t-1} \quad (4.10)$$

$$\pi_t = B_2 - 0.5109 M_{t-1} + 0.0332 a_{t-1} + 0.0089 S_t \qquad (4.11)$$

where a_t is the advertising share of firm i in market segment j at time t, S_t is market share and π_t are price–cost margins. The (structural) entry equation takes the form

$$S_t = \begin{cases} S_t & \text{if } \bar{S}_t > 0 \\ 0 & \text{if } \bar{S}_t \le 0 \end{cases} \qquad (4.12)$$

where

$$\bar{S}_t = B_3 + 0.0627\,\pi_t + 0.0386 a_t + 0.8515 S_{t-1}. \qquad (4.13)$$

Equation (4.12) is a Tobit model that describes market penetration in terms of a latent variable $\bar{S}_t$ that reflects the present discounted value of all future profits (see chapter 3). If $\bar{S}_{t-1} = 0$ but $\bar{S}_t > 0$, then $S_t > 0$ when $S_{t-1} = 0$, and this signals that entry has occurred. B_1, B_2 and B_3 include all the exogenous variables in the system.[14]

The system (4.10)–(4.13) is useful because it enables one to assess the effects of entry on margins under a fairly wide range of counterfactual assumptions. We shall focus on only the simplest of these here, comparing how margins would be affected by shocks were the market to be monopolized and entry blocked by fiat with how it appeared to react in practice. If the market were monopolized (i.e. if $S_t = a_t = 1$), then (4.11) suggests that margins will follow a path given by

$$\pi_t = B' - 0.5109\pi_{t-1}. \qquad (4.14)$$

However, when entry and advertising are allowed to occur, margins change because entry affects both S_t and a_t, and these affect π_t. Using (4.10) and (4.12), margins follow a time path given (at least to the second order) by

$$\pi_t = B - 0.5103\,\pi_{t-1} + 0.0006\,\pi_{t-2} \qquad (4.15)$$

when entry occurs. Clearly the dynamics of margins were not substantially affected by entry in the UK car market, although it is the case that the entry-induced effects of advertising on margins are fairly substantial in the long run (a glance at (4.9) reveals that entry has even less impact in petroleum). To interpret (4.15) imagine that, for all $t < 0$, $B = 0$, but that at $t = 0$ the intercept of (4.15) rises permanently to some positive number B. The short-run effect of this shock is B, while, in the long run, margins settle down to a level of about $0.66B$. Although this is pretty much how one might expect a market to respond to a favourable profitability shock (it is, perhaps, not as large a response as one might want to see), (4.14) traces out almost exactly the same dynamic path under the counterfactual assumption of no entry. Part of the apparent similarity between (4.14) and (4.15) arises from the truncation of the latter at π_{t-2} (meaning that the effects of entry take quite some time to make themselves felt and (4.15) captures these lagged effects rather poorly), but, this said, it is also the case that margins in this sector appear to display a dynamic that is pretty much independent of observed entry flows. This may reflect the nature of the demand for durable goods or, as we shall discuss below, it may reflect the effects of potential competition.

There are, of course, a wide variety of structural models that could be developed to assess the effects of entry. Masson and Jeong (1991) estimated entry and profits equations for Korea, finding that the rate of increase in the number of firms had a negative but rather small effect on profits, one that seemed to be rather more precisely determined in booms rather than recessions. Lieberman (1988b) developed a model of market prices for the US chemical processing industry in which actual rates of price change are compared with those which would occur were the industry to follow Cournot pricing rules. He argued that this benchmark would be attractive to consider as a situation in which incumbents passively accommodate entry, and that the difference between actual and predicted Cournot rates of price change might be considered to be a measure of the aggressiveness with which incumbents respond to entry. Examining entry into 30 chemical processing industries, he observed price cuts of about 6% following entry (although, when entry occurred through vertical integration, price cuts were about 12%). These rates of price change did not seem consistent with the hypothesis of an aggressive response by incumbents, but, perplexingly, they also were not related to those predicted by the Cournot model, and industry concentration had little apparent effect on price dynamics. Reiss and Spiller (1988) modelled entry into small airline markets in the USA, utilizing price equations that allow entry to have an effect on price directly via changes in the number of firms and indirectly via the conjectures that incumbents make about total supply. This, of course, gets rather close to modelling the effects of potential entry, a step made much more explicitly by Hurdle et al. (1989) in another study of US airlines. They identified potential entrants not deterred by scale economies, and found that measures of concentration which included these potential entrants had a significant impact on market performance. Although both of these airline studies give some grounds for believing that entry is likely to have an impact on prices or profits, neither contains much information on the short-run dynamics of the process.

Reduced Form Models

The difficulty with simple structural models is that they model profit dynamics as being driven only by changes in market structure. While traces of such dynamics can be observed (as we have seen), models of this type do not fully capture many of the competitive pressures which in principle are activated when $\pi_{t-1} > \pi^*$. In particular, potential entry, investment competition amongst incumbents, threats of intra-industry mobility and so on are all neglected. The interesting feature of all of these competitive forces is that, when anticipated, they may lead to strategic responses by incumbents which affect prices and profits by way of discouraging entry or intra-industry mobility. However, to the extent that pre-emption occurs, many potential entry threats never materialize, and therefore they are never recorded as 'entry' or in changes in market structure. Thus, prices and profits are affected without a concomitant change in market structure.

To ascertain whether 'potential entry' has a substantive effect on margins, it is necessary to enrich the simple structural model that we have used thus far. If potential entry is not an effective discipline on incumbents, then the model (4.1)–(4.3) provides an adequate (albeit rather simple) basis for assessing the nature of market dynamics. If, on the other hand, proxying the total competitive challenge presented to incumbents using actual entry flows or changes in market structure creates a measurement error which is large, then (4.1)–(4.3) is likely to produce estimates of the speed of market dynamics which exaggerate its slowness. Following Geroski and Jacquemin (1988), a very simple way to get a crude handle on the effect of this possible measurement error on the character and estimated speed of profit dynamics is as follows. Potential entry is impossible to observe directly and, rather than attempting to measure it with error, it is attractive to consider treating actual plus potential entry, E_t in (4.2), as a latent variable. Some fraction of potential entry materializes and affects market structure via (4.3) and then profits via (4.1); the remaining potential entrants do not appear because incumbents engage in a policy of pre-emption at the cost of some diminution in their margins. Thus, the two components of E_t, actual and potential entry, affect π_t through two different channels. However, both are driven by π_{t-1} and, because they both affect π_t, their joint influence can be observed in the relationship between π_{t-1} and π_t without the need to observe either directly. If the various relationships are linear and the lags are short, then one emerges with a dynamic model of margins.

To be more precise, let $E_t = A_t + P_t$, actual plus potential entry. Actual entry affects market structure as in (4.3) and so

$$\Delta S_t = \phi A_t, \qquad (4.16)$$

where $\phi < 0$. Total entry is affected by excess profits as in (4.2) and so

$$A_t = \gamma_0 (\pi_{t-1} - \pi^*)$$
$$P_t = \gamma_1 (\pi_{t-1} - \pi^*) \qquad (4.17)$$

where $\gamma_0, \gamma_1 > 0$. Profits are affected by market structure as in (4.1), but also respond to the threat of potential entry, so (4.1) becomes

$$\pi_t = \beta S_t + \alpha P_t \qquad (4.18)$$

where $\beta > 0$ but $\alpha < 0$. Solving (4.16)–(4.18) and neglecting a second-order lag in π_t, one arrives at an analogue of (4.4):

$$\pi_t = \lambda_0 \pi^* + \lambda_1 \pi_{t-1} \qquad (4.19)$$

where $\lambda_0 = -\beta\phi\gamma_0$ and $\lambda_1 = 1 + \beta\phi\gamma_0 + \alpha\gamma_1$. The short-run effect of actual entry on margins is captured in (4.19) (as before) by $\beta\phi\gamma_0$, but to this is added a second effect, $\alpha\gamma_1$, which occurs because incumbents anticipate – and try to block – entry. Since by assumption A_t and P_t cannot be separately observed, these two effects cannot be separately unscrambled from λ_1 (hence the label 'reduced form' model). Generalizations of (4.16)–(4.18) to allow for longer effects of π_t on entry and of A_t and P_t on margins result in longer autoregressions in (4.19).

To assess the role of potential entry on margins, one needs to make a comparison between (4.1)–(4.3) on the one hand and (4.19) on the other. Estimating (4.1)–(4.3) requires data on actual entry flows or changes in market structure, and the dynamics of margins are presumed to be governed only by these observables. Estimates of (4.19), on the other hand, do not require one to observe either actual or potential entry, and λ_1 reflects the (conflated) effects of both on margins. It follows that the difference between the two sets of estimates – ϕ, β and γ on the one hand and λ_1 on the other – yields information on the effect of potential entry and other unmeasured competitive pressures on margins in the short run (differences in the estimates of π^* reflect long-run effects). Equations (4.1)–(4.3) imply that profits follow a time path described by (4.4), and it follows from comparing (4.4) with (4.19) that, if $\lambda_1 \approx 1 + \phi\beta\gamma$, then potential entry plays no role in determining the character of disequilibrium processes. If, on the other hand, $\lambda_1 < 1 + \phi\beta\gamma$, then estimates of market processes that rely only on the information about competitive forces provided by actual entry are likely to be biased. A simple way to interpret this comparison is to note that if $\pi^* = 0$ (implying that

$\lambda_0 = 0$), (4.4) and (4.19) describe simple decay processes whose half-lives are log $2/\log(1 + \phi\beta\gamma)$ and log $2/\log \lambda_1$ respectively. Thus, differences between λ_1 and $1 + \phi\beta\gamma$ translate directly into the differences in the time it takes competition to eliminate excess profits through entry, potential and actual.

There are a number of indications which suggest that neglecting potential entry in models like (4.1)–(4.3) leads to perhaps major biases in estimates of the speed of market processes. Geroski and Masson (1987) constructed estimates of the parameters of (4.4) for a relatively small cross-section of US industries in the 1950s–1960s from estimates of a model like (4.1)–(4.3) that Masson and Shaanan (1982) estimated using actual entry penetration data over a seven-year period. The values of β, γ and ϕ used were untypical of the literature associated individually with (4.1)–(4.3) only in so far as γ and ϕ were slightly on the high side (in absolute value) of published estimates. Taken together, the estimates implied that $1 + \phi\gamma\beta = 0.9766$. However, while the estimates of (4.1)–(4.3) taken individually all appear to be sensible, they jointly imply an extremely unrealistic time path of margins. From a starting point of $\pi_0 = 13.84\%$, Geroski and Masson found that margins only moved about half way towards their long-run value $\pi^* = 8.42\%$ in 70 years. On the basis of these numbers, one would have to conclude that the effect of actual entry on margins is, at best, non-existent. By contrast, Levy (1987) estimated variants of (4.19) using a large cross-section sample of US industries, with observations on a five-yearly basis from 1963 to 1972. Levy's estimates of λ_1 range from 0.12 to -0.07 (see his Table I, equations (4)–(6), p. 87), the latter of which actually implies weak, damped oscillations toward equilibrium. A value of $\lambda_1 \approx 0.10$ reduces $\pi_0 = 13.84\%$ to $\pi_1 = 8.96\%$ in five years, almost the full adjustment needed to restore equilibrium in the model estimated by Masson and Shaanan. Since $\lambda_1 \approx 0.10$ implies that excess profits are eliminated quickly by actual and potential entry operating together, but $1 + \phi\gamma\beta \approx 0.98$ implies that eliminating excess profits through actual entry alone is slow, one is inclined to conclude that potential entry may play an important role in the dynamics of margins.

Similar conclusions have emerged from studies of the dynamics of profits and market shares at the firm level. Geroski (1978a) collected estimates of β, γ and ϕ derived from studies of the erosion in the market share of dominant firms and constructed an estimate of $1 + \phi\beta\gamma = 0.91$ when time was measured in units of five years. By contrast, Mueller (1986), Geroski and Jacquemin (1988) and others have estimated (4.19) on annual time series of profits data for individual large firms and have generally found λ_1 to be smaller than 0.50, and often considerably so.[15]

Both the firm level estimates and industry level estimates of (4.1)–(4.3) discussed above put $1 + \phi\beta\gamma \geq 0.90$, implying that, if actual entry alone were the only force driving market dynamics, then reducing 10% excess profits to 1% might require nearly 22 time periods (over a century when time is measured in units of five years). Reduced form estimates of the speed of the process using (4.19) are much higher. If $\lambda_1 = 0.50$, then one only requires just slightly more than three time periods, while if $\lambda_1 = 0.10$, one only requires one period to reduce profits of 10% to 1%. Using the somewhat unreliable lags given in the literature, estimates of the reduced form model (4.19) seem to imply that most excess profits are bid away within five years or so, while estimates of the structural model (4.1)–(4.3) suggest that markets might need perhaps as long as a century to perform the same task.

Fuller Structural Models

It would seem, then, that the structural model (4.1)–(4.3) is not quite up to the task of examining market dynamics, and it is of interest to explore a general model that encompasses both the structural model (4.1)–(4.3) and the reduced form model (4.19), a model that enables one to observe (in principle) both some pre-emption of potential entry and the effect of actual entry on margins. That is, one would like to allow for two types of systematic dynamic movement in margins, the former apparently autonomous and the latter associated with entry flows.

The paradigmatic model of this type is, of course, the dominant firm model discussed above. Entry regulation involves both accommodation and pre-emption, and this is probably true even when it involves using a more substantive strategic investment than price. A description of the implications of this type of activity might follow Geroski (1990a). For simplicity, suppose that entrants behave in the manner described by (4.2). Incumbents are assumed to be unable to change this behaviour, but can manipulate it by choosing an appropriate price path. Given a lag in response to high prices or margins by entrants, it is clear that the choice of price by the dominant firm will involve trading off current against future profits: choices in t will affect profits in both period t and period $t + 1$. Maximizing the expected present discounted value of all future profits subject to the constraint (4.2) yields a first-order condition describing margins which can be written as

$$\pi_t + \phi S_t + \delta\pi^e_{t+1} = 0 \qquad (4.20)$$

where π_t are price–cost margins, S_t is the market share in incumbents, π^e_{t+1} is the expectation held at time t of profits in $t + 1$, ϕ is the reciprocal of the elasticity of demand and δ depends on the speed of response of entrants to profits (as measured by γ in (4.2)), the discount rate and the industry growth rate (and ϕ, $\delta < 0$).[16]

Equation (4.20) is in fact a simple generalization of familiar static structure performance models like (4.1), one that introduces an additional term into the contemporaneous relationship between market share and price–cost margins, π_t and S_t, that emerges from static structure performance models (e.g. Cowling and Waterson, 1976; see also Geroski, 1988a, Bresnahan, 1989). Since the future consequences of current price rises are adverse, this additional term reflects the fact that a far-sighted firm concerned to (at least partially) block entry is likely to 'choose' a larger S_t for any given π_t or a smaller π_t for any given S_t than a firm that is willing to tolerate entry would. This reduction in price or margins reflects a long-sighted dominant firm's reluctance to sacrifice future market position for (current) profits. If, by contrast, the dominant firm were myopic, then $\delta = 0$, and (4.20) reduces to a decision rule which says that market shares ought to be proportional to price–cost margins (with a factor of proportionality that depends on the elasticity of demand). As a myopic dominant firm would not try to pre-empt entrants, declines in its market share and margins occur only through the mechanism of actual entry eroding share and 'causing' margins to fall. It follows, then, that the term $\delta\pi^e_{t+1}$ in (4.20) captures movements in π_t which are induced by the strategic efforts of incumbents to block or pre-empt entrants; that is, $\delta\pi^e_{t+1}$ measures the extent to which margins are reduced to maintain market share. Thus, using (4.20), it follows that movements in actual margins π_t are driven by two forces: those of actual entry that act via changes in S_t, with impact ϕ, and those of potential entry that act via the term π^e_{t+1}.

It is not necessary to include terms measuring actual entry flows in (4.20) since their presence and effects are registered by S_t. However, if one wishes to make the role of actual entry A_t explicit, then one must replace S_t by A_t and a collection of its recent past values. More precisely, the dominant firm's market share at any time t is determined by its initial market share and by its reaction to entry; that is, by the extent to which it has chosen to set high prices despite the threat of future entry. If net entry is the sole source of fringe expansion, then

$$S_t = S_{t-1} - A_{t-1} = S_0 - \sum_{j=1}^{t-1} A_j \qquad (4.21)$$

where S_0 is the initial market share of the dominant firm. Equation (4.21) implicitly assumes that entrants always act independently of the dominant firm and, given the structure of the dominant firm model, this means that they are assumed never to assist in raising prices. Preferring to free-ride on the efforts of the dominant firm, their position in the market causes an erosion of the dominant firm's market power which is permanent. Using (4.21), (4.20) becomes

$$\phi S_0 - \phi \sum_{j=1}^{t-1} A_j + \pi_t + \delta \pi_{t+1}^e = 0 \qquad (4.22)$$

The term π_{t+1}^e in (4.20) is the expectation held by the dominant firm in period t about the value its price–cost margin is likely to take in period $t + 1$. This expectation depends upon all the information it has as of date t and on its knowledge about the behaviour of entrants. If one assumes that the expectations of agents – entrants and the dominant firm alike – are rational, then the difference between π_{t+1}^e and its realization π_{t+1} in $t + 1$ is unpredictable in t and thus is uncorrelated with other observables in $t, t - 1$ and so on. Rearranging (4.22) and backdating it one period,

$$\pi_t^e = \beta - \frac{1}{\delta}\pi_{t-1} + \frac{\phi}{\delta} \sum_{j=1}^{t-1} A_j \qquad (4.23)$$

where $\beta \equiv \phi S_0$. Defining ξ_t as

$$\pi_t^e = \pi_t - \xi_t \qquad (4.24)$$

and noting that the assumption of rational expectations means that ξ_t is a white noise random variable, then

$$\pi_t = \beta + \frac{1}{\delta}\pi_{t-1} + \frac{\phi}{\delta} \sum_{j=1}^{t-1} A_j + \xi_t. \qquad (4.25)$$

Equation (4.25) is a simple dynamic model of margins that is written entirely in terms of observables and reflects the twin channels through which entry affects margins: via actual entry A_j and via systematic movements in margins caused by the pre-emptive actions of incumbents designed to meet the threat of entry. As such, it obviously generalizes (4.4) and (4.19).

Equations (4.2) and (4.25) jointly form a simple feedback model between entry and margins that provides estimates of long-run margins π^* and of the short-run dynamics of margins caused by actual and potential entry. Estimates of both were generated by Geroski for 85 three-digit manufacturing industries in the UK from 1974 to 1979 and are shown on table 4.1 (a slightly different version of equation (i) is displayed in (ii) in

Table 4.1 Regression estimates of (4.2) and (4.25)

Dependent variable	*(i)* E_t	*(ii)* π_t
π_t^e	0.9421	–
	(3.287)	
g_{t-1}	0.0092	0.0009
	(0.8745)	(0.072)
z_{t-1}	0.0146	−0.0075
	(0.9054)	(0.325)
k_{t-1}	0.0016	−0.0055
	(0.2999)	(1.17)
π_{t-1}	–	−0.1214
		(1.66)
π_{t-2}	–	0.0312
		(0.543)
π_{t-3}	–	−0.0226
		(0.688)
E_{t-1}	–	−0.1009
		(1.76)
E_{t-2}	–	−0.0681
		(2.11)
R^2	0.080	0.813
Log likelihood	866.266	829.091

Equation (i) explains entry rates E_t while (ii) explains margins π_t. Absolute values of t statistics are given in parentheses below the estimated coefficients; all equations have a full set of fixed effects and time dummies; E_t, net market penetration by entrants, market size being defined as domestic sales (= domestic production plus imports less exports); π_t^e, expected post-entry margins, proxied by using the predictions from (ii); g_{t-1}, lagged rate of growth of industry sales; z_{t-1}, lagged logarithm of domestic sales (= domestic production plus imports less exports); k_{t-1}, capital stock–output ratio, where output is domestic production; π_{t-1}, lagged price–cost margins (= net output less the wage bill less net capital expenditure divided by gross output). All estimates of standard errors are heteroscedastic consistent.
Source: Geroski, 1990a

table 3.3). The data were pooled for four years and (4.25) was generalized to allow for three lagged terms in π_t; only two lags of E_t were available. π^* was proxied by a full set of fixed effects, lagged industry growth g_{t-1}, industry size z_{t-1} and capital intensity k_{t-1}.

As can be seen in (i), the estimate of γ, the effect of (expected) margins on entry, is 0.9421 and clearly significant, while π^* was estimated to be 0.1927 (using the estimated parameters of (i) or, for that matter, (ii) since both equations produced virtually the same estimates of π^*). This suggests that incumbents were able to maintain prices above costs by 15–20% on average without attracting entry; that is, that barriers to entry are rather high in the UK on average. The short-run effect of actual entry on margins was estimated to be about -0.0805, while that which operates through pre-emption was -0.1243, slightly larger (both of these estimates come from a statistically acceptable simplification of (ii) in which the coefficients of π_{t-2} and π_{t-3} were set equal to zero while those on E_{t-1} and E_{t-2} were constrained to be the same). That is, actual and potential entry seem to have a similar impact on the dynamics of margins. Substituting the estimates of (i) into (ii) produces a dynamic equation for margins analogous to (4.4) and (4.19), namely

$$\pi_t = C - 0.2001\pi_{t-1} - 0.0758\pi_{t-2}, \qquad (4.26)$$

and these estimates indicate that an initial level of profits of C will be reduced by about 25% in the long run. The whole process appears to take three to five years and involves some slight overshooting. Geroski also found clear evidence in the data suggesting that both ϕ and δ varied enormously across industries, and that both were larger (i.e. closer to zero) in more advertising-intensive, more highly concentrated, slower growing sectors. That is, both pre-emption and entry-induced dynamics were weaker in highly concentrated sectors where advertising was a major competitive weapon.

The estimates in table 4.1 trace only the effects of domestic entrants on margins. Foreign competition, however, may prove to be a more substantial source of competitive discipline and table 4.2 shows some estimates of (4.2) and (4.25) that allow for both domestic entry E_t^d and foreign entry E_t^f. Equation (i) tracks domestic entry and is reproduced from table 4.1, while foreign entry is described by equation (ii). The two flows of entry are not highly correlated (as we discovered earlier), and the estimates in (i) and (ii) show why: they respond in quite different ways to the four observables. Foreign entry appears to respond perversely to expected profits but, as π_t^e are the expectations held by domestic firms of domestic profits, the perversity of $\gamma^f < 0$ may be more apparent than real.[17] Neither equation provides a terribly good fit of the data, suggesting that both data series are (at best) extremely noisy signals of π_t^e. The fixed effects in both equations were roughly the same size on average; they were positively correlated with each other, and most were individually significant. The important comparison to make between tables 4.1 and 4.2, however, is between estimates of the profits equation with (equation (iii) in table 4.2) and without (equation (ii) in table 4.1) foreign entry. It is clear at a glance that foreign entry has little impact on margins:

Table 4.2 Estimates of (4.2) and (4.25) for domestic and foreign entrants in the UK

Dependent variable	(i) E_t^d	(ii) E_t^f	(iii) π_t
π_t^e	0.9421	−2.426	–
	(3.287)	(3.02)	
g_{t-1}	0.0092	−0.0879	0.0016
	(0.8745)	(2.299)	(0.1251)
z_{t-1}	0.0146	0.1316	−0.0038
	(0.9054)	(2.194)	(0.1628)
k_{t-1}	0.0016	−0.0013	−0.0048
	(0.2999)	(1.19)	(1.142)
π_{t-1}	–	–	−0.1219
			(1.697)
π_{t-2}	–	–	0.0251
			(0.4143)
π_{t-3}	–	–	−0.0184
			(0.5324)
E_{t-1}^d	–	–	−0.0981
			(1.701)
E_{t-2}^d	–	–	−0.063
			(1.915)
E_{t-1}^f	–	–	0.0390
			(0.9468)
E_{t-2}^f	–	–	−0.0112
			(0.3517)
R^2	0.080	0.049	0.8133
Log likelihood	866.266	655.750	830.169

Equations (i) and (ii) explain entry rates E_t^d and E_t^f while (iii) explains margins π_t. Absolute values of t statistics are given in parentheses below the estimated coefficients; all equations have a full set of fixed effects and time dummies; E_t^f, the change in the import share; E_t^d, net market penetration by entrants, market size being defined as domestic sales (= domestic production plus imports less exports); π_t^e, expected post-entry margins, proxied by using the predictions from (iii); g_{t-1}, lagged rate of growth of industry sales; z_{t-1}, lagged logarithm of domestic sales (= domestic production plus imports less exports); k_{t-1}, capital stock–output ratio, where output is domestic production; π_{t-1}, lagged price–cost margins (= net output less the wage bill less net capital expenditure divided by gross output). All estimates of standard errors are heteroscedastic consistent.
Source: Adapted from unpublished estimates in Geroski, 1990a

neither the coefficients on E_{t-1}^f nor that on E_{t-2}^f is very large, and neither is remotely statistically significant. What is more, the estimated effects of domestic entry on margins are extremely robust to the inclusion of foreign entry, meaning that (4.26) is still a reasonable description of the dynamics of margins in the typical UK industry of the late 1970s. Foreign entry is not, it seems, much of a substitute for domestic entry from the point of view of market performance.

A Summing Up

The evidence that we have discussed in this section is not extensive, but its import does seem to be fairly clear. However one measures it, the dynamic movements in margins associated with actual entry flows are extremely modest. Potential entry (and intra-industry competition between incumbents) also seems to have an effect on the dynamics of margins, but it too is quite modest. Autonomous movements in margins apparently due to potential entry do occur; they are somewhat larger in size than those associated with actual entry and they seem to account for some (and perhaps much) of the perhaps not extremely extensive dynamics in margins that we do observe.

A useful way to summarize these results is to think of profits as varying over time and across industries. The total variation across these two dimensions can be decomposed into 'within' variation, the variation in profits over time within the typical industry, and 'between' variation, the variation in profit across industries at any given time. The permanent differences between sectors reflected in the between-industry variation in margins depend on the height of entry barriers, while the differences over time capture the effects of short-run dynamics associated with both potential and actual entry (and other dynamic effects on margins unrelated to entry). Essentially, the data show extremely high ratios of between- to within-industry variation in margins, indicating that differences in margins between industries are far larger than variations over time in margins within industries. One concludes that the dynamics of margins is modest in most sectors and therefore that the short-run effect of entry is relatively modest. Yet margins do differ widely between sectors, and these differences persist over longish periods of time. It follows, then, that entry barriers probably play the major role in explaining the profit outcomes that we observe year by year, and certainly play a bigger role than do actual entry flows or observed changes in market structure. Margins generally appear to be fairly near their long-run levels most of the time.[18]

138　　　*Entry and the Dynamics of Prices and Margins*

It is possible to be slightly more precise about the within- and between-variation in profits that mirrors the results for the dynamics of π_i that were shown on tables 4.1 and 4.2. Geroski and Toker (1988) decomposed the total variation in margins across 112 UK industries from 1970 to 1979 into between and within variation and discovered the former to account for about 80% of total variation. Table 4.3 shows the partial correlations in margins across these 112 industries over time, correlations that are large, positive and fairly stable (rank correlations were quite similar). Both calculations suggest that permanent structural factors are the major determinants of margins and that transitory factors (including systematic disequilibrium dynamics induced by entry) do not have much impact (not surprisingly, much the same seems to be true of inter-industry wage differentials; see, for example, Krueger and Summers, 1988). By contrast, the between-industry variation in various measures of entry in the UK over the period 1974–9 was in the region of 20–25% for net penetration, net entry rates and gross entry rates (it was 49% for gross penetration). Correlations in gross entry rates and penetration across industries over time were never above 0.5–0.6 during that period, while correlations in net penetration were virtually zero (see chapter 2 above). At a purely statistical level, this difference in the type of statistical variation characterizing the two series 'explains' why variations in the one (entry or margins) appear to have little effect on variations in the other (margins or entry). More fundamentally, it suggests that the two series do not share the same underlying determinants. Margins depend, it seems, on stable underlying structural factors (like entry barriers), while entry depends on more transitory and idiosyncratic features of current and recent past market activity (like those market conditions which mediate the effects of barriers on entrants).

Table 4.3　Partial correlations in margins across 112 UK industries over ten years

	1970	1971	1972	1973	1974	1975	1976	1977	1978	1979
1970	1.0									
1971	0.8239	1.0								
1972	0.7838	0.8811	1.0							
1973	0.7030	0.7129	0.8054	1.0						
1974	0.6965	0.6020	0.7384	0.7656	1.0					
1975	0.7010	0.7804	0.8039	0.7116	0.7306	1.0				
1976	0.7334	0.8015	0.8484	0.8116	0.7767	0.8698	1.0			
1977	0.7141	0.7781	0.8086	0.7430	0.7842	0.8562	0.9100	1.0		
1978	0.7354	0.7748	0.7969	0.7047	0.6955	0.8283	0.8670	0.9003	1.0	
1979	0.6254	0.7602	0.7579	0.6459	0.6726	0.8384	0.8030	0.8718	0.8445	1.0

Before finally concluding that the short-run effects of entry on margins are modest, there are, perhaps, four caveats that must be noted. First, drawing conclusions about the extent of competition using average industry price–cost margins as a measure of the relative deviation of price from marginal cost is risky, since difficulties of measuring the user cost of capital ensure that the signal is noisy and, perhaps, biased.[19] Indeed, one can go further and argue that the typically rather conservative valuation techniques used by accountants will often tend to 'smooth out' extreme profits outcomes, and that such practices will produce a series of observed profit outcomes that have already had much of the interesting dynamics filtered out of them. Second, the rather modest effect of entry on margins that we have observed may actually understate the effect that entry has on prices, largely because competition from entrants may lead to reductions in x-inefficiency and so in unit costs, reductions which may maintain margins to some extent in the face of price decreases. There is certainly plenty of evidence (see chapter 6) to suggest that entry often induces a tightening of belts (at least when a major entrant or a large number of entrants is expected), and this inclines one to suspect that prices may move somewhat more in response to entry than margins appear to do. Third, modest as it is, these results may actually overstate the effects of entry on margins, largely because we have attributed all of the systematic movements in margins unrelated to actual entry to the workings of potential entrants. This, of course, ignores the forces of competition within an industry, competition between the dominant group and existing fringe firms and/or competition within the dominant group, as well as purely stochastic exogenous factors that affect particular sectors.[20] Fourth and finally, entry penetration is a slow and costly process and the failure rate of new entrants is, as we have seen, extremely high. The data we looked at in chapter 2 suggest that it may take perhaps five or ten years for new entrants to establish themselves and begin seriously to challenge incumbents. If this is true, then examining the effects of entry over a five-year period or so may not give entrants enough time to make their effects felt; 15 or 20 years might be a more appropriate time scale in which to track their activities and look for effects on margins. If it truly takes that length of time for entrants to have an impact, then the use of short time series (as we have done above) is bound to lead to understatement of the short-run dynamics of margins in response to entry and to overstatement of the permanence of high margins and the height of entry barriers.

Methods of Entry Deterrence

The effect of entry is usually thought to be mainly on price because entry is usually conceived of as an increase in industry supply. Our goal in this section is to lay bare the mechanism by which this happens. At the simplest level, price effects will be initiated either by the incumbent (through limit pricing or entry regulation) or by the entrant (in the absence of an initial response by the incumbent). To observe such effects, one must be able to associate observed price changes (or their absence) with potential entry (if one wishes to observe limit price strategies) or with actual entry (if one wishes to observe entry regulation or entrant-initiated price wars), and this can often be done with well-constructed case studies. The hypothesis that we wish to explore here, however, is more involved than this. If, as we argued above, non-price weapons of entry deterrence are likely to dominate the use of price, then one will only ever observe the use of prices pre- and post-entry when all else has failed. That is, price wars will often be an almost unintended consequence of entry. Gathering evidence on this second argument is rather difficult, and in what follows we shall have to rely on a rough intuitive impression derived from numerous case studies and one or two slightly broader cross-section studies.

To detect limit pricing in the data, one must be able to associate price movements with the threat of potential entry. The latter, however, is all but impossible to observe directly. One slightly indirect way to spot potential competition is to look for very public, large-scale reductions in entry barriers, changes that one might legitimately suppose will attract new competitors. Changes in entry barriers occur all the time, but they are particularly spectacular and easy to observe when they involve some form of deregulation of markets. In the UK, for example, the monopoly of conveyancing that solicitors have long enjoyed ended in May 1987, opening up the possibility that licensed conveyancers will compete with solicitors. In consequence of what was, in fact, a long-awaited change, prices dropped by as much as 20% over the period 1983–6, before entry could occur. Further, the structure of conveyancing fees altered, with prices falling much more at the bottom (28%) than at the top (7%) of the market (Domberger and Sherr, 1987). Similarly, the Airline Deregulation Act of 1978 was designed to open up domestic US airline markets to entry in 1981, and it led to a reduction in revenue per passenger mile from $8.24 in 1977 to $8.02 in 1979 (a fall that may also have been due in part to a diminution in quality – see Trapani and Olson, 1982). One can also make some inferences about potential entry from regulations that restrict entry in certain ways. In the USA, for example, only certain states allow branch banking (although often with numerous restrictions). If one can presume that this implies that entry into local banking markets will in general occur through branching rather than the establishment of new banks, then it is possible to make some inferences about potential entry into these markets by identifying those banks capable of setting up branches in particular local markets. A study of banking in Pennsylvania by Hannan (1979) that was designed along these lines suggested that entry threats had an impact on price (in this case, on the interest rate paid on savings accounts), and that this was larger the less competitive was the host market.

The difficulty of spotting limit pricing in practice arises because there are numerous reasons why prices may be low, and in some cases low prices caused by efficiency may block entry entirely innocently. Consider, for example, the pricing of frozen foods in the UK by the market leader in the 1960s, Birds Eye (Geroski and Vlassopoulos, 1989). In the early stages of the market, its objective appears to have been to maximize the growth of its sales volume, a natural strategy to follow when scale economies or learning effects are important, and one that has the happy consequence of both reducing costs and making entry more difficult. In practice, Birds Eye apparently acted as a price leader, and it did not raise its prices across the board so much as increase the weight of the pack offered to customers, increasing the prices only of those of its products which had a large market share (where, of course, rivals' low volumes gave them a cost disadvantage). In addition, Birds Eye offered discounts on published trade prices to a small number of retailers selected on the basis of the turnover of its products at that retailer in the previous year as well as on the cabinet space offered (and allocated to Birds Eye's products) at retailers' shops. 'The company told us that its criterion in discount negotiations was to achieve a consistent level of gross profitability from various customers. This meant that discounts were related to differences in the costs of distributing to different customers as well as such other factors as the mix of products bought by a customer. The main differences in the delivery cost per ton of the product to different customers were due to differences in the size of delivery' (MMC (Monopolies Commission), 1976, p. 32). In fact, discounts related to turnover represented 70% of the total discounts offered, and total discount payments totalled 6% of the gross revenues from all retailers. Frequency and size of delivery were other factors that influenced Birds Eye's discount and, as a consequence, large retailers received the bulk of the discounts. In 1973–4, discount payments to the largest retailers exceeded 10% of the gross value of their purchases and, in the judgement of the Monopolies Commission, 'exceeded the costs savings in supplying them'.

Although it is not clear who the potential entrants into this market might have been, this price discounting strategy has all the appearance of an entry-deterring pricing strategy designed to exploit scale economies or absolute cost advantages. The major problem facing an entrant seeking a position in the market is that of supplying retailers with its product. Large retailers are particularly valuable in this respect, and any entrant forced to fight for sales by serving a wide variety of small-scale retailers is likely to have faced relatively severe cost disadvantages *vis-à-vis* Birds Eye as a consequence. This is particularly the case with Birds Eye's discounts based on the allocation of cabinet space by retailers and the 'over-riding discounts' it offered, discounts paid retrospectively to retailers who attained some target level of sales volume. Such discounts were particularly hard for rivals to match, since Birds Eye's greater sales volume forced smaller rivals to offer a larger discount to produce the same cash payment. If scale economies are important, such obstacles to access effectively raise the rivals' costs and block entry. However, their effects on entry may be no more than an 'innocent' by-product of prices that are set by a firm to exploit scale-related efficiencies. The difficult question is that of deciding whether there was actually an entry threat that the incumbent was responding to, and whether the observed pattern of prices would have emerged in the absence of an entry challenge.

It is not difficult to observe price changes timed to precede known changes in entry barriers, nor to think that these price changes reflect the increase in competition that incumbents expect to follow. The number of examples of apparent limit pricing generated in this way is not very large, however, and the sample of examples tends to be dominated by sectors where government regulation has long protected incumbents from challenges by new firms. Whether this means that limit pricing really is infrequently used, or whether the sample evidence is scanty because the unobservability of potential entry threats typically leads one erroneously to attribute observed price falls to non-entry related factors that are easier to detect in the data is simply not clear. The problem is also compounded by ambiguities in what one might mean by 'pre-entry' (although, as argued in note 6, these may actually exaggerate the observed incidence of limit pricing relative to entry regulation).

By contrast, post-entry price responses are more straightforward to detect but, as they can reflect either entry regulation by incumbents or entrant-initiated price cuts, they too can be difficult to interpret. When entry occurs and leads to an erosion of the market hitherto served by incumbents, prices are likely to fall whether they are regulated by incumbents or not. The effect of regulation (when successful) is to slow the rate of market penetration by entrants (and other 'fringe' producers), modifying the speed by which prices fall. Price cuts will be timed by incumbents to occur when the threat of expansion by entrants and the fringe is highest, times which may or may not coincide exactly with periods of maximum fringe expansion. By contrast, when prices are not regulated, then price decreases of a somewhat greater magnitude ought to occur more or less exactly when entry or fringe expansion occurs. Thus, the difference between entry regulation and unregulated post-entry competition runs in terms of quantitative and not qualitative differences in short-run price dynamics. To get a real feeling about whether entry regulation is occurring, one needs to have a sense about whether incumbents are behaving myopically or whether the market penetration of entrants is being restricted, something one can only ascertain with careful counter-factual construction.[21]

The example of entry (and fringe firm) regulation which is most often cited is that which was alleged to occur while US Steel lost about 40 percentage points of market share in the production of steel ingots between its formation in 1901 and the late 1960s (more recently, it has also lost its name!). However, the evidence to support this interpretation of US Steel's decline is not terribly impressive. Stigler (1965) examined the financial returns to investors in US Steel between 1901 and 1925 and showed that holders of US Steel stock did better than investors in all other steel companies except for Bethlehem Steel. This, however, only indicates that the market expectations of US Steel's future returns did not change too much over that period, and it may also reflect pricing strategies followed in pig iron, a market that US Steel did not lose control of (Parsons and Ray, 1975). In fact, vertical price squeezes and a very passive response to imports have been a major feature in US Steel's pricing policies (e.g. Adams and Dirlam, 1964), behaviour which suggests that US Steel may have conceded ground in one market as part of a process of exploiting its power in another more strategically important one.[22] A second fairly well known example of entry regulation was discussed by Shaw (1974), who examined the response to entry in the UK retail petrol market and observed that three types of strategies were adopted by incumbents: crowding out through the buying up of retail outlets, advertising, and a 'measured price response' which consisted of price cuts timed to coincide with advances in entrants' market shares. However, these price cuts also occurred during periods when the supply of petrol eased relative to demand, and that makes it difficult to be certain whether the 'measured price response' that he observed would have occurred in the absence of entry. Further, it is not clear whether price was used in this case because the other non-price strategies failed to stem the flow of entry or whether price was at the centre of attempts to block entry.[23]

One reason why it is often difficult to decide whether entry regulation accounts for observed post-entry price falls is that entry regulation is not always the optimal response to entry for a long-sighted incumbent. When markets grow very fast or when entrants respond very slowly to profitable opportunities, there may be little reason to slow the rate of entry, and profit maximizing incumbents are likely to set prices near short-run monopoly levels. Brock (1975) (see also Sengupta et al., 1983, for a similar analysis) applied a fairly precise formalization of the standard model of entry regulation to data on IBM's market share in the late 1950s and 1960s in the US computer industry, concluding that the erosions in share which he observed could not have been due to entry regulation because it was 'probably not in IBM's interest to let its market share decline' (p. 71). The arrival of competition in the peripherals market in the late 1960s also provoked no initial response from IBM, although 'in retrospect, it appears that a substantial price cut early in 1969 on exposed peripheral products would have largely prevented the plug compatible industry from developing' (p. 112). By the early 1970s, a more aggressive response to entry by IBM became evident, and there are a number of instances where IBM appeared to use price strategically against entry (e.g. see the discussion on pp. 126, 132). IBM also attempted to lock in consumers using long-term leasing policies (and other devices), effectively trying to deny consumers access to the market. In aluminium, Suslow (1986) observed that Alcoa's market power in the interwar years was limited by competition from used or recycled aluminium, the supply of which was fairly elastic. Nevertheless, pricing to regulate the growth of this source of competitive supply was not a major problem, in this case because 'the source of Alcoa's market power was not so much inelastic fringe supply as it was less than perfect substitutability with the fringes product' (p. 339).

An extreme form of post-entry regulation involves pricing not so much to limit the expansion of entrants as to drive them out. It may involve dropping prices below rivals' (and even one's own) marginal costs or, less spectacularly, limiting entry penetration in such a way as to ensure that entrants are unable to reach a profitable size quickly enough. From the point of view of interpreting the exit of an entrant following a price war as predation, what might be predation is often hard to distinguish from the failure of a genuinely uncompetitive entrant. Still, this said, several instances of apparently predatory behaviour have been aired in the courts. Hoffman la Roche, for example, tried to block Frank W. Horner Ltd in the market for diazepam (Hoffman la Roche's brand was Valium) in Canada. Entry was facilitated in this case by a liberalization of provisions for compulsory licensing, and Horner initiated an assault against Valium in 1970 that mirrored previous competitive inroads made against Hoffman la Roche's other major branded drug, Librium. Hoffman la Roche launched a number of responses to entry in addition to using prices, but all were unsuccessful (one marketing tactic stressed that Hoffman la Roche had developed diazepam, presumably implying that that made their product somehow superior to those of entrants). Its price response was targeted at the obvious port of entry for a new seller (the hospital market), and it occasionally involved selling Valium well below its costs and, indeed, giving it away at times. The mechanisms by which this occurred (some of which were also used in the chlordiazepoxide market where Librium was under threat) included special offers targeted at the date of entry, quality discounts applied to all of Hoffman la Roche's products, and giveaways of the 'try one and get three free' variety (this involved giving away a 'really obsolete' 10 mg dosage at one point). Predation was not successful in the case – Horner exited and then re-entered after the predatory episode ended, Hoffman la Roche was prosecuted, and prices continued to tumble, so much so that by the mid-1970s, one hospital was paying only 10% of the 1960s' monopoly price of Valium (Gorecki, 1986b).

These several examples of pre- and post-entry pricing responses are, in the main, difficult to interpret unambiguously as limit pricing or entry regulation. However, the difficulties of deciding whether the observed declines in price were deliberately engineered by incumbents are not, perhaps, as severe as those involved in deciding whether price was the major weapon used against entrants. It is interesting to speculate on whether the observed price responses were a consequence of the use of other non-price strategies that failed to have the desired effect on entrants. We have already noted US Steel's vertical price strategies, and the advertising and space packing strategies that were used by UK petrol retailers in addition to their 'measured price response'. Similarly, price responses attendant on deregulation might legitimately be regarded as the consequence of a failure by regulated firms to ensure that the government continues to protect their markets. Indeed, although it is somewhat speculative, one can read the case study evidence as suggesting that price often is used as a last resort, as a means of gracefully and profitably exiting from a market for which the battle had already been lost. In the US copying machine industry, Xerox had a cost advantage in supplying its xerographic machines to high volume users but, in the early 1960s, it concentrated on low and medium volume markets. As entrants using electrofax technology appeared in the 1960s, Xerox gradually retreated to the high volume end of the market, pricing its products in the low and medium usage segments somewhat below monopoly prices (apparently) to retard but not block entry (Blackstone, 1972). In this case, it appears that pricing behaviour was a consequence (not a cause) of a strategy choice to cede market share. A similar sequence of events may also have led to Kodak's decision to concentrate on selling equipment to film processors in the UK as demand shifted from colour slides to prints, market segments which Kodak did not dominate (Shaw and Simpson, 1985).

If it is indeed the case that price is used as a weapon of last resort, then one suspects that the major responses by incumbents to the threat of entry will be non-price responses. It is certainly not difficult to find plenty of examples of non-price strategies used against entrants. The entry of Golden Wonder into the UK potato crisp industry provoked Smiths, the incumbent, to advertise much more heavily and to introduce various types of flavoured crisps. No sign of pricing to deter or retard entry seems evident in the data (Bevan, 1974). Entry into the UK domestic washing machines market also provoked retaliation via advertising and product innovation (not all of which was motivated by entry deterrence), but not price (Shaw and Sutton, 1976). Price effects can be observed in these essentially non-price competitions, but there is little reason to think that they were provoked by any strategic thinking on the part of incumbents. In the UK dry cleaning industry, for example, the response by incumbents to entry in the late 1950s and early 1960s involved massive defensive investments which, by adding substantially to industry capacity, ultimately provoked a price war (Shaw, 1973).

Similarly, entry into plain paper copiers was blocked for a long period of time by a strategy in which Xerox 'patented every imaginable feature of the copier technology' (Bresnahan, 1985, p. 15). When the Federal Trade Commission (FTC) consent decree required Xerox to license its patents to all copiers in 1975, prices fell rapidly, although Xerox's prices lagged behind entrants until the late 1970s (because of its large stock of leased machines). The entire process of entry and bidding down prices took three to five years from the time that the FTC required Xerox to license its patents to all copiers. Although this was not a particularly rapid response by entrants, there is little evidence to suggest that Xerox's price strategy played any role in delaying their arrival (or that it was designed to do so). The loss of patent protection in the European polyester fibres industry also seemed to signal the end of any attempts of incumbents to block entry. In particular, no attempt was made to limit price, although entry did in the end lead to a price war (Shaw and Shaw, 1977). West (1981) observed the use of space packing strategies amongst supermarkets located in Vancouver, and pre-emption in product space seems to have blocked entry in the US ready-to-eat breakfast cereals market without the need for incumbents to use prices against entrants (Schmalensee, 1978b).

Finally, Alemson (1969) has discussed a number of examples of entry into Australian markets that provoked a wide range of non-price responses by incumbents (cigarettes, processed soups, automobiles, chocolate drinks etc.), concluding that 'price does not change subsequently over time in oligopoly situations', despite what are often quite large changes in market shares (p. 240).

We have, then, a fairly lengthy list of examples of price and non-price responses to entry, and a vague, rather poorly established presumption (if the feeling is as strong as that) that the latter are likely to dominate the former both in the sense of being used more often as well as in the sense of being used first whenever there is a choice between them. Underlining this presumption is, of course, the further presumption that responding to entry is likely to be the optimal strategy for incumbents to follow in most situations. Case studies, however, are a rather unsatisfactory basis on which to make generalizations since they are a non-randomly selected sample of industries where interesting entry deterrence strategies were used. More satisfactory evidence requires a broader based inter-industry study.

The evidence on these issues at the cross-section level is somewhat limited, but that which we have is fairly clear. Biggadike (1976) asked his (not very random) sample of 35 entrants in the USA (all subsidiaries of large, diversified firms) about their perception of incumbent reactions, and discovered that 46% perceived no reaction to entry whatsoever. In 93% of the sample, price either did not change or declined by less than 5% in the face of entry. In 68% of the sample, there was no change in incumbents' marketing expenditures whatsoever when entry occurred, although marketing expenditures did rise in response to entry in 32% of the cases studied. Finally, in 92% of the sample incumbents' capacity rose by less than 10%. Yip (1982a) examined 36 'important' entrants, finding no response at all to entry by acquisition and only a response incidence of 10–20% for direct entry. Smiley (1988) reported the results of a questionnaire sent to 293 US firms asking about the incidence in use of different types of strategies. For incumbents defending new products, advertising and patent policy were used most frequently. Thirty-two per cent of the respondents indicated that they used advertising 'frequently', 31% used R&D and patent protection 'frequently', and only 2–3% indicated that they used limit pricing or entry regulation 'frequently'. Learning curve and excess capacity strategies were used 'frequently' by only 6–9% of the sample. For incumbents defending mature existing products, learning curve advantages are not available, but profits can be hidden and the product space packed. Together with advertising, these two strategies were used 'frequently' by 31%, 26% and

24% of the respondents respectively. R&D and patent protection were used by 11% 'frequently', while excess capacity and pricing strategies were used by about 7% of the respondents 'frequently'. About half the respondents felt that decisions about entry were as important as other types of strategic decisions, with 54% reporting frequent use of entry-deterring instruments to protect new products and 58% reporting their use to protect mature markets. As with Biggadike, the clear moral seems to be that advertising is among the more important strategic weapons that are used against entrants (and not price), but that the response to entry is fairly selective. This conclusion is broadly consistent with work reported by Cubbin and Domberger (1988) who studied entry into 42 UK advertising-intensive markets. They perceived an advertising response to entry in only about 40% of their cases by looking for structural changes in advertising at or near the entry date (a procedure that may understate pre-entry responses).

Selectivity in response is a clear feature of the data, and a number of studies provide rather weak evidence to suggest that the likelihood of response varies systematically across markets (to some degree). Cubbin and Domberger found responses to be more likely in static markets dominated by a single firm and, similarly, Smiley (1987) found responses more likely in highly concentrated markets dominated by large firms. Using a multinomial logit model with a fivefold classification of strategy use (from 'never' to 'frequently'), Smiley also found that market growth did not affect the likelihood of responding to entry and, less surprisingly, that responses to entry were less likely in markets where barriers to entry (as conventionally measured) were high. Price strategies tended to be used (if at all) in slow growth or contracting markets, while learning, capacity pre-emption, R&D and hiding profitability were all more likely to be employed against entrants in highly concentrated markets. Patenting tended to be used where relatively little was spent on advertising, although advertising was used in markets where firms also made large expenditures on R&D.

The major difficulty with evaluating this evidence on the selectivity of response by incumbents to entry (and, in particular, with confronting the arguments made in the second section with it) is interpreting what 'no response' means. At the simplest level, the lack of a price response to entry may, of course, mean that incumbents are already pricing very near to costs, possibly because of entry. More subtly, maintaining high pre-entry output levels post-entry involves literally no response to the fact of entry, even though these output decisions pre- and post-entry may be driven by a concern to block entrants. That is, 'no response' in the sense of not changing current levels of activity in the fact of entry differs from accommodating entry by cutting back on current activities and making room for the entrant, and it might therefore be regarded as a somewhat hostile reaction to entry. In addition, no response to entry in the short run does not imply that incumbents will never respond to entry, particularly when entrants are slow to penetrate into the market. Responses – accommodating or hostile – do not necessarily need to be timed exactly with the arrival of an entrant to be well judged or effective. Still, these caveats aside, it is hard to draw much support from this evidence for the notion that incumbents find the fact of entry to be sufficiently disruptive to dislodge them from their current activities. Responses to the fact of entry are, apparently, rather selective.

Thus, one is inclined to conclude that price does not seem to be the major weapon used against entrants, pre- or post-entry. That is not to say, of course, that entry has little effect on price, but it does suggest that price effects are often the consequence of other, more fundamental non-price actions taken by incumbents against entry. There is a considerable amount of evidence to suggest that responses to entry (when they occur) tend to be marketing based, and involve alterations in the incumbents' marketing mix (such as increased advertising and product proliferation). Not only may such activities have much more profound effects on demand than price, they may have rather perverse effects on price and on margins (as we saw earlier in the case of the UK car industry). It is hard to avoid the impression that most firms allocate marketing instruments to the targets of creating and sustaining monopoly positions, and price to the target of using such a position to generate a large flow of rents. Applying an instrument such as price to a target like blocking entry may have attractions from a public policy point of view, but that should not persuade anyone to think that it necessarily makes much sense from a business strategy perspective.

Conclusions

Some economists have looked to the force of competition between firms to bring prices into line with marginal costs, and many who think that at least some degree of collusion and co-operation in pricing amongst incumbents is endemic in most markets have stressed the role that potential entry can have in affecting prices. The evidence from numerous econometric case studies of pricing behaviour is that price taking behaviour is not very common; that is, that at least a certain amount of output restriction occurs in many markets (e.g. see the surveys by Geroski, 1988a, and Bresnahan, 1989). If it is true that price competition between incumbents is often less vigorous than it might be, then the contribution that potential entry might, in principle, make to industry performance is large. In practice, however, the evidence that we have examined here leads one to think that potential entry does not often greatly affect prices, or, more important, pricing behaviour in the short run. In particular, there is little case study evidence to suggest that the threat of entry regularly has a major effect on pricing behaviour pre-entry. When entry occurs, prices often fall somewhat (although not always), but it is generally rather hard to see most post-entry price wars as the consequence of a consciously pursued entry regulation policy. At best, the evidence is ambiguous. When firms choose to respond to entry – and they do so only selectively – they often choose a broad-based marketing campaign involving a much wider range of strategic actions (e.g. advertising) than just price cuts. Indeed, one has the sense that the level of price is more often than not determined after all the interesting non-price choices associated with entry have been made.

Although it is not necessarily the case that the typically modest price effects which have been associated with entry in the case study literature translate into the modest and quite unexciting short-run dynamics in margins associated with entry that a number of econometric studies have produced, one cannot help feeling that the two sets of observations are not unrelated. There are, perhaps, two considerations that lead one in this direction. First, the fact that responses to entry are selective almost certainly means that broad cross-section times series studies of entry-induced changes in margins will contain relatively few instances of post-entry price wars. The vast majority of entrants in most markets – that is, the firms that have generated most of the entry recorded in the data – seem to come and go at furious speeds without, however, much disturbing the placid calm of industry price–cost margins. To observe major price (or margin) dynamics associated with entry, one has to be rather selective in collecting (or at least filtering) one's data, concentrating only on major entry assaults into particular, well-defined and often rather narrow market segments. Second, the fact that most of the selective responses to entry that occur do not involve price (at least in the first instance) may mean that margins do not change much as a consequence of entry even when entry has a tremendous impact on the activities of firms in the market. Strategic investments in capacity, major advertising campaigns, the proliferation of products and so on all affect both costs and prices, and there is no reason to think that the result will be a simple monotonic convergence of price–cost margins towards their long-run level.

Nevertheless, margins do move systematically (with just a hint of oscillation) towards their long-run levels, and part of this movement can be associated with flows of entry by new and diversifying firms. More interesting is the observation that there are systematic movements in margins that are not correlated to changes in market structure. It is possible to interpret these as reflecting the workings of a latent competitive force such as potential entry, although there are clearly other interpretations of this dynamic motion that are consistent with the data. If one does accept this interpretation, then the results discussed above lead one to conclude that actual and potential entry have rather similar effects on the dynamics of margins in the short run, but that the total effect of both is rather modest. However much of this systematic dynamic in margins that one chooses to attribute to potential entry, the implication is surely that the effect of potential entrants on market performance is easy to exaggerate. Actual and potential competitors – and, indeed, new entrants and established incumbents – are not close substitutes from the point of view of providing competitive discipline in markets in the short run.

What comes out from the rather shortish times series that have been examined in this context is that margins often appear to be at, or fairly near, their long-run levels. That most markets may not be very far from their long-run equilibrium positions for most of the time is (as we have seen) a conclusion that one can also read into the raw data on entry, and into the results that have emerged from applying various models of entry to those data. From the point of view of understanding the short-run dynamics of prices and margins, this conclusion suggests that changes in market structure may be the important determinant of the dynamics of market performance in the short run, and of the level of performance reached in the long run. After all, if prices are always at or near a level determined by the height of entry barriers, then it is changes in barriers (and not behaviour) that will lead to changes in prices (with or without the fact of entry). One concludes, then, that if strategic price and non-price entry-deterring behaviour matters (that is, if they have an effect independent of those generated by changes in market structure), it does so because the non-price actions of firms affect entry barriers and, if this is truly the case, then the affect of such behaviour on prices (although not, perhaps, on entry flows) will be indirect and, quite possibly, of second order. One way or the other, it seems clear that barriers to entry are likely to be a major determinant of market performance, even in the short run.

Notes

1 For surveys of theories of oligopoly, see Shapiro (1989), Scherer (1980, chs 5–8) and, on collusion, Jacquemin and Slade (1989).

2 Following Demsetz (1968) and Baumol et al. (1982), one might think of these effects as the consequence of a bidding process between incumbents and entrants for profitable market positions (see also Waterson, 1981, for further remarks in this vein). 'Contestability' theory goes some way to making plain the conditions under which this process can generate competitive-looking outcomes even when scale economies exist.

3 It is worth emphasizing the effects that expected future entrants may make to the expectations of incumbents and current entrants. If current entrants are just the first of many likely entrants, then the post-entry behaviour of incumbents is unlikely to be accommodating (see Omori and Yarrow, 1982, compared with, say, Dixit, 1979). Bernheim (1984) has argued that reductions in barriers to entry may make markets less attractive to current entrants who perceive that such reductions carry a short-run gain in facilitating their own entry which must be set against the cost of a decline in long-run market profitability. Entry deterrence in models where a sequence of entrants appear over time is discussed in Hay (1976), Prescott and Visscher (1977), Eaton and Ware (1987) and others.

4 Traditional limit price models are presented and discussed in Modigliani (1958) and Bhagwati (1970); Milgrom and Roberts (1982) give a limit price model that relies on informational asymmetries which are exploited by incumbents against sophisticated entrants, a theory not inconsistent with much in the rich, pioneering discussion by Bain (1956). Bagwell and Ramey (1987, 1990) extend this type of model to consider advertising and pricing strategies jointly. Dixit (1979) and Osborne (1973) examine the 'rationality' of limit pricing; that is, the conditions under which it is preferred to a myopic pricing strategy.

5 See Gaskins (1971), Kamien and Schwartz (1971, 1972, 1975) and Baron (1972, 1973) for various models along these lines. Judd and Peterson (1986) explore the link between finance and the expansion of entrants, Lippman (1980) considers the case where entry rates are uncertain, Encaoua et al. (1981) the case where the eventual erosion of its market share induces the leader to change its pricing behaviour over time and De Bondt (1976) the effects of entry lags on the optimal strategy of incumbents.

6 Deciding what is pre- and what is post-entry is a delicate question, since the act of investing in plant and equipment – the irrevocable first step into the market – may pre-date the appearance of output by quite some time. Entry regulation may well commence post-investment but pre-market-appearance and, being designed to limit the investment undertaken by the entrant, may erroneously be mistaken for limit pricing. It follows that one runs the danger of identifying more instances of limit pricing than actually occur in the data, and of understating the incidence of entry regulation.

7 An implication of the argument in the text is that market processes may be hysteretic, with perhaps random short-run shocks altering market conditions in a manner which changes long-run equilibria because they give rise to relatively irreversible entry flows. Arguments to this effect have been put forward with respect to imports in the USA in the 1980s as a consequence of an

overvalued dollar; see, for example, Baldwin (1987) and references cited therein. On the interrelated effects of entry and exit barriers more generally, see Caves and Porter (1976), Eaton and Lipsey (1980) and others.

8 This argument is due to Eaton and Lipsey (1979); see also Gilbert and Newberry (1982) and, more generally on the tendency toward monopolization that is inherent in sequential entry models, see Prescott and Visscher (1977, section 3).

9 Stating this argument verbally leads to a slight risk of creating confusion, and it is worth being somewhat more precise. The entrant's problem is to choose x to maximize its profits, $\pi = xp(x, y) - vk - F$, given y. Call the solution to this problem $x = x(y)$. y^*, by definition, is that value of y for which $p[x(y), y] = v + F/x(y)$. By contrast, the best post-entry output for the incumbent, y, maximizes its profits given $x = x(y)$.

10 Although apparently prosaic, the point is of some importance in terms of the gaming that goes on between entrant and incumbent. If, for example, the entrant is able to persuade the incumbent that it has not or cannot perceive the threat to produce y^* post-entry, then there is little point in trying to make y^* credible. Any strategy implemented by the incumbent whose effects are clear to see would make such posing by the entrant less than credible.

11 On the depreciation of the effect of advertising, see the survey in Comanor and Wilson (1979). Schmalensee (1983) and Baldwin and Masson (1981) differ on the issue of whether advertising can, in principle, be a credible strategic investment.

12 See, for example, Schmalensee (1978b), Eaton and Lipsey (1978), Bonanno (1987), Judd (1985) and others; Ireland (1987) looks at product differentiation models more generally. It is a moot point whether incumbents actually need to proliferate their products prior to entry in order to deter entry if it is common knowledge that incumbents can 'move faster' than entrants. A strategy of launching new products at exactly the same time that entrants launch their new products (i.e. creating 'fighting brands') has much appeal as a tactic to block or at least to limit the market penetration of entrants.

13 On using capacity to block entry, see Wenders (1971), Spence (1977), Dixit (1980), Kirman and Masson (1986), Bonanno (1988) and others; on inventories, see Ware (1985) and Saloner (1986); on maintenance costs, obsolescence and the effect of sunk costs, see Eaton and Lipsey (1980), Baumol et al. (1982, pp. 296–301) and others.

14 The estimates in (4.10)–(4.13) are derived from table 1 of Geroski and Murfin (1990b) using equations (iv), (iii) and (i) respectively. Equation (4.11) suppresses a term in a_{t-1}^2 and S_{t-1}, while (4.13) takes (in the notation of that table) $D = 1$, $T = 0.3$ (its sample mean) and $\pi_t^c = \pi_t$ and suppresses R_{t-1} and various constants into B_3. B_1 and B_2 are also firm and market segment specific.

15 These individual firm time series studies also suggest that there is considerable heterogeneity in market dynamics within industries. Speeds of adjustment appear to be lower for firms with large market shares, and can vary between situations where $\pi_{t-1} > \pi^*$ and $\pi_{t-1} < \pi^*$; see also Mueller

(1977), Connolly and Schwartz (1985), Ogadiri and Yamawaki (1986) and the papers contained in Mueller (1990). Cubbin and Geroski (1987) develop and estimate a model which suggests that firm-specific and not industry-wide forces are the major factor propelling the profits of firms towards their long-run levels.

16 Briefly, the dominant firm chooses a price p_t in period t which has effects on its profits π_t in the future because it affects the expansion rate of the fringe. With a discount of ρ, the present discounted flow of profits that it expects are

$$ V_t = \sum_{\tau=0}^{\infty} \rho^\tau \pi_{t+\tau}^e $$

where $\pi_{t+\tau}^e$ is the expectation held at t of future profits. Assuming for simplicity that the future effects of p_t are confined to one period, then the optimal price trajectory is given by

$$ \frac{\partial V_t}{\partial p_t} = \frac{\partial \pi_t}{\partial p_t} + \rho \frac{\partial \pi_{t+1}^e}{\partial p_t} = C. \tag{4.20'} $$

The first two terms in (4.20) emerge from the first term in (4.20'), δ turns out to be proportional to ρ ($\rho = 0$ implies $\delta = 0$), and the third term in (4.20) is derived from second term in (4.20'); for details, see Geroski (1990a).

17 On the other hand, Geroski and Murfin (1990b) observed a negative γ for foreign-based producers in the UK car market, suggesting that this result may be more robust than one might imagine. Note that both sets of estimates use a full set of fixed effects, relying only on the 'within' variation in the data. The fact that within-industry variations in the *change* in import share are negatively correlated to π_t^e does not, of course, imply that between-industry variations in the *level* of import shares will be negatively correlated to π_t.

18 This may, of course, reflect the application of a limit pricing policy by incumbents who believe themselves to be continually under threat. The numbers estimated by Geroski (1990a), for example, generate an estimate of the elasticity of demand which implies values of monopoly mark-ups far in excess of the estimated levels of long-run margins.

19 See, for example, Fisher and McGowan (1983) and Fisher (1987a); Edwards et al. (1987) is a better balanced view of the subject, showing *inter alia* that persistently high accounting profits imply persistently high economic profits.

20 In essence, we have solved the latent variables problem of potential entry by using π_{t-1}, π_{t-2} etc. as an indicator of the extent of potential entry, the theory being that π_{t-1}, π_{t-2} etc. ought to fulfil this role as they are a major determinant of entry. The two substantive problems with this are that high π_{t-1}, π_{t-2} etc. also set off other reactions (intra-industry investment competition, high wage demands by prices and so on), and that π_{t-1}, π_{t-2} etc. are not particularly strong determinants of actual entry. There is no doubt that other solutions to the problem of modelling potential entry are worth exploring.

21   At first sight, it might seem that any substantial investment activities under-
      taken by incumbents at the time of entry are *prima facie* evidence against the
      null hypothesis of myopia, particularly if they appear to be targeted against
      entrants. Given this, any observed price cuts might then be taken as evidence
      of entry regulation since it is clear that incumbents are responding to entry.
      On the other hand, if non-price strategic entry deterrence dominates the use
      of price, then the fact that these strategic investments take place may mean
      that entry regulation by price is not occurring.

22   Yamawaki (1985) has analysed the dynamics of price and capacity expansion
      in the US iron and steel industry during the period 1907–30, discovering that
      fringe market share had a negative effect on price (with elasticity approx-
      imately −0.9) and that price had a positive effect on fringe capital stock and
      output (with elasticities approximately 0.4 and 1.4 respectively). Although
      this appears to be consistent with entry regulation, it is very hard to see why
      this pattern of correlations is not also consistent with myopic behaviour by
      US Steel. Yamawaki argues that the alternative hypothesis might be that the
      fringe was not myopic and that levels of capital stock held by US Steel under
      this alternative would not affect the capital stock held by the fringe. He
      observed no such effect and concluded that the hypothesis of entry regulation
      was consistent with his data.

23   Not all instances of entry lead to price declines. For a reputation good – like
      physician care – entry may lead to a deterioration in consumer information,
      giving firms the opportunities to raise price. Pauly and Satterthwaite (1981)
      document this in the case of private physician care in the USA.

5

The Empirical Analysis of
Barriers to Entry

Introduction

It is often argued that 'market structure' is the important determinant of market performance. The link from structure to performance is generally thought to follow from more fundamental causal relations that run from market structure to market conduct, and the classic example of this kind of argument is, of course, that which suggests that a highly concentrated market is likely to be one where producers are able to collude tacitly or overtly, maintaining prices well above marginal costs for substantial periods of time. While there is no doubting the proposition that market structure is potentially an important determinant of market performance, what is open to question is what one means by 'market structure' and whether the links from structure to performance are simple and systematic enough to give the hypotheses any kind of useful empirical bite. More fundamentally, one must ask what these links are: is structure important because it uniquely determines one particular pattern of conduct, or is it important because the stability of market structure ensures a continuity in behaviour over time, however the latter is determined?

Roughly speaking, the evidence of countless cross-section studies is that structure–performance correlations between market concentration (or market shares) and profits exist, but they are often imprecisely measured and account for only a modest percentage of observed variations in profitability (for a recent survey, see Schmalensee, 1989). Yet, both market concentration and profitability vary relatively little over time: their between-industry variation dwarfs their within-industry variation. This co-variation across industries coupled with a high degree of persistence in each series over time must derive from some common cause, from some factor that provides a stable framework within which competition occurs in markets. Indeed, the interesting feature of industry price–cost margins is not that they are positively (but weakly) correlated to concentration, but that they are (like concentration) relatively stable over time. It is this persistence in profitability that needs to be explained, and it seems reasonable to believe that some feature of 'market structure' will be able to account for it. The obvious candidate is barriers to entry. Particular types of barrier give rise to particular types of competitive behaviour and an associated degree of concentration. More fundamentally, the fact that barriers condition behaviour means that the persistence of barriers over time ensures that the same associated market outcomes (e.g. profits and concentration) will also tend to persist over time, however idiosyncratic their relation is to each other or to particular barriers.

The arguments involved are much the same as those that one encounters in debates on the genetic determinants of human behaviour. That certain types of disorder are genetically transmitted and, indeed, that an individual's phenotype has a genetic basis does not imply that there is one gene for homosexuality, another for intelligence, humour and so on. Nor is it the case that any simple relationship exists between genotype and phenotype, much less between phenotype and behaviour. Similarly, the fact that the initial development of an individual is genetically programmed does not mean that the environment into which the individual is born plays no role in shaping its development; nor does it mean that the individual cannot affect its own development by exercising some control over its immediate environment. Genes matter because they set (rather broad) limits on what individuals can do and, more importantly, because they provide some continuity in basic human characteristics between generations. In exactly the same way that genes delimit the broad features of potential human behaviour, so entry barriers provide a stage upon which the nuances of competitive market behaviour can be played out. However, what is important about market structure defined in this way is not the possibility that every stage may be uniquely suited to a different play, but rather that the existence of the same stage period by period helps to establish a continuity in the behaviour that we observe on it. That is, market structure matters not so much because it gives rise to certain types of market conduct and associated performance outcomes, but because it ensures that certain patterns of conduct and associated performance outcomes persist over time.

Thus, it seems reasonable to think that market structure helps to establish continuity in market performance, providing the basic foundation for the persistent inter-industry differences in profitability over time that we observe. This does not, of course, mean that market structure has to be thought of as completely fixed or exogenous. Not only is it possible that agents may consciously try to refashion some of the permanent features of their environment, but it may also be the case that actions designed to exploit certain elements of market structure will, in the process, transform that structure. Firms may, for example, consciously try to alter the structure of their costs by engaging in R&D into alternative manufacturing processes, and successful process innovations may push back technological frontiers in unexpected ways that open up new opportunities for further innovations. In addition to this endogenous process of change, market structure is also likely to change exogenously, often in ways that are rather difficult to predict. These changes, when transmitted through the rather uncertain link between structure and conduct, eventually induce changes in performance, longer-run secular drifts that are superimposed in the day to day performance variations caused by noisy variations in conduct and their noisy effect on performance. The argument that structure is important, then, relies not so much on the premise that structure is exogenous and fixed, as on the premise that changes in structure are slow and exogenous from the point of view of the pricing decisions made by agents at any given time. As long as the dynamics of market structure operate glacially, then structure can bring continuity to market performance in the short to medium run.

This observation suggests a second, slightly deeper point. Much of the debate on the role of market structure has turned on the question of precisely what definition of structure is appropriate. Convention definitions generally run in terms of market concentration or market shares; recent definitions (including the one given above) run in terms of entry barriers. The conflict between them, however, is more apparent than real. The precise operational definition of market structure that is appropriate in any situation depends on how short run the decisions are that one is trying to describe, and on how long a period one expects to observe continuity in market conduct and performance. Characterizations of market structure that run in terms of the number and size distribution of suppliers in the market are, in a sense, appropriate for very short-run static analyses. For problems of pricing and for tracing the very short-run dynamics of profits, one can reasonably take market structure defined in these terms as exogenous and fixed. Sooner or later, however, other firms wil react to these short-run market outcomes by making decisions that lead to entry, exit and, more generally, changes in market shares. The structural factors that determine how much entry, exit and intra-industry mobility occur are barriers to entry, and from the point of view of investment decisions that affect market performance in the medium term they can be thought of as being both relatively fixed and exogenous. However, many of the investment decisions made by incumbents to exploit barriers are likely to change them (however subtly) at the same time, and this is certainly likely to be the case (or at least the intention) with almost all the investment decisions made by entrants. Barriers to entry are therefore also likely to change over the longer run, often in ways not wholly independent of persistently recurring patterns of market conduct. The exogenous variables that help to guide the gradual evolution of entry barriers are the culturally determined patterns of behaviour that establish the needs which consumption is designed to satisfy, and the basic scientific knowledge that determines the rate and direction of technological advance. Culture and technological opportunity are the fundamental determinants of both the structure of costs and demand and, more important, their evolution in the long run. As such, they are the truly long-run elements of market structure.

Our goal in what follows is to view market performance over the medium to long run, looking at the extent to which barriers to entry affect the number and size distribution of firms and the persistence of supernormal profitability. What is of most interest, then, is how barriers impede entry and, by this means, give rise to the relatively permanent interindustry differences in performance that we observed in chapter 4. However, since barriers only matter to the extent that they are exploited strategically by incumbents, any examination of barriers inevitably involves a complementary examination of the methods by which they can be exploited and the manner in which they change over time. This, in turn, is an essential input into any examination of how long differences in current period profitability caused by barriers are liable to persist. The discussion will proceed in three stages. We start in the next section with a definition of barriers to entry. Since assessing the height of barriers to entry is an inherently speculative exercise, it is important to be clear about exactly what type of counterfactual constructions one must make. In the following section we consider the major sources of barriers, relying on the famous three-part classification given by Bain. Most of the evidence that we have on particular types of barriers has emerged from case studies, but there is no sense in which this evidence can be said to do anything other than illustrate the wide variety of factors that can impede entry. Gathering these factors together into one overall figure that measures the height of barriers in a particular sector is a problem that is discussed in the penultimate section, and here most (but not all) of the evidence that we have is derived from econometric studies of profits or from the types of entry equations discussed in chapter 3. Putting the two types of empirical evidence together paints a fairly consistent picture, one that suggests that most markets do not approach the ideal of perfect competition (or contestability) very closely in the short run. Barriers are not immutable, however, and many markets often appear to be reasonably competitive in the long run.

The Condition of Entry

The notion of entry barriers is a subtle one because it involves a comparison between two equilibria, only one of which can ever be observed. As a consequence, measuring the height of barriers and ascertaining the specific structural factors that give rise to barriers is inherently conjectural. The main sources of uncertainty arise from the fact that barriers are affected both by the type of entrant under consideration and by mediating market conditions, including the response of incumbents to entry. Somewhat more troubling, attempts to infer 'what could be' from 'what is' by using observed entry flows or by taking too static a view of the immutability of costs or demand when estimating the size of barriers can have a tendency to exaggerate their height. Barriers are always likely to seem larger to the uncritical eye.

It is natural to commence by defining barriers in terms of their principal consequence, namely positive profits in the long run. Barriers to entry are obstacles which inhibit the ability of firms outside a market to enter and compete with established insiders. As such, they protect positions of market power and enable incumbents to earn supernormal profits in perpetuity. Any concern with the long-run performance of markets is therefore bound to be translated into an interest in the height of entry barriers. High profits in the long run are not, however, the same thing as supernormal current profits, and to identify the existence and measure the height of barriers to entry, one must probe beneath the profit outcomes observed in any particular period. Indeed, the effects that barriers have on market performance in the long run may be difficult to distinguish from transitory fluctuations in profits that arise from a variety of causes in the short run. Members of a perfectly competitive industry which has no barriers to entry may nevertheless earn high profits because of rapid and unanticipated demand growth, and such profits are likely to persist for as long as it takes capacity to adjust to demand. Only if supernormal profits persist in the long run can one infer that barriers exist.

Somewhat more formally, barriers are 'the advantages of established sellers in an industry over potential entrants, these advantages being reflected in the extent to which established sellers can persistently raise their prices above a competitive level without attracting new firms to enter the industry' (Bain, 1956, p. 3). Implicit in this definition is a comparison between the profits that incumbents realize pre-entry and those that entrants can earn post-entry. This is a natural comparison to make since expected pre-entry profits are what (in principle) attracts the attention of entrants, and expected post-entry profits are what determines the likelihood that entry actually occurs. Barriers exist when entrants are attracted to the market but cannot enter. Notice that except in cases where entry is the vehicle of some innovation which transforms the market or where the market exogenously expands *pari passu* with entry, the pre-entry profits of incumbents are bound to exceed an entrant's post-entry profits simply because the supply side of the market is transformed by entry, say from a monopoly to a duopoly. As long as tastes and technology are static, there will almost always be a natural limit to the number of firms that can simultaneously operate in a market, and profits per firm will decline as the number of market participants increases. This does not mean, however, that entry is unattractive: as long as post-entry profits are positive, entry will occur whether or not the profits of new firms are less than those earned by incumbents just prior to entry. Barriers to entry exist when such a supply side transformation necessarily results in negative profits post-entry for the entrant. Given this, entry will obviously not occur and the incumbent will continue to enjoy positive profits at 'pre-entry' levels. Barriers are important not because most markets can accommodate only a finite number of firms but, rather, because of the possibility that the point at which the marginal entrant is deterred may be such as to leave incumbents earning substantial 'pre-entry' profits in perpetuity.

To put this definition of entry barriers into perspective, it is worth recalling the somewhat different definition proposed by Stigler, who argued that barriers are 'a cost of producing which must be borne by a firm which seeks to enter an industry, but is not borne by firms in the industry' (Stigler, 1968, p. 67). This is a comparison between the post-entry profits of the incumbent on the one hand and those of the entrant on the other. If the two differ, it may be that the cause of this difference leads to a set of post-entry equilibrium prices at which entrants make no profits. However, such a differential is not a reliable indicator of the height of barriers for two reasons. First, it is entirely possible for the differential to be zero when barriers exist. Suppose that, pre-entry, the incumbent earns $M_1 > 0$ and that, post-entry, the incumbent and entrant earn V_1 and V_2 respectively. If $V_1 = V_2$, then Stigler's comparison suggests that no barriers exist. However, if $V_1 = V_2 < 0$, then no entry will, in fact, occur and the incumbent will earn $M_1 > 0$ in the long run. Clearly a barrier exists despite the fact that $V_1 = V_2$. Second and more subtly, consider the case where $V_2 = 0$, so that $V_1 - V_2 = V_1$. Because the post-entry market structure would involve a duopoly if entry occurred, then almost surely $V_1 < M_1$. But, since $V_2 = 0$, entry will not, in fact, occur. Hence, $V_1 - V_2$ is likely to understate the true level of barriers simply because it is M_1 that the incumbent will actually enjoy in the long run and not V_1.[1]

In fact, it is hard to see what the comparison between a V_1 and V_2 contributes to identifying barriers to entry. The post-entry returns of incumbents, V_1, are not those that will be realized in the long run if entry is blocked; nor are they likely to be sustainable if $V_2 > 0$ unless further entry is blocked. If further entry is blocked, then V_1 and V_2 are, in fact, pre-entry returns to the crucial marginal entrant who is blocked, and are relevant for this reason only. The Stigler criterion is really concerned more with the ability of entrants to compete with incumbents as ongoing concerns than with problems of entry *per se*. From the point of view of entry, what matters is whether $V_2 > 0$ or not. The difference $V_1 - V_2$, on the other hand, is a measure of the disadvantages that entrants would face were they to be established as competitors. In some sense, it measures the kind of competitive pressure that entrants are likely to present to the original incumbents when they too are established as incumbents. As such, it contains information on whether the force of actual competition will equalize returns across firms who are present in the market. Whether, in addition, profits will be driven to zero in the long run is another question altogether. In short, if $M_1 > 0$ but $V_2 < 0$, incumbent firms will all earn positive profits in the long run; if $V_2 > 0$, they will earn less than M_1 in the long run; and if $V_1 \neq V_2$ then some firms will earn more than others in the long run if further entry is blocked.[2]

The comparison between Bain's and Stigler's criteria for identifying barriers suggests that it is one thing for an entrant to be able to enter in a market where positive profits are being earned by incumbents, and it is another thing altogether for a successful entrant to compete on a par with incumbents in that market. In making their preparations to enter or defend markets, different firms clearly make different strategic decisions, investing in certain types of assets and neglecting others. Such differences in strategy are likely to be reflected in the types of investment decisions which firms make, decisions that create assets which give rise to differences in costs or demand between firms. If it is difficult for rivals to overcome such cost or demand differences, then the result is likely to be persistent profitability differentials of the type identified by Stigler. Collecting together into 'strategic groups' all firms in the same industry that follow a similar competitive strategy, then the existence of such groups implies the existence of what might be called 'mobility barriers' which sustain permanent profit differences between groups of firms in the same industry (Caves and Porter, 1977).

Although interesting in their own right, mobility barriers also enrich the notion of entry barriers in an important way. If mobility barriers exist, then it matters where in the market an entrant chooses to compete. Clearly, entry into a market which contains a number of different strategic groups can be inhibited by a range of different types of entry barrier, depending on which market niche the entrant attempts to penetrate. More fundamentally, the existence of mobility barriers raises the question of what the best route to take to a particular desired niche is; that is, of what the appropriate 'entry path' is. Thinking of an industry as a map with a number of distinct niches, the question which entrants face is whether it is better to attempt to enter some desirable niche B directly, or to enter and produce at a less attractive niche C first and then move on to B from there. Several considerations suggest that indirect entry paths may often be optimal. The ability of a firm to compete successfully in niche B may depend on the accumulation of production experience in the industry, and generating consumer goodwill for the good produced in niche B may require that the entrant offer a range of other products in other niches like C. Further, when entrants must make substantial commitments before entering highly profitable niches, then a sequential sinking of smaller commitments built up by operating first in less profitable niches may be much less risky. One way or another, the implication is that the barriers facing an entrant into market niche B are likely to depend on the particular path to B that it chooses to follow. More generally, the existence of mobility barriers means that 'entry' will consist of not one but a whole sequence of decisions. The fact that entrants can take faster or slower routes to their desired market niche means that their post-entry profits may exhibit different profiles over time, an effect analogous to that created by time–cost trade-offs in R&D programmes. The implication is that entry decisions cannot be made in isolation from subsequent market penetration decisions. Entry will occur if the expected present discounted value of post-entry profits is positive, and this depends on the height of entry barriers in the niche where the entrant first attempts penetration, as well as on the height of mobility barriers throughout the rest of the industry.

Having acknowledged this complication, let us return to the somewhat simpler scenario of entry into a relatively unstructured market, and focus on what the comparison between the incumbents' pre-entry profits and the entrants' post-entry profits reveals about the sources of barriers to entry. Since, by definition, barriers to entry exist if $M_1 > 0$ and $V_2 < 0$, then clearly the source of such barriers lies in the differences between the profit functions of entrants and incumbents. To explore these, we need to extend our notation somewhat. Let firm $i = 1$ be the incumbent and $i = 2$ be the entrant. Each produces output x_i (which, for simplicity, we take to be i's choice variable), and each expects the other to respond according to some best reply function $x_j = F_{ij}(x_i)$. Using $F_{ij}(x_i)$, one can express each firm's profits π_i in terms of its own output alone. Profits depend on costs and revenues and so, using obvious notation, $\pi_i = R_i(x_i) - C_i(x_i)$.[3] In the absence of entry, the incumbent sets output as a monopolist at $x°$ and earns $M_1 = \pi_1(x°) > 0$. The difference between M_1 and V_2 can be thought of as having two components, $\pi_1(x°) - \pi_2(x°)$ and $\pi_2(x°) - \pi_2(x^*)$, where x^* is the post-entry output chosen by the entrant (i.e. $V_2 = \pi_2(x^*)$). The first component is the difference between $\pi_1(x°)$ and $\pi_2(x°)$, a comparison of different profit functions evaluated at the same level of output. This comparison is rather Stigleresque in the sense that entrant and incumbent profits are compared at the same equilibrium output configuration, and it will reveal the existence of any type of barrier which operates as a cost of generating net revenue which the entrant must incur but which the incumbent need not. This type of barrier exists if either $R_1(x°) > R_2(x°)$ or $C_1(x°) < C_2(x°)$, differences arising from *product differentiation* or *absolute cost advantages* respectively. However, the fact that firms must share the market is likely to imply that output per firm post-entry is less than the level produced by the incumbent pre-entry; that is, that $x^* < x°$. Hence, a second source of difference between M_1 and V_2 may be caused by scale advantages, advantages that are revealed by comparing the entrant's profit function evaluated at different levels of output, say by comparing $\pi_2(x°)$ with $\pi_2(x^*)$. If the two differ – say, if $\pi_2(x^*) < \pi_2(x°)$ – then this must be because $R_2(x)/x$ rises or $C_2(x)/x$ falls with x in the range $[x°, x^*]$.[4] This second comparison, then, is rather Bainian, being a comparison of profit outcomes between pre- and post-entry equilibria, and it will reveal the existence of any type of barrier that is scale related.[5]

The factors which generate one or both types of difference between M_1 and V_2 are those which determine the shape of the profit functions. We shall refer to them as structural, meaning that to be barriers to entry they must be exogenous to current price or output decisions. It is now widely recognized that the conditions which create barriers to entry must be unalterable in the immediate post-entry period if they are credibly to deter entry, and this is why one wishes to focus only on those factors which are exogenous to current output decisions. If these structural conditions arise from strategic investments made previously by incumbents, then the costs incurred must be sunk; if they arise innocently or exogenously, then they must not easily be removed in the short or medium run.

More important is the question of whether any entry barrier is wholly structural in the sense that it can be identified independently of the precise type of competitive pricing behaviour which prevails post-entry. The comparison between $\pi_1(x^\circ)$ and $\pi_2(x^\circ)$ is in principle to be made at x°, the incumbent's pre-entry output level. It follows that both product differentiation and absolute cost advantages can be identified independently of the nature of post-entry pricing behaviour. Scale advantages, however, are identified by a comparison between equilibria, and so cannot be identified without knowledge of the nature of the post-entry competition that helps to determine the nature of one of these equilibria. In assessing the difference $\pi_2(x^\circ) - \pi_2(x^*)$, structural factors determine how $\pi_2(x)/x$ varies with x, but the actual difference in output produced pre- and post-entry, $x^* - x^\circ$, depends on pricing conduct (amongst other things). Certain types of post-entry pricing behaviour by incumbents may result in an outcome in which entry is blocked (if x^* is quite a bit less than x° and scale advantages are strong), while others will result in duopoly even when scale economies exist.

Assessing the nature of the response of incumbents to entry when scale advantages are present is only one of the reasons why calculating the height of entry barriers is an inherently conjectural exercise. The second complicating feature of the exercise is that barriers are likely to be entrant specific, and what may be a barrier from the point of view of one entrant may not necessarily be so from the point of view of another. To overcome this type of problem, Bain suggested using a counterfactual construction which pits the most advantaged potential competitor possible against the incumbent. The height of entry barriers faced by this most formidable of opponents was labelled the 'immediate condition of entry' by Bain (1956, pp. 9–11). Clearly, this particular counterfactual may understate the height of the barriers that most entrants will face in practice, but this is not the problem that it seems to be at first sight. If, as seems plausible, the supply of such superior entrants is less than perfectly elastic, then, as entry occurs over time, a larger and larger percentage of the profits realized just prior to the arrival of each entrant will persist in the long run. To reflect this diminution in the competitive challenge of entry, Bain defined the 'general condition of entry' as the 'succession of values of the immediate condition of entry to the industry as entry occurs . . . beginning with the most favoured firm' (p. 9). The important point about this procedure is that it divorces the measurement of barriers from the vagaries of actual entry. There are two reasons why this is desirable. First, entry may not actually occur during the period in which a particular industry is being studied. If there are no entrants observed in a market, then measuring entry barriers by comparing actual entrants to incumbents is impossible. Further, it would be incorrect to claim in this situation that the absence of entry implies that barriers are high and that all observed profits will persist in the long run, if only because entrants may respond to market opportunities with substantial lags. Second, even if entry actually occurs, there is no guarantee that the entrants that one observes are the most advantaged entrants possible.

Thus, even if one observes a certain level of profits to be successfully defended against some actual entrants, that is no guarantee that they will be sustained in the long run after all possible entrants have attempted entry. Using actual entry to infer the existence of barriers to entry is rather hazardous, and seems prone to exaggerating the height of those barriers which do exist. On the other hand, although the use of counterfactual constructions to estimate the height of barriers is, in principle, a more satisfactory way to proceed, they can also lead one to exaggerate the height of barriers. Building a counterfactual requires one to imagine what the best possible manner of entering an industry is, and to calculate how much it will cost to mount such a campaign. Given enough careful study, there seems to be little reason to think that one cannot become as well informed about a market as any putative entrant. The problem is that it is easy to slip into the temptation of presuming that the possibilities open to an entrant are defined by the incumbent's current operations; that is, of thinking that the entrant can do no better than imitating the actions of the incumbent. Since the definition of a product or a production process is at least as elastic as the collective imagination of all currently successful producers, there always exists the possibility that a little creativity can engineer a leap into the (apparently) safest of markets. Indeed, it is in precisely those situations where purely imitative strategies are apparently blocked that entrants must, perforce, be innovative to succeed. It follows that any inclination to measure entry barriers by calculating how successful an entrant will be in replicating the activities of incumbents is likely to exaggerate the barriers to entry which a more innovative entrant will face.

Structural Determinants of Entry Barriers

The difference between M_1 and V_2, the pre-entry profits of the entrant, has, as we have seen, two components, $\pi_1(x^\circ) - \pi_2(x^\circ)$ and $\pi_2(x^\circ) - \pi_2(x^*)$. The first identifies product differentiation or absolute cost advantages that incumbents might enjoy, while the second identifies possible scale advantages on the cost or demand side. Whatever their specific source, barriers to entry exist if $M_1 > 0$ but $V_2 < 0$, in which case M_1 be sustained in perpetuity. Our first task is to identify the specific sources of barriers, the structural factors that cause $R_1(x^\circ) > R_2(x^\circ)$, $C_1(x^\circ) < C_2(x^\circ)$, and $R(x)/x$ rising in x or $C(x)/x$ falling in x. We shall consider each of the three generic categories of barriers in turn.

Product Differentiation Advantages

Advantages to incumbent firms associated with barriers created by product differentiation refer to 'buyers' preferences for one of some variety of very similar substitute products . . . and also to the fact that different buyers have different product allegiances or preference patterns, so that the preferences in question do not result in some universally agreed upon system of grading or rating of the competing products' (Bain, 1956, p. 114). A preference by consumers for an incumbent's products rather than those of a putative entrant is likely to be created by the costs of making consumption decisions. Evidently, to make a choice amongst 'experience goods' (those goods whose intrinsic characteristics cannot be fully discovered merely by inspection prior to purchase and consumption; see Nelson, 1970), consumers must acquire information. However, such expenditures on information are sunk costs from the point of view of consumers, and so investment in learning about one particular brand will weaken a consumer's interest in other brands which arrive on the market later (see Bain, 1956, p. 116; Comanor and Wilson, 1974, chs 3, 4; Schmalensee, 1982). With 'search goods' (whose intrinsic characteristics can be ascertained before purchase) or even with frequently purchased experience goods (for which experimentation to discover intrinsic characteristics is not too costly), it may still be costly for consumers to re-evaluate their consumption programme with the arrival of every new product. The consequence is that late coming entrants may have to incur additional costs of generating revenue in the form of price cuts, massive advertising campaigns and so on to achieve market penetration (on the effect of switching costs on competition, see *inter alia*, Klemperer, 1987a, b, c, and Farrell and Shapiro, 1988). That is, such entrants will need to persuade consumers already settled in their ways to collect information, compare products with different specifications and re-evaluate their purchasing habits. Of course, the original innovating firm which first entered (and so created) the market in question had to persuade consumers to buy the original good in the first place, but the disadvantage that later entrants face is that, by the time they attempt to persuade consumers to switch to their product, consumers have the alternative of a similar brand with which they are already familiar.

These observations on the source of product differentiation advantages suggests that an obvious way to examine whether they exist is to examine the experience of pioneering brands in markets when they are faced by late entry (for a survey on first mover advantages see Lieberman and Montgomery, 1988). Urban et al. (1984) examined 129 frequently purchased consumer brands in 12 US markets, explaining the market share of nth movers relative to the first movers in terms of the order of entry, entry lags, relative advertising and brand positioning. The order of entry turned out to have a strong effect on relative success. At equilibrium, the second brand in the market had a share of less than 75% of the pioneer, the third of about 66%, the fourth of about 50% and so on, all for the same level of advertising and brand positioning (entry lags were not significant). Put another way, if the second brand wanted to achieve the same share as the pioneer, it would have had to have done nearly 3.4 times the volume of advertising as the pioneer, an appreciable increment in the costs of generating revenue. Lambkin (1988) used two cohorts of firms drawn from the PIMS data bank, and discovered noticeable differences between pioneers in markets, early followers and late entrants. Pioneers entered at a larger scale (broader product line, bigger distributive network, more capacity) than their rivals, while later entrants entered on a smaller scale using heavy promotion aimed at intensive exploitation of a particular market segment. Early followers seemed to rely on price to gain competitive advantage. Pioneers enjoyed both a larger market share and persistently higher profits than early followers or late entrants.

Numerous case studies (particularly of the pharmaceutical industry) also suggest that early movers do, in fact, appear able to sustain their market positions against later 'me too' entrants. Grabowski and Vernon (1982), for example, observed that heavy brand promotion in the US pharmaceutical industry tended to protect pioneering firms from entry even long after patents expired (see also Bond and Lean, 1977). A case study of the Canadian drug industry by Gorecki (1986a) found that late entrants succeeded in capturing a decent market share only in regional markets where price competition was enforced and pharmacists were allowed to select lower priced brands. However, this relatively successful market penetration seems to have been won at the cost of having to sell late arriving brands at something of a discount relative to the incumbent pre-entry (and, in fact, often relative to the incumbent post-entry), indicating that a barrier exists (see also McRae and Tapan, 1985). Much the same effects can often be observed when early firms are able to impose their product standards on the market, or can lock-in consumers by their control of necessary complementary goods. One of the many allegations made about IBM's market behaviour is that it has long exploited the 'software lock-in' that arises when customers come to depend on specific computers and computing systems to handle vital calculations (for a popular account, see De Lamarter, 1988).

It is easy, however, to exaggerate the power of first mover advantages, and it is worth considering at least one counter-example to put them into perspective.[6] Drugs are a sector where first mover advantages are often linked to patent protection and/or to the substantial switching costs associated with the investments made by doctors in learning about new drugs (and, perhaps, to their understandable risk aversion). Tagamet was a pioneering anti-ulcer drug launched by SmithKline in 1976 that became the world's best selling drug by 1981, and it was the first drug ever to achieve sales in excess of $7 billion per year. It was supplanted 1987, however, by a drug called Zantac that was launched in 1981 by a small British pharmaceutical firm called Glaxo and sold for a higher price than Tagamet. There are, perhaps, three reasons why Tagamet failed to maintain its lead and capitalize on first mover advantages. First, Tagamet's technological leadership was neutralized and its patent protection was circumvented when Glaxo developed a 'me too' drug based on a simple molecular modification of the original drug that produced similar therapeutic effects from a slightly different chemical structure. Although Zantac was not a major innovation, it did embody a number of minor advantages relative to Tagamet (e.g. it could be taken in lower dosages and had fewer side effects). Second, the market grew by over 200% after Zantac's entry, an expansion that was mostly the result of more doctors being convinced of the benefits of anti-ulcer drugs. That is, market growth took the form of 'new' doctors who faced no switching costs and, in particular, over two-thirds of the consumers that bought the drug (on the recommendation of a doctor) in 1989 had not tried (or been prescribed) either product at the time of Zantac's launch. Third and finally, SmithKline failed to come up with a convincing defensive strategy. Its early success and superiority at the product level led SmithKline to underestimate the competitive strength of Zantac, and its marketing effort was inadequate and poorly targeted. SmithKline used the US market (the world's largest consumer of medicines) to anticipate and fight any possible threat from a competitor. Since Glaxo entered this market last, SmithKline started to fight back too late. The costs of this complacency were increased by Glaxo's use of alliances and simultaneous testing to enter the US and numerous markets very rapidly (Dell'Osso, 1990).

There are several types of structural factors which appear to give rise to product differentiation barriers in a fairly wide range of circumstances.

A naturally limited product space may be pre-empted by incumbents to restrict the demand attainable by entrants for a given outlay whilst, on the other hand, the necessity to produce products with high set-up costs may make small- or moderate-scale entry unprofitable. Either way, product differentiation advantages can combine with scale effects to the detriment of entrants. An example of the former can be seen in the US ready-to-eat breakfast cereal market in which economies of scale are small (3–5% of the market necessary for an optimally sized plant), technology is simple and capital costs are modest. Nevertheless, the various brands of cereal differ from each other in several relevant dimensions (sweetness etc.). Given a wide distribution of consumer preferences over these characteristics, competition is inevitably localized and entrants can be squeezed out if incumbents proliferate brands. Between 1950 and the early 1970s, the number of brands of cereal rose by about a factor of 3, profits remained consistently high and no entry by new firms occurred (Schmalensee, 1978b). Very similar types of crowding effects have been observed in the UK fertilizer industry (e.g. Shaw, 1980, 1982a, b), and cement is a famous example of a market where purely geographic space packing has often kept entrants at bay (e.g. Scherer, 1980, p. 256). Automobile styling costs are a classic example of working a similar strategy from the cost side, inflating fixed marketing and packaging costs to the disadvantage of relatively small-scale producers (e.g. Fisher et al., 1962, or White, 1971).

Another source of asymmetry between entrant and incumbent arises when provision of the good requires a basic interaction between buyers and the seller, such as when pre- or post-sale services are supplied. In these circumstances, retailers can often play a major role in helping to differentiate the product, not least because they are often (at least in non-convenience goods markets) a crucial source of information for consumers (e.g. Porter, 1976a). This may, for example, create substantial problems for entrants in local loan markets where the personal relationship between banker and borrower is crucial to the evaluation and acceptance of risk (e.g. Alhadeft, 1974). Bain (1956, appendix D) calculated that personal sales representation, assistance with technical services and special treatment in the matter of delivery dates created a 'slight' entry barrier in the US steel market, necessitating an expenditure of about 2% relative to price by entrants. In much the same vein, control of retail and wholesale networks can be used to help differentiate a product and, at the same time, restrict access to the market by entrants. This second effect is more akin to an absolute cost advantage than a product differentiation advantage, but the consequence of such a barrier may be to encourage entrants to differentiate their products in order to overcome this obstacle.

The 'Solus' system of long-term contracting between garages and suppliers of retail petrol (e.g. Shaw, 1974), the existence of tied houses blocking entry by new brewers in the UK (e.g. Shaw and Sutton, 1976; MMC, 1989), and leasing arrangements and long-term sales contracts with buyers in the US metal container industry (e.g. Hessian, 1961) are all examples of such barriers. In the USA, Bain found 'moderate' barriers (i.e. a 2.5–5% higher price net of selling costs) for leaders in the replacement market for rubber tyres largely as the result of such control, and entrants into the typewriter market were estimated as needing five to ten years to build up competitive repair and maintenance services. Dealer systems were also important in another industry with 'great' entry barriers, namely automobiles.

Attempts to measure product differentiation barriers often focus on advertising. Comanor and Wilson, arguing that advertising expenditures 'are both a symptom and a source of differentiation' (1967, p. 423), identified absolute cost, economies of scale and capital requirements sources of barriers due to advertising (see also Comanor and Wilson (1974, 1979) and, more generally on advertising, Schmalensee (1972), Ferguson (1974) and Cowling et al. (1975)).[7] The major conceptual problem with thinking of advertising as a barrier to entry is that it is not structural; that is, the choice of advertising is not likely to be independent of output choice (e.g. Dorfman and Steiner, 1954). Rather, it is one of the methods by which incumbents and entrants compete in certain types of markets. The basic determinants of the choice of advertising levels are consumer preferences, consumer informativeness and the technology of information transmission (e.g. Butters, 1976, especially p. 395), and these are clearly the same structural conditions which create product differentiation advantages. Firms choose their advertising levels given the existence of these conditions, and advertising may not be a reliable proxy for them. Thus, there are some markets where advertising will never occur no matter what other product differentiation advantages exist (e.g. producers' goods), and some markets where advertising will be used to compensate for the lack of basic product differentiation advantages. For example, Bain observed that, despite heavy persuasive advertising, entry was not blocked in the US soap industry because brand allegiances were slight; incumbents were not able to maintain price premia and plenty of scope existed for entry into specialty lines. By contrast, cigarettes, another heavy advertising industry, was classified by Bain as having 'great' barriers, with brand allegiances built up over long periods of heavy advertising, forcing entrants to incur advertising costs 'ten to twenty times that of established firms for seven years to get a market position comparable to the largest sellers' (1956, p. 290). Although it is possible that this result reflects product differentiation advantages created by advertising in the cigarette industry, it is hard to see why the same effects on brand loyalty were not present in soap. In fact, the barrier in cigarettes could well be due to scale effects of advertising alone (see below) and, since advertising is clearly not a structural feature of markets that creates differences in the profit functions of entrants and incumbents at all levels of output, one is inclined to think that advertising may be important less as a proxy for underlining product differential advantages than as a source of scale advantages.

The debate about the effects of advertising on entry and, more generally, on the state of competition in markets has been long and, to some extent, difficult to follow. The usual argument is that advertising can be both informative (and so pro-competitive) and persuasive (and so anti-competitive), meaning that its effect on competition is ambiguous. To support this conclusion and counterbalance the type of evidence discussed above, reference is often made to Benham (1972) who studied the pricing of eye glasses in the US using data on 634 individuals who had an eye examination or bought glasses in 1963. He found that the price of eye glasses was lower in those states where opticians were allowed to advertise (the difference was about 20%), despite little apparent variation in costs. He tried to explain the differences in prices paid by the characteristics of the individuals concerned, by other restraints on competition that differed across states and by quality (the types of firms providing eye glasses tended to differ somewhat in states where advertising was allowed). None of these alternatives seemed (to him) to be consistent with the data, leaving one to accept the null hypothesis that advertising was responsible. This conclusion is consistent with the view that advertising provides real information to consumers and improves their choice amongst competing products.[8] The distinction between informative and persuasive advertising, however, is a false one, not least because what is at issue is whether a consumer changes his/her mind or not, an event that can occur no less because he/she becomes persuaded that some alternative to his/her current choice is preferable than because he/she becomes better informed about the product in question. What is true is that advertising can stimulate competition by allowing firms to call attention to their product (a particular boon for new entrants), but advertising is also costly and, in certain circumstances, may create scale advantages that impede entry or intra-market mobility.

To understand the effect that advertising has on competition, it is necessary to consider how consumers make choices between various brands of a product. Although it is by no means a general one, Schmalensee has advanced a particular model of choice that is suggestive in this regard (see Schmalensee, 1978a, and the brief discussion in chapter 3 above). Consider an experience good. For this kind of good, a single purchase is not sufficient to give the consumer complete information about its characteristics, characteristics which, in any case, may often change relatively more frequently than the good is purchased by a typical individual. In these circumstances, there is always some chance that a consumer will switch brands no matter what the characteristics of his/her current choice are. Further, suppose that the price of different brands varies much less than important non-price characteristics of the good. This may occur because competitors tend to favour non-price over price modes of competition, because the product is inherently complex or because buyers are better informed about price than quality. The implication is that buyers will in all probability use something other than price in helping them to decide whether or not to switch to some other rival brand. Suppose that the probability of being satisfied with brand *i* depends on its overall quality. If quality is high, then the probability of a switch to some other brand *j* is low; if quality is low, then a switch is much more likely.

The problem with switching is that the overall qualities of rival brands are not known and the consumer must decide which of them is better than brand *i*. Numerous sources of information are likely to be consulted in making this decision, and at least some of them can be strategically affected by the producers of different brands. In many markets, advertising is bound to play a role, and it is not unreasonable to think that consumers will be induced to switch towards those brands which are heavily advertised. At least two sets of considerations support this view. First, the heavy advertising of such brands may provide useful information or, more simply, it may remind the consumer of the brands' market presence and encourage him/her to seek information on them. Second, it is possible that consumers will take the volume of advertising itself as a signal of brand quality, deciding that the need to establish and maintain a reputation will keep producers and advertisers fairly honest and willing to advertise only when there is some substantive basis (e.g. selling a relatively high quality product) for doing so (e.g. Nelson, 1974; for some further work see Mizuno and Odagiri, 1988, and references cited therein). One way or the other, then, it seems reasonable to believe that the probability of a switch from brand *i* depends on *i*'s quality, and that the probability that brand *j* will be selected instead of *i* depends on the relative volume of advertising by *j*, as measured by its advertising share.

The equilibrium (or, more accurately, stationary state) of this model is surprisingly simple. Brands with high quality and high advertising shares will have large market shares because relatively few consumers switch to consuming other brands (because of the high quality), and those who do switch from other brands are likely to choose highly advertised brands. By contrast, low quality, low advertising share brands will suffer from a high exit and low entry of consumers and will therefore have low market shares. Either way, market shares will be proportional to advertising shares with a factor of proportionality that depends on the relative quality of the brand in question. It is worth stressing that advertising and product quality play quite different roles in affecting consumer choice in this model. In particular, advertising is used to attract dissatisfied users of other brands, but the gain in market share that this gives rise to will only be temporary if product quality is not adequate. A firm with a low quality, highly advertised brand will suffer a high exit rate of dissatisfied consumers which offsets the high inflow of consumers that its advertising attracts, and the firm will therefore have a lower market share than a highly advertised, high quality good. Conversely, a firm offering a high quality product but not advertising heavily will take much longer to attract dissatisfied consumers of other brands than a heavier advertiser, but will keep any given consumer loyal for much longer than a producer of a lower quality product would.

Consider now the situation facing an entrant who wishes to chisel away customers who are loyal to incumbent firms. In the short run, its principal weapon will be advertising used to attract customers dissatisfied with the brands produced by incumbents (to retain the loyalty of these customers, the entrant will, of course, have to keep product quality high). Thus, to achieve a market share sufficiently large to enable the entrant to offset its fixed entry costs, the entrant must advertise sufficiently heavily to capture a certain share of total industry advertising. This is likely to generate an escalation in total industry advertising as incumbents respond in kind, making the acquisition of advertising share by later entrants that much more expensive. It follows that entry is likely to occur in periods when industry advertising is slack, when the quality of incumbent brands can be bettered and when incumbents are thought to be unable or unlikely to respond fully to a post-entry advertising war. The fact that the consequence of entry is likely to be an advertising war which inflates the cost of acquiring market share implies that flows of entry are likely to be short in duration, occurring in bursts or waves. Early entrants, in their scramble for a viable market position, create conditions which make the same scramble for market position that much more expensive for later entrants, and therefore that much less likely to occur. Advertising in this model is pro-competitive in the sense that acquiring a large advertising share attracts a large market share, but anti-competitive in the sense that the costs of following such a strategy are higher the more intensive is the advertising done by incumbent rivals.

To observe the pro- and anti-competitive effects of advertising identified by this model, one needs to observe the competitive process over time. Alemson (1970) examined advertising strategies pursued by entrants in the Australian cigarette industry. Certainly entry had an enormous effect on advertising in this market, which rose by a factor of 23 over the period 1954–67, about ten times faster than sales. Prior to entry (in 1956), advertising was general in nature, but post-entry competition focused advertising on brand promotion, shifting it from press to television advertising in the process. Subsequent entrants (two in 1958 and another in 1964) did much less well than the first entrant in 1956 (market shares by 1967 were 32%, 15.2% 10% and 1%; the incumbents' 96% share in 1954 fell to 40.6% in 1967), and the last entrant exited in 1968. Alemson observed a 'ratchet' effect on industry advertising following new entry and new brand introductions, and a rough and ready association between market shares and relative advertising expenditure. Although it is difficult to be sure without an explicit counterfactual, advertising was clearly a vehicle that facilitated the entry of early moving entrants, but it also appears to have made entry by later moving new firms more difficult and, eventually, impossible.

Geroski and Murfin (1990a) (see also their 1990b and 1987 papers discussed in chapter 3) also observed a relationship between advertising and entry in the UK car industry that was not inconsistent with this model. Incumbents, long used to operating in a cosy protected domestic market, proved to be extremely vulnerable to an entry-induced advertising war in the late 1960s, not least because, prior to entry, they were advertising 'too little'. The market shares of entrants and incumbents alike correlated closely with advertising shares, and the escalating volume of industry advertising (it rose by a factor of 7 post-entry) made entry progressively more difficult for later entrants. Although the evidence is only anecdotal, there is some reason to think that the estimated effectiveness of advertising in gaining market share in the UK car industry was related to dimensions of product quality like reliability. Advertising in this market first facilitated and then inhibited entry, and, at the end of the day, Geroski and Murfin observed high advertising and no entry in the market, a state of affairs often (but in this case quite incorrectly) cited as consistent with the proposition that advertising is anti-competitive. As with the case of Australian cigarettes, the effect of advertising can only be observed by tracking the dynamics of the process of post-entry competition. In both cases, entry induced a major escalation in industry advertising which inflated the costs of acquiring an advertising (and so, it appears, a market) share of any given size, so (one presumes) deterring further entry. The pattern is one in which early entrants 'crowd out' later entrants, and is reminiscent of the kinds of dynamics of entry flows over time that were observed using autoregressive models in chapter 3.

Both the Alemson and the Geroski–Murfin papers suggest that advertising must have something to bite on to have an effect on consumers (new brand introduction and market segmentation in the one case, and product quality in the other). Further, in both studies, it seems to be the case that it is the volume of industry advertising that deters entry (at least for entrants whose product is good enough to compete with those of incumbents) and thus that the behaviour of incumbents matters. Although it is probably over simple, the implication seems to be that advertising has an effect on entry for reasons to do with scale. Anything that forces entrants to spend more to get a given advertising and therefore market share raises its fixed costs per unit of revenue, making entry less likely (and post-entry profitability will be much lower for those who do enter – see the evidence presented by Biggadike, 1976, discussed in chapter 2), particularly when these expenditures are sunk. Furthermore, the effect of advertising on consumer behaviour may be only transitory. Advertising often acts as an attractor, but it may not create a permanent bond between consumer and product. By contrast, factors like product quality that differentiate the products of entrants and incumbents at all levels of output are the basic source of whatever product differentiation advantages incumbents enjoy relative to entrants. These factors are the ones that bring product specifications into line with the demand by consumers for specific product characteristics. Unlike advertising, they can often have a long-run effect on consumer behaviour.

To sum up then, there are a wide variety of structural factors which can give rise to entry barriers based on product differentiation. The evidence gives one little reason to doubt that imitative entrants can be severely handicapped in markets for experience goods, in markets where reputation matters, in markets where competition is localized and/or where fixed design and set-up costs matter, and often (but not always) in markets where advertising is heavy. However, most of the studies cited (at least implicitly) presume that entrants can do no better than match the actions of incumbents and this, as we have argued, is liable to overstate the strength of barriers to entry (for a prescriptive discussion of entry strategies that turns on this point, see Yip, 1982b). Any critical reading of these various case studies leaves one with the strong feeling that this is very much the case with product differentiation barriers. For example, Raleigh's attempt to control the differentiation of its bicycles in the UK market by only supplying specialist retail outlets opened the UK market up to a wave of entry through imports that supplied department stores and discount houses (MMC, 1981). The entry of Rolls Razor into the UK domestic washing machines market in 1958, although not ultimately successful, used a marketing strategy which bypassed traditional retail outlets (Shaw and Sutton, 1976) in much the same way that Laker's entry into the North Atlantic airline market with Skytrain involved a redefinition of both the product and the means used to sell it to consumers. Finally, as long as entrants merely replicated the activities of incumbents in producing brands with slightly different combinations of the same basic characteristics already contained in existing goods, entry proved to be difficult if not impossible in the US ready-to-eat breakfast market. However, when the natural cereals segment of the market began to grow in the early 1970s, entrants were able to introduce new brands successfully in an area of the market that was both poorly covered by incumbents and deep enough to enable them to cover their fixed costs (Schmalensee, 1978b).

That product differentiation barriers are often not proof against an innovative entrants is clearly illustrated in the case of entry into the UK crisps market (e.g. Bevan, 1974). Prior to 1960, Smiths dominated the market with a 65% share, selling a product that was conceived as a consumption activity complementary to beer drinking. Since this was rarely done at home, Smiths crisps were sold mainly in pubs, and Smiths forged powerful links with the major brewers that gave it a lock on these distribution channels. In 1961, Golden Wonder, a small Scottish producer (acquired by Imperial in 1961), chose to launch an ambitious campaign to become a national producer largely on the basis of expanding the market (rather than by stealing sales from Smiths). To this end, it launched a heavy television advertising campaign aimed at persuading consumers that crisps could (and should) be consumed as snacks at home by the whole family (beer and non-beer drinkers alike), coupling this with a strategy of selling through major supermarkets that bypassed Smith's control over distribution through licensed premises (Golden Wonder also improved the quality of its crisp relative to Smiths by using a new continuous frying process). Largely as a consequence of these tactics, a hitherto stagnant market doubled in size between 1960 and 1965, and Golden Wonder was able to enter and acquire a position of market leadership in short order. At least part of Golden Wonder's success (it had the largest market share – 45% – by 1965) can be traced to a lack of response by Smiths (who, not perceiving the expansion in the market, consistently overestimated their market share and underestimated Golden Wonder's market penetration), and in part to the 1960s revolution in UK retailing that made this type of distribution outlet far easier to serve than hitherto. When Smiths finally did respond, it did so by producing new flavours in crips, initiating a 'product quality' war that resulted in a flowering of product variety but did not preclude further entry (at least two major regional producers entered post-1968).

The bottom line, then, is that the definition of a product is only as elastic as the collective imagination of those firms that produce it, and consequently the structure of product differentiation barriers in many markets is far more malleable than it often appears at first sight. Product differentiation barriers are often high for merely imitative entrants, but that is not to say that they are often a major impediment to entry by innovative firms.

Absolute Cost Advantages

Absolute cost advantages to incumbent firms exist 'if the prospective unit costs of production of potential entrant firms are generally, and more or less at any common scale of operations, higher than those of established firms' (Bain, 1956, p. 144). These advantages arise when entrants must use inferior techniques or pay higher prices for factors of production, advantage which, in turn, stem from strategic control of factor markets or production techniques by incumbents, or from other imperfections in factor markets which work to the advantage of incumbents. 'For a given product, potential entrant firms should be able to secure just as low a minimal average cost of production after entry as established firms had prior to this entry. This in turn implies (a) that established firms should have no price or other advantages over entrants in purchasing or securing any productive factor (including investible funds); (b) that the entry of an added firm should have no perceptible effect on the going level of any factor price; and (c) that established firms have no preferred access to productive techniques' (Bain, 1956, p. 12).

Numerous illustrations of absolute cost advantages exist. The strategic control of natural resources by well-placed incumbents seems to have created 'substantial' barriers in the US copper industry, 'moderate' ones in steel (Bain, 1956), 'high' barriers in the US sulphur and nickel industries (Mann, 1966) and non-negligible barriers in both the Mid-Western coal industry (Comanor, 1966) and the UK retail petrol industry (Shaw, 1974). However, although control of material resources can block entry and guarantee incumbents a steady stream of high returns over time, ownership of a scarce resource does not necessarily create an absolute cost advantage. A scarce factor of production has an opportunity cost of use that is a key component of any decision to continue to exploit it or sell up, and, where this opportunity cost is properly imputed, absolute cost disadvantages *may* disappear. If a scarce resource is valued at its opportunity cost but is available to all firms – incumbents and entrants alike – at that price, then no barrier exists no matter how restricted in supply it is. If, however, incumbents are able to obtain it at lower costs than entrants can, then a barrier exists. A natural resource that is valued at its true opportunity cost will also give rise to a barrier if its value is owner specific, that is, if its use is enhanced by combining it with complementary assets that are not available to rivals. In this case, the value of the package – natural resource plus complementary asset – exceeds its market value, and an absolute cost advantage exists. For example, as copper mining companies exploited lower grade ores in larger deposits in the period 1870–1930, US production became increasingly large scale and capital intensive. This, in turn, prompted vertical integration into refining and fabricating, a move that 'owed more to the greater value added that accrues there compared with the earlier stages of production' and ensured that the major US producers enjoyed relatively high profits at least until 1930 (Schmitz, 1986, p. 406). Whether it be control over scarce resources (never complete and eroded after 1930 by the emergence of African copper), the rise of vertical integration to deny non-integrated entrants access to refining or fabricating, or just the vastly increased capital costs that an entrant would need to mine larger but lower grade ore deposits, the result seems to have been a notable escalation in entry barriers.

Asymmetries between new and well-established firms are often created when incumbents exploit superior technology, particularly when it is protected by patents. Direct calculations suggest this to have been the case in the US gypsum industry (Bain, 1956) and the US ethical drugs industry (Mann, 1966). Somewhat indirectly, in the UK polyester fibres industry (Shaw and Shaw, 1977), the UK metal boxes industry (Prais, 1981, ch. 8; Shaw and Simpson, 1985) and the US plain paper copiers market (Bresnahan, 1985), the expiry of patent protection generated a flood of entry which, presumably, had previously been blocked. Of course, the fact that incumbents control access to a particular technology does not necessarily mean that entrants will suffer an absolute cost disadvantage. The obvious reply to barriers generated by patents is for entrants to develop new technologies to compensate for their lack of access to existing ones. The advent of small, on the premises, cleaning shops in the UK dry cleaning industry, for example, followed from basic changes in the technology of dry cleaning that otherwise well-entrenched incumbents were slow to adopt (Shaw, 1973). More generally, the extent to which patents protect incumbents depends on how difficult imitation is. Mansfield et al. (1981) examined 48 product innovations and discovered the ratio of imitation to innovation cost to be about two-thirds, similar to the ratio between imitation and innovation times. Patents did not appear to present imposing obstacles to imitators – 60% of the successful patented innovations in their samples were imitated in four years – although patents did raise imitation costs by about 11% on average. Patents in drugs seemed to afford the most protection to innovators (imitation costs were raised by about 30%) Levin et al. (1987) used a large-scale questionnaire survey to generate information on the appropriability of returns to R&D and patents. Aside from uncovering evidence that corroborates Mansfield et al., they found major innovations to be more costly to duplicate than others, no appreciable difference in imitation costs between product and process innovations, and no lead time or learning curve effects on imitation costs or time.

Patents or other factors which delay the arrival of entrants can often give incumbent firms time to develop other types of cost advantage. Interesting in this respect are cost advantages associated with learning and experience in producing products. Freeman (1963) observed that even relatively efficient entrants required 15–30 years to challenge patent-protected market leaders in the plastics industry, and similar advantages have also been observed to accrue to technological leaders in the semiconductor industry (Spital, 1983; Flaherty, 1983) and the synthetic fibres industry (Shaw and Shaw, 1984). Learning by doing in production is often alleged to bring substantial advantages to early movers. In semiconductors, for example, accumulated production experience can improve yields considerably, and the average cost of producing a semiconductor can fall by 20–30% every time its cumulative production doubles. Many of these learning advantages come from deliberately managed efforts to improve production processes, and often require considerable R&D expenditures to realize. However, the intense proliferation of new products in this sector has meant that (until recently perhaps) the exploitation of learning advantages has not been a serious impediment to entry; most firms, new and established, have concentrated on developing new product lines rather than intensively investing in producing existing products more efficiently (e.g. Tilton, 1971, pp. 85–7; Levin, 1982, p. 20). Lieberman (1984) discovered that pervasive learning effects in the chemicals processing industry were associated with cumulative output and investment (but not calendar time), that such learning was augmented by R&D expenditures and that the effects of learning on costs and thus on prices far exceeded those attributable to scale economies. However, subsequent work on entry suggested that cost advantages based on cumulative production did not block entry (it did, however, contribute to a reduction in the survivability of entrants), largely because incumbents could not limit access to technology (Lieberman, 1988a). Clearly, learning brings advantages only when it can be fully appropriated by incumbents, and entrants who do suffer some cost disadvantages due to learning can often compensate by careful product positioning. Aircraft design and production, for example, is widely thought to involve substantial learning, yet Airbus Industry effected a rapid entry (capturing nearly 50% of the wide-bodied aircraft market within a decade) at least partly because it located in the important and hitherto empty market niche for wide-bodied medium to short haul aircraft, and partly because it produced a plane with noticeably lower maintenance costs than its rivals (e.g. Majumdar, 1988).

Control over the infrastructure supporting production and sales can create absolute cost advantages for incumbents (as we saw earlier in connection with control over retail outlets), advantages that often have effects like scale economies because they involve investments which substantially raise fixed costs. Express coaching, for example, was deregulated in the UK in 1980, stimulating entry in most major intercity routes. However, most of the hopeful entrants into the market have subsequently exited and National Express, one of the two original public sector companies, retains a dominant position in most of the routes that it initially monopolized. Although several factors are at work, one is that National controls the coaching terminals in many of the larger cities and has refused access to rivals (Davis, 1984). This continued dominance of incumbents has been a feature of many deregulated markets in the UK, often for reasons similar to that in coaches (for a brief summary, see D. Thompson, 1987). Among a number of advantages that the newly privatized British Gas holds relative to entrants is its control of the pipeline network to which any entrant must gain access. It also enjoys statutory protection against entry into the domestic market (the largest and most profitable segment) and favourable unit gas costs (Vickers and Yarrow, 1988, p. 258–9). The ability of incumbents to control the infrastructure of their markets often varies over the industry life cycle. The expansion of the frozen foods industry in the UK post-Second World War, for example, was limited by the need to develop a distribution network capable of handling frozen foods, an infrastructure that included the need to build refrigerated transport, cold storage capacity and refrigerated display cabinets. Birds Eye managed to seize control over the distribution network and, as a consequence, to dominate the market for more than a decade until its position was undermined by the growth of specialist distributors and large supermarket chains (Geroski and Vlassopoulos (1989) and, for an account of how Birds Eye used its control over distribution to raise prices without attracting entry, see chapter 4).

Bain and many subsequent scholars have harboured deep suspicions that a major source of absolute cost advantages might lie in the need to finance entry attempts.[9] Entry is a risky enterprise, and a failed entry attempt is likely to yield very little in the way of salvageable assets. In the UK financial leasing industry, this was identified as a major source of entry difficulties and led to entry attempts mainly by well-established diversifying financial institutions (Morgan et al., 1980). The main difficulty in evaluating the height of this type of entry barrier arises from the fact that assessing the future requires imagination, and often turns on intuitive hunches which are difficult to defend rigorously. Risks that seem daunting to one individual (say, a banker) may, quite reasonably, be thought to be relatively minor by another (say, an enthusiastic young entrepreneur); what appear to be substantial capital-raising barriers may be transformed by new pieces of information, or shifts in 'animal spirits' (see also Martin, 1989). The US computer industry presents a particularly clear example of this. In its early days, new firms generally found little difficulty in raising small or moderate amounts of capital because of investor enthusiasm. For example, a firm call Viatron managed to achieve a stock market value of $217 million in 1969 before it made any deliveries (it closed two years later). However, by the early 1970s, a general credit squeeze and IBM's apparently aggressive market behaviour turned capital costs into a 'significant' barrier to entry in the peripherals market (Brock, 1975). Similarly, the early enthusiasm and then sudden collapse of venture capital markets had a major effect on entry rates into the US semiconductor industry (Levin, 1982). One should be careful, however, of attributing too much to examples like these. Scott (1981) focused on post-entry capital costs arising, *inter alia*, from systematic risk and argued that they are smaller in more highly concentrated markets, *ceteris paribus*. The theory here is that competitive firms, being price takers, have less control over their environment than firms with market power who can alter market conditions (somewhat) to reduce risk. Since markets typically concentrate as they mature, Scott's empirical result that a 10% rise in concentration may cause a 1% fall in capital costs is inconsistent, however, with the computer and semiconductor industry examples that were just cited (although there may be an offsetting increase in capital costs for entrants associated with the fact that they are new and untried, an increase that, in the cases of computers and semiconductors, overwhelms the Scott effect). Note, however, that since entry affects the degree of competition in a market, Scott's results suggest that early entrants can affect the entry conditions facing later ones (as we saw earlier in the case of advertising).

The effect of excess capacity in deterring entry turns on a kind of absolute cost barrier that arises from the fact that the incumbent has sunk investments in plant and equipment while the entrant has not, as yet, done so. As we noted in chapter 4, if output costs v per unit to produce and capacity α per unit to install, then an incumbent who has sunk an investment in capacity of $\bar{k}$ can effectively produce output up to that limit at a cost of v per unit; by contrast, output effectively costs $v + \alpha$ for an entrant (if one unit of capacity is needed to produce each unit of output). Work by Hilke (1984), Lieberman (1987) and Masson and Shaanan (1986) on rather different samples provides (at best) rather weak support for the hypothesis that excess capacity blocks entry. Possibly more important, start-up costs can have very similar effects on entrants' cost functions, creating a scale advantage if they are fixed or an absolute cost advantage if they depend on the scale of entry. Beesley, for example, estimated these costs to be about a third of the £1.2 million that London Express Aviation needed to enter the airline market for tourist flights between London and Singapore in 1983 (Beesley, 1986).

Absolute cost advantages can also be created by various devices that raise rivals costs by more than they raise the costs of incumbents. Computer reservation systems are now the predominant method by which most travel agents book airline flights. These are owned by the airlines (by and large) and have been (it has been alleged) offered to travel agents at or below cost. For example, United Airlines is alleged to have offered a travel agent $500,000 cash, five years' free use of its system and other goodies as an incentive to install its reservations system. Although this raises the costs of the airline proprietors of these systems, the compensating gain (raising rivals' costs) comes because the system can be used to shift bookings towards certain flights. Not all possible flights or routings can be listed first (or on the first page) on the computer display, and booking agents have a tendency to choose flights listed on the first line or first page of the flight listings. American airlines apparently found that 92% of ticket sales are taken from the first screen page of displayed flights, and 53% from the first line (i.e. flight) displayed. It is a simple matter for proprietors of these systems to list their own flights first, and this can put rivals at a considerable disadvantage since they can end up flying with empty seats or having to make extra efforts (*ceteris paribus*) to fill them (Fisher, 1987b).

Finally, there is no doubt that legal restrictions and various types of government policies can create absolute cost advantages for incumbent firms. Changes in cigarette taxes induced by EEC tax harmonization and the slow speed with which market leaders reacted to them made entry possible in the UK king-sized cigarette market (Prais, 1981, ch. 9; and more generally on barriers to trade in Europe, EEC, 1988). The banking industry has also afforded several examples of entry blocked or induced by legal regulations (e.g. Peltzman, 1965; Spiller and Favaro, 1984; Gelfand and Spiller, 1987). Legal restrictions which act as a barrier to entry are particularly easy to observe in the case of imports, which can be seriously impeded by tariffs an non-tariff barriers to trade. Geroski and Murfin (1990b) observed that entry by foreign producers into the UK car market in the late 1960s followed a fall in effective tariff rates from about 0.30 in 1958 to 0.05 in 1983, and many other similar examples exist. Since the Second World War, successive General Agreement on Tariffs and Trade (GATT) treaties have lowered tariff barriers and protectionism has shifted towards use of non-tariff barriers such as subsidies and voluntary export restrictions. Intervention appears to be most common in industries such as textiles, clothing, footwear, steel, autos and shipbuilding (OECD, 1985). Subsidies are notoriously difficult to observe, of course, but most industrial policy support (at least in Europe) is general and non-discretionary, or is functional and directed at exports, R&D, employment or location decisions (e.g. Carlsson, 1983). Procurement policies by national governments, by contrast, are often directed at advanced sectors such as telecommunications and aerospace and are deliberately used to protect 'national champions'. This said, governments can also encourage entry through subsidies. Airbus Industries is often cited as an example of an entrant whose success in the wide-bodied aircraft market depended on massive support by the governments who backed it (amongst other things), although it seems likely that its US rivals did not suffer from a lack of official assistance (Majumdar, 1988). Possibly more clear cut is the $50 million assistance provided by local, state and US federal government when Volkswagen decided to set up assembly operations in the USA (wage concessions of about $40 million were also wrung from the United Automobile Workers; see Baldwin, 1986). Of course, not all officially backed entrants succeed, as John De Lorean's $100 million venture in Northern Ireland illustrates.

As in this case of product differentiation advantages, what emerges from these cases is an impression that there is a rather wide range of factors which can create absolute cost advantages for incumbents. In the case of product differentiation advantages, the malleability of consumer tastes gives one the sense that it is possible to exaggerate the height of barriers, and innovative entrants often seem to be able to succeed where imitative aspirants have failed. Much the same observation applies to absolute cost barriers, although in this case it is often changes in technology or in the structure of vertically related markets that undermine the cost advantages enjoyed by incumbents. For example, the kinds of advantages that Birds Eye's strategy of vertical integration into distribution gave it were undermined by a range of changes in the UK frozen food market in the mid-1960s, a set of changes that were largely exogenous to Birds Eye's actions. The abolition of resale price maintenance and a growth in market demand stimulated changes in the structure of retailing that, in turn, chipped away at the barriers to entry protecting Birds Eye. The size of the market tripled in the decade prior to 1972, with growth over the period 1956-81 averaging 15% per annum. Although the number of retailers stocking frozen foods fell over the period 1966-74, this period saw the rise of large supermarkets chains (by 1980, there were 7000 supermarkets in the UK, an increase of 40 times in 21 years). These chains had their own distribution systems and used them to promote entry (mainly but not exclusively through own brand labels). Further, new types of distribution companies emerged (such as cold storage companies) to serve parts of the newly expanded market. The consequence of the marketing muscle of the new chains plus the increasing vertical disintegration in distribution was a wave of entry that seriously eroded Birds Eye's position. Falling sales and profitability were the outcome. Birds Eye's market share fell from 60% in 1972 to 32% in the late 1970s, and then to 18% in the early 1980s, and it recorded a post-tax loss in 1977, barely breaking even in 1979 (Geroski and Vlassopoulos, 1989).

The bottom line, then, is that numerous sources of absolute cost advantages exist, but that none is completely proof against the occasional clever entrant operating in a favourable market environment. Although it is entirely impressionistic, a reading of the evidence can (but does not necessarily have to) leave one with the general impression that tastes vary a good deal more over time than technology, and thus that absolute cost advantages may (outside of high growth, new technology sectors) sustain market positions far longer than product differentiation advantages. That said, it also seems fairly evident that many absolute barriers are created (or at least strengthened) by the strategic actions of incumbents. One concludes, then, that while they may often be relatively permanent, the existence and height of absolute cost advantages are not always (or often) exogenous to the competitive process.

Economies of Scale

Economies of scale create problems for entrants through a 'percentage' effect and through an 'absolute capital requirements' effect (Bain, 1956, p. 55). The former depends on the size of the minimum efficient scale plant relative to the market. If an entrant attempts to enter at efficient scale when the latter is a sizeable fraction of industry size, then its addition to industry output will undoubtedly reduce price (to an extent which depends, of course, on the specific details of post-entry pricing behaviour). If, on the other hand, it enters at less than efficient scale, it will face a cost penalty whose severity depends on the slope of the cost curve at less than efficient production levels. Thus, either way, it is at a disadvantage and, if this disadvantage is large and is astutely exploited by incumbents, it may find entry into an otherwise profitable market impossible. The absolute capital requirements effect arises from difficulties in financing what may be rather large investment outlays to build an efficiently sized plant. If these outlays are very large and capital markets are imperfect, then entrants may suffer an absolute cost disadvantage *vis-à-vis* incumbents. The fact that the barrier created by the percentage effect depends on pricing behaviour means that there is no unique mapping from the size of minimum efficient scale to the height of barriers created by scale economies. Nevertheless, it is useful to have a kind of benchmark estimate of one or more of the critical points in this mapping, and it seems reasonable to imagine that any industry in which at least 10% of the market must be captured to ensure efficient production is one where at least some (if not much) difficulty will be experienced by an entrant.[10]

To calculate the size of a minimum efficient plant requires a counterfactual construction showing the cost per unit that could be achieved by an entrant using the best practice technology at current factor prices and how large the cost penalties associated with producing at suboptimal scale are. Although extremely expensive, these estimates (called 'engineering estimates') have been made for a number of industries. The results of most studies are that, except in rather small economies closed to international trade, minimum efficient scale tends to be a rather modest fraction of market size, and is often considerably below 10% (for a thorough discussion and extensive references, see Scherer, 1980, pp. 81–118). These engineering estimates probably overstate the size of minimum efficient scale by concentrating on what is technically possible, and neglecting problems associated with managing large plants. The facts is that large plants are difficult to manage, not least because they are noticeably more strike prone than smaller establishments. Further, the industries for which engineering estimates have been calculated were (as a rule) selected for study because they were thought likely to exhibit extensive scale economies, a sample selection bias which suggests that this type of evidence may, if anything, generate an upward bias in the impression we have of the height of scale-induced barriers across the whole population of manufacturing industries. One concludes from the relatively small number of engineering estimates that are available, then, that economies of scale are unlikely to be a substantial barrier in many – if not most – sectors (see also Schmalensee, 1981, whose argument is rather more subtle than the 10% critical point used here).

Of course, the number of industries which have been studied in this manner is fairly limited, and it would be useful to have a somewhat less expensive method of making such estimates. The problem here is that 'the best possible' is not directly observable, and must be inferred from the actual plant sizes that one observes. Virtually every alternative method of estimating minimum efficient scale requires one to assume that some or all existing incumbents are as efficient as it is humanly possible to be. Statistical cost function estimates and cost or production function estimates utilize data on all firms in the market, assuming each to be on the cost curve, cost function or production function estimated (Johnston, 1960; Fuss and Gupta, 1981; and others). However, the practice of inferring best practice costs from actual costs observed at differently sized plants is not likely to be very reliable without a critical awareness of how the data are generated. Thus, a small establishment that reports high costs might be taken as evidence that scale economies exist, it might signal the existence of a managerial team too inefficient to minimize costs and gain market share, or it might identify a small niche producer of, say, a customized product. There are, in short, many reasons why plants may be small and apparently cost inefficient, and not all of these are related to scale economies.

Rather less draconian are methods which produce estimates by assuming that 'the largest plants in the market are likely to be at least as large as is required for maximum efficiency' (Bain, 1956, p. 69). The idea here is that multi-plant firms which serve a large market often have the option of building as large a plant as is necessary at a particular location, unconstrained by insufficient demand. Smaller firms, by contrast, may not be willing to risk building one optimally sized plant if it is likely to be run well below capacity levels. This type of assumption has been used to generate a wide range of estimates of minimum efficient scale, such as the average plant size, median plant size, the average size of the largest plants (those responsible for 50% of industry output) and so on (for a number of the more popular proxies generated in this fashion, see Bain, 1956; Pashigan, 1968; Sawyer, 1971; Weiss, 1963; Comanor and Wilson, 1967; amongst others). In an interesting variant of this approach, Lyons (1980) argues that firms producing at the true minimum efficient scale will be equally likely to operate one or two plants, thus identifying minimum efficient scale as the actual size of those plants which, on average, operate 1.5 plants.

It is difficult to accept purely *a priori* arguments which purport to identify that subset of firms in an industry which are efficient, and one's disbelief is strengthened by even a cursory inspection of the actual distribution of plant sizes in markets. In general, the most striking feature of that distribution is its extremely high variance and enormous range. Most markets are composed of a few large firms producing in one or more establishments, a range of single-plant enterprises of medium size, and an enormous number of small firms. This observation makes it seem unlikely that anything like a single minimum efficient scale exists or, if it does, that cost curves are anything other than rather flat on either side of the efficient point. Still, if such an efficient plant size exists, it is possible that the application of 'survival of the fittest' arguments will be more useful than the purely *a priori* guesses discussed above. Following Stigler (1958) it is natural to identify 'efficiency' with the ability to survive and prosper, and the most common method used to generate estimates of efficient size is that proposed by Stigler: 'if the share of a given (size) class falls, it is relatively inefficient, and in general is more inefficient the more rapidly share falls' (p. 73). In practice, such 'survivor' estimates of minimum efficient scale are not very stable over time, and they are rather sensitive to market definitions (Saving, 1961; Weiss, 1964; Rees, 1973; Shepherd, 1967; and others). The most serious problem with this technique, however, is the vagueness with which the notion of 'survivability' is defined: is a 1% market share decline indicative of a non-optimally sized plant or firm, is it just random noise, or is it the result of measurement error? In fact, the survivor technique often generates several different estimates of minimum efficient scale for the same market, implying that plants of widely different size are able to prosper side by side. This at least is consistent with the conclusion that scale advantages are unlikely to inhibit entry in general.

The general impression that one gets, then, is that the advantages of scale in production are often rather modest. This conclusion is consistent with productivity studies that fail to find plant size to be an important factor in explaining productivity differentials across countries (e.g. Prais, 1981). In the UK, for example, productivity performance appears to be rather poor in those sectors where plants are particularly large, mainly because of the poor productivity performance of the large plants in those sectors (e.g. Caves and Davies, 1987, p. 68). There are, no doubt, several reasons for the unimpressive productivity performance of many large plants, but one is that they are often not very efficient in situations that demand the production of a range of differentiated products whose specifications often change. In the European washing machines industry, for example, engineering estimates place minimum efficient scale at about 1,000,000 units per year, but productivity is highest in plants sized 200,000–300,000 units per year. The answer to this apparent puzzle arises from the fact that small plants specialize in one or two models, while large plants produce a variety of slightly different models (typically, top loaders or front loaders with various drum sizes or spin speeds) in rather short production runs that require regular expenditures on set-up costs (Baden-Fuller and Stopford, 1987). Economies of scale exist in this sector, but there is no apparent competitive advantage to be gained from exploiting them.

More generally, in many markets where products are differentiated, entrants may overcome the disadvantages of scale economies either by specializing in specific, often custom-made, products or by adopting more flexible production techniques. Essentially, this second choice involves choosing a cost curve that is 'flatter' than that of incumbents (even if it is higher), trading off the ability to produce very efficiently at only one specific output level against the ability to do fairly well across a range of outputs (e.g. see Carlsson, 1989a, on the notion of flexibility in production). Both specialization and flexibility may, perhaps, sacrifice some scale advantages, but, thought of as an element of a product differentiation strategy, they can give entrants a competitive advantage over incumbents that rely on mass production methods to produce a standardized good. In machine tools, for example, the development of numerical control has undermined the use of mass production methods, making small-scale, almost handicraft methods of production viable and perhaps, in some cases, optimal. Although there are still clear advantages to making long productive runs, the ability to produce a range of products in short runs seems to be an increasingly important determinant of commercial viability (Carlsson, 1989b). To take a second example, in the UK clothing sector, UK firms tend to manufacture relatively standard products in long runs, while German firms produce a great variety of high quality goods in small batches and enjoy a level of output per employee at least twice that typically realized in the UK (Steedman and Wagner, 1989). The moral, then, is that scale economies in production may matter (in principle) only where entrants and incumbents strive to secure a great number of homogenenous consumers wishing to purchase a single standardized good.

Scale advantages can also arise on the demand side, from advantages which large firms enjoy in generating revenue (e.g. Spence, 1980). By far the most interesting possibility in this respect arises in connection with advertising, and the debate on this particular subject is extensive (see Comanor and Wilson, 1979, pp. 467–70, for an overview). Economies of scale may arise from thresholds in the effect of advertising, from variations in rate structures with respect to size of advertising budget and from variations in the effectiveness of different media (e.g. television versus the rest) whose use requires expenditure of different orders of magnitude. Evidence from both beer (Peles, 1971) and cigarettes (Brown, 1978) lends support to the notion that such economies exist. In cigarettes, for example, Brown calculated that a new entrant might be required to achieve an advertising–sales ratio 48% higher than incumbent firms to compete on a par (p. 437), particularly for newer brands. Two cases do not prove a rule, but one's feeling that scale advantages lie behind the effectiveness of advertising is much strengthened by studies which show that television advertising is much more effective at generating profits than other types of advertising (Porter, 1976b, and others), since access to this medium is effectively only open to very heavy advertisers.

Advertising is not the only factor that may give rise to scale advantages in generating revenue. Just as large lumpy investments in infrastructure may enable a firm to produce far more efficiently, so investments in the provision of complementary goods or in constructing a network of users may make a product more attractive to consumers. Large fixed expenditures of this type that are made by a particular incumbent firm may, in effect, produce a bundle of characteristics that consumers find sufficiently attractive to justify purchasing that firm's product at rather higher prices than those charged by rivals. Video cassettes, for example, require both satisfactory machines and large, easily accessible libraries of tapes to be attractive, and any video cassette producer able to ensure provision of both has an enormous advantage over rivals (Grindley and McBryde, 1989a). The existence of 'network externalities' (see Katz and Shapiro, 1985, and others) means that returns revenue per unit realizable by a producer almost certainly rises with the number of units of the product sold, and this will give large-scale producers a scale advantage over entrants. Product standardization is also a marketing strategy that can involve substantial fixed costs but, at the same time, confer substantial advantages on the firm that selects the standard. Taken together, the two effects can lead to sharply increasing revenues per unit of output sold. The erection of a standard is likely to have adverse effects on entrants, essentially because it reduces the possibility of using niche strategies and forces them to compete on a cost basis with incumbents. Octane grading of petrol in the UK, for example, seems to have reduced both the overall number of retail petrol stations in the UK and the number of independently owned ones (Grant, 1986). Standards that are 'open' (as opposed to 'proprietary' standards that restrict adoption), however, may facilitate the emergence of numerous new competitors – as IBM discovered to its cost in the personal computer market (Grindley and McBryde, 1989b). Whether choosing an 'open' standard is worth it or not from the point of view of the incumbent depends, *inter alia*, on whether the quick expansion and development of the market that it brings can be exploited before entrants eliminate the profits from doing so.

The evidence on scale advantages, then, is somewhat unbalanced. There is a lot of evidence (some of which is not wholly satisfactory) that economies of scale in production do not, in general, matter much from the point of view of entry. There seem to be very few instances where entrants need to mass produce a standardized good in order to effect entry successfully – competitive advantage is as likely to be realized by carefully differentiating products or adopting flexible productive strategies as it is by building long assembly lines. It does seem to be the case, however, that scale advantages originating on the demand side may often matter. Here the evidence is rather weaker, and consists of rather cursory evidence on the effects of advertising, complemented by a few examples of markets with network externalities or product standards. These cases complement the broader survey evidence of Biggadike discussed earlier (chapter 2) which suggests that fixed costs associated with advertising and R&D are primarily responsible for the low profits of many entrants, even those who appear to be particularly advantaged. What seems to be clear, then, is that there is little reason to think that small-scale entry is not, in general, a viable entry strategy, even if the strategies that sustain entry at small scales do not always give much promise of subsequent market expansion. Although it is not wholly clear why they would usually want to do this, entrants that wish to challenge market leaders on their own terms may face problems associated with scale, problems that are as likely to be marketing related as not.

Measuring the Height of Barriers to Entry

Having isolated the various factors which give rise to entry barriers, the next step is to measure the height of barriers to entry overall. The natural units in which to measure them is in terms of profitability (and price–cost margins in particular), and the basic methodology involves attempting to estimate the level of profits which would be observed at a long-run equilibrium. There are two considerations which suggest that this exercise is not quite as simple as summing up the heights of barriers to entry created by product differentiation advantages, absolute cost advantages and scale economies. First, it is often difficult to express the height of barriers created by particular structural factors in terms that make them easy to compare, much less to sum. For example, the effect on entrants of a minimum efficient plant size of 10% of the market is difficult to compare with the effect that strategic control by incumbents of a natural resource will have on entrants. Of course, a comparison is possible if both can be expressed as a percentage elevation of prices sustainable in perpetuity, but, as we have seen, there are very few estimates of individual barriers which have been expressed in these terms. Second, and more importantly, one cannot simply sum up barriers of specific types into an overall condition of entry because many barriers derive their strength by interacting with other barriers. For example, modest scale economies can completely rule out entry in geographically segmented markets but, in densely packed product spaces or in homogeneous good national markets, the same degree of scale economies will have little or no effect on entry (e.g. Eaton and Lipsey, 1978; see also Williamson, 1963). Many of the specific examples of entry barriers listed above involved a mix of scale and absolute cost or product differentiation advantages, and their effects on entrants were scale related in certain circumstances but took the form of absolute cost advantages in other circumstances. There is, in short, some risk that starting from the particular and summing up to the general will understate the true height of barriers overall, not least because the substitution between barriers, from the point of view of a most advantaged entrant, is unlikely to be infinite.

It follows that while one might make some progress by first isolating specific barriers and then amalgamating them into an index of barriers overall, a more natural procedure might start from the outset by modelling long-run profitability directly in terms of observables such as observed profitability or observed entry. These two alternative paths correspond to the basic methods that have been used in practice to measure the height of barriers to entry. The first, pioneered by Bain, utilizes the subjective judgement of the researcher to weight the various individual barriers and to trace their interactions. The alternative involves constructing an econometric model which enables one to estimate the size of excess profits in the long run, and to test whether it differs significantly from zero. Naturally, there can be as many different types of econometric model as one cares to imagine, but we shall concentrate on the two simple types of model that have been used most often in the literature, equations modelling profits and those modelling entry (such as those discussed in chapters 3 and 4). The Bainian technique relies on counterfactual comparisons with the hypothetical 'most advantaged entrant' while the econometric approach, which relies on information about actual entry flows, implicitly uses actual entrants as the basis of its counterfactual comparison. Thus, we expect that both types of estimates of barriers may be biased upwards somewhat, although possibly to different degrees and for quite different reasons.

The method used by Bain (1956; see also Mann, 1966) starts with a thorough investigation of the sources of specific types of barriers, and then relies heavily on the judgement and experience of the researcher to convert a ranking of industries by each specific type of barrier into an overall scale. To make this conversion, one must, in effect, form a view about the likely consequences of an attempt at entry by a most advantaged entrant handicapped by the full range of specific barriers, solving for the levels of prices or profits sustainable in the long run. Given the fairly imprecise nature of this exercise, it is natural to work with a discontinuous overall scale which ranks industries by the height of barriers overall. Bain, for example, considered barriers to be 'high' if they enabled incumbents to raise prices persistently above costs by about 10%; 'substantial' and 'moderate to low' barriers would support prices 7% and not more than 4% above costs respectively (1956, p. 170).

Bain's method seems particularly attractive when very different types of specific barriers are being assesed, or when specific barriers interact in important ways. Indeed, his estimates of the height of barriers overall often seem to be more accurate than the impression one would get either by summing specific barriers or, even more simply, by just counting their number. Thus, for example, automobiles were judged by Bain to have high scale economies, high product differentiation barriers, high capital requirements and low absolute cost barriers. Virtually everyone would agree from this that barriers are 'high' in this sector. However, Bain judged the level of barriers in the cigarette market to be 'high' as well, despite the fact that the only structural factors impeding entry were high product differentiation barriers and capital-raising requirements. Similarly, barriers were judged to be 'high' in the fountain pens market despite the fact that the only source of barriers was product differentiation. By contrast, the steel sector was observed to have high absolute costs and capital requirements barriers, medium scale economies, and low product differentiation barriers and yet, overall, barriers were judge to be 'substantial'. 'Substantial' barriers were also judged to exist in shoes, where only medium levels of scale economies and, perhaps, product differentiation advantages existed.

A major drawback of this methodology is the absence of any measure of the uncertainty attached to the estimates generated. Needless to say, Bain recognized the many possible sources of error in his estimates, and for this reason presented only ordinal rankings of industries. However, compressing what are, in principle, cardinal rankings into ordinal ones simply because of uncertainty over their estimation is a crude way to make allowance for estimation errors, and it sacrifices much useful information. Bain, for example, lumped together industries which could sustain prices of both 10% and, say, 17% above costs in the same 'high' barriers class, although long-run profits of 17% are of far more concern than those of 10%. Further, one might reasonably ask whether those industries with 'moderate to low' barriers actually do earn excess profits significantly different from competitive levels (as might be the case if an estimate of 4% were subject to much error). It is therefore not unreasonable to think

194   *The Empirical Analysis of Barriers to Entry*

that a method which produces cardinal rankings with precise estimates of their uncertainty might also be useful. This is, of course, one of the two big comparative advantages of using an econometric model (the other being its potential ability to make judgements applicable to a very wide range of industries) This said, it should also be added that this gain comes at the very real cost of sacrificing the ability to measure specific sources of barriers with accuracy and trace their interactions. In practice, this gain has only been realized using extremely simple models of the determinants of long-run profitability.

If barriers to entry are high, then incumbent firms in an industry are likely to earn persistently high profits. It follows that one ought to be able to detect the presence of barriers from the observation of persistently high profits, and to measure their height from estimates of the level of profitability achieved in the long run.[11] However, long-run profit levels are not directly observable. To make inferences about profits in the long run from observed profits one needs to establish some kind of link between the two (such as those discussed in chapter 4). It is a common presumption of many scholars that cross-section data enable one to test assertions about the properties of long-run equilibria directly, that observables in cross-section regressions somehow differ from their long-run values by purely random amounts. If this is indeed the case, then one can take observed profits (or, more prudently, observed profits averaged over, say, a five-year period) to be a direct if noisy signal of long-run profitability. If, however, observed data are contaminated by systematic disequilibrium dynamics, then this type of procedure is invalid and may lead to bias. Instead, one has to model the dynamics inherent in the observed data and solve for long-run profits using the estimated parameters of that model. As we saw in chapter 4, there are some systematic – if fairly modest – disequilibrium dynamics in profits data associated with observed entry flows and other unobserved factors (such as potential entry). While profits never seem to be far from their long-run levels, it would probably be a little imprudent to assume that observed profits were necessarily accurate and unbiased estimates of long-run profits. It is therefore worth devoting some effort to developing models for use in generating estimates of long-run profits in different sectors.[12]

Observed profits will yield useful information on long-run profits only if entry occurs quickly when profits are high and quickly reduces them back to normal levels. With such a quick and efficient error correction mechanism in operation, profits that do deviate from their long-run levels π^* will only do so far an instant. It follows that fluctuations in observed profits π_t will occur randomly around π^*, and will not exhibit any systematic short-run dynamic movements. Suppose that profits in the long run are constant over time and are determined by the height of some barrier X which varies across industries. Say,

$$\pi^* = \beta_0 + \beta_1 X. \qquad (5.1)$$

Then, if the random fluctuations of π_t around π^* are truly independent of X, it follows that a cross-section regression of π_t on a constant and on X will yield estimates of β_0 and β_1, and thus estimates of π^*.

There are now a great many studies in the literature which proceed on this basis. The general thrust of the results reported from countless cross-section regressions is that advertising appears to be highly positively associated with long-run returns, and that measures of the absolute cost requirements for building a minimum efficient sized plant are generally significant determinants of long-run returns (although its effect often cannot be easily disentangled from that associated with minimum efficient scale or with corrections for inter-industry variations in capital intensity), as is industry concentration (whose effect is also often difficult to distinguish from that associated with scale economies).[13] Interesting as these results are, what is also worth commenting on is the extremely low degree of explanation that these regressions typical achieve. R^2s of 0.30 or less suggest that observed profits are, at best, no more than an extremely noisy signal of long-run profits. Indeed, this very low signal to noise ratio inclines one to suspect that the assumption that entry is instantaneous is rather strong and ought not be adopted as a maintained hypothesis.

Assuming that entry responds to excess profits with a lag effectively implies that observed profits are no longer directly proportional to long-run profits. Following our earlier discussions, assume that profits depend on entry E_t and a range of transitory factors collectively described by μ_t,

$$\pi_t = \alpha E_t + \mu_t, \qquad (5.2)$$

and that entry responds to profits in excess of π^* with a short one-period lag:

$$E_t = \gamma(\pi_{t-1} - \pi^*) \qquad (5.3)$$

Clearly, $\alpha < 0$ and $\gamma > 0$. Substituting (5.3) into (5.2), it follows that

$$\pi_t = \gamma\alpha\pi_{t-1} - \gamma\alpha\pi^* + \mu_t. \qquad (5.4)$$

Equation (5.4) reveals that if entry does not respond strongly to excess profits (γ is 'small') or have a large impact on profits (α is 'close to' zero), then π_t will provide little useful information on π^*. At the extreme, if $\gamma\alpha = 0$, then observed profits will fluctuate from period to period in a manner largely determined by transitory factors, and a cross-section of values of π_t in any particular period is unlikely to be highly related to the same cross-section of π^*. If, by contrast, the product $\gamma\alpha$ is significantly different from zero and less than unity, then systematic autoregressive movements in profitability may be observed over time. Using (5.1), a cross-section regression of π_t on π_{t-1}, a constant, and on X yields estimates of β_0, β_1 and the product $\gamma\alpha$. Using these, one can calculate the level of profits sustainable in the long run (i.e. at which no incentives to entry exist) as being

$$\pi^* = \frac{-\gamma\alpha}{1 - \gamma\alpha} \left(\beta_0 + \beta_1 X \right). \tag{5.5}$$

Further, standard errors for β_0, β_1 and $\gamma\alpha$ can be used to produce standard estimates for π^*, enabling one to test whether profits do differ significantly from zero in the long run. Finally, note that the model (5.4) is more general than any which assumes that entry is instantaneous, and thus can be used to test whether that maintained assumption is consistent with the data.

As we saw in the last chapter, there is now a growing literature devoted to modelling profitability in the manner of (5.4), estimating both long-run levels of profits and charting the short-run dynamics which, in part, determine movements in observed profits. The literature is in fairly strong agreement that observed profits do fluctuate systematically over time and that π^* differs systematically across industries at any given time. More to the point, estimates of these models also generally suggest that profits in the long run differ significantly from zero, and that factors such as advertising and industry concentration (or market share) are systematically associated with variations in long-run profits. These results are similar to those that have been obtained from (5.1), not least because (as we have seen) the within-industry variation in profits is fairly small relative to the between-industry variation in profits. Although the difference between π_t and π^* is systematic, the two are never sufficiently different for the two regressions – (5.1) and (5.4) – to produce strikingly different patterns of correlation with X.

Although one can make inferences about the height of entry barriers from observed profit levels, the procedure is clearly rather indirect and the accuracy of one's inferences depends on the accuracy of one's model of profit dynamics. It therefore seems reasonable to look at entry flows rather than profits in search of a more direct and reliable indicator of barriers. The difficulty with observed flows of entry is that it is seriously misleading to think that high observed entry rates imply low barriers to entry, or that low observed entry rates imply that barriers are high. Entry barriers only impede entry in situations where entry might otherwise have occurred. Therefore, in order to use observed entry rates to make inferences about the height of entry barriers, one must calculate the amount of entry that would have occurred in a particular industry at a particular time had there been no entry barriers whatsoever. The difference between this counterfactual flow and the actual flow of entry is a natural measure of the height of barriers. The precision with which one can do this calculation clearly depends on the care one puts into modelling the determinants of entry. Equation (5.2) is (as we saw in chapter 3) a simple example of the kind of calculation that must be made. Profits in $t - 1$ are assumed to attract entry with a one-period lag, the volume of entry in the absence of barriers being $\gamma \pi_{t-1}$. When barriers exist, $\pi^* > 0$ and the amount of entry that is blocked is $\gamma \pi^*$. If π^* depends on various entry barriers X in the manner of (5.3), then a cross-section regression of E_t on a constant, π_{t-1}, and on X yields estimates of γ, β_0 and β_1, and thus of π^*. Further, one can compute a confidence interval for the resulting estimates of π^* and see whether it contains zero.

Numerous applications of this model have produced a fairly consistent view of the determinants of π^*.[14] By and large, the results suggest that π^* increases with increases in advertising intensity, capital intensity, minimum efficient scale and, rather less well attested, the extent of diversification, multi-plant economies and economies of scope. All these correlations are roughly similar to those which have been produced using static profits models like (5.1) and dynamic profit models like (5.4). However, unlike profits models, entry models tend to show mixed and rather uncertain effects of industry concentration on π^*. Although extremely speculative, one might argue that this contrast implies that concentration has no major role to play in determining long-run profits, despite having an effect on profits in the short run (presumably by affecting entry). If, as is often argued, concentration proxies both the likelihood and intensity of entry-deterring activities that entrants expect to (or actually do) face, then this conclusion is consistent with the view that types of strategic entry deterrence which do not alter barriers to entry (such as limit pricing or entry regulation) have no more than a transitory effect on profits. Other transitory factors like industry growth tend to lower π^* in entry models, but have mixed effects in profit models. Industry size also tends to have a negative effect on π^* in entry models, presumably reflecting other scale advantages not captured in estimates of minimum efficient scale.[15]

It is also worth noting that there have been inconsistencies between studies in the detailed results pertaining to various specific determinants of π^*. Table 5.1 illustrates this point by showing the output for this kind

Table 5.1 Estimates of (5.3) for six countries

	Sample	Measure of entry	Measures of barriers
UK	95 MLH industries in 1983 and 1984 (panel data)	(i) Net market share penetration of new firms in year of entry (ii) Net change in import penetration	* Size * Growth (−) * Fixed effects
West Germany	79 four-digit industries 1983–5	Gross entry rate (entrants/all firms)	** MES (−) * Product differentiation dummy (+) Capital requirements R&D
Norway	141 five-digit industries 1981–5 (panel)	Gross absolute entry (log of)	* Size (−) ** Growth (+) * Sunk cost ** MES (+) ** Log capital requirements (−) ** Concentration (−) R&D Growth ** Log size (+) ** Exit rate (+) Risk

Portugal	Gross absolute entry (log of)	* Sunk costs (−)
		** MES (−)
		** Capital requirements (−)
		** ADV (−)
		** Diversification (−)
		** Patents (−)
		** Size (+)
		** Growth (+)
		Concentration dropped because collinear with size
Belgium	109 three-digit industries 1980–4	
	(i) Net entry rate	** Fixed assets (−)
		* Growth (+)
		* Product differentiation (US adv) (−)
	(ii) Gross entry rate	** R&D (+)
		** MES (+)
	(iii) Gross exit rate	* MES (−)
Korea	62 four- or five-digit industries 1977–81	
	(i) Net entry rate	** Advertising intensity (−)
		Capital requirements
		Loan subsidy
	(ii) New entry rate	** Concentration (+)
	(iii) Entry shares	* Growth (+)

MES, minimum efficient scale; **, significant at 5%; *, significant at 1%; the estimated sign is shown after each variable name when significant. The results shown are (in the words of Cable and Schwalbach) 'representative' for each country.

Source: Cable and Schwalbach, 1991

of exercise drawn from studies done in six countries (necessarily suppressing within-study variations in the estimates of β_0, β_1 and so on). Generally, measures of capital requirements and sunk costs attracted negative signs (i.e. they raised π^*), although the former were not always significant. Market growth, market size, advertising and product differentiation and minimum efficient scale, however, displayed a mixture of signs. Further, the degree of fit of these models varied from $\overline{R}^2 = 10\%$ to $\overline{R}^2 = 78\%$. This slightly mixed bag of results should not, however, cause concern. There is little reason to believe that barriers to entry are uniform industry by industry across a range of countries, and the various samples used in the different countries do not, in any case, have the same coverage of the total population of industries. More fundamentally, it is clear that the effects of many entry barriers on entrants depend on a range of mediating market circumstances, and these will vary in effect over time within the same country and cross countries. Minimum efficient scale may inhibit entry in stagnant or declining markets but not in fast growing markets, and, as we have seen, advertising may encourage entry in some situations. Some instability in the estimates of the β_0, β_1 and so on is therefore to be expected. This said, it must also be noted that equation (5.2) has a number of shortcomings as a model of entry, and misspecification may create bias and instability in repeated applications.

Although the detailed estimates of β_0, β_1 and so on are subject to some specification-induced uncertainty (in addition to the usual uncertainty arising from sampling errors), what are of interest are the estimates of π^* that emerge from using (5.3). Unfortunately, very few direct estimates of π^* have been reported in any of this literature. Masson and Shaanan (1982) estimated $\pi^* = 8.43\%$ on average for a small sample of US industries in the late 1950s and early 1960s, where π^* was defined as a return on assets. Orr (1974a) calculated an index of entry barriers related to π^* for 71 Canadian industries in the 1960s. The index of barriers overall was only weakly correlated to measures of individual barriers such as capital requirements and advertising, and suggested that barriers were highest in smelting and refining, aircraft, brewing and so on (see his table 1, p. 42). Finally, Geroski (1990a, 1991) estimated entry equations for both domestic entrants and foreign entry for the UK in the early 1980s. The estimates of π^* were in the range 15–20% for both on average, where π^* was defined as a price–cost margin.[16] Similar work was done by Morch van der Fehr (1991) for Norway and tables 5.2 and 5.3 show lists of industries with high and/or low barriers for the UK and Norway. The rankings of industries by the height of barriers facing domestic and foreign entrants in the UK seem to be fairly similar, and the two are not dissimilar to the ranking (by *de novo* domestic entrants) of high barrier

Table 5.2   The height of barriers by industry in the UK

SIC	Name	π^* for domestic entrants	π^* for foreign entrants
Highest barriers to domestic-based entrants			
242	Cement, lime and plaster	0.73	0.36
231	Stone, clay and gravel	0.51	0.50
423	Starch	0.42	0.21
424	Spirit distilling	0.38	0.29
324	Machinery for food etc.	0.36	0.39
241	Structural clay products	0.34	0.32
257	Pharmaceuticals	0.33	0.33
475	Printing and publishing	0.30	0.29
330	Office machinery	0.28	0.23
426	Wines, cider etc.	0.25	0.25
Highest barriers to foreign-based entrants			
231	Stone, clay and gravel	0.51	0.50
324	Machinery for food etc.	0.36	0.39
495	Miscellaneous manufacturing	0.14	0.38
242	Cement, lime and plaster	0.73	0.36
257	Pharmaceuticals	0.33	0.33
241	Structural clay products	0.34	0.32
245	Working of stone etc.	0.22	0.31
323	Textile machinery	0.19	0.31
412	Processing of meat	0.16	0.30
475	Printing and publishing	0.30	0.29

Source: Geroski, 1991

industries in Norway. Although these lists differ somewhat from those produced for Canada by Orr and for West Germany by Schwalbach (1991), the actual industries that appear at the top and bottom are not unreasonable or too surprising. They are also similar to the lists one gets using (5.1) and (5.4). Geroski (1990a), for example, found almost identical estimates of π^* and associated ranks for sectors using both a profits equation like (5.4) and an entry equation like (5.3).

All these estimates of π^* are, of course, rather imprecisely estimated (this is truer for those derived from (5.3) than for those from (5.1) or (5.4)). They do, however, vary widely across industries and are generally individually significantly different from both zero and each other.

Table 5.3 The height of entry barriers by industry in Norway

Sector	Highest barriers	Sector	Lowest barriers
425	Fertilizers and pesticides	305	Made-up textile goods
525	Primary aluminium	570	Other metal products
290	Tobacco products	330	Outer garments of textile and plastic
260	Cocoa, chocolate, sugar, confectionery	345	Leather products
460	Petroleum refining	595	Repair of machinery
385	Sulphate and sulphite pulp	635	Building of boats
235	Vegetable oils	370	Building materials and other wood products
510	Iron and steel	355	Sawing and planing of wood
495	Cement and lime	265	Food products not elsewhere classified
275	Spirits and wine	395	Fibre boards

Source: Morch van der Fehr, 1991

Although the precise point estimates of π^* (and the size of the effect on π^* of its individual determinants) may be open to a good deal of dispute, the overall conclusion – that a considerable margin between prices and average costs persists in the long run – it is not difficult to accept.

Finally, given the numerous problems associated with the use of accounting profits, there is something to be said for applying the methodology associated with (5.1) to data on prices rather than profits. Jaffe and Thompson (1986) examined the UK express coach market, regressing the log of price (i.e. fares) on a range of factors correcting for costs plus variables purporting to reflect various barriers to entry. Their results suggest that terminal access appears to have enabled incumbents like National Express to raise prices by 10–20% (which is consistent with the case study by Davis, 1984). R. Thompson (1987) looked at the Irish car market and estimated a discount associated with entrants' models of about 10.5%, at least in the small and medium car range. Estimates like these – which combine data on entrants and incumbents and look for significant differences in the intercept of hedonic price regressions between the two – are rather more informative than those based on average industry profits, but can have a tendency to understate the differences between entrant and incumbent to the extent that they neglect differences embodied in observed characteristics (entrants may not be able to build cars as long as those of incumbents, say). Needless to say, they are only as useful as the corrections for costs for production that they embody.

One final observation is in order, and that is that the height of entry barriers calculated by Bain seems to be rather lower on the whole than the econometric estimates of π^* that have been generated subsequently. Part of this difference may, no doubt, be attributed to differences in the time periods examined or in the countries and industries used in the different samples. More fundamentally, Bain's technique relies on counterfactual comparisons between actual incumbents and hypothetical 'most advantaged entrants', while the econometric estimates of π^* project the effects of actual entrants on incumbents' profits into the long run. Since many actual entrants are unlikely to be amongst the most advantaged (particularly the small and fragile *de novo* entrants who dominate the data), these econometric estimates are probably rather more likely to overstate the height of barriers than Bain's do. One might (rather speculatively) combine the two types of estimate on a rough and ready basis by arguing that Bain's estimates come close to measuring the 'immediate condition of entry', while the relatively higher econometric estimates of π^* suggest that the 'general condition of entry' increases fairly substantially when one looks beyond the one or two most advantaged entrants that Bain focused on.

Conclusions

Whether or not markets reach competitive outcomes in the long run depends on whether or not barriers to entry exist. Even a cursory glance at the data supports the view that there is a wide variety of factors which can give rise to barriers in some circumstances. One's impression is that, of the three basic sources of barriers identified by Bain, economies of scale in production are, in general, the least likely to be of real importance (scale effects in raising revenue may be important, however). Absolute cost advantages, on the other hand, do certainly appear to be important in a wide range of circumstances. Product differentiation advantages are the most difficult to pin down. They often afford considerable protection against imitative entrants, but are not proof against the actions of more innovative entrants who can shift the basis upon which consumers make choices, or on which markets are defined. It also seems clear that advertising is associated with high long-run profits and low entry on average, although there are reasons to believe that it may facilitate bursts of entry by advertising-oriented new firms in 'under advertised' markets. Although difficult to think of as a structural entry barrier, its influence on entry (particularly but not exclusively for scale-related reasons) is hard to deny. Somewhat more broadly, the evidence discussed in chapter 4 suggested that the response by incumbents to entry often involved the use of various marketing weapons (when, of course, there was a response to entry). Needless to say, any proclivity by incumbents and entrants alike to use advertising or other marketing tools to create or overcome product differentiation advantages may make product differentiation barriers somewhat unrobust and unstable over time, and indeed it may make them endogenous to the process of entry in the very long run.

What this all adds up to is difficult to determine with certainty. Calculating the level of profits sustainable in the long run is an inherently speculative exercise. On the whole, Bain's calculations some 30 years ago produced a range of fairly modest estimates of long-run profitability for the USA. Subsequent work with profits and entry equations generally detect levels of profitability significantly different from zero in the long run but, accepting that they may be upwardly biased, one is inclined to think that the numbers are large but not terribly large (although they are larger than Bain's were). These estimates are drawn from cross-section work, and thus the fact that long-run profits are, on average, not very large is of course consistent with the possibility that a sizeable group of industries do enjoy protection from very high barriers to entry (and that is certainly borne out in the data). One is therefore inclined to conclude that most markets appear to be protected by at least modest barriers (particularly against imitative entry), and some by very high barriers. Barriers seem to be high enough in many cases to allow managers some discretion in their pricing choices, and to enable firms to co-operate in their pricing to some degree. Since market discipline is, in this sense, generally not too tight, we also expect to observe a considerable diversity between firms choices in short-run disequilibrium situations, an observation that is consistent with empirical findings which suggest that the movements in profitability of the leading firms in many markets are not highly correlated with each other or with movements in average industry profits (e.g. Cubbin and Geroski, 1987). Firm-specific influences in profits matter in both the short and the long run, meaning that entry (or mobility) barriers are not negligible.

The effects that we have observed advertising to have on entry suggest an alternative way of thinking about barriers to entry. Advertising, we have argued, has only a transitory effect on entrants. To retain customers in the long run, an entrant's product must have some quality or differentiation advantage that separates it from that of the incumbent in the mind of consumers. Advertising does not work in a vacuum. That advertising can, nevertheless, inhibit entry means that time is on the side of the incumbent. An entrant proffering a high quality product will sooner or later acquire a respectable market share. Later may be too late, however, for a firm with limited finance (or an inability to stimulate the imagination of its bankers). Advertising matters to the entrant because it can be a way of attracting customers quickly, and it may block entry if doing so is impossibly expensive. Somewhat more generally, the 'special assets' which are widely thought to determine the competitive ability of firms cannot simply be created overnight, and indeed many of them (such as learning enough about a production process to have lower costs than rivals) require a good deal of time and experience to create. While it may be the case that some entrants are more or less adept at learning than others, one senses that the important differences between entrants may be in their ability to survive long enough to see the learning process through.

The observation, then, is that entry programmes may have characteristics in common with R&D programmes that give rise to time–cost trade-offs. For entrants unable to wait forever for 'natural' market processes to bring them their just rewards, forcing the pace of market penetration will be an important component of their entry strategy. This means surmounting entry barriers rapidly – requiring a set of actions which may inflate the costs of entry in a manner that rises with the attempted speed of penetration. The moral is that entry barriers may not truly be barriers in the sense that even plodding entrants can make a place for themselves in most markets sooner or later. Rather, they are a form of adjustment cost that plagues new competitors who have only a limited time in which to prove themselves, and are no different in kind (or effect) from a wide range of other factors that induce agents to respond less than instantaneously to market opportunities.

One final set of remarks on the material discussed in this and the preceding chapter is in order. Market structure (however defined) may affect market performance either because the features of structure rigidly determine the details of market conduct or because the stability and continuity of structure in most markets provides a basis for persistent patterns of conduct to form, leading to persistence in performance outcomes. Although we have not tried to test or compare these two views systematically, even the most cursory examination of the data leads one to take the second view very seriously. That is, market structure (in the sense of barriers to entry) do seem to give rise to quite persistent differences in performance, despite the fact that the specific structure–conduct–performance link is rather idiosyncratic considered industry by industry. The principal implication of adopting this second view about how market structure affects performance is that it suggests that much of the dynamics in performance that one observes are driven by structural changes that disrupt behaviour patterns and so induce what are often rather unpredictable changes in conduct. Again and again, case studies of entry start from some structural change that upsets the existing pattern of activities undertaken by incumbent firms, and, while the strategic decisions made by entrants and incumbents in the ensuing melée play a major role in determining the character of the final equilibrium, conduct often seems to play no major independent role in initiating change. One must therefore conclude that the key to much of the dynamics we observe is structural in origin.

Needless to say, one should not push too hard on the view that structure determines the (particularly long-run) performance of markets, if only because we have seen several examples where structure has not proved to be absolutely inviolate or, for that matter, exogenous to the entry process. Innovative entrants can often successfully surmount apparently high entry barriers essentially by changing the terms under which competition occurs – developing product differentiation strategies to overcome cost disadvantages caused by economies of scale, devising new production techniques to circumvent patents and so on. This, of course, means that the link between market structure and performance is likely to be stable only in the short and medium run, but not necessarily in the very long run. Further, the possibility that barriers may be (in a long-run sense) endogenous means that current market behaviour can affect future market structure in a way that makes the long-run evolution of market structure path dependent. In a nutshell, history can matter and, when it does, it records its influence in the elements of market structure that we see at any given time. Many firms operate in markets which – in some very long-run sense – they have created.

Notes

1 I have interpreted Stigler's definition in terms of relative net earnings rather than reading it literally as relative costs, not least because a definition of barriers that neglects potential barriers associated with product differentiation (as well as those associated with scale economies) seems to be a non-starter. Stigler's definition may have been motivated by a (laudable) desire to separate the effects of entry barriers (which affect the profits of entrants and incumbents in different ways) from that caused by an increase in the number of firms (which reduces the profits of all firms alike without necessarily blocking entry). As indicated in the text, this distinction creates no problem for the Bainian definition of barriers.

2 Von Weizsacker (1980) has suggested that one ought to require 'the existence of certain inefficiencies as an attribute of entry barriers' (p. 400; see also Demsetz, 1982, in a similar vein). While the notion that there may exist situations where less rather than more entry is desirable is a valuable one, there seems little point in consciously mixing normative evaluations with positive measurement decisions. For work on the conditions in which 'too much' entry may occur, see Perry (1984), Mankiw and Whinston (1986), Gilbert and Vives (1986), Suzumura and Kiyaro (1987), Vives (1988) and others.

3 When firms compete not only using price but also using advertising and other non-price weapons, it makes more sense to think of a firm producing 'revenue' than producing output, understanding that the cost of generating 'revenue' is minimized by appropriate choices of the various competitive weapons at hand. Spence (1980) uses this idea to transform complex profit functions into simpler ones which appear similar to those which one might encounter in homogeneous goods markets. The argument in the text can easily be recast along these lines.

4 Notice that the definition of product differentiation advantages presented in the text is slightly different from that which one often finds in the literature where $R_1(x^\circ) > R_2(x^\circ)$ and $R(x)/x$ rising in x are often considered together under the same heading.

5 Schmalensee (1987) has suggested the useful terminological distinction between *operating advantages*, which correspond to the comparison between π_1 and π_2 at x°, and *strategic advantages*, which loosely correspond to the comparison of π_2 between x^* and x°. The latter 'may arise . . . simply because (the incumbent) appears on the market first and can acquire assets before potential entrants make their decisions' (1987, p. 64). Scale economies can provide such a strategic advantage essentially because the entrant's

decision involves adding the level of industry capacity already chosen by the incumbent.

6   That first movers may derive considerable advantage from their speed of movement does not mean that moving first is always a sensible strategy. In particular, the costs of (and risks inherent in) creating a new market may exceed those involved in trying to join an established one; see Glazer (1985) amongst others.

7   Getting the right counterfactual to calculate entry barriers is important. The debate on advertising as an entry barrier, for example, turns in part on these points. Schmalensee has argued that advertising does not create an entry barrier if capital markets are not too imperfect and 'if potential entrants can produce and promote as efficiently as established firms' (1974, p. 587). However, as is clear from his equations (11) and (12) (p. 583), he bases this assertion on a comparison between the profits of incumbent and entrant post-entry. Cubbin (1981) correctly points out that this is insufficient to reveal the existence of a barrier essentially because, in the absence of entry, the incumbent would advertise as a monopolist; if entry occurred, it would be one of two advertisers in the market. The ability to advertise as a monopolist will yield it higher returns than advertising as a duopolist for a given level of advertising and price, and this is neglected in the comparison between post-entry outcomes. Thus, when $V_2 = 0$, $V_1 < M_1$ since the former is calculated at a duopoly outcome and the latter at a monopoly position.

8   Further work by Leffer (1981) and Rizzo and Zeckhauser (1990) suggests a somewhat more subtle view of the effects of advertising. Leffer found that advertising promoted the entry of superior new drugs but not the entry of low-price substitutes. Similarly, Rizzo and Zeckhauser found that advertising acted as a complement to experience, providing higher earnings for more established physicians (who advertise less). Although both studies suggest that advertising promotes competition, both suggest that it favours some competitors rather more than others. In this sense, then, it may also inhibit competition.

9   These capital-raising disadvantages are related to those faced by small (relative to large) firms and unquoted (relative to quoted) firms: see Prais (1976), Reinganum and Smith (1983), Hay and Morris (1984) and others.

10 If production is impossible at suboptimal levels, if there is no growth in demand, if entrants accept the Sylos postulate and if the elasticity of market demand is -1, then, following Modigliani (1958), the percentage mark-up of price over marginal cost which can be persistently maintained without threat of entry is 10% when minimum efficient scale is 10% of the market. As demand becomes more elastic, the percentage mark-up falls; if positive growth occurs, the mark-up also falls (Bhagwati, 1970). Thus, for a minimum efficient plant of 10%, one imagines that a less than 10% long-run elevation of prices will possible, and so less than 'substantial' entry barriers will exist.

11 As we have noted in chapter 4, there are a whole host of well-known hazards involved in making inferences from accounting profits (see, for example, Scherer, 1980, for a good discussion). Fisher and McGowan (1983) have constructed a number of examples in which accounting and economic profits

diverge spectacularly, but these measurement errors do not appear to be strongly correlated with anything but firm size (Salamon, 1985). Further, and more to the point, persistently high accounting profits imply persistently high economic returns (Kay and Mayer, 1986), suggesting that inferences based on persistently high accounting profits over a period of time are likely to be less unreliable than those made on the basis of accounting profits in any single period.

12   Failing to allow for systematic deviations of observed profits from long-run equilibrium profits may generate bias in estimating the effects of variables of interest on long-run profits whenever the incidence or extent of disequilibrium across industries is correlated to variables of interest. At least two examples of this seem to have occurred in the literature concerned with estimating the effect of concentration on profits. Weiss (1974) observed that the correlation was noticeably weaker during inflationary periods, while Martin (1983) and others noticed that the profits–concentration correlation became negative in the mid-1970s. In both cases, it is reasonable to believe that observed profits not only differed from their long-run equilibrium levels, but also that the difference was much larger in highly concentrated sectors. In the first case, profits in highly concentrated industries were undoubtedly lowered by the much longer lag in adjusting prices to increases in costs which is generally observed in such industries, while in the second case, highly capital-intensive and concentrated industries were thought to be particularly susceptible to sharp increases in materials prices and to the effects of the recession.

13   For surveys, see Weiss (1974), Scherer (1980), Geroski (1987), Schmalensee (1987) and others. There have been several explorations of mobility barriers using a variant of this methodology, the basic idea being that firms in different strategic groups within an industry ought to have different values of β_0 and β_1; see Newman (1978), Porter (1979) and Oster (1982a).

14   Orr (1974a) first suggested something rather similar to the procedure discussed in the text. Results from exploring models of this type are reported by Mansfield (1962), Orr (1974b), Duetsch (1975, 1984). Gorecki (1975, 1976), Harris (1976), Hirschey (1981), Yip (1982a), Baldwin and Gorecki (1983, 1987), Khemani and Shapiro (1983, 1986, 1987), Shapiro (1983), Hamilton (1985), MacDonald (1986), Schwalbach (1987), Morch van der Fehr (1991), Masson and Jeong (1991), Mata (1991) and others.

15   In a number of instances (e.g. Orr, 1974b), estimated values of γ were reported to be significantly different from zero. Taken literally, these imply estimates of π^* which are extremely large. A more reasonable interpretation is that this weak link between entry and profitability casts real doubt on how informative observed values of either π_t or E_t will be on the size of π^*.

16   Unlike the majority of studies cited in note 12, Geroski used panel data, enabling him to estimate π^* using fixed industry effects. This effectively frees estimates of π^* from problems associated with omitting unobserved barriers, or neglecting interactions between barriers. There is no reason, of course, why econometric models need to neglect interactions between barriers – with two barriers X and Z, (5.1) can be written as $\pi^* = \beta_0 + \beta_1 X + \beta_2 Z + \beta_3 (XZ)$.

6

Entry, Technical Progress, Efficiency and Productivity

Introduction

Entry is generally conceived of as a force of discipline in markets, an error correction mechanism which helps to bring about competitive market outcomes. The theoretical basis of this view is easy to appreciate. Departures from perfect competition are founded on restrictions in supply designed to elevate prices, and entry is an additional source of supply outside the control of incumbent firms which, in principle, will materialize when prices are pushed too far above costs. Indeed, entry need not actually materialize in order to have this effect, since the mere anticipation of entry might lead incumbents to cut prices in an effort to forestall entry and maintain their market positions. While there is nothing wrong (in principle) with the view of entry as a force of discipline, it is rather static. Entry can also play a more creative role in markets, serving as a vehicle for the introduction and diffusion of innovations which embody new products or processes that fundamentally alter conditions of supply and demand. Further, the mere threat of entry of this type may induce incumbents to generate new innovations or to adopt existing ones more rapidly.

In fact, as we have seen, the evidence seems to indicate that entry is not a particularly powerful force of discipline in markets. The short-run dynamics in profits that can be attributed to entry, actual or potential, are fairly modest, and significant inter-industry (and, for that matter, inter-firm) differences in margins of at least modest size appear to persist for considerable periods of time. That market performance is (one way or the other) largely (but not entirely) determined by market structure (in the sense of entry barriers) suggests that structural change may be a major source of market dynamics. And, while entry may not have much effect on market performance given the level of barriers in any given market, entry-induced strategic non-price competition can (as we have seen) change both the nature and the height of barriers over time. That is, entry may play a role in the process by which market structure evolves over time.

Taking a broader view, then, entry can be both an equilibrating and a disequilibrating force in markets and, at the risk of some over-simplification, one might again invoke the distinction between 'imitative' and 'innovative' entry in this context. Imitative entry occurs whenever profits can be made merely be replicating the actions of incumbents. The process of replication is equilibrating in the sense that it drives markets towards the competitive equilibrium that would prevail given existing conditions of cost and demand. Imitative entrants are likely to be attracted by the existence of excess profits on existing activities for, taking cost and demand conditions as given, profits from imitative entry can only be made if prices exceed average costs. By contrast, innovative entry is designed to shift market demand or to take advantage of new cost functions. This type of activity is, of course, inherently disequilibrating, shifting markets away from existing equilibria and towards new equilibrium configurations. Whether or not an attempt to transform market demand or supply in this fashion will be profitable for an innovative entrant does not depend a great deal on the level of excess profits that incumbents realize on existing activities, and for this reason the rate of innovative entry may have rather different determinants from imitative entry. Innovative entry involves the displacement of current activities by new ones, activities which can be profitable even if current activities are not. Further, imitative entry is likely to be endogenous to the current price and output choices of incumbents in a way that innovative entry is not. If it is endogenous to current market outcomes, innovative entry is so because it is affected by the current and past technological and marketing decisions made by incumbents. Needless to say, barriers to the entry of imitative firms are unlikely to apply with equal force to innovative entrants.

While neither of these two ideal types of entrant are likely to be easily observable in practice, the distinction between innovative and imitative entry is conceptually useful as a reminder that, in principle, entry can be both an agent of and a response to change in markets. Indeed, there is a clear analogy between the notion of entry as a creative force in markets and natural selection arguments that is worth exploring. In biological systems, survival requires successful adaptation to the environment, and it is the competitive pressures created by scarce natural resources that form the basis for discrimination amongst alternative adaptations. Selection occurs amongst individuals: those well suited to their environment are favoured and increase in relative numbers. This relative expansion in the number of well-adapted individuals induces a general change in the characteristics of the population, producing a better fit with the environment. In terms of markets, the unit of selection is the firm, and the analogue of genes are its products and the routines or operating procedures which underlie the production, distribution and marketing processes it uses (for a stimulating discussion, see Nelson and Winter, 1982). 'Better fit' might be interpreted as 'maximizing consumer welfare subject to resource constraints', and involves, *inter alia*, driving prices down to the level of marginal costs. The 'relative expansion of well-adapted individuals' is no more than the increase in the supply of existing products, and may occur literally through an expansion in the number of producers via imitative entry or indirectly through an expansion in production by incumbents who anticipate the arrival of imitative entrants.

However, the analogy between natural selection and market processes is not perfect. In natural settings, the expansion of well-adapted individuals almost never (except in the simplest organisms) occurs through perfect replication. Instead, essentially random (meaning not so much stochastic as exogenous to current survival struggles) genetic mutations occur from time to time, producing individuals slightly different from their parents. Genes provide a basic continuity between the characteristics of successive generations, but the fit is not perfect. The process of genetic mutation is, in effect, a method of investigating the suitability of all possible sets of characteristics that individuals can possess, and, as such, it is the mainspring of change in natural selection processes. Since the search for an optimal fit to any given environment is not consciously directed and is totally exogenous in natural settings, it often requires an extraordinary amount of time to complete – the human eye did not emerge by chance one bright Thursday afternoon (e.g. Dawkins, 1986). By contrast, amongst humans and, more particularly, in markets, the process of search, testing and change is both better directed and a good deal faster than it is amongst animals – the human leopard can willingly change its spots.

Although much of the push stimulating the development of new innovations may be random in the sense of being exogenous to current market activities, the potential for learning and the conscious choices that are made by agents mean that innovation as a source of change will operate in a more complex manner than genetic mutation. In particular, innovations need not be introduced through the addition of new individuals to the population, since learning and adaptation enable existing individuals to change (some of) their characteristics (and pass these on in a Lamarkian manner) in response to both internal as well as environmental pressures (Gould (1980, ch. 7) discusses human cultural evolution in not dissimilar terms). The fact that the human leopard can change its spots means two things in this context. First, innovative and imitative entry need not actually occur during the process of adaptation to change, since the mere anticipation that innovative entry may occur can provoke incumbents to pre-empt entrants by innovating or initiating the introduction of necessary changes. That is, human agents can anticipate future selection pressures and begin to adapt to them before they fully emerge. Second, and more speculatively, it is at least conceivable that the evolution and development of markets could occur without entry, real or imagined, and this for reasons having to do with the internal dynamics of human institutions. Competition within firms may be at least a partial substitute for competition between firms, and may have a similar effect on innovation.

This last point starts from the premise that all firms, large and small, old and new, operate on the basis of a set of routines implementing a strategy which embodies a conception of what ought to be produced, how it ought to be produced and how it ought to be sold. Many alternative possible strategies exist in each of these dimensions, and new ideas are continuously generated endogenously and exogenously by individuals operating within the firm, or in rival firms. As the environment in which the firm's routines are implemented constantly changes, so the rate at which new ideas are generated changes, and their relative merits vary over time. Competition amongst these different possibilities – the debate between different ideas – occurs not only between firms, but also within firms. Indeed, in a fundamental sense, what a firm actually chooses to do depends upon the nature of the competitive conflict between individuals and factions within it, and how this conflict is resolved (e.g. Cyert and March, 1963). Even if the viability and profitability of a particular firm is not affected by competitive threats emanating from other firms, new or old, the division of the profits within a firm between management, shareholders and workers always remains a source of conflict, as does the division of spoils within each of these broad classes. As long as the extent of competition between firms leaves some surplus residual to be distributed, competition within firms will occur; as long as different individuals and factions within the same firm express their different demands for part of the surplus in the form of new operating routines or strategic initiatives, then innovations of some sort will always emerge as part of the ultimate resolution of intra-firm conflict.

The implication, then, is that competition in the sense of 'new firms' is by no means the same thing as competition in the sense of 'new ideas'. The distinction between imitative and innovative entry reflects the fact that new firms do not always serve as the vehicle for new ideas; the distinction between competition within and competition between firms reflects the fact that new ideas do not necessarily need new firms to effect their entrance to the market. Still, this said, it is of no small interest to explore the role that new firms play in the process of change and development in markets. Not only is it possible in principle that entry may play an important creative role in market processes, it is also possible that this role brings more benefits to consumers in the long run than does the market discipline which entry provides in the short and medium run.

Our discussion of this question will focus on the effects of entry on innovation and on productivity growth. The effect of competitive rivalry on innovation has long been a source of debate, and both this debate and much of the evidence – econometric and case study – is summarized in the next section. This discussion is followed by an examination of the causal relations between entry and innovation using a latent variables model similar to those discussed in earlier chapters. In general, the evidence on the relation between competitive rivalry and innovation is fairly mixed, and in the following section we shall discuss a possible resolution of this dilemma – that the effects of rivalry on innovation vary over the product life cycle in various systematic ways. This view, not unpersuasive on strictly *a priori* grounds, is made all the more plausible by a number of case studies that show fairly clearly when entry does and does not affect innovation. In the penultimate section, the relationship between entry and productivity growth (and technical efficiency more generally) is explored, again using a mix of case study and econometric evidence. Productivity growth across and within industries is quite unlike profitability in its statistical properties, and there are reasons to think that both entry and, more important, innovation are major determinants of it. These various and slightly disparate pieces of evidence are drawn together in the concluding section, where some implications of the results are discussed.

Assessing the Schumpeterian Hypothesis

To assess the role of entry as a creative force in markets, it is useful to adopt a broad conception of entry that makes at least some allowance for the notion of competition as 'new ideas'. What is indisputably the case is that most markets have a core (and are often defined by that core) of a few firms producing relatively standardized products which collectively account for the great majority of sales. Considering entry as the promotion of a new firm into this core almost certainly requires thinking of entry as being based on an innovation that changes the core product in certain ways; the source of potential entrants to the core is that amorphous mass of potential entrants to the industry plus existing fringe producers.

Thus, in what follows in this section, we shall generally understand 'entry' to mean the commencing of relatively large-scale mass production of a new good (or the use of a new process) that is almost certainly an innovation relative to the existing core good (or production process) which currently dominates the market, by a firm not already a market leader. One strength (and weakness) of this stylization is that it concentrates attention on 'major' innovations. It is probably the case that one can often find an innovation of some sort at the bottom of most entry attempts, but this reduces the relationship between entry and innovation almost to tautology. It is also the case that this stylization blurs the distinction between large firm size in an absolute and a relative sense. This is probably not too serious a problem. Market leaders are, in general, large both in terms of the scale of their activities and in terms of the percentage of market activity that they account for. In what follows, we use the phrase 'market power' generically to describe the advantages of both aspects of large size. Combining entry and intra-industry mobility by aggregating fringe producers and potential entrants into a single competitive block, one can think of the leading enterprises as *insiders* and the rest as *outsiders*, where outsiders have no market power themselves but may limit the market power possessed by insiders (see Averill (1968), Berger and Piore (1980) and others for a discussion of the 'dual' economy that rests on a stylization similar to this).

With this usage in mind, the question to be addressed is whether the seeds of market growth and development lie in a market selection process fuelled by the innovative activity of outsiders. This will clearly be the case whenever outsiders are more flexible and imaginative than insiders, and whenever insiders are so committed to existing activities as to make them resistant to change. Although this seems to be a reasonable position to take when expressed in general terms, it runs counter to a range of extremely influential, popular Schumpeterian hypotheses about the technological progressivity of large firms that enjoy market power. The several strands of Schumpeterian assertions extant in the literature all stress one or more of a range of relatively favourable opportunities for innovation available to insiders, and they must be answered if the case for entry as a creative force is to be accepted. Indeed, taking the Schumpeterian hypothesis seriously actually carries the rather strong implication that the advantages of insiders in producing new innovations may actually be enhanced if outsiders are absent. Any amount of entry may, in this view, prove to be socially excessive.

To understand Schumpeterian arguments fully, it is useful to distinguish *actual* from *anticipated* market power (e.g. Kamien and Schwartz, 1982, p. 27, or Scherer, 1980, pp. 428–9). Anticipated market power refers to the post-innovation state of the market, and describes an innovator's ability to enjoy the full benefits of its innovation by blocking imitation and appropriating a large share of the potential post-innovation returns on offer. A firm which is able to ensure a post-innovation monopoly is more likely to innovate than one that is unable to do so, and in this sense anticipated market power always stimulates innovation. This is hardly a controversial argument, and were the Schumpeterian hypothesis to be expressed in these terms it would be relatively uninteresting. What is controversial is the role of actual market power. Actual market power refers to the pre-innovation state of the market, to the degree of monopoly currently exercised by the putative innovator, and the question of interest is the effect that it has on the probability than an innovation will be produced or adopted within a given time period. Do monopolists innovate more or less than firms operating in more competitive conditions? The complicating feature of the question is that the anticipated market power of a firm may depend on its actual market power. Thus, actual market power can have an *indirect effect* as innovative activity via the effect it has an anticipated market power (or, more simply, on the level of post-innovation returns), and a *direct effect* on innovative activity for a given degree of anticipated market power (that is, for a given level of post-innovation returns). Let us consider each effect in turn (what follows is drawn from Geroski, 1990b).

The indirect effect of actual market power on innovation is likely to be positive and thoroughly pro-Schumpeterian (if it exists). It operates via the effect that actual market power has on anticipated market power, and the effect that anticipated market power has on innovation. The effect of anticipated market power on innovation reflects no force more subtle than that which leads those who perceive a higher post-innovation return to innovate faster and more extensively than those who anticipate less abundant rewards. Anticipated market power describes the (expected) ability to appropriate a greater degree of any given potential post-innovation return, and there are at least two reasons for believing that actual market power readily translates into anticipated market power. In the first place, it is likely that those firms who enjoy pre-innovation market power will be better placed to erect barriers to post-innovation imitative entry than pre-innovation fringe producers or new entrants. This may be the case for a variety of reasons: current period market power may generate the excess profits necessary to finance the strategic investments designed to create barriers, it may bring sufficient relief from day-to-day competitive pressures to enable a firm to take the long-term view required for such investments, and so on. Furthermore, the actual degree of market power that exists pre-innovation is likely to depend on entry barriers, and if these are durable and are not displaced by the innovation, then they will afford protection post-innovation.

Second, and somewhat more subtly, the returns to innovation realizable by insiders can exceed those that outsiders expect, and this differential in post-innovation returns may translate into a relatively higher level of innovative activity by insiders. Two different mechanisms can operate to bring this about, one on the demand side and one on the cost side. To appreciate the first of these, note that positions of market power must, at bottom, be based on some innovation introduced at some time in the past. If the new innovation complements the original one in the sense that there are gains to co-ordinating the pricing of the two associated products, then this new innovation will always be worth more to an insider who possesses the original innovation than to any outsider.[1] On the cost side, there may be economies of scope which bring benefits from joint production of the products associated with the two innovations, new and old. If no benefits of scope exist, but if the returns to an innovation depend on the scale of its usage (such as might occur for a process innovation that reduces per unit production costs), then clearly insiders will benefit more from the innovation than outsiders if they are able to maintain larger production volumes. Either way, firms that currently enjoy market power (in the sense of being large, absolutely and relatively) will enjoy a higher level of post-innovation returns for any given innovation, and are therefore likely to be more innovative than outsiders, *ceteris paribus*.

However, the incentive to act in response to a post-innovation return of any given size may differ between insiders and outsiders, and this second, direct, effect of market power may more than outweigh the indirect effect just discussed. In fact, most of the controversy associated with the Schumpeterian hypothesis is concerned with whether the direct effect of actual market power on innovation is positive or negative. The main lines of discussion set the 'material advantages' of insiders against various 'behavioural advantages' that outsiders are presumed to possess (e.g. Rothwell, 1984). Insiders, and particularly those who enjoy market power, are likely to have a far greater command of financial and technical resources than outsiders. They have distribution networks in place, and can command the well-developed marketing skills necessary to ensure a reasonable probability of success in innovation. Further, the high profits derived from actual market power weaken their reliance on external finance, a step which may enable them to act more quickly, to act on a larger scale and to absorb more risk than firms without market power would. By contrast, small outsider firms are generally thought to be somehow more likely to behave in an innovative, entrepreneurial fashion. Their organizational structures are typically much simpler and more easy to control than those of large firms, their goals are likely to be more straightforward and, perhaps, elemental and, as we shall see in a moment, they often have no rents to protect. The consequence is that they are generally thought to be more flexible, adaptable and more responsive to events than large market leaders whom, it is thought, can easily mire themselves in a muddle of bureaucratic inactivity. Material advantages present insiders with numerous opportunities to innovate quickly and efficiently, but it is not clear that they are capable of seizing more than a small percentage of them. Smaller, leaner and fitter outside firms may prove to be so much more capable of exploiting a more limited opportunity set that, in the end, they outperform their larger rivals.

There is more to the story of the direct effects of actual market power on innovation, however, than material versus behavioural advantages. Two further considerations hinge on the observation that, while insiders may have the ability to respond more rapidly to a post-innovation return of any given size, they are unlikely to have the incentive to do so unless they are prompted by the competitive challenge provided by the outsiders. The first incentive effect arises whenever new innovations displace old ones and the stream of earnings associated with them (e.g. Fellner (1951), Arrow (1962) and, for a popular discussion, Foster (1986)). If the pre-innovation stream of earnings earned by an insider is π_0 and the post-innovation one is π_1, then the net return to innovation for an insider is $\pi_1 - \pi_0$, while an outsider who does not share any of the returns on existing activities gains π_1. Since $\pi_1 > \pi_1 - \pi_0$, it is clear that the incentives for insiders to act are weaker for any given level of post-innovation returns π_1, and they are weaker the more actual market power the insider enjoys (i.e. the larger is π_0). Insiders, however, may gain by jointly pricing the complementary products of new and old innovations, or by exploiting the innovation more effectively than outsiders, earning, say, $\pi_2 > \pi_1$. Despite this, they will still be slower to act if $\pi_1 > \pi_2 - \pi_0$. It follows from these observations, then, that innovations will be introduced largely because of the activities of outsiders (unless $\pi_2 \gg \pi_1$) for one or both of two reasons. First, whenever $\pi_1 > \pi_2 - \pi_0$, outsiders are likely to have more incentive to act than insiders, and second, the existence of imitative entrants and the possible arrival of innovative entrants threatens the level of returns on pre-innovation activities, π_0. To an incumbent facing the certain loss of π_0 because of the imminent arrival of an innovative outsider, the opportunity cost of innovation is effectively zero and, if $\pi_2 \geqslant \pi_1$, it may act to pre-empt the challenger. In this case, the innovation may be introduced at some date t by the insider, but only because of the actions of the outsider.

The second incentive effect of competition on innovation that may play a role in this context is the incentive that insiders and outsiders have to do research more intensively and to generate more innovations per unit of time. The strength of this effect depends on how many firms are competing to discover 'the' innovation, and on how the post-innovation returns are likely to be shared out. If only those firms who first introduce the innovation gain the rewards to innovating, then competition takes the form of a first-past-the-post race. In these circumstances, the more firms there are searching for 'the' innovation, the more intense is each firm's search likely to be, and the more certain it is that one will stumble upon the important clue by date t.[2] Competition in the supply of innovations will therefore lead to more innovative output than monopoly, *ceteris paribus*. If, on the other hand, imitators can share some of the gains to innovation with first movers without incurring substantial development costs, then the risk of losing a race to innovate will diminish and, as a consequence, firms may do less intensive research and so may innovate less.[3] As with the first incentive effect associated with the competitive challenge of outsiders, the consequence of research or innovation races is to increase the response of insiders to post-innovation returns of any given size. The direct effects of actual market power on innovation associated with material versus behavioural advantages can be positive or negative depending on which advantage is larger; those associated with the incentives created by the challenge of outsiders, by contrast, are based on the possibility that insiders will not respond as rapidly as outsiders to post-incentive returns of any given size. Overall, then, the direct effect of actual market power on innovation will be positive only if the material advantages that flow from market power outweigh both behavioural disadvantages and incentive effects. The overall effect of actual market power on innovation depends on whether the indirect effects of market power (which are likely to be positive) outweigh any negative direct effects that exist if the material advantages of insiders are not too large.

In short, it seems to be the case that insiders have a greater potential for innovative action than outsiders. Not only may they enjoy various and sundry material advantages but, more compellingly, they are likely to be able to generate a higher level of returns for any given innovation. The major problem lies in the incentives they have to take advantage of their favourable opportunities. In this connection, the opportunity cost of innovation plus any inclination to opt for the quiet life or to pursue managerial ambitions in other directions are all likely to lead to a more relaxed response by insiders to a post-innovation prize of any given size.

The net effect, in principle, is ambiguous, but in practice one is inclined to think that incentives are more important than opportunities in stimulating activity. This, of course, implies that at base much innovative activity is likely to be driven by the activities of outsiders. Indeed, a pattern that one might expect to observe is that of innovations undertaken by outsiders and then taken over by insiders who would be only too happy to pay the present discounted value (to the outsider) of the innovation in the not infrequent situations where it is worth more to the insider than to the outsider. A careful reading of the evidence suggests that insiders often do require added incentives to innovate, and that these are often provided by outsiders.

To sort out the respective roles of insiders and outsiders in the innovation process it is necessary to ascertain whether the major innovations that we observe can be attributed to large firms or to firms operating in situations where insiders clearly enjoy market power. Most empirical work on the issue of firm size and innovation has tended to focus on relating the intensity of R&D inputs, measured either by R&D expenditure expressed as a percentage of sales or by the employment of research personnel, to firm size. The evidence surveyed by Scherer (1980), Kamien and Schwartz (1982), Baldwin and Scott (1987) and Cohen and Levin (1989) suggests that R&D tends to rise more than proportionately with firm size but that, after some threshold of R&D intensity is reached, it remains constant or declines. The threshold varies across industries, but appears to lie somewhere near the bottom range of *Fortune's* 500 industrial listing. Our interest, however, lies with the output of innovations rather than with inputs of R&D, and there are two reasons for believing that the picture may be rather different when one focuses on innovative output. First, because smaller firms generally do not have formal R&D programmes, their research inputs are not picked up in the statistics, and second, there may be systematic differences in the efficiency with which firms undertake R&D, leading to more or less innovative output from a given set of research inputs. For one or both reasons, then, the apparent proclivity of large firms to do R&D need not necessarily translate into more innovations, much less into more important innovations.

Certainly the available evidence suggests that, in fact, smaller firms appear to be more efficient than larger rivals at generating innovative output.[4] For example, investigations of expenditure per patent and of parallel product development efforts both reveal the smaller firms incur lower costs (see Kamein and Schwartz, 1982, pp. 66–70). It is often observed that small firms are quicker in bringing new products to the markets: engineering new products in 70% of the time taken by large firms, developing prototypes twice as fast, establishing production marginally faster and starting up sales in about two-thirds of the time taken by large firms (Ergas, 1984, p. 46, who cites a study by Gellman Research Associates). Evidence based on looking at the generation of innovations – major and minor – suggests that small and medium-sized firms do make a major contribution to the flow of innovative activity, and one that is far in excess of their employment or value added shares. In the UK, for example, nearly 29% of the major innovations introduced over the period 1945–83 were produced by firms with less than 200 employees. Firms larger than 50,000 employees, on the other hand, produced a mere 21% of the total, despite accounting for the lions share of R&D (e.g. Pavitt et al., 1987). Feinman and Fuentevilla (1976, cited in Scherer, 1984, ch. 11) examined 500 important innovations which were first introduced in the USA during the period 1953–73. Of the 319 which originated from US firms, 24% came from firms with less than 100 employees, 24% from firms employing between 100 and 1000, and only 35% from firms with more than 10,000 employees. Edwards and Gordon (1984) studied 8074 major and minor innovations introduced into the USA in 1982, and found that small firms (less than 500 employees) innovated at about 2.4 times the rate of large firms. In short and more or less regardless of how one looks at it, the evidence based on various measures of innovative output suggests that it is smaller rather than larger firms that account for a major share of new innovations.

Looking at aggregate data that are based on simple counts of innovations or patents can, of course, be slightly misleading. For example, the relative contribution of large and small firms to total innovative activity exhibits considerable inter-industry variation. Data from the UK suggest that firms of less than 1000 employees are important in machinery and instruments, where they account for more than 45% of all innovations. Firms of more than 10,000 employees, on the other hand, produce more than 75% of all innovations in mining, food, chemicals and electrical products. In a sector like electronics, firms of less than 1000 workers account for 26% of all innovations but these are heavily concentrated in electronics instruments and computers; firms larger than 10,000 account for 61% of all the innovations produced in the sector, but these are concentrated in telecommunications and electronics capital goods. In fact, 64% of all small-firm innovations are concentrated in machines, mechanical engineering, and instruments, while 45% of large-firm innovations are in chemicals, electrical engineering and electronics (Pavitt et al., 1987, and, for work on the USA, Acs and Audretsch, 1988). Although there is no direct evidence on this, inter-industry differences in the innovativeness of small firms and entrants more generally may reflect not only differences in technological opportunities but also differences in innovativeness by entrant type. Industries differ in the relative proportions of domestic entrants, foreign entrants, independent *de novo* entrants, diversifying entrants (by firms established elsewhere) and so on that they host, and this may affect their technological progressivity. Indeed, corresponding to waves of entry by type of entrant (see chapter 2) one can observe waves of innovation by slightly different types (see, for example, the discussion of computers and semiconductors below for some suggestive hints along these lines).

It also appears to be the case that large firms often produce rather minor innovations, relying heavily on small firms for basic ideas which they then develop for commercial application (see Schott, 1976, and, more generally, Scherer, 1980, pp. 416–18; Kamien and Schwartz, 1982, pp. 68–70). Even when large firms innovate faster than smaller rivals, the inventions that their innovations were based on originated, as often as not, from the efforts of independent outsiders. Jewkes et al. (1969) attributed only 12 of 61 major twentieth-century innovations to the laboratories of large corporations, and Hamberg (1963) found only seven of 27 major US innovations introduced between 1946–55 to have sprung from large firms. Of 25 of the leading innovations introduced by DuPont in the USA between the World Wars, only 11 originated in that company's research laboratories (Mueller, 1962). Post-war innovation in petroleum and aluminium also appears to have exhibited the same basic pattern (Enos, 1962; Peck, 1962). Freeman (1963) observed that 43% of the patents issued for principal groups of plastics went to individuals in the period up to 1930. This dropped to 8% in the period 1946–55 as R&D costs rocketed and insiders began to protect their positions through strategic patenting. It is, of course, a moot point whether many of these inventions subsequently developed by large insiders would have appeared had they not been taken over by them (Scherer, 1980, p. 417), but the rather defensive nature of much corporate patenting makes one wonder whether it would have been a good deal later than sooner. For example, AT&T's research programme in radio communications early this century seems to have been geared more towards creating a blanket of protection against rivals than towards actually commercially pioneering radio communications, if only because this work threatened its own position in wired telephones (Reich, 1980).

Of course, the Schumpeterian hypothesis involves more than just the assertion that large firm size encourages innovation. Possibly more far reaching is the further assertion that an absence of rivalry in markets is also conducive to innovativeness. The available evidence on this subject is largely based on tests which regress measures of innovative input or output on measures of market structure and rivalry, and other factors. A positive correlation between measures of industry concentration and innovative input or output is generally interpreted as consistent with the view that the net effect of monopoly power on innovativeness is positive, and many studies seem to record positive and generally significant coefficients on industry concentration (for surveys, see Kamien and Schwartz, 1982, ch. 3; Baldwin and Scott, 1987; Scherer, 1980, pp. 433–6; or Cohen and Levin, 1989). However, the problem with these results is that the correlation is extremely sensitive to corrections for variations in the degree of 'technological opportunity' across industries.

Technological opportunity refers to the fecundity of an industry's scientific and technological base (see Rosenberg, 1974, for a classic discussion). In the literature, it has been measured in numerous ways (Scherer, 1967; Schrieves, 1978; Waterson and Lopez, 1983; and others; the most ambitious attempt to proxy technological opportunity using observables is by Levin et al., 1985), and the interesting consequence of introducing these various proxies is that they generally cause the estimated effect of industry concentration on innovativeness to diminish considerably, and, indeed, to become insignificantly different from zero. In Geroski (1990b) an almost complete correction for these effects was achieved by using panel data, extracting inter-industry variations in technological opportunity through the introduction of a full set of industry-specific fixed effects. This procedure yielded an estimated coefficient on industry concentration in an equation determining innovation counts which was negative and significant. The first column of table 6.1 shows the basic set of estimates produced by Geroski, and the negative coefficient on concentration displayed there proved to be extremely robust to a wide variety of re-specifications of (i), including endogenizing concentration. The estimates shown in column (i) reveal that, were levels of concentration to decline without any diminution in technological opportunity, then innovation would rise in these sectors. However, dropping the fixed effects (i.e. neglecting to correct for inter-industry variations in technological opportunity) yielded a positive estimated coefficient on concentration (shown as (ii) in table 6.1) and a dramatic reduction in the degree of explanation achieved (a similar result can be found in Cohen et al. (1987), who examine the firm size and innovative link). It follows, then, that the apparently positive correlation between innovation and industry concentration seems to arise because industries rich in technological opportunity also tend to be highly concentrated.

Thus, the evidence provided by correlations between industry concentration and innovation input or output does not provide much support for the Schumpeterian hypothesis. Although this conclusion is informative, one ought not to hinge the whole test of a proposition on the sign of a

Table 6.1 The direct and indirect effects of actual monopoly on innovation

	(i)	(ii)	(iii)	(iv)	(v)
log π	2.27*	21.96*	–	–	–
	(0.146)	(3.70)			
CON	–58.42	7.12	0.323	–0.499	–58.919
	(2.34)	(0.695)	(0.270)		
ENTRY	18.40	41.03	–0.838	–1.890	16.51
	(1.05)	(0.780)	(2.56)		
IMPORT	–0.401	10.43	–0.0049	–0.011	–0.412
	(0.129)	(0.941)	(0.017)		
SFIRM	(3.63)	–15.73	–0.260	–0.5902	3.37
	(1.09)	(1.09)	(1.87)		
EXIT	–25.94	59.45	0.445	1.010	–24.93
	(1.36)	(1.28)	(1.48)		
DCON	–10.01	–20.08	–0.102	–0.231	–10.241
	(2.22)	(1.42)	(1.20)		
SIZE	4.24	8.51	–0.239	–0.542	3.698
	(0.614)	(3.45)	(1.71)		
GROW	3.46	1.14	–0.056	–0.127	3.333
	(1.91)	(0.246)	(1.81)		
KAYO	0.854	–4.36	–0.017	–0.038	0.816
	(1.26)	(3.66)	(1.30)		
EXPORT	6.84	16.56	0.020	0.045	6.885
	(0.857)	(2.77)	(0.139)		
UNION	–2.618	–16.417	0.040	0.09	–2.52
	(0.489)	(1.02)	(0.234)		

The dependent variable in (i) and (ii) is a count of major innovations. The data pool two cross-sections each covering successive five-year periods in the 1970s. (i) is a tobit estimate that includes fixed effects whilst (ii) duplicates (i) suppressing the fixed effects into a single constant common to all industries. t values (in absolute value) are in parentheses below the estimated coefficients. I, number of innovations; CON, five-firm concentration ratio; GROW, percentage change in domestic production over the period; SIZE, log of industry capital stock; DCON, percentage change in industry concentration; KAYO, capital–output ratio; IMPORT, imports as a percentage of sales; ENTRY, market share of entrants in year of entry; EXPORT, exports as a percentage of sales; SFIRM, the number of firms with 99 employees or fewer as a percentage of the total number of firms; EXIT, market share of exiting firms in the year of exit; UNION, percentage of the workforce covered by collective agreements; log π_1, expected post-innovation price–cost margins. The dependent variable in (iii) is log π and (iii) also includes fixed effects, risk = 1.17 (1.32), an instrument for $I = 0.0159$ (3.59), and $CON^2 = -0.806$ (0.704). Risk is measured as the standard deviation of price–cost margins within the relevant five-year period. The direct effects of competition on rivalry can be taken from (i), column (iv) gives the indirect effects calculated from the coefficient in log π in (i) (the indirect effect for CON is evaluated at the mean, CON = 0.51) and the estimates shown in (iii) and, finally, column (v) shows the total effects of actual monopoly on innovation.
Source: Geroski, 1990b

single estimated coefficient, particularly when it is liable to reflect a number of direct and indirect effects of market power on innovation. The results shown in table 6.1 push beyond correlations between industry concentration and innovations, showing that there exist positive correlations with entry rates and the percentage of small firms operating in the industry, and negative correlations with exit rates and increases in concentration.[5] Thus, it appears that the notion that rivalry is conducive to innovativeness is robust to the precise proxy that one uses to measure the degree of rivalry. Columns (iii)–(v) show calculations of both indirect effects (effects of actual market power that operate via expected post-innovation returns) and direct effects (effects that operate given the level of expected post-innovation returns), letting various proxies of rivalry affect each. Column (iii) is an estimate of an equation showing how expected post-innovation returns depend on the various measures on rivalry used in (i), and this is used in (iv) to calculate the indirect effects of rivalry (e.g. for entry, the indirect effect is $2.27 \times -0.838 = -1.9$). The direct effects of each measure of rivalry on innovation is given in (i), and the sum of direct and indirect effects is shown in column (v). As we have just seen, the direct effects of market power appear to be negative. The indirect effects – estimated using a rational expectations proxy for expected post-innovation returns – were positive as expected (i.e. increases in expected post-innovation returns increased innovativeness, and rivalry diminished these returns, weakening the incentive to innovate). However, the indirect effects of actual monopoly power on innovation were more than dominated by the direct effects. Rivalry in the form of entry, small-firm activity and changes in concentration reduces expected post-innovation profits (exit and concentration raise them), but the impact of these indirect effects on innovativeness are small, not least because the effect of expected post-innovation returns on innovation appears to be rather modest. The conclusion, then, is that rivalry – as reflected in five measures of market structure – appears to stimulate innovativeness unambiguously, notwithstanding the slightly depressing effect it has on post-innovation returns and thence on innovativeness.

Thus, much of the statistical evidence on the effect of actual market power on innovativeness provides little more than weak support for the Schumpeterian hypothesis, if that. Entrants and small firms do innovate, contributing a share of innovations far in excess of their share of employment or value added, and the positive association that is sometimes observed between industry concentration and innovative inputs or output almost certainly arises because highly concentrated industries are frequently also those that are rich in technological opportunity. Innovation by market leaders and in concentrated industries often occurs, one

226   *Entry, Innovation and Productivity*

suspects, despite and not because of the market power enjoyed by insiders. Indeed, one's strongest impression from the data is that it is deep structural features of markets such as technological opportunity which play a rather more important role in stimulating innovation than rivalry. Still, this said, one comes away from the data without much doubt that rivalry does stimulate innovation to some extent in industries where technological opportunity is rich – that insiders are likely to require regular prodding by outsiders to keep them progressive. Although it would be rash to draw any firm conclusions from this rather mixed body of statistical experiments, there exists a wealth of case study evidence that reinforces these views.

The importance of entry and rivalry is often clearly recorded in cases that focus on changes in innovativeness which occur in a given market as an industry becomes deconcentrated or on differences in the progressiveness of the same industry in two different countries. For example, the initial monopolization through patents of the diesel engine in the USA considerably slowed down competition with steam power (perhaps by 'some ten years') at a time when the more fluid and open European industry was able to forge ahead of American firms and produce a variety of engines to suit the variety of uses to which they were increasingly put (Lytle, 1968). The aluminium industry in the USA saw a quickening in its innovative pace post-Second World War when the number of refiners rose from one to three and then to five. In any case, many of the innovations introduced came from the highly competitive fabricating industry, not from the refiners (Peck, 1962). The much more rapid development of computer-aided design and semiconductors in the USA (relative to Europe) is almost certainly due to small (often spin-off) firms leading the commercial exploitation of inventions, often right across the manufacturing sector (Rothwell, 1984; see also Porter, 1990, for a number of international comparisons that reach this type of conclusion). Not all cases show this pattern, however. In plastics, the dominance of West Germany in production and exports appears to have been largely due to the effects of IG Farben and its post-war successor firms (Freeman, 1963). The US industry, by contrast, appears to have been both less concentrated and less progressive, and the post-war deconcentration of the industry in West Germany did lead to an apparent loss in that country's technological leadership. Still, this conclusion may be an artifact of these two particular comparisons. The UK, France and Italy were all highly concentrated industries which never produced more than 25% of world patents in this area. Further, at a global level, DuPont, IG Farben, ICI and a few others have as a group kept the industry fairly competitive with low international technological diffusion lags, and it is not clear that IG Farben's dominant position in the West German market amounted to much in the way of substantial market power globally.

It is also frequently the case that insiders are too wedded to existing activities to respond quickly to the arrival of new opportunities, thus making themselves vulnerable to entry. In the alkali industry, large investments in the nineteenth century by some British producers in plant and equipment embodying the Leblanc process made them loath to invest in the newly developed Solvay process and, indeed, they attempted to maintain the value of their assets by trying to enter into price-fixing agreements with other British producers using the Solvay process (Rothwell and Zegveld, 1985, pp. 40-1). Rapid entry into the UK dry cleaning industry in the late 1950s and early 1960s was based on a technology known since the 1930s, and the great rush of entry forced incumbents to convert from factory-based to on-site cleaning operations well before they would have wished. For incumbents, this conversion meant not only scrapping factory cleaning operations, but also initiating large-scale changes in internal organization that they were reluctant to implement (Shaw, 1973; Shaw and Sutton, 1976, pp. 108-26). Although not (until recently) terribly vulnerable to entry, the innovative activity of IBM has many of these features. Of 21 major innovations in the computer industry examined by Brock (1975), only six could be credited to IBM (although IBM successfully replied to most of them extremely rapidly). Each of the three generations of computer was introduced by an entry challenge. Although in most cases, IBM has managed to establish a standard to which the industry has adhered, it has rarely initiated the process which resulted in those standards (see also Shaw and Sutton, 1976). Other responses by incumbents faced with entry challenges of this type include withdrawal into market segments less vulnerable to challenges and minimizing changes to operations involving existing products, behaviour observed in the post-war electronic components industry by Soukup and Cooper (1983).[6]

Examples of existing firms with no good reason to be too wedded to their existing activities to innovate are plentiful. As we saw in chapter 5, in the UK potato crisp market, the market incumbent (Smiths) proved extremely vulnerable to entry (by Golden Wonder) based upon major (but by no means mysterious) marketing and some rather minor technological innovations, eventually responding by increasing product variety in a manner which was not beyond their capabilities pre-entry. The ultimate consequence of entry was a much wider variety in products sold in a wider variety of retail outlets than hitherto, changes previously constrained only by the lethargy of a dominant incumbent (see Bevan, 1974). Similarly, Rolls Razor's entry into the UK washing machine market in 1958 was

228 Entry, Innovation and Productivity

'founded on the inadequacies of established firms' (p. 51), and had a similar effect in transforming a previously languishing market (Shaw and Sutton, 1976, pp. 43-53). However, it would be a mistake to presume that incumbents are always (or frequently) wedded to existing activities and unable to meet innovative challenges simply because they are blind, stupid or lazy. Bresnahan (1985) found Xerox to be vulnerable to entry in the plain copier market because of its large stock of rented units, the problem being the large capital loss on existing units which it would be forced to bear for each new unit put on the market. The consequence was that it was reluctant to match the prices that entrants charged. More fundamentally, the core products and processes which define a firm's major activities often have a ways of embedding themselves so thoroughly into the fabric of a firm's organization that they condition the ways in which that firm innovates. A well-defined core product – like a large luxury car propelled by an internal combustion engine – often breeds an extensive division of labour amongst the scientists and engineers responsible for product development that makes incremental innovation possible, but only at the expense of an inability to redesign the core product itself. When a division of labour is used to organize new product development, everyone is a specialist at something and, as long as the core product remains the dominant design, that design defines how they interact. However, new designs require new specialists and new methods of interaction; above all, they require generalists, not specialists. The relatively feeble response of the major US car producers to the growing competitive challenge of small, compact economical cars can be traced (at least in part) to how they organized their product development effort (e.g. Clark, 1988).

Although it is rather hazardous to generalize from a number of non-randomly selected cases, there is enough evidence in these cases to suggest that insiders – large, incumbent firms whose domination of core industry activities gives them market power – play an important but by no means overwhelming role in *generating new innovations*. They do not always move with alacrity, however, in using their own – or others – innovations, and outsiders – smaller fringe and new firms with little market power – often play a major role in *stimulating diffusion*. The main problem seems to be a lack of incentives rather than a lack of opportunities. Large insider firms are often wedded to existing activities, and they are often reluctant to abandon them in favour of new ones. This may simply be a case of not pursuing new activities whose displacement of an existing earnings stream does not yield a major net increase in returns, but one often sense that the apparent attractiveness of old familiar ways are the consequence of a limited imagination and a bloated sense of complacency.[7] Outsider firms are less sleepy and less committed to existing activities and, as a consequence, are far more flexible than insiders. This flexibility may or may not overcome a range of other disadvantages that weaken their ability to generate new innovations, but it is almost certainly likely to make them quicker and more enthusiastic about adopting innovations generated elsewhere. The implication, then, is that entry and outsider firms are almost certainly likely to play a major role in the diffusion of new innovations, whatever their contribution to the process of generating new innovations is.

Indeed, the evidence suggests that market leaders do not often adopt new innovations as fast as their smaller rivals, or as fast as entrants. A classic example of this is provided by (what was then) US Steel who reacted much more slowly to innovations like continuous costing and the basic oxygen furnace than most of its rivals (see Oster, 1982b, and references therein). Other examples are not difficult to track down as, it must be said, are counter-examples (see, for example, Metcalf's study of the UK textile industry (1970) and, for both examples and counter-examples, the work surveyed in Baldwin and Scott (1987, pp. 128–38)). As with the evidence relating firm size to the generation of innovations, so there is no real basis in this evidence on diffusion for thinking that large incumbent firms are particularly fast adopters, and there is at least some suspicion that one observes them to be so mainly in situations where the competitive threat of smaller, outsider firms encourages them. Evidence on the diffusion of numerical control machines across ten US industries suggests that diffusion is slower in sectors where there are large inequalities in firm sizes (Romeo, 1977a, b; Davies, 1979) and, more generally, that diffusion speed seems to be adversely affected by high level of concentration (Mansfield et al., 1971). The evidence in Davies and Mansfield is that, within industries, larger firms are often relatively slower to adopt new technology. Certainly, the sigmoid diffusion pattern which characterizes the diffusion of most innovations suggests that, sooner or later, insider firms will be forced to adopt simply because a number of their competitors have already done so and, as a group, are beginning to make competitive inroads in the sales of non-adopters. Thus, even if the competitive effects of outsiders are not completely evident at the outset, the cumulative impact of their actions is likely to hasten a diffusion process already under way.

Causal Relations between Entry and Innovation

Sorting out the respective roles of insiders and outsiders in the innovation process also requires one to look more directly at the innovative activities of outsiders. The natural place to start an empirical examination of this issue is with the question of whether innovative entry actually exists – do at least some entrants use innovation as a vehicle of entry, and if so, how many? This is a rather difficult question to address, and answers are only possible if one takes a broad view of what 'innovation' is (a bias likely to overstate the degree of truly innovative entry).

The data suggest that there is almost no doubt that 'innovative entry' constitutes little more than a small proportion of total entry attempts. For example, the proportion of new or small UK firms founded on the basis of even a fairly minor innovation is quite limited. Johnson and Cathcart (1979) found that only nine of 74 new manufacturing firms in the northern regions of the UK (1971–3) were based on a technical innovation (and three disappeared within three years). In East Anglia (1971–81), Gould and Keeble (1984) discovered that only 10% of new firms in their sample were high technology firms, 58% of which were in electronics (50% alone were in scientific instruments) and 75% of which were located within 30 miles of Cambridge. Lloyd and Mason (1984) found that only one in six new firms in the Greater Merseyside and Manchester areas were innovative, while only one in four were in South Hampshire. O'Farrell and Crouchley (1984) found only four in 100 new small firms in Nottingham to be innovative. Virtually all these authors suggest that their estimates of the rate of innovative entry are biased upwards, since the judgement of what is innovative is often based on the opinion of the founder of the firm in question. The bottom line, then, seems to be that, at most, about 10% of all new firms are innovative entrants. This is not to say that these innovative entrants are unimportant. They typically enjoy remarkable growth rates and low failure rates. They are, in general, product innovators and, being development rather than research oriented, are often rather good at introducing commercially oriented innovations (Bollinger et al., 1983). In short, there is some basis for thinking that only a rather small percentage of (what is, after all, quite a large population of) actual entrants are, in any important sense, innovative.

That innovative entry is only a small percentage of total entry is, of course, consistent with the possibility that entrants are nevertheless directly or, more likely, indirectly responsible for a major share of total innovative activity. Innovation (at least on a fairly major scale) is a relatively infrequent activity while entry is not, and, in any case, entrants can play a valuable role in creating incentives for insiders to innovate. Rather more worrying is the possibility that any association that one observes between innovation and entry arises because innovation creates opportunities which attract entrants to a market, and not because entrants to a market introduce new innovations.

More broadly, it is interesting to ask whether rivalry determines the evolution of technology in markets, or whether technological trajectories shape the competitive structure of markets in systematic ways over time. Although most economists have mainly been interested in the causal links running from concentration and other proxies for the degree of competition in markets to innovation, the causal channel from technology to concentration may be no less important. Blair (1974), for example, has argued that many of the innovations introduced in the twentieth century have been deconcentrating. In contrast with late eighteenth-century advances such as steam power and railroad transportation which encouraged the growth of large production establishments, twentieth-century innovations like electricity, transport using trucks and the use of new materials such as plastics have, he argued, reduced minimum efficient scale in many industries (see also Piore and Sabel, 1984, for a rather broader, more proscriptive discussion in this vein). At a somewhat different level, there is also some econometric evidence to suggest that innovative activity has had a modest negative effect on levels of industry concentration in the UK (e.g. Geroski and Pomroy, 1990, and references cited therein). Thus, it is worth asking whether entry stimulates innovation directly because new firms introduce new innovations or indirectly because they stimulate incumbents to do so, or whether a positive correlation between entry and innovation reflects the stimulating effects that technological change can have on entry by reducing barriers to entry.

The major difficulty with constructing an operational model of entry and innovation to explore this question is that many of the determinants of entry and innovation (both transitory factors like mediating market conditions and permanent factors like entry barriers and technological opportunity) are difficult to observe. One solution to this type of problem is (as we saw in chapter 3) to use a dynamic latent factor model that relies only on information about entry and innovation rates. Since it is not always possible directly or accurately to observe the conditions of entry and innovation in a market, it is frequently impossible to measure the effects of either on entry and innovation. One can make some indirect inferences about these effects, however, because unobserved changes in causes will be recorded in observed consequences. In particular, endogenous variables (like entry and innovation rates) *fully* reflect the *complete* set of exogenous but unobserved variables of interest (like entry barriers and inter-industry variations in technological opportunity) – they are (if you like) observable indices of the conditions of entry and innovation in markets.

Suppose that all the latent transitory determinants of entry and innovation can be summarized by two sequences of serially uncorrelated shocks,

a_t and b_t, and the independent and permanent determinants (entry barriers and technological opportunity respectively) by two fixed factors A and B. Following Geroski (1989a) the two-equation system determining entry and innovation can be written as

$$E_t = \sum_{\tau=0}^{\infty} \alpha_\tau a_{t-\tau} + \sum_{\tau=0}^{\infty} \lambda_\tau b_{t-\tau} + A$$

$$(6.1)$$

$$I_t = \sum_{\tau=0}^{\infty} \theta_t a_{t-\tau} + \sum_{\pi=0}^{\infty} \beta_\tau b_{t-\tau} + B$$

where I_t denotes innovation and E_t denotes entry. Since a_t and b_t are orthogonal by construction, then any correlation that is observed between entry and innovation must be caused by non-zero values of the λ_τ and/or θ_τ. That is, if E_t and I_t are correlated, it can only be because the transitory determinants of innovation summarized by b_t have an effect on E_t, the transitory determinants of entry summarized by a_t have an effect on I_t, or both. The problem is that it is impossible to measure the λ_τ and θ_τ directly because a_t and b_t are not observable. However, E_t contains information on a_t (and a_{t-1}, a_{t-2}, . . .), I_t on b_t (and b_{t-1}, b_{t-2}, . . .), E_{t-1} on a_{t-1} (and a_{t-2}, a_{t-3}, . . .), I_{t-1} on b_{t-1} (and b_{t-2}, b_{t-3}, . . .), and so on. Each observable is therefore a signal of one or more of the unobservables, and using this observation to rearrange (6.1) yields a reduced form expressed entirely in observables:

$$E_{it} = \sum_{\tau=1}^{\infty} \Psi_\tau E_{it-\tau} + \sum_{\tau=0}^{\infty} \eta_\tau I_{t-\tau} + A_i + \mu_{it}$$

$$(6.2)$$

$$I_{it} = \sum_{\tau=1}^{\infty} \xi_\tau I_{it-\tau} + \sum_{\tau=0}^{\infty} \phi_\tau E_{it-\tau} + B_i + \gamma_{it}$$

where $i = 1$, . . ., N indexes industries and $t = 1$, . . ., T time periods. A_i and B_i are industry-specific fixed effects assumed to be constant over time, and μ_{it} and γ_{it} are white noise residuals.

The primary attraction of (6.2) is that it enables one to examine the causal links that exist between entry and innovative activity. Consider first the possibility that the transitory determinants of entry have no effect on innovation; that is, that $\theta_\tau = 0$, $\tau \geqslant 0$. Using (6.1) and (6.2), it is the case that $\theta_\tau = 0$ if and only if $\phi_\tau = 0$, $\tau \geqslant 0$, since $\alpha_\tau \neq 0$. Hence, the hypothesis that the determinants of entry do not cause innovation corresponds to the restriction in the second equation of (6.2) that the terms $\Sigma \phi_\tau E_{t-\tau}$ be excludable.[8] Similarly, the hypothesis that the transitory determinants of innovation have no effect on entry corresponds in (6.1) to the restriction that $\lambda_\tau = 0$, $\tau \geqslant 0$. This will be the case if $\eta_\tau = 0$, $\tau \geqslant 0$, since $\beta_\tau \neq 0$. It follows, then, that an appropriate test of the hypothesis that innovation has no effect on entry is whether one can accept the restriction that the terms $\Sigma \eta_\tau I_{t-\tau}$ can be excluded from the first equation of (6.2). The acceptance of either of these restrictions converts (6.2) into a recursive system.

Geroski (1989a) applied (6.2) to a sample of 79 digit industries in the UK, pooling two cross-sections (for 1978 and 1979) together. I_t was defined as the logarithm of unity plus the number of innovations produced in each sector i; E_t was measured as net entry penetration (although the results proved to be quite robust to the use of gross entry measures and to the use of measures of the incidence of entry). An analysis of variance of the innovations data pooled over the period 1975–9 indicated that roughly 58% of the total variation in the number of innovations was between-industry variation. For net entry, the corresponding percentage was, as we saw in chapter 2, 23%. Further, variations in innovative activity across industries were observed to be rather stable over time, while variations in entry were not. The correlation between variations in innovation across industries in 1979 and that in 1978, 1977, 1976 and 1975 was always about 0.700; that between net entry penetration in these years never exceeded 0.100. Thus, inter-industry differences in innovation are slightly more pronounced than variations over time in the innovative activities of particular industries, not least because some industries simply do not innovate while others do so consistently. Current and near future innovating industries are relatively easy to spot on the basis of their near past innovation records. Inter-industry differences in entry, by contrast, are much less marked, and the substantial variation over time in the entry experience of any particular industry is relatively unsystematic and extremely difficult to predict. This, in turn, suggests that entry is likely to be very sensitive to a wide range of perhaps idiosyncratic market conditions (as we saw in chapter 3). Innovation rates, by contrast, seem to be much less strongly affected by mediating market conditions, and the constraints on innovative activity imposed by technological opportunities divide highly innovating industries from the rest fairly clearly. Given these quite marked differences in the statistical properties of innovative activity and entry, it is not surprising to discover that partial correlations between values of either across industries in 1979 and values of the other in earlier years were all positive but modest in size, never exceeding 0.215.

Partial correlations are, of course, likely to understate the cumulative effect of one variable on the other, and, in any case, they give no information on causal orderings. It is therefore necessary to probe somewhat more deeply using a statistical vehicle like (6.2), and table 6.2 shows OLS estimates of a statistically acceptable restricted version of (6.2). Equation (i) shows the results of regressing I_t on its own history plus that of E_t. The five restrictions that the $\phi_\tau = 0$, $\tau = 0$, . . ., 5 inflated the sum of squared residuals by about 9.3%, and the calculated $\chi^2(5)$ statistic was well above conventional 5% significance levels. Together, the two calculations suggest that it would be imprudent to accept the restrictions $\phi_\tau = 0$, however modest the estimated impact of the $E_{t-\tau}$ is. Equation (ii) shows the results of regressing E_t on its own history, and it is statistically a restriction of a more general model that corresponds to imposing $\eta_\tau = 0$, $\tau = 0$, . . ., 5. That the restrictions $\eta_\tau = 0$ are acceptable but

Table 6.2 Estimates of (6.2)

Dependent variable	(i) I_t	(ii) E_t
I_t	–	–
I_{t-1}	−1.062	–
	(8.48)	
I_{t-2}	−0.6142	–
	(4.96)	
I_{t-3}	−0.0943	–
	(0.8241)	
I_{t-4}	0.1933	–
	(1.334)	
E_t	−3.842	–
	(3.089)	
E_{t-1}	−2.440	−0.7367
	(1.509)	(12.70)
E_{t-2}	−1.736	−0.6257
	(1.097)	(6.146)
E_{t-3}	−2.493	−0.2587
	(1.174)	(2.484)
E_{t-4}	−2.336	−0.0491
	(3.129)	(1.608)
$\bar{R}^2$	0.800	0.4850
Log likelihood	20.65	478.348
SSR	7.1227	0.02170

All equations include 79 industry-specific industry dummies and one time dummy, and all estimates are heteroscedastic consistent.
I_t, log of unity plus the count of innovations; E_t, net entry penetration.
Source: Geroski, 1989a

$\phi_\tau = 0$ are not suggests that the fully interdependent two-equation model (6.2) can be simplified to the recursive model shown in table 6.2 in which E_t has an effect on I_t but I_t has no effect on E_t. That is, if one focuses only on the transitory determinants of entry and innovation, it appears that entry causes innovation, but that innovation does not cause entry. However, entry and innovation rates are also driven by relatively permanent factors such as technological opportunity and entry barriers. These are captured in (6.2) by the fixed effects A_i and B_i, and the correlation that arises between innovation and entry through them was, in fact, strong and positive. Estimates of the fixed effects retrieved from equations (i) and (ii) in table 6.2 were found to be correlated with coefficient 0.730. Regressing estimates of B_i on those of A_i yielded

$$\hat{B}^i = \underset{(5.69)}{0.7542} + \underset{(11.90)}{29.88\hat{A}^i} + \underset{(8.28)}{244.08\hat{A}^2_i} \tag{6.3}$$

with $R^2 = 0.71$, where t statistics are given in parentheses beneath the estimated coefficients.

Thus, there appear to be two sources of correlation between entry and innovation rates, and the two partially offset each other. The correlation that arises because the permanent determinants of each are similar is positive, and it is consistent with the notion that entry barriers and technological opportunities are highly related across industries. Industries that are rich in technological opportunity appear to have lower entry barriers in general, and therefore high levels of entry and innovation activity simultaneously occur in these sectors. Transitory determinants, however, work the other way, and the correlation that arises between innovation and entry through the lagged values of the observables – a correlation that reflects the apparent causal influences of entry on innovation – is negative. Figure 6.1 shows some simulations designed to show these two offsetting forces at work. Case 1 shows a simulation of equations (i) and (ii) from table 6.2 that set $A = 0$, $B = 0.75$ and $E_t = I_t = 0$, $t = 1, \ldots,$ 4. Increasing A_i facilitates entry, as shown in case 2 where A_i increases to 0.01 and, for this reason, reduces the count of innovations through the transitory effects registered in equation (i) in table 6.2. The reduction in innovation turns out to be about 5% in total over 15 periods. However, (6.3) suggests that A_i and B_i cannot be treated as if they were independent parameters, and case 3 shows what happens when the increase in A_i is mirrored in an increase in B_i by an amount given by (6.3). Innovation rises considerably – by about 37% relative to case 1 and by about 45% relative to case 2. Finally, were only B_i to change, case 4 shows that innovation would be higher still. As before, the negative offset from the

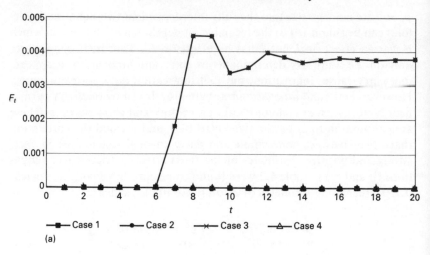

(a)

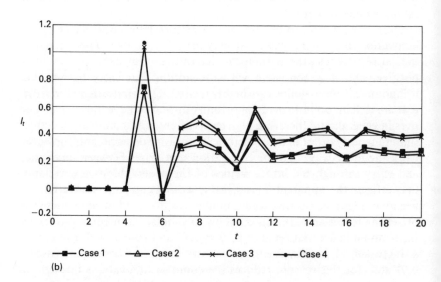

(b)

Figure 6.1 Simulations of the relationship between entry and innovation.

effects described in equation (ii) in table 6.2 leads to about a 5% decrease in innovativeness. It follows, then, that positive association between entry and innovation is driven by the positive correlation between entry barriers and technological opportunity, a positive association that is more than strong enough to overwhelm a negative causal effect running from entry to innovation that is driven by more transitory market conditions.

The evidence that we have just discussed is both consistent and inconsistent with that discussed in the previous section (particularly table 6.1). What is common to both tables is the important role played by the fixed effects in explaining innovation rates. These, we have argued, proxy conditions of technological opportunity, relatively permanent features of market structure that condition both the speed and direction of technological advance. All the results that we have discussed are quite consistent with the argument that it is technological opportunity which determines innovativeness, and that competitive rivalry has only second-order effects. However, tables 6.1 and 6.2 point in slightly different directions when it comes to the question of how competition affects innovation. Overall, both suggest that rivalry increases innovation, but table 6.2 suggests that purely transitory factors induce a negative causal effect running from entry to innovation, while table 6.1 shows that entry has an imprecisely estimated but nevertheless positive effect on innovation. Further, the results in table 6.1 suggest that highly concentrated industries are often liable to be those where technological opportunities are rich, while table 6.2 leads one to think that industries with rich technological opportunities may have lower entry barriers (*ceteris paribus*). Although not strictly inconsistent with each other, these different results are slightly disconcerting.

There are, no doubt, several possible ways to reconcile them. One line of approach simply asserts that rivalry may have only a second-order effect on innovation, and that small effects will always be difficult to discern with any accuracy in these kinds of data. A second asserts that indices of concentration and measures of entry reflect competitive conditions in two quite different subsectors of an industry (at the top and at the bottom) which are effectively separated by high mobility barriers. Rich technological opportunities, in this case, can encourage concentration at the top and entry at the bottom of the same industry; more or less rivalry at the top may have an effect on innovation that is quite different from more or less rivalry at the bottom. Perhaps the most attractive reconciliation, however, asserts that taking a rather static and timeless view of what is a dynamic process may distort one's view of the process. In particular, it may be the case that the effects of rivalry at the top and the bottom vary systematically over time as markets evolve, and that apparently small effects of rivalry are observed because a static view of the process conflates periods in an industry's history when rivalry matters with periods when it does not. One way to explore this conjecture is to look at the co-evolution of entry and innovation over the product life cycle.

Entry and Innovation over the Product Life Cycle

The evidence that we have just reviewed seems to provide little support for the view that market power and innovativeness necessarily go hand in hand. To be sure, large firms do innovate and innovations do occur in highly concentrated industries – the contributions of IBM, IG Farben, AT&T, DuPont or GE cannot simply be dismissed out of hand. However, the evidence is consistent with the view that such events may have occurred more frequently had those particular firms been a bit smaller and had they operated in industries that were a bit more competitive. On the other hand, the evidence associating innovative activity directly to entry – to new firms – is not exactly overpowering. Most entrants are not particularly innovative, and those that are often require many years of growth to bring them up to a competitive basis with industry leaders. While it is probably the case that the types of outsiders whose innovative activity most effectively challenges insiders in generating innovations are fringe producers already established in the market, market leaders in nearby markets together with high technology new firms do occasionally constitute a major threat to insiders, and this threat may be sufficient to keep an industry fairly progressive. However important they are in generating innovations, it does seem to be the case that both entrants and fringe producers play a major role in stimulating the diffusion of innovations. The distinction between generation and adoption can often be a rather fine one, and this is particularly the case in the early stages of a product's life when technical innovation and commercial application generate a variety of different products which struggle amongst themselves to form the basis or core of the emergent industry. In fact, one can make sense of many of the ambiguities in the data by setting the process of competition between new firms and new ideas into an explicit life cycle framework. The message that emerges when one does this is that entry plays a potentially crucial innovating role early in the life cycle of most industries.

Gort and Klepper (1982) have argued that markets typically evolve through a number of stages which can be defined in terms of net entry rates. Following the commercial introduction of a product and an initial monopoly phase, net entry occurs, often at a phenomenal rate. Over time, net entry falls to zero and then becomes negative as exit occurs. Industry structures tend to concentrate at this stage, and the number of active firms declines until, again, net entry is zero. This final stage 'continues until the eventual shrinkage of the market induced by obsolescence of the product, or until fundamental changes in technology launch a new product cycle . . .' (p. 631). Examining 46 products spanning up to about 73 years, they found few instances of commercial introduction followed immediately by rapid entry (the mean lag was 14–15 years, and only seven of the 46 saw rapid entry within five years). When entry began, however, it was generally extensive. The rapid entry phase lasted an average of ten years (and as much as 25 years in one case) and, on average, saw a net increase of nearly six firms per year. The subsequent contraction phase was much quicker (about half the length of the expansion phase on average, and noticeably longer in only five of 46 cases), leading to a net reduction of about five firms per year. For those 19 products that Gort and Klepper were able to observe well into their mature phase, the number of producers removed during industry rationalization averaged 40%, exceeding 50% in six cases. Using industry life cycles defined in terms of net entry, they observed that the number of 'major' innovations peaked during the expansion phase, the number of 'minor' innovations peaked just before contraction occurred, and the number of patents turned down after the contraction phase. Gort and Klepper interpreted their data not only as showing that the pace of innovative activity varies with net entry over the life cycle, but also as suggesting that, in early stages, outsiders are the source of most innovations and use these as a vehicle of entry. As time goes on, insiders provide relatively more of the innovations introduced, innovations that are 'minor' more often than not.

It is not difficult to winkle out a reasonable story from this data. When products are first introduced, they and the market that they serve are often very poorly defined. Consumers often have only a vague idea of which product characteristics are of most value, and producers have yet to explore fully the range of product specifications which are technically possible. This uncertainty on both sides of the market makes it difficult for any substantive barriers to entry to build up, and new entry is often associated with new ideas, leading to a very high ratio of innovative to imitative entry.[9] The competitive process at this stage is very much a selection process, and one expects that relatively high entry and exit rates will be a concomitant of the process of weeding out and winnowing down. At some point, however, the product begins to standardize, and the range of product variants available often shrinks considerably. Firms that happen to produce the good which becomes the standard (or part of the core of standardized products) begin to enjoy advantages arising from consumer recognition and loyalty on the demand side, and, on the supply side, proprietary knowledge about producing the good and the exploitation of any economies of scale in production that are opened up by the possibilities of mass producing a standardized good. These barriers make entry more difficult, and, if the early entry intensive selection process fully explored all the technological opportunities available in the industry, then the possibilities for further innovative entry will in any case diminish. Innovations that occur will increasingly originate from insiders, and, both because technological opportunities become exhausted and because the challenge of entry has fallen off, they will be more infrequent and, perhaps, increasingly less important.[10]

In fact, it is possible to push this argument a step further and argue that this process of market evolution can often be accompanied by a shift from product towards process innovation. This can come about for several reasons, but the main ones are the consequence of product standardization and the shifting from competition between firms on the basis of unusual product attributes to competition based on price. As standardization occurs, the locus of innovation shifts away from entrants who, as non-producers, are unlikely to be as familiar with the production process as insiders, and, within firms, from personnel associated with marketing (those geared to identifying new user needs) to personnel familiar with the technology (those geared to producing well-defined products more efficiently). Market needs give way to technological imperatives, the urge to define and expand markets gives way to competitive strategies based on serving the market cheaply. As this process continues, production often becomes increasingly systemic, more highly elaborated and highly integrated to control the production of a specific product, and this, in turn, makes it expensive for firms to contemplate introducing new products that require new production systems. Expressed somewhat differently, the shift to process innovation can commence a trip down the product learning curve which generates increasing productivity at the cost of increased inflexibility (Abernathy and Wayne, 1974).

In support of this hypothesis about product and process innovations, Utterback and Abernathy (1975) examined data on 330 commercially successful innovations from 77 firms operating in five industries. These 330 innovations came from a wider study of 567 innovations, of which 237 proved difficult to allocate to early or later phases of product life cycles. They observed that about two-thirds of the product innovations in their sample were introduced in early stages of the life of the product, while nearly 70% of innovations introduced in latter phases of the product cycle were process innovations. Many of these early innovations also apparently incorporated new technology rather than existing technology adapted from other uses, appearing to be 'major' rather than 'minor'. Firms in different stages of product development were quizzed on the priority that they placed on research, and the proportion that accorded it high (low) priority fell (rose) steadily as the product they were concerned with matured. Finally, they observed that the innovations introduced in early phases of the life cycle were, on the whole, rather more likely to originate from small firms; large firms predominated as innovators in later phases.

Further support for this hypothesis emerged from a study of technological changes in engine plant development at Ford Motor Company reported by Abernathy (1976; see also Abernathy, 1978; Abernathy et al., 1983; Clark 1983), who documented the transition of production technology from an initial, highly fluid state to a much more organized and specific final state. Noticeable features of this process included a sharply increasing cost of product change (from zero in the days of the Model T to at least $20 million with the advent of the Model A and the V8 engine) and a continual rise in backward integration. In general, the shift towards process innovation and the increase in backward integration is likely to be part of a process of industry concentration and rationalization which raises entry barriers and reduces the competitive challenges of outsiders. This is perhaps rather unfortunate, since these same developments often gradually envelop the industry in a sort of sclerosis which substantially weakens an already diminished tendency to introduce major new products and, perhaps, process innovations. Reviewing the history of the car industry, it seems clear that the consolidation of the industry has occurred *pari passu* with a slackening in innovation rates, and that the areas in which the leading insiders in the USA have actively innovated are, in the main, those where they have been challenged by entrants or by government regulatory bodies (White, 1971). Industry maturity, it seems, may be no more than a synonym for stagnation, and can be, in large part, endogenous to the competitive process.

There is no need to accept the full set of hypotheses associated with the product life cycle to be persuaded that entry often plays a major role early in the life of most products, or, to phrase the same idea in a more causally neutral fashion, that the emergence of new products is often accompanied by a flurry of entry or small-firm activity. The British aircraft industry before 1914 contained at least 200 firms and, stimulated by the Great War, the number of producers rose to 771 in November 1917 and 1529 by October 1918. The number of competing designs was enormous, and efforts made during the war to standardize production were not successful. Serious rationalization (aided by government procurement practices) did not occur until the mid-1930s (Fearan, 1969). The car industry in both the USA and the UK emerged from the hurly-burly of extensive early entry. In the UK, there were more than 400 competing motor car producers pre-1914 (Saul, 1962), while in the USA the existence of producers almost too numerous to list ensured that: 'anyone trying to buy a car in 1900 was confronted with a bewildering array of products and technologies. There were cars powered by steam, electricity or gasoline;

cars with three wheels or four . . . structural features, mechanical principles and performance characteristics varied widely from car to car' (Clark, 1983, p. 103). Katz and Phillips (1982) counted 48 variants of the second generation, commercial transistorized computers which appeared in the five years following November 1958, 'something akin to a Schumpeterian "swarming" of entrepreneurs . . .' (p. 212). Much the same swarming occurred in the mid-1960s, with the arrival of minicomputers, microprocessors and so on. In the UK, the number of suppliers of disc packs and disc drives rose by factors of 13 and 18 within four years of new product introduction in 1968 (Shaw and Sutton, 1976, p. 105).

There are, of course, exceptions to the rule. Television, for example, emerged in the USA largely (but not entirely) through the efforts of RCA, who spent in excess of $9 million between 1930 and 1939 doing the basic and developmental research, having bought out work done in the late 1920s by Westinghouse (Maclaurin, 1950). Similarly, fluorescent lamps were introduced in the late 1930 more or less simultaneously by the four leaders (with a joint share of 86%) in the incandescent lamp industry (Bright and Maclaurin, 1943). In both cases, however, entry (into both the new industry and the old one from which it sprang) appears to have been blocked by a welter of patents cross-licensed amongst incumbents, and in both cases one senses that potential competition from other insiders spurred innovators on, and that more potential competition would have produced more innovations or at least a much quicker introduction of those that did appear. In television, Philco supported an independent research team which, eventually, incorporated and entered as an independent (but short-lived) competitor. This, of course, is hard to construe as a major competitive challenge, and Maclaurin argued that 'the historical evidence in radio and television suggests that more competition among GE, Westinghouse and AT&T would have resulted in greater technical progress from 1920–40 than actually occurred' (p. 156). In fluorescent lamps, much of the early basic research was done in Europe, and GE (together with Westinghouse) commenced development research rather late in the day (1935), well after its smaller more ambitious rival, Sylvania, began. GE, apparently, felt quite secure in the domestic lamp market and directed most of its efforts into the improvement of its existing line of activity, incandescent lighting. As a consequence, Sylvania's competitive push eventually resulted in a market share in fluorescent lighting four times its share of the incandescent lamps market. Very little in the way of an independent technical challenge to GE emerged from Westinghouse (the number two firm in incandescent lamps, with a market share of 20%, just less than a third of GE's). In fact, the introduction of fluorescent lamps in 1938 was prompted by lighting engineers working for the New

York and San Francisco Worlds Fair, much sooner than GE and Westinghouse would have wished (p. 439). Once again, one senses that the absence of innovative entry (there was a certain amount of imitative entry, producing to the GE-Westinghouse standard) considerably retarded the emergence and development of this market. Certainly developments post-1940 have been much more rapid, not least because Sylvania matured into a major, technologically competent challenger (p. 449).

One emerges from all of this, then, with a strong sense that entry may provide the key to understanding many of the broad features of how markets evolve and develop in their early stages. Most markets commence with a flurry of entry. In some cases, the new products originate from the R&D laboratories of large firms in related areas; in other cases, the basic science and know-how already exists. In either case, however, commercial application often follows from the activities of a wide variety of new firms not inhibited by current activities which the innovation might displace. Product variety widens during the early life of the new market, and an increasing body of consumers are treated to a diversity of products suited to an ever wider range of needs and applications. Even when the basic invention originates from the activities of large, incumbent insiders, there seems to be little doubt that entry can play a crucial role in expediting its commercial application and diffusion. This is not the full story, however, and the picture often changes as the industry matures. Increasing competitive pressures often make firms more cost and price conscious, and, as a consequence, innovative activity often becomes more focused on process innovation. This, in turn, generally means that barriers to entry – to initiative and innovative entrants alike – rise, and the role of insiders in the innovation process increases, a transformation which (in all likelihood) hastens the decline of the industry into maturity. The conclusion must be that the standard, popular version of the Schumpeterian hypothesis, if it is not simply wrong, is at least far too simple to account for what we observe. The concentration of inventive activity in the hands of market leaders is a concomitant of the process by which market power is created, although, to be sure, it reinforces the market power that insiders accumulate from other sources. What is more, the association between insiders and innovation that one can see at this point in an industry's life is one that characterizes the descent into maturity. The creative flood of innovation, the flow of new ideas and new products that defines the character and evolution of the market, occurs much earlier, and generally requires an absence of market power to ensure that it reaches full flower.

The semiconductor and computer-aided design industries provide fairly vivid illustrations that may bring this stylization to life. As virtually every school child knows, the transistor was developed in 1951 by AT&T, and production quickly took off in the early 1950s, led by a number of firms already established in the production of receiving tubes who, quite rightly, perceived the threat that transistors posed to their existing business. For a variety of reasons (including AT&T's liberal licensing policies and willingness to tolerate the defection of skilled personnel into new spin-off firms), much of the impetus behind the growth of the market came from new firms who rapidly eroded the market position of the early leaders. These new firms tended to specialize in commercial applications, and were far more effective (at least initially) in encouraging diffusion of the new product to a wide range of users by developing numerous applications than they were in contributing to the generation of this basic invention. In 1951, four companies on the USA made transistors commercially; by 1956 there were 26 (Braun and MacDonald, 1982). Between 1961 and 1965, the number of firms producing integrated circuits rose to more than 30 and, in 1972, there were at least 1220 firms in the semiconductor industry (p. 122). The diversity of products they introduced was enormous. By 1957, there were no fewer than 600 different types of transistor on the market, a tenfold increase in four years (p. 56); between 1956 and 1962, about 6000 different transistor types were produced, 75% of which were still available in 1962 (p. 77). Similarly, the first microprocessor, the 4004 introduced by Intel at the end of 1971, was followed by 19 different microprocessors introduced by mid-1974, and over 40 before the market was five years old (p. 110). The competitive process engendered by these entrants also led to an extraordinarily high turnover among market leaders, and 'each significant new product innovation launche(d) a technology race from which one or two firms usually emerge(d) with the lions share of the market. At any point in time, there (were) dozens of product markets, and most firms (were) unlikely to be among the leaders in more than a few' (Levin, 1982, p. 31).

This rather frantic pace of change and market development could not, of course, be sustained forever (although it still remains rapid by any standard). The technology of the industry followed a trajectory towards process innovation which gradually shifted technological leadership back toward the large established firms. New firms tended to account for a far higher share of product than process innovations, and did less patenting than incumbents who, it appears, concentrated their work in basic research and (often fruitlessly) tried to protect their activities with patents. Entry barriers were initially quite low, largely because of the availability of ready venture capital, the existence of only modest capital requirements, the ease of access to technology, and a number of features of US government procurement policy (on which, see Levin, 1982). Since the 1970s, however, the costs of entry appear to have risen quite rapidly, largely owing to the increasing costs of manufacturing increasingly complex products, and entry from the late 1970s onwards tended to involve niche strategies based on customized products or production. The rise in entry barriers was also caused in part by a rise in vertical integration occasioned by the blurring of distinctions between electronic components and systems, and a slow down in the rate at which key technical personnel could abscond with ideas that established firms had not yet developed. Clearly this market would have developed in the absence of entry, but it is probably the case that it would have done so with less variety, less product innovation, a smaller range of industrial and consumer applications, and, most clearly of all, much more slowly without entry. This, it has been argued (e.g. Tilton, 1971), can be seen by examining the evolution of the industry in Europe and Japan. In fact, the technology diffused somewhat more rapidly in the USA than in Europe and Japan, and in Europe diffusion was largely prompted by the activities of new subsidiaries set up by US entrants. Neither Europe nor Japan saw the swarming of new indigenous entrants that greeted early users and consumers in the USA, and established firms in Europe would almost certainly have responded much more slowly in the absence of foreign investment by US firms.

Much the same sort of pattern can be perceived in the development of the market for computer-aided design (CAD) systems (e.g. Kaplinski, 1983). The initial (pre-1969) years of development largely occurred in the laboratories of large aerospace, computer mainframe and defence industry firms, often with heavy support from the US Department of Defense. From the late 1960s to early 1970s, the product rapidly defused to the electronics sector, largely through the actions of new software specialist firms who broadened the range of CAD applications. By the late 1970s, when CAD equipment began to be sold widely across the manufacturing sector, the industry began to concentrate, with predators amongst many of the major users gobbling up suppliers (and, of course, some suppliers systematically winning sales at the expense of others). The increase in vertical integration raised entry barriers, and entrants post-1980 have, in the main, sold specialist or customized systems. They apparently have not been able to compete with the comprehensive application program systems offered by market leaders using mini and mainframe computers, but are able to exploit microprocessor-based systems (p. 53).

The conclusion seems to be that entry is an integral part of the process of industry evolution, an important cog in the wheel that propels the process of change and development through innovation. Following the discussion in the previous section, one might identify two sources of association between entry and innovation. The first and probably most important is that between conditions of technological opportunity and entry barriers. These two sets of structural factors appear to be highly interdependent, and one conjectures that they together evolve systematically as the industry pushes out along its technological trajectory. The consequence is the joint occurrence of entry and innovation in the early development of many markets, the one serving as a vehicle to carry the other to consumers. Subsequent (and partly endogenous) developments in the market tend to shut down entry possibilities while, at the same time, shunting the development of new technologies from a product to a process orientation. Both entry and the rate of (at least major) innovation typically slow at this point as a consequence of these structural changes. The second source of association between entry and innovation arises from direct causal effects that run between the two for given levels of entry barriers and technological opportunity. These causal channels are rather difficult to assign a clear sign to (particularly the one running from entry to innovation), much less to measure in size. This is almost certainly because there can come a time in industry evolution where the advantages of insiders become very large relative to outsiders. Nevertheless, a considerable amount of evidence exists to persuade one that insiders do have incentive problems, and that outsiders are frequently necessary to spur them into action. What does seem to be true is that the role of entry – and of outsiders more generally – in stimulating the generation of innovations is probably less clearly positive than it is in stimulating the diffusion of innovations. Further, whatever the size of these direct causal effects of entry on innovation, it is probably the case that they are dwarfed by the association created between entry and innovation caused by changes in entry barriers and technological opportunity. Entry and innovation rates might best be thought of as signals of the same deep underlying phenomenon rather than as mutual stimulants.

Competition, Efficiency and Productivity

That entry may speed the diffusion of new products and processes implies that entry is a force can which help to bring actual operating costs into line with a best practice cost function which shifts over time. Although it is very difficult to do so practically, one can conceptually distinguish this effect (a movement of the productive frontier) from the effect that entry may have on x-inefficiency (a movement to the frontier). Suppose that technology is stable and well known, and that it has been so for sufficiently long to have enabled all firms to adjust their plant and equipment in the appropriate manner. Even in these circumstances, one can expect to observe slack in production operations if firms have some degree of market power. By restricting output and raising price, firms can generate supernormal profits which will be shared out amongst shareholders, managers, workers and, possibly, other relevant parties (e.g. suppliers) in a manner that depends on the precise resolution of the intra-firm competition that their existence provokes. Whatever the details of how it occurs, the resolution of that conflict may involve bloated dividends, inflated wages and salaries, the tolerance of a variety of restrictive or inefficient working practices, and, perhaps, a series of self-indulgent acquisitions. In effect, excess profits enable firms to finance an 'easy life' in which they choose not to make the best of current circumstances, and one expects to observe an actual or anticipated increase in competition to provoke a search for cost-saving actions by incumbents. Indeed, as firms gradually lose control over price in the face of increased competition, the only way that they can maintain their margins is to reduce their costs. Perfectly competitive firms are often thought of as price takers who passively accept that the environment that they operate in is exogenous. This, however, does not mean that their relative position and, indeed, survival in the market is exogenous, and one expects that the struggle for survival in a perfectly competitive market will reverberate within firms and then be transmitted backwards to input markets.

Possibly the simplest way to observe the effects of entry or increased competition on efficiency is to compare directly the cost or productive efficiency of entrants and incumbents, looking to see whether more efficient entrants displace less efficient incumbents, and measuring how much of an impact on industry productivity performance this change in the composition of its population may have. Hazeldine (1985) found that entrants in Canada actually had slightly higher costs than incumbent surviving firms, and that the change in the performance of survivors is what accounted for the 1973 productivity slowdown and the post-1976 boom. On the other hand, Baldwin and Gorecki (1991) tracked Canadian entrants over the period 1970-9 and discovered that new entrants were rather more productive than exiting firms. New firms can take some time to grow into their optimal size, and correcting for variations in plant size (as Baldwin and Gorecki did) suggests that new firms were clearly more productive than continuing firms. One of Baldwin and Gorecki's estimates suggested that entry and displacement accounted for about 24% of productivity growth in the typical Canadian industry. However, entry may have a salutary effect on incumbents even when entrants have no cost advantage, and to observe this indirect effect one needs to examine the differences in the performance of incumbents between high and low entry industries or differences over time in the same industry associated with variations in entry over time. Here the evidence that entry can stimulate productivity growth (see below) is a little clearer, and one concludes that what may be a modest productivity gain arising from the displacement of old inefficient firms by new efficient ones can be magnified by the incentives that incumbents have to improve their own efficiency in the face of entry. That is, what might be called *displacement effects* may induce further *demonstration effects*, the two adding up to a positive effect overall.

Other ways in which one might hope to observe the effect of entry and increased competition on efficiency include examining what happens when collusive arrangements or positions of protected market power break down. For example, Erickson (1976) looked at price conspiracies in gymnasium seating (mid-1940s to 1960 in the USA), rock salt (early 1930s to the 1960s in the northern USA) and structural steel (early 1950s to 1962 in the upper Mid-West in the USA). In all three cases, he observed an escalation in costs attributable to collusion (particularly, it seems, in the salaries of upper and middle management), with costs eventually reduced by 23% in gymnasium seating and 10% in steel when collusion was eliminated. It is interesting to note that the costs both of non-participants sheltering under the price umberalla and of entrants who arrived at the end of the collusive agreement were also affected.

In much the same vein, one often observes that the initial reactions of incumbents to the arrival of new entrants in a market include an exercise of savage cost cutting that enables them to cut prices without necessarily sacrificing margins. It is not difficult to find examples of this type of activity, and, as before, the demolition of legally created entry barriers provides a natural, easy-to-observe experimental setting. The deregulation of public enterprises which swept the USA in the late 1970s in a range of industries and the privatization policies introduced by the UK in the early 1980s show the cost side effects of competition quite clearly. Many of these industries – airlines, refuse collection, railways and so on – were protected, and many were monopolized. The workers in these firms were often the beneficiaries of a weak and vacillating industrial relations policy, and the inefficiencies and restrictive working practices that grew up within these firms are legion. The effects of deregulation have been plain to see. Bailey (1986) examined four US industries following decontrol. In airlines, for example, deregulated incumbents initiated a broad range of cost cutting policies (although they appear not always to have been able to match entrants' costs (p. 7)), and pressures to renegotiate labour contracts in airlines, freight transport and telecommunications have been high. Productivity gains have been substantial, not least from the movement towards hub systems in airlines and freight transport, and unionized labour has been one of the main losers.[11] In the UK, a certain amount of deregulation has accompanied a major series of ownership changes (most of which did not, however, result in a change in senior management). However, a fairly wide range of studies have suggested that there exist very little in the way of effects on efficiency that can be associated with the switch from public to private ownership, and that it is the interaction of ownership and competition that leads to improvement (see, for example, the surveys by Kay and Thompson (1986) and Vickers and Yarrow (1988)).

It is much more difficult to evaluate the effects of competition on x-efficiency in the absence of 'experiments' like deregulation or the collapse of a collusive arrangement simply because the degree of competition is only one of a great many factors which cause cost and cost functions to vary across industries. Regional variations in the structure of a given industry are one way to break this deadlock, since a comparison across firms in different regions enables one to hold a number of characteristics of technology constant. Primeaux (1977), for example, compared the costs of municipally owned electricity firms facing competition with those which enjoyed monopoly power, and found that average costs were reduced by nearly 11% because of competition (but see Nelson, 1990). White (1976) compared capital labour ratios in the USA and Pakistan for 31 industries, 1968-9, finding evidence that the absence of competition in Pakistan encouraged (or, at least, failed to discourage) the use of labour-intensive technology. Capital equipment was 'indulged in' for (apparently) reasons of prestige, and all the more so in more highly concentrated industries (for further work, see the survey by Siegfried and Wheeler, 1981).

These various experiments suggest that competition can have a major impact on cost structures and, taken together with the evidence discussed earlier in this chapter, point to the conclusion that an increase in competition can, in general, be expected to induce both movements to and movements of the production frontier. If the various effects discussed thus far are at all substantive, then one ought to be able to observe their collective outcome by relating variations in productivity growth across industries and over time to variations in the degree of competition. The simplest exercise one can perform is to relate variations in productivity growth across industries over some given time interval to various measures of competitiveness, and this is most frequently done using indices of market concentration. The usual outcome of this type of experiment is that the effect of market concentration on productivity growth is positive and statistically significant, but that it is extremely small. Greer and Rhoades (1976), for example, estimated an effect which suggested that the *complete* elimination of monopoly would raise productivity growth by about 1-2% (see also Amato et al.,1981). On the face of it, this result seems to cut across the presumption that competition increases efficiency, and rationalizing it tends to lead one into a number of dubious arguments that conflate the alleged effects of economies of scale, more efficient managers in large firms and higher innovation rates in highly concentrated industries. Other results reported in the literature are also not wholly persuasive. Dickson (1979) and Gupta (1979) present evidence suggesting that the extent of suboptimal capacity is lower in more highly concentrated industries, evidence which seems to follow from little more than the tautological relationship that exists between the distribution of firm and plant sizes. Carlsson (1972) also presents evidence suggesting that concentration has a positive effect on efficiency, but his results do not appear to be robust to the method of calculating concentration ratios.

It would probably be rather impudent to take these results as suggesting that the absence of competition encourages productivity growth for four reasons. First, the results do not appear to be very robust and the effects are, in any case, rather small. Sveikauskas and Sviekauskas (1982) reported no effect, as did several studies prior to Greer and Rhoades, while Caves and Davies (1987) reported that UK–US productivity differentials were negatively (but, in general, not significantly) related to UK concentration. Klotz et al. (1980) examined the percentage difference in productivity within 195 four-digit US industries in 1967 and found that the intra-industry dispersion was rather higher in more highly concentrated markets than in less concentrated markets. Second, virtually all studies that have included exchange rate or tariff variables have found that they have the expected (positive and negative) effects in productivity growth. This is also true of one further study (to be discussed below) that correlated entry rates to productivity growth. As these reflect competition-induced pressures no less than concentration ratios, they call into question the rather common and uncritically accepted interpretation of concentration as a proxy which is inversely related to the degree of competition. Third, it is not entirely clear exactly what concentration indices measure or proxy for in this context. Observed productivity growth depends on movements to and movements of the production frontier. Innovation rates, however, depend on the degree of technological opportunity in each sector and, as we saw in the second section, there are good reasons to think that more highly concentrated sectors are richer in technological opportunity. Thus, it is not unreasonable to think that innovation rates are high *despite* and not *because* markets are concentrated. It follows, then, that a positive association between productivity and concentration may reflect variations in technological opportunity (for some results consistent with this, see Scherer, 1983), and that productivity growth would have been even higher in industries rich in technological opportunity were they less concentrated, more open to trade and so on.

The final reason for doubting that a positive correlation between industry concentration and productivity growth exists is that even a purely cursory inspection of the data suggests that the two have such wildly different statistical properties that it is unlikely that the one will ever account for much of what we observe about the other. Industry concentration is relatively constant over time – it exhibits a lot of between-industry variation but very little within-industry variation. As an explanatory variable, then, it can account for differences in performance between industries but not within industries over time. By contrast, the interesting thing about productivity growth is its enormous variability across industries at any time and, even more interesting, its unusually high variation over time within industries. Geroski (1989b) examined annual labour productivity growth rates for a sample of 79 three-digit industries in the UK over the period 1970–9 and discovered that well over 80% of the variation in labour productivity growth across industries and years was within-industry variation. While the distribution of productivity growth rates across industries in any given year was normal, the location of particular industries on that distribution varied enormously year by year. High productivity growth rates did not persist over time, and partial correlations across industries never exceeded 0.3 between any pair of years over the period 1970–9. While total factor productivity growth varied somewhat less across industries and over time than labour productivity growth, its variation over time was still large enough to suggest that explaining the purely cross-section variation that one observes (which is, effectively, all that a concentration ratio is capable of doing) is not of major interest.

Thus, productivity growth rates seem to respond to a variety of forces whose strength varies over time. Entry rates, as we have seen earlier, are one of these, as are, to a lesser degree, innovation rates. Pooling data for four years (1976–9) across these 79 industries, allowing each industry to have its own production function and allowing for both short- and long-run effects associated with entry and innovation rates, Geroski found that roughly 30% of observed productivity growth could be attributed to the effects of entry. Table 6.3 shows two of his estimated equations, tracing the effects of domestic entry E_t, foreign entry M_t and the number of innovations I_t on productivity growth (the second equation uses instruments for E_t, M_t and I_t). The effect of domestic entry and innovations is clearly positive, while that of foreign entry is negative but small.[12] The long-run effects of domestic entry are about 50% larger than its initial impact on productivity, while those of foreign entry are perhaps 15% larger. The contribution of domestic entry to productivity growth is about

252   *Entry, Innovation and Productivity*

Table 6.3   The effects of entry and innovation of productivity growth in the UK

	(i)	(ii)
F_t	0.0851	0.4947
	(0.5427)	(0.4641)
E_{t-1}	0.4202	0.4529
	(2.281)	(1.669)
E_{t-2}	−0.2682	−0.2382
	(2.616)	(2.352)
M_t	−0.0411	−0.1141
	(3.705)	(4.33)
M_{t-1}	−0.0312	−0.0183
	(1.094)	(1.014)
M_{t-2}	0.0176	−0.0031
	(1.277)	(0.3579)
I_t	0.0030	0.0114
	(1.536)	(2.195)
I_{t-1}	0.0024	0.0071
	(0.9184)	(1.75)
I_{t-2}	0.0053	0.0062
	(1.824)	(2.208)
R^2	0.8846	0.8917
SSR	0.221172	0.207535
Log likelihood	699.415	709.471

The sample is 79 three-digit UK industries pooled over the four years 1976–9. All estimated equations include 79 industry and three-time intercept dummies, and allow for 79 + 3 slope coefficients on the rate of growth of labour and materials per unit of capital. The dependent variable is the rate of growth of real output per unit of capital. Equation (i) takes E_t, M_t and I_t to be exogenous, while (ii) uses instruments for E_t, M_t and I_t. E_t is net entry penetration, M_t is the change in the import sales ratio, and I_t is the number of innovations produced in each sector. Absolute values of t statistics are given in parentheses below the estimated parameters; all estimates are heteroscedastic consistent.
Source: Geroski, 1989b

1.6 percentage points, half (or less) of that of innovations; for foreign entry, the corresponding figure is −0.62.

   Table 6.3 suggests that innovative activity makes a more substantial contribution to productivity growth than entry does,[13] but it is probably unwise to try to separate out the separate effects of the two since they are (as we have seen) positively correlated. Not only are the effects of the two intertwined with each other, but they are probably also bound up with more general cyclical effects on productivity growth. An inspection of the raw data underlying table 6.3 reveals that rates of growth of industry output are two to four times more variable than are rates of growth of labour, capital or materials inputs, and the within-industry variation in output growth rates is nearly 90% of its total variation. The result is pro-cyclical variations in productivity growth. Entry (as we saw in chapter 2) is probably pro-cyclical, and innovation rates may also be pro-cyclical too. The consequence is that separating out the effects of cycles and competition (whether that takes the form of new firms or new ideas) is bound to be difficult to manage. One is tempted to speculate that the intertwined effects of entry and innovation are unleashed during cyclic upswings – that markets are subjected to surges in the strength of competitive forces during booms which make a not inconsiderable mark (in total) on their productivity performance.

Thus, neglecting the occasionally observed positive correlation between concentration ratios and productivity growth, one has little difficulty in seeing entry – and, more generally, the activity of outsiders – as reducing inefficiency and stimulating productivity growth. Parts of these effects are, of course, attributable to the effect of competition and rivalry on the innovation process, and many of them may vary in intensity over the trade cycle. However, it seems clear that even a generous assessment of the size of innovation and cyclical effects leaves plenty of room for thinking that competition reduces x-inefficiency. It is tempting to speculate that the effects of restrictions on competition are, in the first instance, registered on costs, and that they spread from there to prices, aided and abetted by any inflation in margins that market power enables firms to make. The modest effects of entry on margins that we observed in chapter 4, coupled with the altogether larger (seemingly) effect that entry appears to have on costs, suggest that it may be the effect that reducing competition has on costs which matters most in explaining the variations in prices that are associated with variations in monopoly market power.

Conclusions

Economists are fond of using natural selection arguments to describe market processes, occasionally succumbing to the dreadful temptation of talking about 'the competitive jungle' as if it were the hotbed of conflict that they (erroneously) suppose most jungles to be (see Colinvaux, 1980, ch. 13). However, the habit of static thinking that underlies the standard conception of markets often leads economists to stress the role of selection as a force of discipline, and to neglect its role in stimulating industry development. This practice generally leads to the view of entry as an error correction mechanism that propels markets back toward equilibria that, from the point of view of entry, are exogenously given. Aside from the fact that this use of the natural selection analogy is based on a misunderstanding of what selection actually does in the wild, the problem with this line of thought is that it largely relegates the dynamics of industry evolution and development to exogenous forces.

In fact, the important feature of natural selection processes is not the fact of selection but, rather, the occurrence of mutation. In the absence of mutation, no changes occur in genetic structure, and there is nothing for selection pressures to operate on. All change, save the possibility of extinction, ceases: species either fit their environment or they do not, and that is all there is to it. Mutation creates diversity, allowing selection pressures to exert an (at least local) choice between characteristics, and given enough time and enough stability in the environment, choice amongst various local adaptations may well result in a global best fit. In short, selection provides discipline, but mutation generates the seeds of creative change in natural settings. Thinking of competition as a selection process in this way focuses attention on two roles that it may play in affecting market performance. As a disciplinary force, entry and fringe firm activity can spur the diffusion of new ideas largely because large incumbent insider firms are often too wedded to their existing activities to adopt new product or major process innovations quickly (as countless case studies attest). In this context but at a somewhat more prosaic level, it also seems to be the case that competition can play an important role in reducing x-inefficiency, a role that may actually be the principal way through which entry affects prices. That is, as a force of discipline entry may affect prices only indirectly, via the effect that competitive discipline has on incumbent firms' efficiency (which may, of course, help to explain why examples of limit pricing or entry regulation are hard to find). As a creative force, competition not only stimulates product innovation, it also plays a major role in generating, or at least in delivering, a wide diversity in the range of products on offer in markets. As we have seen, many responses to entry involve the use of marketing weapons, and this may be a consequence of the effect that entry has on product development.

One of the reasons why it is difficult to sort out the respective roles of insiders and outsiders in the innovative process is that these appear to vary systematically over time. Indeed, the evidence suggests that the creative role which entry can play in markets often seems to be concentrated in early stages of the product life cycle, and its absence often seems to be related to the process of maturation and stagnation in markets. The products that eventually define the core of an industry – the specification of product characteristics which eventually becomes the industry standard – often emerge from a wide range of alternatives that arrive early in the life cycle of the product. Entry is a crucial part of this selection process since it can be the source of many of the alternatives which form the basis of the choice set. Although entrants may continue to stimulate innovative activity throughout the full life cycle of many products, acting either directly or indirectly by stimulating insiders to act, it seems that much of the useful creative work done by entrants is finished by the middle or end of the first major phases of industry growth. The possible exception to this rule occurs (if it actually does occur) much later in the product life cycle. Mature industries where core products are no longer as well adapted to the environment (consumer tastes, the relative abundance of different factors of production) are also industries that, by and large, stand in need of the burst of innovative creativity that entry brings, or, at least, is associated with. Many of the leading firms in these markets – pioneers of the initial core good in earlier days – are far too wedded to their existing activities to undertake the necessary innovative activities, and a regeneration of the market through entry-induced revisions in the definition of the core good is often part and parcel of the process by which they decline. It is not so much that they lose market shares to imitative entrants, as that innovative entrants shift markets out from underneath them.

It is, of course, possible to overstate the association between competition and innovation and, more worrying, to misjudge levels of causation. Even a cursory reading of the evidence reveals that new firms do not always serve as the vehicle for new ideas, and that new ideas do not necessarily need new firms to carry them to the market. Further, it is probably the case that the role of competitive rivalry in stimulating innovation is modest compared with that played by fundamental supply side forces like technological opportunity. Indeed, many of the regression results that have been reported leave one with the overpowering feeling that it is variations in technological opportunity that account for much of the variation in innovative activity that we observe, not rivalry. More subtly, there are reasons to think that the state of technological opportunity is not unrelated to the height of entry barriers, meaning that both entry and innovation rates may be joint outcomes of more fundamental underlying causes.

Notes

1 If an outsider gets the innovation then, as possessor of the new and old innovation, it sets jointly profit-maximizing prices and earns π_1 say. If the outsider innovates, the two firms compete, with the insider earning π_2 and the outsider π_3, where $\pi_1 > \pi_2 + \pi_3$. The gain to innovating for the insiders is $(\pi_1 - \pi_2) > \pi_3$, the gain to innovating for the outsider, as asserted in the text. See Gilbert and Newberry (1982), who apply this argument to

pre-emptive patenting, and Eaton and Lipsey (1979), who apply it to pre-emptive capacity expansion (a variant of this type of argument was used in ch. 4 to suggest why incumbents might often have an incentive to block entry). Notice that the argument is not unambiguously pro-Schumpeterian, since pre-empting outsiders requires insiders to act before they otherwise would. There is therefore a sense in which outsiders drive innovative activity since, without their challenge, it might be much reduced or delayed.

2 Whether or not each firm searches more intensively when the number of searching firms rises depends on whether development costs are contractual; that is, on whether firms must pay the same amount regardless of whether they win the race to the innovation. On this issue, see Loury (1979), Lee and Wilde (1980), Dixit (1989b) and, for overviews, Kamien and Schwartz (1982) and Dasgupta (1986).

3 This effect may, of course, ultimately lead to stagnation in the innovativeness of an industry. If one firm continually acts as a 'fast second' follower, parasitically free-riding on the development research of others, then their incentives to do research will weaken and innovation rates will fall.

4 One must be careful with interpreting these data. If the marginal productivity of research inputs declines and if, as seems reasonable, large firms enjoy the benefits of lower marginal costs in obtaining research inputs, then their average productivity may be lower than that registered by smaller firms (for some critical remarks in this vein, see Fisher and Temin, 1973). Much the same effect on relative efficiency will emerge to the extent that the informal R&D done by smaller firms is either mis-recorded or not recorded at all.

5 Comanor (1967) and others have provided complementary evidence suggesting that an N-shaped relationship between entry barriers and R&D inputs exists: when barriers are low or very high, the incentive to invest in R&D is low, and thus 'there is some indication . . . that the incentive is related to the goal of impeding entry' (p. 657). See Acs and Audretsch (1991) for a survey of empirical work on innovation and entry.

6 Steam locomotive builders in the USA are a clear example of defensive activity by threatened incumbents leading to disaster. The American Locomotive Company, in particular, developed the capacity to enter the diesel switching market more or less in step with General Motors, the leading outsider firm, but entered a good six years after GM pioneered the first successful diesel passenger locomotive. Its entry into diesel freight locomotives was also delayed by the Second World War, and the delay allowed GM to build up a dominating position, leading to exit by the American Locomotive Company in the late 1960s. Baldwin Locomotive Works and Lima Locomotive Works were even less progressive than American, eventually merging and concentrating on non-locomotive steam-powered equipment (Marx, 1976).

7 An examination of the record of dominant firms suggests that they often become rather sleepy – that the lack of persistent innovative entry challenges often dulls their critical awareness and causes an atrophying in their competitive skills. They lose track of routines or procedures for dealing with

entry, and thus can succumb to a sudden surprise attack; see Geroski (1987a).

8   This is essentially a test of Granger causality (Granger, 1969) and, as such, is a test of whether the terms in E_{t-r} add anything to the linear predictor of I_t that uses information only on its own history (i.e. the I_{t-r}). Note that one cannot make any inferences about simultaneous causality using (6.2).

9   Swann (1990) has argued that a very rapid expansion in product characteristics will be a feature of this process. This, in turn, suggests that many early entrants may proliferate varieties as fast as they can until an industry standard emerges. Evidence that successful component manufacturers in semiconductors followed such a strategy is discussed in Flaherty (1984).

10 Mueller and Tilton (1969) discuss R&D as an entry barrier in a manner not inconsistent with this scenario, while Winter (1984) examines a rather different stylization of industry evolution that runs in terms of successive technological regimes. Klepper and Grady (1989) examine the effect that chance events and exogenous factors have on entry and the growth rate of incumbents during the course of industry evolution.

11 The extensive entry into these deregulated industries has also substantially affected the range of services offered. In many cases, this has taken the particularly transparent form of the emergence of discount no-frills suppliers, or other specialist niche suppliers. Davis (1984), for example, observed that the deregulation of express coaches in the UK has led to alterations in the frequency of services on a wide range of routes, as well as to the introduction of a number of innovative services such as the use of videos, refreshments, hostesses, toilets and so on. There has also been an increase in the variety of buses used, particularly in local services.

12 That foreign-based entry has a negative effect has perhaps three explanations. First, given total demand, an increase in import penetration displaces domestic production without, however, reducing domestic capital stock, thus lowering the rate of growth of output per unit of capital. Second, it is often the case in the UK that high quality foreign imports displace high quality domestic goods, forcing domestic producers down market. Wherever this causes domestic firms to specialize in lower value-added goods, one will observe a diminution in productivity growth during the displacement process. Finally, it is possible that low productivity sectors attract a growing volume of imports.

13 Geroski (1990d) has pursued the relationship between innovation and productivity growth more deeply, discovering that the use of innovations contributes far more to productivity growth than the production of innovations does, that those innovations produced in the engineering sectors have a far greater impact on users' productivity than other innovations do, and that intersectoral spill-overs are very small in size.

7

Entry and Industry Evolution

A Summing Up

Our goal in this book has been to try to push past the rather static mind set that economists often bring to discussions about markets and to focus on the kinds of dynamics that make up the world as we frequently observe it. Although a number of interesting things have been said by various theorists on the subject of market dynamics, there is a case (as we argued in chapter 1) for letting the data do some of the work. In quite different (but complementary) ways, both case studies and econometric analyses can provide a structured organization of 'the facts', even if this does not always take the form of classical hypothesis tests and even if the contributions of different studies of either type are not always mutually consistent. To deal effectively with data in this form, one must work at the level of developing rather broad conceptions of what market processes typically look like, and subject these conceptions to the 'test of consilience'. That is, one must ask whether these conceptions are robust enough to weave together successfully a large number of disparate bits of information collected from many independent sources. Most of what has passed above has been written in this spirit, and it is time to try to pull together the various strands into a more coherent whole.

The natural place to start is, of course, with the raw data on entry (as we did in chapter 2). What one learns from data gathered in a wide variety of countries is that entry into most markets is relatively easy, but that post-entry market penetration and survival is not. The relatively rapid turnover that one observes at the bottom of the size distribution in most industries suggests that the entry process is not so much one by which industry supply is expanded as it is a means by which the population characteristics of firms (and products) in a market are chosen. Indeed, one can occasionally see this selection process at work in a very clear form. Markets often seem to be invaded by successive waves of entrants of different types, particularly, it seems, during periods of rapid expansion. There is no doubt that members of these successive cohorts of entrants displace (at least in part) their predecessors (although this is not true of all types of entrants), and that early members of any cohort can crowd out later members of the same cohort. Even if the number and size distribution of firms in an industry change very little, an active selection amongst firm types can profoundly alter the character of an industry's population, a development that may have important implications for industry performance. Still, for all of the blood and thunder occasioned by entry, there is no doubt that the first appearance in a market of a new firm (even a particularly advantaged one) is almost always followed by a long struggle to gain a solid foothold in that market and to expand in it, one that frequently ends in tears.

Whether viewed across markets, over time, or both, the raw data make it plain that entry is an extremely noisy activity. Unlike rather more conventional measures of competitiveness (such as concentration ratios), the rate of entry often varies enormously over time within any given industry, and its purely cross-section variation is also substantial. The challenge that this poses for those who wish to explain inter-industry and inter-temporal variation in entry flows is plain. As we saw in chapter 3, a number of observable characteristics of markets (such as their size, growth and profitability) have effects on both the incidence of entry and entry penetration into markets. However, it is more than clear that the usual observable variables (including a number that purport to reflect particular types of entry barriers) account for only a rather modest proportion of the variation in entry flows that we observe. That fixed permanent features of market structure (like entry barriers) do not seem to matter all that much as determinants of entry flows is an impression which is reinforced by the rather modest success one enjoys by using autoregressive models of entry that include fixed effects. The data suggest that the permanent factors which determine entry flows are overwhelmed by more transitory factors that can have sustained effects on entry well beyond their immediate initial effects. These transitory factors are probably best thought of as mediating market conditions of some type or another, and, indeed, models of entry that have tried to allow for systematic variations in market conduct have often significantly outperformed entry models that relied on structural determinants (observable or not) of entry alone.

There are two ways that one can interpret these results. The first is to argue that most markets are in a state of long-run equilibrium for most of the time, and that, as a consequence, almost everything that one observes in the way of disequilibrium dynamics is unsystematic noise. This view is also consistent with the evidence on the dynamics of price – cost margins that was discussed in chapter 4. There we discovered some systematic disequilibrium dynamics in margins, but between-industry variations thoroughly dominated within-industry variations. Since this is more or less exactly the pattern that one expects to observe if markets are fairly near to a long-run equilibrium determined by relatively permanent but industry-specific entry barriers, it is natural to conclude that most markets are frequently near or at that state. The second way that one can interpret the (rather mixed) results that have emerged from applying the various models of entry to the data is that it is very-short-run local factors that matter most to entrants, factors that may well be (in part) endogenous to the entry process itself. Autoregressive models of entry do reveal a pattern of entry over time that is consistent with the view that early entrants can crowd out later ones, and cases exist which suggest that some types of (early) entrants can affect market conditions in ways that either encourage or discourage later entrants of different types. Much more prosaically, the very small size of most entrants suggests that local market conditions in particular market niches are bound to matter a lot to individual entrants, and these are the kinds of factors that researchers using broad cross-sections composed of three-, four- and five-digit industries in national markets are likely to find all but impossible to proxy.

These two interpretations of the data are probably not as mutually inconsistent as they may appear to be at first sight. Markets generally have complex internal structures that are defined by product characteristics, geography, production methods and so on. Aggregation is often the only way in which one can sensibly handle these details, but it is not without its costs. At a broad aggregate level, many industries undoubtedly do look as if they are in long-run equilibrium, and, at this broad level, one is often struck by the rather placid calm that they reveal. Yet, apparently stable industries are often subject to considerable internal turbulence and, while the whole may look to be more or less in equilibrium, many of the parts definitely are not. Entry is almost certainly part of the rough and tumble of life in the various market niches which exist in every industry, and one's view of the process may, accordingly, be rather sensitive to the precise level that the data have been aggregated to.

This same observation probably applies to any attempt to assess the effects of entry on market performance. In chapter 4, we focused on the short-run effects of entry on prices and margins in markets. Although it is possible to find numerous instances where entry has had an effect on prices, it is generally rather difficult to interpret this evidence as consistent with the hypothesis that price is an important part of the pre- or post-entry response of incumbents to the arrival of new firms into their markets. Most incumbents respond only selectively to entry. Although it is not always optimal for an incumbent to respond to entry, one senses that the fact that we observe only selective responses means that incumbents do respond to some of the relatively rarer types of entrants (such as large-scale entrants diversifying from well-established activities elsewhere in the economy) and do not respond to more common types (like small-scale *de novo* entry). Further, when they do respond, many incumbents seem to use marketing tools (such as advertising) rather than price. This pattern of behaviour is consistent with the view that incumbents allocate rather different instruments to the twin targets of maintaining and exploiting positions of market power. It is hard to see price as an important part of the fight to protect a market, and it seems much more likely that it is determined by what the market can bear and by the outcome of any fight using non-price weapons amongst firms which takes place in that market.

Price–cost margins and price are both likely to settle in the long run at levels determined by the height of barriers to entry. The evidence discussed in chapter 5 suggests that most markets are protected by at least moderately high barriers, and that imitative entrants in particular often face substantial obstacles in their path. If, as we conjectured earlier, most markets (broadly defined) are in or near long-run equilibrium, then there is unlikely to be much room for an expansion in industry supply, and entry will necessarily be difficult. However, while the total volume of industry supply may be roughly in equilibrium, the precise specifications of what is supplied can vary in response to numerous small changes in tastes and technology, and the market response to these changes may occur through entry. If entry barriers also act as mobility barriers against subsequent market penetration into desirable niches, then the entry process may take on some of the character of a selection process that tries to slot various more or less square pegs (i.e. entrants of different types) into a number of round holes (i.e. market niches of different types, protected by different sorts of barriers). That is, the existence of barriers to imitative entry but not necessarily innovative entry means that entry will be part of a broader market experiment designed to enable consumers to choose among alternative goods and services, and a fairly high turnover of new small firms is a likely outcome of this kind of market process.

Absolute cost advantages seem to be the most important source of entry barriers in a wide range of circumstances, and it may well be the case that they are also the most durable. Economies of scale in production, on the other hand, are not likely to be of real importance in many markets, although fixed costs in raising revenue caused by the need to erect a large distribution system, advertise extensively and so on often matter. Product differentiation barriers are ubiquitous, but do not always prove to be durable or to afford incumbents with much protection in the long run. They are clearly effective against imitative entrants, but innovative entrants can often redefine markets in ways that facilitate their own entry. One conjectures that it is this malleability of product differentiation barriers – their susceptibility to the challenge of innovative entrants – which accounts for the observation that many of the responses of incumbents to entry are marketing based. What can be made can be unmade, and then remade.

As countless cases attest, particular entry barriers are not immutable, and the competition between entrants and incumbents to surmount and defend them can add no little momentum to their gradual evolution over time. The dynamics in market performance that we observe are therefore composed of three distinctly different elements. First, price and non-price dynamics can arise from differences in the behaviour of incumbents for any given level of barriers. That is, changes in conduct can drive changes in performance for any given structural configuration, an event that may not occur often. Second, market structure may itself change exogenously, changing performance directly or indirectly through what are often rather unpredictable changes in market conduct. Markets grow and contract, government regulations change and technology evolves, and these changes can often transform the performance of particular markets. Third and finally, market conduct can change market structure and for this reason induce changes in market performance over time. Conduct may directly affect performance in the short run and, at the same time, plant the seeds of longer-run changes in peformance through its effect on structure.

There is simply no body of evidence strong enough to enable one to rank these three sources of market dynamics in order of importance. At best, one can work backwards from observations about the dynamics of market performance. Markets are clearly more competitive in the long run than in the short run, but they are not tremendously so. Profit differences between firms and industries persist for quite long periods of time, and long-run outcomes (long run from the point of view of the data sets typically used to analyse these questions) do not differ all that much from the short-run outcomes that we see recorded in the data. However, we also observe that rivalry in markets protected by entry barriers is often fierce, and one can see in many markets a steady rise and fall in the importance of particular barriers to entry. Various specific barriers are sometimes more and sometimes less important in affording protection against entry, but one senses that entry is often difficult – one way or the other – most of the time. An obvious conclusion is that barriers are – and remain – fairly high overall in many markets even though their composition changes over time. The evolution in market structure, then, may involve less a change in the height of barriers and more a change in their composition.

These speculations suggest that many of the most interesting market dynamics may be bound up with the dynamics of market structure, and the evidence discussed in chapter 5 and, more substantively, in chapter 6 shows that entry can at least occasionally play a major role in restructuring markets. Entrants are occasionally the vehicle of major innovations in markets, and, apparently more often, they provide the kinds of incentives that incumbents require to keep themselves innovative. Perhaps more interesting is the observation that the role which entry plays in stimulating innovativeness in markets can vary substantially over the product life cycle. Both in young markets and, to a lesser degree, in mature markets, entry is often a vehicle by which markets experiment amongst different types of products. Extensive entry is often observed to occur at the same time that product variety flowers, and the selection that consumers make between product types is often implicitly a selection between entrants, or, less frequently, between insider and outsider firms. Entrants probably also have a big effect in the local market niches that they inhabit. Although most entrants do not introduce anything like a major innovation, many entrants are bound to offer some slight difference in service to consumers that differentiates them from other firms in their niche. The development of such niches and their colonization by a range of different firms offering a range of goods and services is a major way in which markets customize goods. The considerable inflow and outflow of firms from these niches, then, is part of a selection process in which individual (or small groups of) consumers seek out goods with a preferred set of characteristics.

There are several dimensions along which market performance can be measured, and many people are more concerned with the speed of productivity growth or innovation rates in markets than they are with the divergence of price from marginal cost. The lack of statistical concordance between entry flows and measures of market performance such as profitability that was observed in chapter 4 is much less marked when one examines measures of market performance like innovation rates and productivity growth (as we saw in chapter 6). Both exhibit much higher ratios of within- to between-industry variation, and both are rather more clearly and somewhat more strongly positively correlated to entry than was the case with margins. Productivity growth is noticeably pro-cyclical, as is entry and (probably) innovation, and one conjectures that the effects of competition on innovation and productivity growth are bound up with the effects of a range of cyclical factors. It may not be too fanciful to think of major cyclical booms as a kind of rebirth of a market, and to see in the events that occur during a boom many of the forces which are observed to operate during the birth and early emergence of a market. Needless to say, this may also be the time when major structural changes occur, leading to a realignment in the types of barriers which protect a market, as well, perhaps, as to some change in the height of barriers overall.

In short, the character of particular markets (defined as a set of products of a certain types) evolves over time hand in hand with their structure (defined in terms of particular barriers to entry and the height of barriers overall) and the process by which this co-evolution occurs involves a selection between different firms which have different ideas that are embodied in the different products and services that they offer. Selection also seems to occur at an uneven speed over time, being particularly prominent in the early stages of markets and, perhaps, during cyclical booms. At any one time, most markets are not tremendously competitive in the sense that price is often not very close to marginal cost, but, over time, most markets are pretty competitive in the sense that market rivalry changes the environment that particular firms face. Competition is not, for the most part, a process that affects the quantity of supply of any particular product offered for sale in a market. Rather, it seems to be a selection process which determines the types and ranges of goods and services that are offered to consumers. That is, entry is as much about choosing quality as it is about producing quantity.

Two Analogies with Natural Selection Processes

When one begins to think about selection processes and how they affect market dynamics, one often finds it difficult (or, in my case, impossible) to avoid drawing analogies with the kinds of phenomena that are observed by evolutionary biologists and ecologists. As a source of new ideas this is probably no bad thing, but it is important not to let it get out of hand. Thus, in the spirit of being suggestive but with no aspirations higher than that, I should like to speculate a little about the nature of industry evolution using two metaphors drawn from natural selection.

Markets are often moulded by successive waves of entrants who play a major role in the experimentation amongst product characteristics that eventually results in the standardized core good which comes to define the market. This colonization process is one that occurs regularly in natural settings, and it does so in surprisingly systematic ways. The 'progressive occupation of abandoned fields by a secession of different plant communities has often been observed. It always happens. First come in the annual weeds, plants whose niches include the ability to have tiny seeds spread far and wide on the off-chance that there will be a patch of bare earth in which they can grow for a season and scatter some more seeds. Next come the perennials, herbs that bite into the ground with resistant root systems and hold onto the fields year after year – then the bushes, then the scrub trees of woodlands. This much is fact. That the process will end with the coming of the primeval forest is conjecture because scientific man has not been around long enough to see the whole process through. It is, however, a rather safe conjecture. We can see the forest trees coming in and we can look at ancient forests disturbed in olden times and see how the mix of trees changes ever more closely towards the original virgin growth. The whole complicated proceeding of a secession of plant communities always occurs when disturbed land is let alone. It is so regular, predictable and orderly a process that a good local botanist can tell you the date a farmer quit farming merely by looking at the plants that are now growing on his land' (Colinvaux, 1980, p. 106).

Two things of importance occur in a mutually reinforcing fashion during this process of recolonization: an increase in species diversity (accompanied by a considerable amount of displacement), and an increase in soil richness. Annual weeds – the early pioneers – use 'opportunist' strategies that take advantage of sudden opportunities for growth in poor environments, spreading a large number of seeds quite widely and relying on the sun for much of the calories that they require. Some types of weeds are able to compete for scarce resources with subsequent immigrants, and these so-called 'equilibrium species' tend to set down roots and underground storage organs, drawing nutrients from the soil as well as from the sun. Many weeds, however, are thoroughly opportunist, and they tend to disappear as a wide variety of herbs and then briars and shrubs begin (literally) to climb all over them and cut off their source of nourishment. These subsequent types of plant are more resilient, and their investment in survival is made manifest in a tangle of wooden thickets that, eventually, are partly (but not completely) replaced by a succession of different types of trees. It may actually be the case (and this is a source of considerable controversy amongst ecologists) that species richness eventually diminishes, resulting in a forest dominated by a relatively small number of towering giants with not much in the way of undergrowth on the forest floor. Be that as it may, soil enrichment occurs as a cause and consequence of this secession of plant types because each successive plant effectively digs and cultivates the soil. Early plants almost literally decompose into the seed beds from which spring later arrivals.

This is a story which has at least a passing resemblance to several of the case studies that we have discussed. Markets are often colonized by waves of entrants of different types, and, at any time, many markets display an often bewildering variety of firms, survivors of different entrant cohorts. As colonization occurs, innovation and selection gradually define a product space from what was once no more than a bright idea by some engineer or marketing specialist. Consumers learn to use and then appreciate the new product, and producers learn how to manufacture it more efficiently. Subsequent innovations build on earlier ones in a way that often first facilitates and then inhibits entry, and, in due course, a relatively small number of firms come to dominate the market producing a variety of standardized goods in large volumes. Some types of products are more prone to standardization than others (tastes may be more homogeneous and economies of scale may be more extensive), and, as a consequence, some markets support a less extensive 'fringe' of smaller, more customized producers than others.

Although the analogy is not perfect, it appears to be suggestive enough to prompt one to ask two questions. First, is the process of colonizing markets by entry as regular and systematic as it is in natural settings? The answer is probably 'not to such a marked degree'. As we mentioned earlier, the difference between market selection and natural selection is that the human leopard can change its spots, and this means that market selection processes are likely to be both faster and more consciously directed than natural selection processes. Since firms can anticipate selection pressures by changing their strategies, the link between particular strategies and the survival of a particular firm is weaker than it is with plants. Further, the power to anticipate carries with it the possibility of skipping over particular evolutionary stages. However, the very high turnover of firms that one sees in market selection processes coupled with the often sluggish reactions to change of market leaders suggests that changing spots is easier said than done. Whether there is a sufficient degree of continuity in the corporate strategies of particular firms to make the analogy with natural selection processes useful is simply not clear. If, however, business strategies become embedded in corporate structures and in the mobility barriers that surround and protect market leaders, then it seems reasonable to work with the analogy and look for the kinds of regular and systematic patterns that are observed in the wild.

Taking the analogy on board raises a second question, and that is whether there is anything general that can be said about the succession of strategies used by entrants that one observes as a market unfolds, or about the types of strategy choices that firms ought to make. Again, a number of cases suggest that a great many opportunistic entrants arrive relatively quickly in markets (often originating in nearby markets), but that many of them are displaced by later, more substantive entrants who come to dominate the market against even later imitative entrants. Strategies based on product innovation seem to give way to strategies based on process innovation, technical innovation of all kinds may give way to marketing strategies, and prices may be used first to penetrate markets and then to harvest them. Whether there is anything about particular generic strategies that induces a natural ordering in their use over time in markets is simply unclear. Furthermore, given the wide variety of costs of arriving early or late (and the many externalities that affect this choice), there is no doubt that each type of strategy is optimal in some (shorter or longer run) sense. When costs of adjustment and evolutionary uncertainties are large, strategy choice is as much a matter of how long one stays in the market as it is a matter of how one does so. The optimal strategy to follow depends on the state of market evolution, and the commitment that a firm ought to make to it depends on how long it wishes to stay in the market.

Thinking about successive waves of entrants colonizing markets raises a second broad question about market evolution, and that is how product spaces evolve and whether there is anything systematic about the way that they do so. Is it the case that the product space of a market gradually fills out, that product diversity gradually increases as a market evolves, or does product diversity first widen and then narrow as a market matures? In either case, what are the lines that product diversity follows as markets evolve? The second analogy with natural selection that I wish to pursue here develops this theme at the broadest level possible by tracing the anatomical development of individuals during the process of evolution. 'Major lineages seems able to generate a remarkable diversity – early experimentation. Few of these designs survive an early decimation, and later diversification occurs only within the restricted anatomical boundaries of these survivors – later standardization. The number of species may continue to increase and may reach maximal values late in the history of lineages, but these profound diversifications occur within restricted anatomies' (Gould, 1989, p. 30).

Although this view of the evolution of life forms is based on a rather limited, distinctly imperfect fossil record, it is not inconsistent with a number of cases that we have discussed (what follows relies in particular on the stimulating discussion in Clark, 1988). There is often a hierarchy amongst the characteristics that define a product. Some are more fundamental than others, and choices made between more fundamental product characteristics have a big effect on the kinds of ancillary characteristics that one might choose between. All markets are born in a cloud of confusion about what exactly is being offered to consumers. This arises partly because many new products are supply driven – they are spin-offs from some technological trajectory or another – and partly because goods conceived for one purpose often reveal themselves to be suitable for a much wider range of unanticipated purposes. Either way, the lack of a clear product definition effectively means that the choice between fundamental characteristics has yet to be made. At this early stage of market development, a wide variety of possibilities, each defined by a different vector of fundamental and ancillary characteristics, is on offer to consumers. As consumers gradually learn about what can be done with the product and what they would like to see done, so the choice amongst fundamental characteristics is gradually and imperceptibly made. At some point a core product emerges, a standard version of *the* good appears, and the market begins to look like markets that we are familiar with. The important point about this standardization of product definition is that, since it is a choice between fundamental product characteristics, it effectively defines the channels along which subsequent choices about ancillary characteristics come to be made. If true, this argument suggests that product variety both narrows (in the sense of choice between fundamental product characteristics) and widens (in the sense of choice amongst ancillary characteristics) as markets mature.

The most interesting stage of market evolution is the process of product standardization, the emergence of a core good from a wide range of seemingly good ideas. The precise way that it happens depends partly on how consumers learn about the potential uses of the new good, and partly on how producers learn about how to produce it efficiently. As we have seen, progress along this front often occurs as part of the process by which different types of entrant successively attempt to colonize the market. At some stage, a wide enough consensus amongst users develops to make an investment in large-scale production viable, and learning and economies of scale that lead to price cuts persuade even more consumers that they might as well climb on board. The emergence of these mass producers leads to sharp increases in market concentration, and these are the 'first movers' or dominant firms who often come to dominate their markets for decades. In short, much of what is interesting about what a market develops into and when it does so seems to be bound up with this process of standardization.

The early development of a market is not the only time that choices about fundamental product characteristics are made. Core products are those that best suit the needs of a fairly wide range of users early in the life of a product. Substantial investments in learning and exploiting scale economies, in developing process innovations, in constructing plant and internally structuring firms to deliver the product in question tend to freeze leading firms into this core product. However, as time passes and the industry matures, user tastes change. Other complementary and substitute goods appear, goods that were once considered luxuries come to be thought of as substitutes and a certain degree of boredom sets in. In these circumstances, the case for restructuring the core product can become overpowering. Given the substantial investments made by incumbents in the original core product, it is almost certainly the case that restructuring will be led by outsider firms or new entrants. Restructuring a mature market may, of course, be much less extensive and require a lot less experimentation than establishing the original core good did, and consequently the amount of entry required to get the job under way may also be less than earlier. Nevertheless, just as in the early stages of market evolution, so in mature markets there is often a case to be made for experimenting with new product possibilities. And just as entrants are likely to play a leading role in facilitating this process at an early stage in industry evolution, so they may need to do so again later on.

Although it is extremely speculative, one might conjecture that much the same kind of process occurs in miniature during major cyclical upswings. Booms are a time when markets expand, and this expansion involves drawing in consumers who, in a well-defined sense, are more and more marginal. Many were constrained by income from buying during the previous recession, which is to say that the opportunity cost of purchasing a good not well suited to their needs was just too high. As more and more of these marginal consumers join the swelling boom of sales in the market, the alignment between the basic core good and the needs of the now vastly increased market that it is serving may weaken somewhat. This plus any tendency for affluence to encourage people to consume more customized products is likely to encourage a modest flowering in product variety, one that may in part be delivered by a surge of new entrants.

These are, of course, only speculations. Those who, like me, find them reasonably compelling can often have little trouble in reading them into particular case studies. Those who do not find themselves moved by these analogies will have no trouble in dismissing them as unfalsifiable (and, in any case, there are no doubt plenty of cases that do not conform closely to either or both of these patterns). In many ways, however, hypothesis testing is beside the point. Any given market only evolves once, and explaining why it follows the route that it does requires the skills and methods of a historian as much as it does those of an experimental physicist. Further, analogies are not theories (much less theorems), and their role is to be suggestive rather than conclusive. The two analogies that we have explored here are helpful because they raise a number of interesting questions about how the composition of products and firms evolve over time in a market, about how, why and when markets concentrate, and about the kinds of setting in which firms must make strategy choices. Most of all, they raise the fundamental question of how systematic, orderly and predictable market evolution is.

Market Selection Processes

While natural selection analogies stimulate one to think about the process of growth and development in markets, there is also much of interest to consider in the selection process itself. The questions that we have raised (many of which remain unanswered) about selection between entrants apply more widely within industries. Selection pressures operate on all members of the industry population to a greater or lesser degree. Some firms fail and others survive, some firms grow and prosper while others stagnate and decline, and this changing composition in the population of firms is bound to affect how markets perform.

At the moment, we have only fairly faint clues about how selection pressures vary within industries. At the bottom of the industry size distribution of firms, selection pressures seem to be reasonably strong. As we have seen, turnover rates can often be very high, and the post-entry performance of survivors is very variable. At the top of many industries, however, selection pressures seem to be rather weaker. Market leaders often maintain their positions (expressed in terms of both market shares and rankings) over considerable periods of time, and their exit is generally more likely to be due to takeover than to failure (see, for example, see Davies et al., 1990, who track the fate of the top five firms in 54 UK three-digit industries over the period 1979–86). One senses that as an entrant first comes into a new market and then expands over time it faces fewer and fewer substantive hurdles. With each challenge that it successfully surmounts, it becomes somewhat stronger and better prepared to meet the next challenge.

There are several reasons why one might expect to observe a diminution in selection pressures as one climbs through the size distribution of firms in a market. First, size disparities between firms widen as one gets closer and closer to market leaders, and this means that the increment in sales that the nth firm needs to achieve to overtake the $(n - 1)$th firm increases as n goes to 1. One simply has to do more and more to overtake one's rival the larger that rival is. One might also think of the importance of size in more dynamic terms. Natural selection in the wild operates because favoured individuals reproduce more rapidly than less favoured ones, thus increasing in relative numbers, and much the same process occurs in markets as successful firms are rewarded with ever increasing sales. If, as is often the case in markets, absolute size confers some competitive advantages on its possessor, then early success breeds continued success and a progressive weakening in selection pressures.

Second, selection pressures may diminish at the top of a market because market leaders are protected by mobility barriers. Smaller rivals who first enter and then try to expand in the market will in this case have to cross a number of thresholds in order to get to the top. Different challengers are liable to take different routes to the top, depending on their special skills, their expectations, their time horizons and so on. Further, those who successfully cross the first thresholds that they meet may find themselves progressively more able to cross subsequent thresholds. For this kind of process to lead to a weakening of market selection pressures as one rises through the industry size distribution, it must be the case that the increasing ability of the surviving challengers is more than offset by the reduction in their numbers as the race to the top continues. This certainly seems to be the case in most markets.

It is possible that the structure of mobility barriers which protects market leaders emerges from the characteristics of the core product that they supply, and from the relationship between the core product and more customized variants. Entrants are often fringe producers located in local market niches, and their expansion must, perforce, take the form of expanding into more and more such niches. To do this, they need to produce a product that is suited to a wider and wider range of buyers, and this means moving away from a strategy of customizing their product and towards one of standardizing it. The relatively intense selection pressures that we observe at the bottom of most industries may be the consequence of having to expand into a succession of local market niches. At first, this creates a tension between serving niche A and niche B, a tension that is exacerbated by the need to satisfy the slightly different consumers who inhabit niche C. However, once the trick of serving A, B and C is mastered, then the process of moving on to serve D, E and F may prove to be rather easier. Thus, the selection pressures that arise from the need to satisfy increasingly diverse consumers may progressively weaken with the accumulation of more and more experience of doing so.

Of course this process of serving more and more diverse consumers is likely to be accompanied by a gradual proliferation of products offered for sale by the gradually expanding entrant. This increase in

272 *Entry and Industry Evolution*

multi-product activity is, perhaps, the third reason why selection pressures may be weaker at the top than at the bottom of most markets. The local market for any specific brand of any particular good is bound to be far more turbulent than the demand for a range of similar goods across a number of local markets is likely to be. Whilst the specialist always has the competitive advantage of serving a particular niche particularly well, it suffers the great disadvantage of being subject to the vagaries of that particular market without any relief from diversification. Market leaders are often the producers of multiple brands, and they often pick off and customize the products demanded by relatively large buyers. Entrants and small firms more generally serve a small market of relatively small buyers and are therefore relatively more vulnerable to demand shifts or cost shocks than large firms are.

The fourth and final reason why selection pressures may appear to weaken as one rises through the size distribution of firms may be bound up with the process of innovation, and the nature of the rivalry that surrounds it. As we have seen, large dominant firms often lack the incentive to generate or adopt new innovations, despite having a richer set of opportunities open to them. This, of course, makes them vulnerable to the competitive challenge of smart, aggressive outsider firms that have something to prove and no rents to protect. If, in addition, innovations are likely to be rather more valuable to market leaders than to the outsider firms that introduce them – if the post-entry returns anticipated by a market leader exceed those of an outsider for the same innovation – then one is likely to observe a pattern of innovations introduced by outsiders and then subsequently taken over by market leaders. Since merger or takeover is often the easiest and most reasonable way to do this, the process by which innovations are introduced and then developed in markets is likely to be mirrored by a process in which market leaders consolidate their hold at the top by buying out their most challenging rivals. What looks like a diminution in selection pressures, then, may just be the consequence of a process in which the fat and rich buy out the lean and hungry, to the considerable advantage of both.

Again, these are no more than speculations. At the moment, we know relatively little about how the selection process operates within markets. However important a role one thinks that entry plays in market processes, we know enough already to be sure that it is only the tip of an iceberg. Those who think that competition thrives on market turbulence, that the sign of a strong and healthy competitive process is a frequent turnover in size rankings and a considerable instability in market shares over time, will be justifiably anxious to explore the rest of the terrain.

Can There Be Too Much Entry?

Chapter 2 opened by posing an apparently simple question, 'is there too much or too little entry in most markets?', and it seems worth devoting a final few paragraphs to trying to answer it. Two observations in particular are worth making.

First, any concern with the quantity of entrants that neglects to consider the quality of entrants is, quite simply, concern misplaced. Most markets, as we have seen, are flooded with new firms year in and year out, and many of these entrants do not survive for long enough to make much of an individual contribution to industry performance. Entrants are not only not perfectly substitutable with incumbents from the point of view of providing market discipline, but different types of entrants are not perfectly substitutable with each other. Competition provided by imports is unlikely to have the same impact on the pricing policies of large domestic incumbents that entry by large subsidiaries of firms established elsewhere will have, and the effects of entry by small firms created *de novo* will be different again.

Somewhat more generally, any concern with the number and size distribution of firms in a market is likely to be misplaced if it neglects to consider types of firms. A market composed entirely of specialist firms is almost certainly going to operate differently from a market dominated by the same number of diversified firms, and market performance in the latter case may also depend on whether those diversified firms are conglomerates, multinationals or vertically integrated upstream or downstream. Markets are populated by a mix of firms following quite different strategies. Some are specialized, some diversified, some are marketing based and some research oriented, some are long sighted and others are slow and stupid. From the point of view of market performance, what may matter as much as the size of the population of competing firms is the mix of types in that population.

Thus, to the question of 'how much entry should there be?', one must append the supplementary question 'of what type?' Before one becomes obsessively concerned with the quantity of competition, one ought to reflect on its quality. Although much of what has passed earlier in this volume gives one a presumption in favour of more rather than less entry, it is possible that it should be read to mean more different types of entrant rather than less regardless of the absolute numbers involved.

The second observation to be made about the question of 'how much entry is optimal?' is that the answer depends very much on one's underlying conception of the role that entry plays in markets. Those who see entry as an error correction mechanism, as a device to increase an artificially restricted supply of the product to the market, are, in a sense, unconcerned with entry *per se*. All that matters is that prices drop to competitive levels, and it simply makes no real difference whether it takes five or 500 entrants to affect this. Indeed, it may not even require any entrants at all if the mere threat of entry by 500 new firms encourages incumbents to behave less monopolistically. More sophisticated versions of this argument recognize that efficiency can dictate some restrictions on entry when there are scale economies or when cannibalization is possible. However, as with arguments about optimum tariffs, these arguments are often accepted in principle and neglected in practice.

If one views entry as a selection process and argues that the role it plays in markets is bound up with choices about product diversity, then the number of entrants begins to matter. That entry helps markets to make better choices means that entry is a generator of positive externalities. While any specific innovation that any particular entrant uses as a vehicle of entry may be valuable, generating for it a positive private rate of return, the fact that this innovation contributes to a broader search process can inflate its social rate of return above this level. A new innovation, however modest, has value in and of itself, and also has value because it fits as part of a broad mosaic in which supply caters to the diverse needs of consumers. Put another way, for selection to generate the best fit between a population (or several populations) and its environment, it requires alternatives to be put forward and compared. The more alternatives considered, the better the fit and the faster it will be achieved. Since the more grist there is for the selection mill to grind on the better will be its output, it is hard to have too little of any reasonably potent source of new ideas. Entry is one of these, and both the quality and quantity of entrants matters.

Of course no activity is costless, and it is easy in principle to imagine an entry process that throws up too many trivial new ideas, that produces too many free-riding new firms that cannibalize their more successful rivals. Yet, before one translates this observation into a set of (perhaps purely theoretical) restrictions on entry, one needs to reflect on the process of change that creates a need for selection. The engine of change in markets is, of course, deep-seated changes in tastes and technology that throw up opportunities for new products and processes to be introduced. Some of these deep-seated changes are (as we have seen) endogenous to the process of competition, while many are exogenous (and therefore analogous to mutations). One way or the other, there are at least two reasons why this kind of process of change undermines any notion that entry and variety ought to be restricted. First, since this kind of change involves changes in tastes, it necessarily changes the yardsticks by which market performance is measured. Any restrictions in entry based upon how markets perform when judged by current standards will inhibit the almost inevitable change in those standards that occurs over time, and such restrictions are unlikely to be justifiable from the point of view of future standards. Second, deep-seated changes (and particularly those that are exogenous) are often very complex and difficult to antici-pate. However clever the human leopard is at changing its spots, it is always likely to encounter an unexpected demand for certain types of spots. Market selection processes might seem both slow and relatively undirected, but these apparent drawbacks can give them a considerable advantage in searching out and finding the best fit possible with a complex and often impenetrable environment.

References

Abernathy, W. (1976) 'Production process structure and technological change', *Decision Sciences*, 7, 607–19.

Abernathy, W. (1978) *The Productivity Dilemma: Roadblocks to Innovation in the Automobile Industry*, Baltimore, MD: Johns Hopkins University Press.

Abernathy, W. and Wayne, K. (1974) 'Limits of the learning curve', *Harvard Business Review*, 52, 109–19.

Abernathy, W., Clark, K. and Kantrow, A. (1983) *Industrial Renaissance*, New York: Basic Books.

Acs, Z. and Audretsch, D. (1987) 'Small firm entry in US manufacturing', *Economica*, 56, 255–66.

Acs, Z. and Audretsch, D. (1988) 'Innovation in large and small firms', *American Economic Review*, 78, 678–90.

Acs, Z. and Audretsch, D. (1991) 'Innovation as a means of entry: an overview', in Geroski, P. and Schwalbach, J. (eds), *Entry and Market Contestability: An International Comparison*, Oxford: Basil Blackwell.

Adams, W. and Dirlam, J. (1964) 'Steel imports and vertical oligopoly', *American Economic Review*, 54, 626–85.

Aghion, P. and Bolton, P. (1987) 'Contracts as a barrier to entry', *American Economic Review*, 77, 388–401.

Aigner, D.J., Hsiaso, C., Kapteyn, A. and Wansbeek, T. (1984) 'The latent variable model in econometrics', in Griliches, Z. and Intrilligator, M. (eds), *Handbook of Econometrics*, Amsterdam: North-Holland.

Alemson, M. (1969) 'Demand, entry and the game of conflict in oligopoly over time: recent Australian experience', *Oxford Economic Papers*, 21, 220–47.

Alemson, M. (1970) 'Advertising and the nature of competition in oligopoly over time: a case study', *Economic Journal*, 80, 282–306.

Alhadeft, D. (1974) 'Barriers to bank entry', *Southern Economic Journal*, 40, 589–603.

Amato, L., Ryan, J. and Wilder, R. (1981) 'Market structure and dynamic performance in US manufacturing', *Southern Economic Journal*, 47, 1105–10.

Arrow, K. (1962) 'Economic welfare and the allocation of resources for inventions', in Nelson, R. (ed.), *The Rate and Direction of Inventive Activity*, Princeton, NJ: Princeton University Press.

Asmussen, E. (1990) 'Entrées et sorties dans l'industrie: impacts instantanés et cumulés', mimeo, Université de Paris I.

Averill, R. (1968) *The Dual Economy*, New York: W. Norton.

Baden-Fuller, C. and Stopford, J. (1987) 'Global or national?', mimeo, London Business School.

Bagwell, K. and Ramey, G. (1987) 'Advertising and limit pricing', *Rand Journal of Economics*, 19, 59–71.

Bagwell, K. and Ramey, G. (1990) 'Advertising and pricing to deter or accommodate entry when demand is unknown', *International Journal of Industrial Organization*, 8, 93–113.

Bailey, E. (1986) 'Price and productivity changes following deregulation: the US experience', *Economic Journal*, 96, 1–17.

Bain, J. (1956) *Barriers to New Competition*, Cambridge, MA: Harvard University Press.

Baldwin, C. (1986) 'The capital factor: competing for capital via global environment', in Porter, M. (ed.), *Competing in Global Industries*, Cambridge, MA: Harvard University Press.

Baldwin, J. and Gorecki, P. (1983) 'Entry and exit to the Canadian manufacturing sector: 1970–1979', mimeo, Economic Council of Canada.

Baldwin, J. and Gorecki, P. (1986) 'The dynamics of firm turnover', mimeo, Economic Council of Canada.

Baldwin, J. and Gorecki, P. (1987) 'Plant creation versus plant acquisition', *International Journal of Industrial Organization*, 5, 27–42.

Baldwin, J. and Gorecki, P. (1991) 'Entry, exit and productivity growth', in Geroski, P. and Schwalbach, J. (eds), *Entry and Market Contestability: An International Comparison*, Oxford: Basil Blackwell.

Baldwin, R. (1987) 'Some empirical evidence on hysteresis in aggregate US import prices', mimeo, Columbia University.

Baldwin, W. and Masson, R. (1981) 'Economies of scale, strategic advertising and fully credible entry deterrence', mimeo, Cornell University.

Baldwin, W. and Scott, J. (1987) *Market Structure and Technological Change*, London: Harwood.

Baron, D. (1972) 'Limit pricing and models of potential entry', *Western Economic Journal*, 10, 298–307.

Baron, D. (1973) 'Limit pricing, potential entry and barriers to entry', *American Economic Review*, 63, 666–74.

Baumol, W., Panzar, J. and Willig, R. (1982) *Contestable Markets and the Theory of Market Structure*, New York: Harcourt, Brace, Jovanovich.

Beesley, M. (1986) 'Commitment, sunk costs and entry to the airline industry', *Journal of Transport Economics and Policy*, 20, 173–90.

Benham, L. (1972) 'The effect of advertising on the price of eyeglasses', *Journal of Law and Economics*, 15, 337–52.

Ben-Ner, A. (1984) 'On the stability of the cooperative type of organization', *Journal of Comparative Economics*, 8, 247–60.

Ben-Ner, A. (1988a) 'Comparative empirical observations on worker-owned and capitalist firms', *International Journal of Industrial Organization*, 6, 7–31.

Ben-Ner, A. (1988b) 'The life cycle of worker-owner firms in market economies', *Journal of Economic Behavior and Organization*, 10, 287–313.

Berger, S. and Piore, M. (1980) *Dualism and Discontinuity in Industrial Societies*, Cambridge: Cambridge University Press.

Bernheim, D. (1984) 'Strategic deterrence of sequential entry into an industry', *Rand Journal of Economics*, 15, 1–11.

Berry, C. (1975) *Corporate Growth and Diversification*, Princeton, NJ: Princeton University Press.

Bevan, A. (1974) 'The UK potato crisp industry 1960–72: a study of new entry competition', *Journal of Industrial Economics*, 22, 281–97.

Bhagwati, J. (1970) 'Oligopoly theory, entry prevention and growth', *Oxford Economic Papers*, 22, 297–310.

Biggadike, E. (1976) *Entry, Strategy and Performance*, Division of Research, Graduate School of Business Administration, Harvard University.

Blackstone, E. (1972) 'Limit pricing and entry in the copying machine industry', *Quarterly Review of Economics and Business*, 12, 57–65.

Blair, J. (1974) *Economic Concentration*, New York: Harcourt, Brace, Jovanovich.

Bollinger, L., Hope, K. and Utterback, J. (1983) 'A review of literature and hypotheses on new technology based firms', *Research Policy*, 12, 1–14.

Bonanno, G. (1987) 'Location choice, product proliferation and entry deterrence', *Review of Economic Studies*, 54, 37–45.

Bonanno, G. (1988) 'Entry deterrence with uncertain entry and uncertain observability of commitment', *International Journal of Industrial Organization*, 6, 351–62.

Bond, R. and Lean, D. (1977) 'Sales, promotion and product differentiation in two prescription drugs markets', mimeo, Federal Trade Commission.

Braun, E. and MacDonald, S. (1982) *Revolution in Miniature*, 2nd edn, Cambridge: Cambridge University Press.

Bresnahan, T. (1985) 'Post-entry competition in the plain paper copier market', *American Economic Review, Papers and Proceedings*, 75, 15–19.

Bresnahan, T. (1989) 'Empirical studies of industries with market power', in Schmalensee, R. and Willig, R. (eds), *Handbook of Industrial Economics*, Amsterdam: North-Holland.

Bresnahan, T. and Reiss, P. (1986) 'Entry in monopoly markets', mimeo, Stanford University.

Bresnahan, T. and Reiss, P. (1988) 'Do entry conditions vary across markets?', *Brookings Papers on Economic Activity*, 3, 833–81.

Bresnahan, T. and Reiss, P. (1989) 'Entry and competition in concentrated markets', mimeo, Stanford University.

Bright, A. and Maclaourin, W. (1943) 'Economic factors influencing the development and introduction of the fluorescent lamp', *Journal of Political Economy*, 51, 429–50.

Brock, G.W. (1975) *The US Computer Industry: A Study of Market Power*, Cambridge, MA: Ballinger.

Brown, R. (1978) 'Estimating advantages to large scale advertising', *Review of Economics and Statistics*, 60, 428-37.

Butters, G. (1976) 'A survey of advertising and market structure', *American Economic Review*, 66, 392-7.

Cable, J. and Schwalbach, J. (1991) 'International comparisons of entry and exit', in Geroski, P. and Schwalbach, J. (eds), *Entry and Market Contestability: An International Comparison*, Oxford: Basil Blackwell.

Carlsson, B. (1972) 'The measurement of efficiency in production: an application to Swedish manufacturing industries', *Swedish Journal of Economics*, 74, 468-85.

Carlsson, B. (1983) 'Industrial subsidies in Sweden: macroeconomic effects and an international comparison', *Journal of Industrial Economics*, 32, 1-24.

Carlsson, B. (1989a) 'Flexibility and the theory of the firm', *International Journal of Industrial Organization*, 7, 179-204.

Carlsson, B. (1989b) 'The development and use of machine tools in historical perspective', *Journal of Economic Behaviour and Organization*, 5, 91-114.

Carlton, D. (1983) 'The location and employment choices of new firms: an econometric model with discrete and continuous endogenous variables', *Review of Economics and Statistics*, 65, 440-9.

Caves, R. (1982) *Multinational Enterprise and Economic Analysis*, Cambridge: Cambridge University Press.

Caves, R. and Davies, S. (1987) *Britains Productivity Gap*, Cambridge: Cambridge University Press.

Caves, R. and Mehra, S. (1985) 'Entry of foreign multinationals into US manufacturing industries', in Porter, M. (ed.), *Global Competition*, Cambridge, MA: Harvard University Press.

Caves, R. and Porter, M. (1976) 'Barriers to exit', in Masson, R. and Qualls, D. (eds), *Essays in Industrial Organization in Honor of Joe S. Bain*, Cambridge, MA: Ballinger.

Caves, R. and Porter, M. (1977) 'From entry barriers to mobility barriers: conjectural decisions and contrived deterrence to new competition', *Quarterly Journal of Economics*, 97, 247-61.

Chetty, V.K. and Heckman, J. (1986) 'A dynamic model of aggregate output supply, factor demand and entry and exit for a competitive industry with heterogeneous plants', *Journal of Econometrics*, 33, 237-62.

Church, R. (1976) 'Innovation, monopoly and the supply of vehicle components in Britain 1880-1930; the growth of Joseph Lucas Ltd', *Business History Review*, 52, 226-49.

Clark, K. (1983) 'Competition, technical diversity and radical innovation in the US auto industry', in *Research on Technological Innovation, Management and Policy*, Greenwich, CT: JAI Press.

Clark, K. (1988) 'Managing technology in international competition: the case of product development in response to foreign entry', in Spence, M. and Hazard, H. (eds), *International Competitiveness*, Cambridge, MA: Ballinger.

280 *References*

Cohen, W. and Levin, R. (1989) 'Empirical studies of innovation and market structure', in Schmalensee, R. and Willig, R. (eds), *Handbook of Industrial Economics*, Amsterdam: North-Holland.

Cohen, W., Levin, R. and Mowery, D. (1987) 'Firm size and R&D intensity: a re-examination', *Journal of Industrial Economics*, 35, 543–66.

Colinvaux, P. (1980) *Why Big Fierce Animals are Rare*, London: Penguin.

Comanor, W. (1966) 'Competition and performance of the Midwestern coal industry', *Journal of Industrial Economics*, 14, 212–25.

Comanor, W. (1967) 'Market structure, product differentiation, and industrial research, *Quarterly Journal of Economics*, 81, 639–57.

Comanor, W. and Wilson, T. (1967) 'Advertising, market structure and performance', *Review of Economics and Statistics*, 49, 423–40.

Comanor, W. and Wilson, T. (1974) *Advertising and Market Power*, Cambridge, MA: Harvard University Press.

Comanor, W. and Wilson, T. (1979) 'The effect of advertising on competition: a survey', *Journal of Economic Literature*, 17, 453–76.

Connolly, R. and Schwartz, S. (1985) 'The intertemporal behaviour of economic profits', *International Journal of Industrial Organization*, 3, 465–72.

Conte, M. and Svejnar, J. (1988) 'Productivity effects of worker participation in management, profit sharing, worker ownership of assets and organization in US firms', *International Journal of Industrial Organization*, 3, 197–217.

Cooper, A. and Smith, C. (1988) 'Established companies diversifying into young industries: a comparison of firms with different levels of performance', *Strategic Management Journal*, 9, 111–21.

Cowling, K. and Waterson, M. (1976) 'Price–cost margins and market structure', *Economica*, 43, 275–86.

Cowling, K., Cable, J., Kelly, M. and McGuinness, T. (1975) *Advertising and Economic Behaviour*, London: Macmillan.

Cross, J. (1983) *A Theory of Adaptive Economic Behavior*, Cambridge: Cambridge University Press.

Cubbin, J. (1981) 'Advertising and the theory of entry barriers', *Economica*, 48, 289–98.

Cubbin, J. and Domberger, S. (1988) 'Advertising and post-entry oligopoly behaviour', *Journal of Industrial Economics*, 37, 123–40.

Cubbin, J. and Geroski, P. (1987) 'The convergence of profits in the long run: interfirm and interindustry comparisons', *Journal of Industrial Economics*, 35, 427–42.

Cyert, R. and March, J. (1963) *A Behaviourial Theory of the Firm*, Englewood Cliffs, NJ: Prentice Hall.

Dasgupta, P. (1986) 'The theory of technological competition', in Stiglitz, J.E. and Mathewson, G.F. (eds), *New Developments in the Analysis of Market Structure*, London: Macmillan.

Davies, S. (1979) *The Diffusion of Process Innovations*, Cambridge: Cambridge University Press.

Davies, S., Geroski, P. and Vlassopoulos, T. (1990) 'The dynamics of market leadership in UK manufacturing, 1979–1986', mimeo, London Business School.

Davis, E. (1984) 'Express coaching since 1980: liberalization in practice', *Fiscal Studies*, 5, 76–86.

Dawkins, R. (1986) *The Blind Watchmaker*, New York: W. Norton.

De Bondt, R. (1976) 'Limit pricing, uncertainty and the entry lag', *Econometrica*, 44, 939–46.

Defourney, J., Estrin, S. and Jones, D. (1985) 'The effects of worker's participation in enterprise performance', *International Journal of Industrial Organization*, 3, 197–217.

De Lamarter, R. (1988) *Big Blue: IBM's Use and Abuse of Power*, London: Pan.

Dell'Osso, F. (1990) 'When leaders become followers: the market for anti-ulcer drugs', mimeo, London Business School.

Demsetz, H. (1968) 'Why regulate utilities?', *Journal of Law and Economics*, 11, 55–65.

Demsetz, H. (1982) 'Barriers to entry', *American Economic Review*, 72, 47–57.

Dickson, V. (1979) 'Sub-optimal capacity and market structure in Canadian industry', *Southern Economic Journal*, 46, 206–17.

Dixit, A. (1979) 'A model of duopoly suggesting a theory of entry barriers', *Bell Journal of Economics*, 10, 20–32.

Dixit, A. (1980) 'The role of investment in entry deterrence', *Economic Journal*, 90, 95–106.

Dixit, A. (1982) 'Recent developments in oligopoly theory', *American Economic Review*, 72, 12–17.

Dixit, A. (1989a) 'Entry and exit decisions under uncertainty', *Journal of Political Economy*, 97, 620–38.

Dixit, A. (1989b) 'A general model of R&D competition and policy', *Rand Journal of Economics*, 19, 317–26.

Domberger, S. and Sherr, A. (1987) 'Completion in conveyancing: an analysis of solicitors charges 1983–85', *Fiscal Studies*, 8, 17–28.

Dorfman, R. and Steiner, P. (1954) 'Optimal advertising and optimal quality', *American Economic Review*, 44, 826–36.

Duetsch, L. (1975) 'Structure, performance and the net rate of entry into manufacturing industry', *Southern Economic Journal*, 41, 450–6.

Duetsch, L. (1984) 'Entry and the extent of multiplant operations', *Journal of Industrial Economics*, 32, 477–89.

Dunne, T. and Roberts, M. (1991) 'Variation in producer turnover across US manufacturing industries', in Geroski, P. and Schwalbach, J. (eds), *Entry and Market Contestability: An International Comparison*, Oxford: Basil Blackwell.

Dunne, T., Roberts, M. and Samuelson, L. (1988) 'Patterns of firm entry and exit in US manufacturing industries', *Rand Journal of Economics*, 19, 495–515.

Dunne, T., Roberts, M. and Samuelson, L. (1989a) 'Firm entry and post-entry performance in the US chemical industries', *Journal of Law and Economics*, 32, 233–71.

Dunne, T., Roberts, M. and Samuelson, L. (1989b) 'The growth and failure of US manufacturing plants', *Quarterly Journal of Economics*, 104, 671–98.

Eaton, C. and Lipsey, R. (1978) 'Freedom of entry and the existence of pure profit', *Economic Journal*, 88, 455–69.

Eaton, C. and Lipsey, R. (1979) 'The theory of market pre-emption: the persistence of excess capacity and monopoly in growing spatial markets', *Economica*, 47, 149–58.

Eaton, C. and Lipsey, R. (1980) 'Exit barriers are entry barriers: the durability of capital as a barrier to entry', *Bell Journal of Economics*, 11, 721–9.

Eaton, C. and Ware, R. (1987) 'A theory of market structure with sequential entry', *Rand Journal of Economics*, 18, 1–16.

Edwards, K. and Gordon, T. (1984) 'Characterization of innovations introduced on the US market in 1982', Report for US Small Business Administration by the Futures Group.

Edwards, J., Kay, J. and Mayer, C. (1987) *The Economic Analysis of Accounting Profitability*, Oxford: Oxford University Press.

EEC (1988) 'The economics of 1992', *European Economy*, 35, 1–222.

Ehrenberg, A. (1988) *Repeat Buying*, 2nd edn, New York: Oxford University Press.

Encaoua, D., Jacquemin, A. and Michel, P. (1981) 'Strategic dynamic de prix et structures de marche', *Cahiers de Seminaire d'Econometrie*, 23, 153–68.

Encaoua, D., Geroski, P. and Jacquemin, A. (1987) 'Strategic competition and the persistence of dominant firms: a survey', in Matthewson, F. and Stiglitz, J. (eds), *New Developments in the Analysis of Market Structure*, Boston, MA: MIT Press.

Enos, J. (1962) 'Invention and innovation in the petroleum refining industry', in Nelson, R. (ed.), *The Rate and Direction of Inventive Activity*, Princeton, NJ: Princeton University Press.

Ergas, H. (1984) 'Why do some countries innovate more than others?', Report, Centre for European Policy Studies, Brussels.

Erickson, W. (1976) 'Price fixing conspiracies: their long term impact', *Journal of Industrial Economics*, 26, 189–202.

Estrin, S. and Jones, D. (1987) 'Are there life cycles in labour managed firms?', mimeo, London School of Economics.

Estrin, S. and Petrin, T. (1991) 'Patterns of entry, exit and merger in Yugoslavia', in Geroski, P. and Schwalbach, J. (eds), *Entry and Market Contestability: An International Comparison*, Oxford: Basil Blackwell.

Estrin, S. and Jones, D. (1988) 'Can employee owned firms survive?', mimeo, London School of Economics.

Evans, D. (1987a) 'The relationship between firm growth, size and age: estimates for the US manufacturing sector', *Journal of Industrial Economics*, 35, 567–82.

Evans, D. (1987b) 'Tests of alternative theories of firm growth', *Journal of Political Economy*, 95, 657–74.

Farrell, J. and Shapiro, C. (1988) 'Dynamic competition with switching costs', *Rand Journal of Economics*, 19, 123–37.

Fearan, P. (1969) 'The formative years of the British aircraft industry, 1913–1924', *Business History Review*, 42, 115–48.

Feinman, S. and Fuentevilla, W. (1976) 'Indicators of international trends in technical innovation', Report to National Science Foundation by Gellman Research Associates.

Fellner, W. (1951) 'The influence of market structure on technological progress', *Quarterly Journal of Economics*, 65, 556–77.

Ferguson, J. (1974) *Advertising and Competition: Theory, Measurement, Fact*, Cambridge, MA: Ballinger.

Fisher, F. (1987a) 'On the misuse of the profits–sales ratio to infer monopoly power', *Rand Journal of Economics*, 18, 384–96.

Fisher, F. (1987b) 'Pan American to United: the Pacific division transfer case', *Rand Journal of Economics*, 18, 492–508.

Fisher, F. and McGowan, J. (1983) 'On the misuse of accounting rates of return to infer monopoly profits', *American Economic Review*, 73, 82–97.

Fisher, F. and Temin, P. (1973) 'Returns to scale in research and development: what does the Schumpeterian hypothesis imply?', *Journal of Political Economy*, 81, 56–70.

Fisher, F., Griliches, Z. and Kaysen, C. (1962) 'The costs of automobile model changes since 1949', *Journal of Political Economy*, 70, 433–51.

Flaherty, M.T. (1983) 'Market share, technology leadership and competition in international semi-conductor markets', in *Research in Technological Innovation, Management and Policy*, Greenwich, CT: JAI Press.

Flaherty, M.T. (1984) 'Field research on the link between technological innovation and growth', *American Economic Review, Papers and Proceedings*, 74, 67–72.

Foster, R. (1986) *Innovation: the Attackers Advantage*, London: Pan.

Freeman, C. (1963) 'The plastics industry: a comparative study of research and innovation', *National Institute Economic Review*, 26, 22–62.

Freeman, C. (1982) *The Economics of Industrial Innovation*, 2nd edn, Cambridge, MA: MIT Press.

Fuss, M. and Gupta, V. (1981) 'A cost function approach to the estimation of minimum efficient scale, returns to scale and suboptimal capacity', *European Economic Review*, 15, 123–35.

Gable, H.L. (1979) 'A simultaneous equation analysis of the structure and performance of the United States petroleum refining industry', *Journal of Industrial Economics*, 28, 89–104.

Ganguly, P. (1985) *UK Small Business Statistics and International Comparisons*, London: Harper & Row.

Gaskins, D. (1971) 'Dynamic limit pricing optimal pricing under threat of entry', *Journal of Economic Theory*, 3, 306–22.

Gelfand, M. and Spiller, P. (1987) 'Entry barriers and multiproduct ologopolies: do they forbear or spoil?', *International Journal of Industrial Organization*, 5, 101–14.

Geroski, P. (1987) 'Do dominant firms decline?', in Hay, D. and Vickers, J. (eds), *The Economics of Market Dominance*, Oxford: Basil Blackwell.

Geroski, P. (1988a) 'In pursuit of monopoly power: recent quantitative work in industrial economics', *Journal of Applied Econometrics*, 3, 107–23.

Geroski, P. (1988b) 'The interaction between domestic and foreign based entrants', in Audretsch, D., Sleuwaegen, L. and Yamawaki, H. (eds), *The Convergence of International and Domestic Markets*, Amsterdam: North-Holland.

Geroski, P. (1988c) 'Competition policy and the structure–performance paradigm', in Davies, S. and Lyons, B. (eds), *Economics of Industrial Organization*, London: Longman.

Geroski, P. (1989a) 'Entry and the rate of innovation', *Economics of Innovation and New Technology*, 1, 203–14.

Geroski, P. (1989b) 'Entry, innovation and productivity growth', *Review of Economics and Statistics*, 71, 572–8.

Geroski, P. (1990a) 'The effect of entry on profit margins in the short and long run', *Annales d'Economie et de Statistique*, 15–16, 333–53.

Geroski, P.A. (1990b) 'Innovation, technological opportunity and market structure', *Oxford Economic Papers*, 42, 586–602.

Geroski, P. (1990c) 'Entry, exit and structural adjustment in European industry', mimeo, London Business School.

Geroski, P. (1990d) 'Innovation and the sectoral sources of UK productivity growth', *Economic Journal*, forthcoming.

Geroski, P. (1991) 'Domestic and foreign entry in the UK: 1983–1984', in Geroski, P. and Schwalbach, J. (eds), *Entry and Market Contestability: An International Comparison*, Oxford: Basil Blackwell.

Geroski, P. and Jacquemin, A. (1984) 'Dominant firms and their alleged decline', *International Journal of Industrial Organization*, 2, 1–28.

Geroski, P.A. and Jacquemin, A. (1988) 'The persistence of profits: a European comparison', *Economic Journal*, 98, 375–89.

Geroski, P. and Masson, R. (1987) 'Dynamic market models in industrial organization', *International Journal of Industrial Organization*, 5, 1–14.

Geroski, P. and Murfin, A. (1987) 'Entry and intra-industry mobility in the UK car market', *Oxford Bulletin of Economics and Statistics*, forthcoming.

Geroski, P. and Murfin, A. (1990a) 'Advertising and the dynamics of market structure: the UK car industry 1958–83', *British Management Journal*, 23, 799–810.

Geroski, P.A. and Murfin, A. (1990b) 'Entry and industry evolution: the UK car industry, 1958–83', *Applied Economics*, forthcoming.

Geroski, P. and Pomroy, R. (1990) 'Innovation and the evolution of market structure', *Journal of Industrial Economics*, 38, 299–314.

Geroski, P. and Toker, S. (1988) 'Picking profitable markets', mimeo, London Business School.

Geroski, P. and Vlassopoulos, T. (1989) 'The rise and fall of a market leader: frozen food in the UK', *Strategic Management Journal*, forthcoming.

Geroski, P., Gilbert, R. and Jacquemin, A. (1990) *Barriers to Entry and Strategic Competition*, London: Harwood.

Gilbert, R. (1989) 'Preemptive competition', in Schmalensee, R. and Willig, R. (eds), *Handbook of Industrial Organization*, Amsterdam: North-Holland.

Gilbert, R. and Newberry, D. (1982) 'Pre-emptive patenting and the persistence of monopoly', *American Economic Review*, 72, 514–26.

Gilbert, R. and Vives, X. (1986) 'Entry deterrence and the free rider problem', *Review of Economic Studies*, 53, 71–83.

Glazer, A. (1985) 'The advantages of being first', *American Economic Review*, 75, 473-80.

Gorecki, P. (1975) 'The determinants of entry by new and diversifying enterprises in the UK manufacturing sector 1958-63', *Applied Economics*, 7, 139-47.

Gorecki, P. (1976) 'The determinants of entry by domestic and foreign enterprises in Canadian manufacturing industries', *Review of Economics and Statistics*, 58, 485-8.

Gorecki, P. (1986a) 'The importance of being first: the case of prescription drugs in Canada', *International Journal of Industrial Organization*, 4, 371-96.

Gorecki, P. (1986b) 'Monopoly, entry and predatory pricing: the Hoffman-La Roche case', in Tucker, K. and Baden-Fuller, C. (eds), *Firms and Markets*, New York: Croom Helm.

Gort, M. (1962) *Diversification and Integration in American Industry*, Princeton, NJ: Princeton University Press.

Gort, M. and Kanakayama, A. (1982) 'A model of diffusion in the production of an innovation', *American Economic Review*, 72, 1111-20.

Gort, M. and Klepper, S. (1982) 'Time paths in the diffusion of product innovations', *Economic Journal*, 92, 630-53.

Gould, A. and Keeble, D. (1984) 'New firms and rural industrialization in East Anglia', *Regional Studies*, 18, 189-201.

Gould, S. (1989) *Wonderful Life*, New York: Hutchinson Radius.

Gould, S. (1980) *The Panda's Thumb*, New York: W. Norton.

Grabowski, H. and Vernon, J. (1982) 'The pharmaceutical industry', in Nelson, R. (ed.), *Government and Technical Progress*, Oxford: Pergamon.

Granger, C. (1969) 'Investigating causal relations by econometric models and cross-spectral methods', *Econometrica*, 37, 424-38.

Granger, C. and Newbold, P. (1986) *Forecasting Economic Times Series*, 2nd edn, New York: Academic Press.

Grant, R. (1986) 'The effects of product standardization on competition: the case of octane grading of petrol in the UK', mimeo, London Business School.

Greer, D. and Rhoades, S. (1976) 'Concentration and productivity changes in the long and short run', *Southern Economic Journal*, 43, 1031-44.

Grindley, P. and McBryde, R. (1989a) 'The use of product standards in business strategy: video cassette recorders', mimeo, London Business School.

Grindley, P. and McBryde, R. (1989b) 'Standards strategy for personal computers', mimeo, London Business School.

Gupta, V. (1979) 'Sub-optimal capacity and its determination in Canadian manufacturing industry', *Review of Economics and Statistics*, 61, 506-12.

Hall, B. (1987) 'The relationship between firm size and firm growth in the US manufacturing sector', *Journal of Industrial Economics*, 35, 583-606.

Hamberg, D. (1963) 'Invention in the industrial research laboratory', *Journal of Political Economy*, 71, 95-115.

Hamilton, R. (1985) 'Interindustry variation in gross entry rates of "independent" and "dependent" businesses', *Applied Economics*, 17, 271-80.

Hannan, T. (1979) 'Limit pricing and the banking industry', *Journal of Money, Credit and Banking*, 10, 438-46.

Hannan, T. (1983) 'Price, capacity and the entry decision: a conditional logit analysis', *Southern Economic Journal*, 50, 539-50.

Harris, M. (1976) 'Entry and barriers to entry', *Industrial Organization Review*, 4, 165-74.

Hause, J. and du Reitz, G. (1984) 'Entry, industry growth and the micro-dynamics of industry supply', *Journal of Political Economy*, 92, 733-57.

Hay, D. (1976) 'Sequential entry and entry deterring strategies in spatial competition', *Oxford Economic Papers*, 28, 240-57.

Hay, D. and Morris, D. (1984) *Unquoted Companies*, Basingstoke: Macmillan.

Hazeldine, T. (1985) 'The anatomy of productivity growth slowdown and recovery in Canadian manufacturing, 1970-79', *International Journal of Industrial Organization*, 3, 307-26.

Hessian, C. (1961) 'The metal container industry', in Adams, W. (ed.), *The Structure of American Industry*, 3rd edn, Basingstoke: Macmillan.

Highfield, R. and Smiley, R. (1987) 'New business starts and economic activity', *International Journal of Industrial Organization*, 5, 51-66.

Hilke, J. (1984) 'Excess capacity and entry: some empirical evidence', *Journal of Industrial Economics*, 33, 233-41.

Hines, H. (1957) 'Effectiveness of entry by already established firms', *Quarterly Journal of Economics*, 71, 132-50.

Hirschey, M. (1981) 'The effect of advertising on industrial mobility, 1947-72', *Journal of Business*, 54, 329-39.

Hurdle, G., Johnson, R., Joskow, A., Werden, G. and Williams, M. (1989) 'Concentration, potential entry and performance in the airline industry', *Journal of Industrial Economics*, 38, 119-40.

Ireland, N. (1987) *Product Differentiation and Non-Price Competition*, Oxford: Basil Blackwell.

Jacquemin, A. (1987) *The New Industrial Organization*, Oxford: Oxford University Press.

Jacquemin, A. and Slade, M. (1989) 'Cartels, collusion and horizontal merger', in Schmalensee, R. and Willig, R. (eds), *Handbook of Industrial Organization*, Amsterdam: North-Holland.

Jaffe, S. and Thompson, D. (1986) 'Deregulating express coaches: a reassessment', *Fiscal Studies*, 7, 45-68.

James, T. (1986) 'The probability of entry and the number of potential entrants', mimeo, University of Southampton.

Jewkes, J., Sawers, D. and Stillerman, R. (1969) *The Sources of Invention*, New York: W. Norton.

Johnson, P. and Cathcart, D. (1979) 'New manufacturing firms and regional development', *Regional Studies*, 13, 269-80.

Johnston, J. (1960) *Statistical Cost Analysis*, New York: McGraw-Hill.

Jovanovich, B. (1982) 'Selection and the evolution of industry', *Econometrica*, 50, 649-70.

Judd, K. (1985) 'Credible spatial pre-emption', *Rand Journal of Economics*, 16, 153-66.

References   287

Judd, K. and Peterson, B. (1986) 'Dynamic limit pricing and internal finance', *Journal of Economic Theory*, 39, 368–99.

Judge, G., Griffiths, W., Hill, R. and Lee, T. (1980) *The Theory and Practice of Econometrics*, New York: Wiley.

Kamien, M.I. and Schwartz, N.L. (1971) 'Limit pricing and uncertain entry', *Econometrica*, 39, 441–54.

Kamien, M.I. and Schwartz, N.L. (1972) 'Uncertain entry and excess capacity', *American Economic Review*, 62, 918–27.

Kamien, M.I. and Schwartz, N.L. (1975) 'Cournot oligopoly with uncertain entry', *Review of Economic Studies*, 42, 125–31.

Kamien, M.I. and Schwartz, N.L. (1982) *Market Structure and Innovation*, Cambridge: Cambridge University Press.

Kaplinski, R. (1983) 'Firm size and technical change in a dynamic context', *Journal of Industrial Economics*, 32, 39–60.

Katz, B. and Phillips, A. (1982) 'The computer industry', in Nelson, R. (ed.), *Government and Technical Progress*, Oxford: Pergamon.

Katz, M. and Shapiro, C. (1985) 'Network externalities, competition and compatibility', *American Economic Review*, 75, 424–40.

Kay, J. and Mayer, C. (1986) 'On the application of accounting rates of return', *Economic Journal*, 96, 199–207.

Kay, J. and Thompson, D. (1986) 'Privatization: a policy in search of a rationale', *Economic Journal*, 96, 18–32.

Kessides, I. (1986) 'Advertising, sunk costs and barriers to entry', *Review of Economics and Statistics*, 68, 84–95.

Kessides, I. (1989) 'Towards a testable model of entry: a study of the US manufacturing industries', *Economica*, 57, 219–38.

Kessides, I. (1991) 'Entry and market contestability: the evidence from the US', in Geroski, P. and Schwalbach, J. (eds), *Entry and Market Contestability: An International Comparison*, Oxford: Basil Blackwell.

Khemani, S. and Shapiro, D. (1983) 'Alternative specifications of entry models: some tests and empirical results', mimeo, Bureau of Competition Policy, Ottawa.

Khemani, S. and Shapiro, D. (1986) 'The determinants of new plant entry in Canada', *Applied Economics*, 18, 1243–57.

Khemani, S. and Shapiro, D. (1987) 'The determinants of entry and exit reconsidered', *International Journal of Industrial Organization*, 5, 15–26.

Kirman, W. and Masson, R. (1986) 'Capacity signals and entry deterrence', *International Journal of Industrial Organization*, 4, 25–42.

Klemperer, P. (1987a) 'Entry deterrence in markets with consumer switching costs', *Economic Journal* (Supplement), 97, 99–117.

Klemperer, P. (1987b) 'Markets with consumer switching costs', *Quarterly Journal of Economics*, 102, 375–94.

Klemperer, P. (1987c) 'The competitiveness of markets with consumer switching costs', *Rand Journal of Economics*, 18, 138–50.

Klepper, S. and Grady, E. (1989) 'The evolution of new industries and the determinents of market structure', *Rand Journal of Economics*, 21, 27–44.

Klotz, B., Madoo, R. and Hansen, R. (1980) 'A study of high and low labour productivity establishments in US manufacturing', in Kendrick, J. and Vaccara, B. (eds), *New Developments in Productivity Analysis*, Chicago, IL: University of Chicago Press.

Krueger, A. and Summers, L. (1988) 'Efficiency wages and the inter-industry wage structure', *Econometrica*, 56, 259–94.

Lambkin, M. (1988) 'Order of entry and performance in new markets', *Strategic Management Journal*, 9, 127–40.

Lane, S. (1987) 'Entry and competition in the ATM market', mimeo, Stanford University.

Lane, S. and Schary, M. (1989) 'The macroeconomic component of business failures, 1956–1988', mimeo, Boston University.

Lee, T. and Wilde, L. (1980) 'Market structure and innovation: a reformulation', *Quarterly Journal of Economics*, 94, 429–36.

Leffer, K. (1981) 'Persuasion or information? The economics of prescription drug advertising', *Journal of Law and Economics*, 24, 45–74.

Levin, R. (1982) 'The semi-conductor industry', in Nelson, R. (ed.), *Government and Technological Progress*, Oxford: Pergamon.

Levin, R., Cohen, W. and Mowery, D. (1985) 'R&D appropriability, opportunity, and market structure: new evidence on some Schumpeterian hypotheses', *American Economic Review, Papers and Proceedings*, 75, 20–4.

Levin, R., Klevorick, A., Nelson, R. and Winter, S. (1987) 'Appropriating the returns from industrial research and development', *Brookings Papers*, 3, 783–831.

Levy, D. (1987) 'The speed of the invisible hand', *International Journal of Industrial Organization*, 5, 79–92.

Lieberman, M. (1984) 'The learning curve and pricing in the chemical processing industries', *Rand Journal of Economics*, 15, 213–28.

Lieberman, M. (1987) 'Excess capacity as a barrier to entry: an empirical appraisal', *Journal of Industrial Economics*, 35, 607–27.

Lieberman, M. (1988a) 'The learning curve, technology barriers to entry and competitive survival in the chemical processing industries', mimeo, Stanford University.

Lieberman, M. (1988b) 'Entry, pricing and vertical integration in the chemical processing industries', mimeo, Stanford University.

Lieberman, M. and Montgomery, D. (1988) 'First mover advantages', *Strategic Management Journal*, 9, 41–58.

Lippman, S. (1980) 'Optimal pricing to retard entry', *Review of Economic Studies*, 47, 723–31.

Lloyd, P. and Mason, C. (1984) 'Spatial variation in new firm formation in the UK', *Regional Studies*, 18, 207–20.

Loury, G. (1979) 'Market structure and innovation', *Quarterly Journal of Economics*, 93, 395–410.

Lyons, B. (1980) 'A new measure of minimum efficient plant size in UK manufacturing industry', *Economica*, 47, 19–34.

Lytle, R. (1968) 'The introduction of diesel power in the US, 1897-1912', *Business History Review*, 42, 115-48.

MacDonald, J. (1986) 'Entry and exit in the competitive fringe', *Southern Economic Journal*, 52, 640-52.

Maclaurin, W. (1950) 'Patents and technical progress - a study of television', *Journal of Political Economy*, 58, 142-57.

Majumdar, B. (1988) 'Upstart or flying start? The rise of Airbus Industrie', *The World Economy*, 10, 497-517.

Mankiw, G. and Whinston, M. (1986) 'Free entry and social economic welfare', *Rand Journal of Economics*, 17, 48-58.

Mann, M. (1966) 'Seller concentration, barriers to entry, and rate of return in thirty industries', *Review of Economics and Statistics*, 48, 296-307.

Mansfield, E. (1962) 'Entry, Gibrat's law, and the growth of firms', *American Economic Review*, 52, 1023-51.

Mansfield, E., Rapoport, J., Schnee, J., Wagner, S. and Hamburger, M. (1971) *Research and Innovation in the Modern Corporation*, New York: W. Norton.

Mansfield, E., Schwartz, M. and Wagner, S. (1981) 'Invitation costs and patents: an empirical study', *Economic Journal*, 91, 903-18.

Martin, S. (1983) 'Markets, firms and economic performance', *Monograph Series in Finance and Economics*, New York: NTU Graduate School of Business Administration.

Martin, S. (1989) 'Sunk costs, financial markets and contestability', *European Economic Review*, 33, 1089-114.

Marx, T. (1976) 'Technological change and the theory of the firm: the American locomotive industry, 1920-1955', *Business History Review*, 50, 1-24.

Masson, R. and Jeong, K.-Y. (1991) 'Entry during explosive growth: Korea during take-off', in Geroski, P. and Schawalbach, J. (eds), *Entry and Market Contestability: An International Comparison*, Oxford: Basil Blackwell.

Masson, R. and Shaanan, J. (1982) 'Stochastic dynamic limit pricing: an empirical test', *Review of Economics and Statistics*, 64, 413-23.

Masson, R. and Shaanan, J. (1986) 'Excess capacity and limit pricing: an empirical test', *Economica*, 53, 365-78.

Masson, R. and Shaanan, J. (1987) 'Oligopolistic pricing and the threat of entry: Canadian evidence', *International Journal of Industrial Organization*, 5, 323-40.

Mata, J. (1991) 'Sunk costs and entry by small and large plants', in Geroski, P. and Schwalbach, J. (eds), *Entry and Market Contestability: An International Comparison*, Oxford: Basil Blackwell.

McRae, J. and Tapan, F. (1985) 'Some empirical evidence on post-patent barriers to entry in the Canadian pharmaceutical industry', *Journal of Health Economics*, 4, 43-61.

Metcalf, J. (1970) 'Diffusion of innovation in the Lancashire textile industry', *Manchester School*, 38, 145-62.

Milgrom, P. and Roberts, J. (1982) 'Limit pricing and entry under incomplete information: an equilibrium analysis', *Econometrica*, 50, 443-59.

290   References

Mills, D. (1986) 'Flexibility and firm diversity with demand fluctuations', *International Journal of Industrial Organization*, 4, 203–15.

Mills, D. and Schumann, L. (1985) 'Industry structure and fluctuating demand', *American Economic Review*, 75, 758–67.

Miyazaki, M. (1984) 'On the success and dissolution of the labour managed firm in the capitalist economy', *Journal of Political Economy*, 92, 909–31.

Mizuno, M. and Odagiri, H. (1988) 'Does advertising mislead consumers to buy low-quality products?', *International Journal of Industrial Organization*, forthcoming.

MMC (1976) *Frozen Foodstuffs*, London: Monopolies and Mergers Commission, HMSO.

MMC (1981) *Bicycles*, London: Monopolies and Mergers Commission, HMSO.

MMC (1989) *The Supply of Beer*, London: Monopolies and Mergers Commission, HMSO.

Modigliani, F. (1958) 'New developments on the oligopoly front', *Journal of Political Economy*, 66, 215–32.

Morch van der Fehr, N.-H. (1991) 'Domestic entry in Norwegian manufacturing industries', in Geroski, P. and Schwalbach, J. (eds), *Entry and Market Contestability: An International Comparison*, Oxford: Basil Blackwell.

Morgan, E., Lowe, I. and Tomkins, C. (1980) 'The UK financial leasing industry – a structural analysis', *Journal of Industrial Economics*, 28, 405–25.

Mueller, W. (1962) 'The origins of the basic inventions underlying Du Ponts major product and process innovations', in Nelson, R. (ed.), *The Rate and Direction of Economic Activity*, Princeton, NJ: Princeton University Press.

Mueller, D. (1977) 'The persistence of profits above the norm', *Economica*, 44, 369–80.

Mueller, D. (1986) *Profits in the Long Run*, Cambridge: Cambridge University Press.

Mueller, D. (ed.) (1990) *The Dynamics of Company Profits: An International Comparison*, Cambridge: Cambridge University Press.

Mueller, D. and Tilton, J. (1969) 'Research and development costs as a barrier to entry', *Canadian Journal of Economics*, 2, 570–9.

Nelson, P. (1970) 'Information and consumer behaviour', *Journal of Political Economy*, 78, 377–99.

Nelson, P. (1974) 'Advertising as information', *Journal of Political Economy*, 82, 729–54.

Nelson, R. (1990) 'The effects of competition on publically owned firms: evidence from the municipal electric industry in the US', *International Journal of Industrial Organization*, 8, 37–52.

Nelson, R. and Winter, S. (1982) *An Evolutionary Theory of Economic Growth*, Cambridge, MA: Harvard University Press.

Newman, H. (1978) 'Strategic groups and the structure–performance relationship', *Review of Economics and Statistics*, 60, 417–27.

Nickell, S. (1978) *The Investment Decisions of Firms*, Cambridge: Cambridge University Press.

OECD (1985) *Costs and Benefits of Protection*, Paris: OECD.

O'Farrell, P. and Crouchley, R. (1984) 'An indutrial and spatial analysis of new firm formation in Ireland', *Regional Studies*, 18, 221–36.

Office of Technology Assessment (1984) *Commercial Biotechnology: An International Analysis*, Washington, DC: Office of Technology Assessment.

Ogadiri, H. and Yamawaki, H. (1986) 'A study of company profits rate time series: Japan and the US', *International Journal of Industrial Organization*, 4, 1–24.

Omori, T. and Yarrow, G. (1982) 'Product diversification, entry prevention and limit pricing', *Bell Journal of Economics*, 13, 242–8.

Orr, D. (1974a) 'An index of entry barriers and its application to the market structure–performance relationship', *Journal of Industrial Economics*, 23, 39–49.

Orr, D. (1974b) 'The determinants of entry: a study of the Canadian manufacturing industries', *Review of Economics and Statistics*, 61, 58–66.

Osborne, D. (1973) 'On the rationality of limit pricing', *Journal of Industrial Economics*, 22, 71–80.

Oster, S. (1982a) 'Inter-industry structure and the ease of strategic change', *Review of Economics and Statistics*, 64, 376–83.

Oster, S. (1982b) 'The diffusion of innovation among steel firms: the basic oxygen process', *Bell Journal of Economics*, 13, 45–56.

Pakes, A. and Ericson, R. (1987) 'Empirical implications of alternative models of firm dynamics', mimeo, University of Wisconsin.

Parsons, D. and Ray, E. (1975) 'The US Steel consolidation: the creation of market control', *Journal of Law and Economics*, 18, 181–220.

Pashigan, P. (1968) 'Market concentration in the United States and Great Britain', *Journal of Law and Economics*, 11, 299–319.

Pauly, M. and Satterthwaite, M. (1981) 'The pricing of primary care physicians services: a test of the role of consumer information', *Bell Journal of Economics*, 12, 488–506.

Pavitt, K., Robson, M. and Townsend, J. (1987) 'The size distribution of innovating firms in the U.K., 1945–83', *Journal of Industrial Economics*, 35, 297–316.

Peck, J. (1962) 'Inventions in the post-war American aluminum industry', in *The Rate and Direction of Inventive Activity*, Princeton, NJ: Princeton University Press.

Peles, Y. (1971) 'Economies of scale in advertising, beer and cigarettes', *Journal of Business*, 44, 32–7.

Peltzman, S. (1965) 'Entry in commercial banking', *Journal of Law and Economics*, 8, 11–50.

Penrose, E. (1959) *The Theory of the Growth of the Firm*, Oxford: Basil Blackwell.

Perry, M. (1984) 'Scale economies, imperfect competition, and public policy', *Journal of Industrial Economics*, 32, 313–30.

Piore, M. and Sabel, C. (1984) *The Second Industrial Divide*, New York: Basic Books.

Porter, M. (1976a) *Interbrand Choice, Strategy and Bilateral Market Power*, Cambridge, MA: Harvard University Press.

292   *References*

Porter, M. (1976b) 'Interbrand choice, media mix, and market performance', *American Economic Review*, 66, 398–406.

Porter, M. (1979) 'The structure within industries and companies performance', *Review of Economics and Statistics*, 61, 214–28.

Porter, M. (1986) *Competition in Global Industries*, Boston, MA: Harvard Business School Press.

Porter, M. (1990) *The Competitive Advantage of Nations*, London: Macmillan.

Prais, S. (1976) *The Evolution of Giant Firms in Great Britain*, Cambridge: Cambridge University Press.

Prais, S. (1981) *Productivity and Industrial Structure*, Cambridge: Cambridge University Press.

Prescott, E. and Visscher, M. (1977) 'Sequential location among firms with perfect foresight', *Bell Journal of Economics*, 8, 378–93.

Primeaux, W. (1977) 'An assessment of x-efficiency gained through competition', *Review of Economics and Statistics*, 59, 105–8.

Rees, R. (1973) 'Optimum plant size in United Kingdom industries', *Economica*, 40, 394–401.

Reich, L. (1980) 'Industrial research and the pursuit of corporate security: the early years of Bell Labs', *Business History Review*, 54, 504–29.

Reinganum, M. and Smith, J. (1983) 'Investor preference for large firms', *Journal of Industrial Economics*, 32, 213–28.

Reiss, P. and Spiller, D. (1988) 'Competition and entry in small airline markets', mimeo, Stanford University.

Rizzo, J. and Zeckhauser, R. (1990) 'Advertising and entry: the case of physicians services', *Journal of Political Economy*, 98, 476–500.

Romeo, A. (1977a) 'Inter-industry and inter-firm differences in the rate of diffusion of an innovation', *Review of Economics and Statistics*, 57, 311–19.

Romeo, A. (1977b) 'The rate of imitation of a capital embodied process innovation', *Economica*, 44, 63–9.

Romanelli, E. (1987) 'New venture strategies in the minicomputer industry', *Californian Management Reviews*, 29, 160–75.

Rosenberg, N. (1974) 'Science, invention and economic growth', *Economic Journal*, 84, 90–108.

Rothwell, R. (1984) 'The role of small firms in the emergence of new technologies', *Omega*, 12, 19–29.

Rothwell, R. and Zegveld, W. (1985) *Reindustrialization and Technology*, London: Longman.

Salamon, G. (1985) 'Accounting rates of return', *American Economic Review*, 75, 495–504.

Saloner, G. (1986) 'The role of obsolescence and inventory costs in providing commitment', *International Journal of Industrial Organization*, 4, 333–45.

Salop, S. (1979) 'Strategic entry deterrence', *American Economic Review*, 69, 335–8.

Salop, S. and Scheffman, D. (1983) 'Raising rivals costs', *American Economic Review*, 73, 267–71.

Sargent, T. (1979) *Macroeconomic Theory*, London: Academic Press.

Saul, S. (1962) 'The motor industry in Britain in 1914', *Business History*, 5, 22-44.

Saving, T. (1961) 'Estimation of optimum size of plant by the survivor technique', *Quarterly Journal of Economics*, 75, 569-607.

Sawyer, M. (1971) 'Concentration in British manufacturing industry', *Oxford Economic Papers*, 23, 352-83.

Schelling, T. (1960) *The Strategy of Conflict*, Cambridge, MA: Harvard University Press.

Scherer, F. (1967) 'Market structure and the employment of scientists and engineers', *American Economic Review*, 57, 524-31.

Scherer, F. (1980) *Industrial Market Structure and Economic Performance*, 2nd edn, Chicago, IL: Houghton Mifflin.

Scherer, F. (1983) 'Concentration, R&D and productivity change', *Southern Economic Journal*, 50, 221-5.

Scherer, F. (1984) *Innovation and Growth: Schumpeterian Perspectives*, Cambridge, MA: MIT Press.

Schmalensee, R. (1972) *The Economics of Advertising*, Amsterdam: North-Holland.

Schmalensee, R. (1974) 'Brand loyalty and barriers to entry', *Southern Economic Journal*, 40, 579-88.

Schmalensee, R. (1978a) 'A model of advertising and product quality', *Journal of Political Economy*, 86, 485-503.

Schmalensee, R. (1978b) 'Entry deterrence in the ready to eat breakfast cereals industry', *Bell Journal of Economics*, 9, 305-27.

Schmalensee, R. (1981) 'Economics of scale and barriers to entry', *Journal of Political Economy*, 89, 1228-38.

Schmalensee, R. (1982) 'Product differentiation advantages of pioneering brands', *American Economic Review*, 72, 349-65.

Schmalensee, R. (1983) 'Advertising and entry deterrence: an exploratory model', *Journal of Political Economy*, 91, 636-53.

Schmalensee, R. (1987) 'Standards for dominant firm conduct: what can economics contribute?', in Hay, D. and Vickers, J. (eds), *The Economies of Market Dominance*, Oxford: Basil Blackwell.

Schmalensee, R. (1989) 'Interindustry studies of structure and performance', in Schmalensee, R. and Willig, R. (eds), *Handbook of Industrial Economics*, Amsterdam: North-Holland.

Schmitz, D. (1986) 'The rise of big business in the world copper industry, 1870-1930', *Economic History Review*, 39, 392-410.

Schott, K. (1976) 'Investment in private industrial research and development in Britain', *Journal of Industrial Economics*, 25, 81-99.

Schrieves, R. (1978) 'Market structure and innovation: a new perspective', *Journal of Industrial Economics*, 26, 329-47.

Schwalbach, J. (1987) 'Entry into German industries', *International Journal of Industrial Organization*, 5, 43-50.

Schwalbach, J. (1991) 'Entry, exit, concentration and market contestability', in Geroski, P. and Schwalbach, J. (eds), *Entry and Market Contestability: An International Comparison*, Oxford: Basil Blackwell.

Scott, J. (1981) 'The pure capital-cost barrier to entry', *Review of Economics and Statistics*, 63, 444-6.

Sengupta, J., Leonard, J. and Vango, J. (1983) 'A limit pricing model for the US computer industry', *Applied Economics*, 15, 297-308.

Sexton, R. and Sexton, T. (1987) 'Cooperatives as entrants', *Rand Journal of Economics*, 18, 581-95.

Shapiro, C. (1989) 'Theories of oligopoly behaviour', in Schmalensee, R. and Willig, R. (eds), *Handbook of Industrial Economics*, Amsterdam: North-Holland.

Shapiro, D. (1983) 'Entry, exit and the theory of the multinational corporation', in Audretsch, D. and Kindleberger, C. (eds), *The Multinational Corporation in the 1980's*, Cambridge, MA: MIT Press.

Shaw, R. (1973) 'Investment and competition from boom to recession: a case study in the process of competition – the dry cleaning industry', *Journal of Industrial Economics*, 21, 308-24.

Shaw, R. (1974) 'Price leadership and the effect of new entry in the UK retail petrol supply market', *Journal of Industrial Economics*, 23, 65-79.

Shaw, R. (1980) 'New entry and the competitive process in the UK fertilizer industry', *Scottish Journal of Political Economy*, 24, 1-16.

Shaw, R. (1982a) 'Product strategy and size of firm in the UK fertilizer market', *Managerial and Decision Economics*, 3, 233-43.

Shaw, R. (1982b) 'Product proliferation in characteristics space: the UK fertiliser industry', *Journal of Industrial Economics*, 31, 69-92.

Shaw, R. and Shaw, S. (1977) 'Patent expiry and competition in polyester fibres', *Scottish Journal of Political Economy*, 24, 117-32.

Shaw, R. and Shaw, S. (1984) 'Late entry, market shares and competitive survival: the case of synthetic fibres', *Managerial and Decision Economics*, 5, 72-9.

Shaw, R. and Simpson, P. (1985) 'The Monopolies Commission and the process of competition', *Fiscal Studies*, 6, 82-96.

Shaw, R. and Sutton, C. (1976) *Industry and Competition*, London: Macmillan.

Shepherd, W. (1967) 'What does the survivor technique show about economies of scale?', *Southern Economic Journal*, 34, 113-22.

Sherman, R. and Willet, T. (1967) 'Potential entrants discourage entry', *Journal of Political Economy*, 75, 400-3.

Sheshinski, E. and Dreze, J. (1976) 'Demand fluctuations, capacity utilization and costs', *American Economic Review*, 66, 731-42.

Siegfried, J. and Wheeler, J. (1981) 'Cost efficiency and monopoly power: a survey', *Quarterly Review of Economics and Business*, 21, 23-46.

Slater, M. (1980) 'The managerial limitation to the growth of firms', *Economic Journal*, 90, 520-8.

Smallwood, D. and Conlisk, J. (1979) 'Product quality in markets where consumers are imperfectly informed', *Quarterly Journal of Economics*, 93, 1-23.

Smiley, R. (1987) 'Who deters entry?', mimeo, Cornell University.

Smiley, R. (1988) 'Empirical evidence on strategic entry deterrence, *International Journal of Industrial Organization*, 6, 167-80.

Soukup, W. and Cooper, A. (1983) 'Strategic response to technological change in the electronic components industry', *R&D Management*, 13, 219–30.

Spence, M. (1977) 'Entry, capacity, investment and oligopolistic pricing', *Bell Journal of Economics*, 8, 534–44.

Spence, M. (1980) 'Notes on advertising, economies of scale and entry barriers', *Quarterly Journal of Economics*, 92, 493–507.

Spiller, P. and Favaro, E. (1984) 'The effects of entry regulation in oligopolistic interactions; the Uruguayan banking sector', *Rand Journal of Economics*, 15, 244–54.

Spital, F. (1983) 'Gaining market share advantage in the semiconductor industry by lead time in innovation', in *Research on Technological Innovation, Management and Policy*, Greenwich, CT: JAI Press.

Steedman, H. and Wagner, K. (1989) 'Productivity, machinery and skills: clothing manufacture in Britain and Germany', *National Institute Economic Review*, 130, 40–57.

Stigler, G. (1958) 'The economies of scale', *Journal of Law and Economics*; reprinted in his *The Organization of Industry*, Homewood, IL: Richard D. Irwin, 1968.

Stigler, G. (1965) 'The dominant firm and the inverted umbrella', *Journal of Law and Economics*; reprinted in his *The Organization of Industry*, Homewood, IL: Richard D. Irwin, 1968.

Stigler, G. (1968) 'Barriers to entry, economies of scale and firm size', in his *The Organization of Industry*, Homewood, IL: Richard D. Irwin.

Storey, D. and Johnson, S. (1987) *Job Generation and Labour Market Change*, London: Macmillan.

Storey, D., Keasey, K., Watson, R. and Wynarczyk, P. (1987) *The Performance of Small Firms*, London: Croom Helm.

Suslow, V. (1986) 'Estimating monopoly behaviour with competitive recycling: an application to Alcan', *Rand Journal of Economics*, 17, 389–403.

Suzumura, K. and Kiyaro, K. (1987) 'Entry barriers and economic welfare', *Review of Economic Studies*, 54, 157–68.

Sveikauskas, C. and Sveikauskas, L. (1982) 'Industry characteristics and productivity growth', *Southern Economic Journal*, 48, 769–74.

Swann, P. (1990) 'Product competition and the dimensions of product space', *International Journal of Industrial Organization*, 8, 281–96.

Thompson, D. (1987) 'Privatization in the UK: deregulation and the advantage of incumbency', *European Economic Review*, 31, 368–74.

Thompson, R. (1987) 'New entry and hedonic price discounts: the case of the Irish car market', *Oxford Bulletin of Economics and Statistics*, 49, 373–84.

Thompson, R. (1986) 'Entry and market characteristics: a logit study of newspaper launching in the Republic of Ireland', *Journal of Economic Studies*, 13, 14–22.

Tilton, J. (1971) *International Diffusion of Technology: The Case of Semiconductors*, Washington, DC: Brookings Institution.

Tirole, J. (1988) *The Theory of Industrial Organization*, Cambridge, MA: MIT Press.

Trapani, J. and Olson, C. (1982) 'An analysis of the impact of open entry on price and the quality of service in the airline industry', *Review of Economics and Statistics*, 64, 67-76.

Urban, G., Carter, T., Gaskin, S. and Mucha, Z. (1984) 'Market share rewards to pioneering brands', *Management Science*, 32, 645-59.

Utterback, J. and Abernathy, W. (1975) 'A dynamic model of product and process innovation', *Omega*, 6, 639-56.

Utton, M. (1979) *Diversification and Competition*, Cambridge: Cambridge University Press.

Van Herck, G. (1984) 'Entry, exit and profitability', *Managerial and Decision Economics*, 5, 25-31.

Vickers, J. and Yarrow, G. (1988) *Privatization: An Economic Analysis*, Cambridge, MA: MIT Press.

Vives, X. (1988) 'Sequential entry, industry structure and welfare', *European Economic Review*, 32, 167-87.

Von Weizsacker, C. (1980) 'A welfare analysis of barriers to entry', *Bell Journal of Economics*, 11, 399-420.

Ware, R. (1985) 'Inventory holdings as a strategic weapon to deter entry', *Economica*, 52, 93-102.

Waterson, M. (1981) 'On the definition and meaning of barriers to entry', *Anti-Trust Bulletin*, 26, 521-39.

Waterson, M. and Lopez, A. (1983) 'The determinants of research and development intensity in the U.K.', *Applied Economics*, 15, 379-91.

Weiss, L. (1963) 'Factors in changing concentration', *Review of Economics and Statistics*, 45, 70-7.

Weiss, L. (1964) 'The survivor technique and the extent of sub-optimal capacity', *Journal of Political Economy*, 72, 246-61.

Weiss, L. (1974) 'The concentration–profit relationship and anti-trust', in Goldschmid, H., Mann, H.M. and Weston, J.F. (eds), *Industrial Concentration: The New Learning*, Boston, MA: Little, Brown.

Wenders, J. (1971) 'Excess capacity as a barrier to entry', *Journal of Industrial Economics*, 20, 14-19.

West, D. (1981) 'Testing for market preemption using sequential location data', *Bell Journal of Economics*, 12, 129-43.

White, L. (1971) *The Automobile Industry Since 1945*, Cambridge, MA: Harvard University Press.

White, L. (1976) 'Appropriate technology, x-inefficiency and a competitive environment: some evidence from Pakistan', *Quarterly Journal of Economics*, 90, 575-89.

Willard, G. and Savara, A. (1988) 'Patterns of entry: pathways to new markets', *California Management Review*, 30, 57-76.

Williamson, O. (1963) 'Selling expense as a barrier to entry', *Quarterly Journal of Economics*, 77, 112-28.

Williamson, O. (1968) 'Wage rates as a barrier to entry', *Quarterly Journal of Economics*, 82, 85-116.

Winter, S. (1984) 'Schumpeterian competition in alternative technological regimes', *Journal of Economic Behavior and Organization*, 5, 287-320.

Worcester, D. (1957) 'Why dominant firms decline', *Journal of Political Economy*, 65, 338-47.

Yamawaki, H. (1985) 'Dominant firm pricing and fringe expansion: the case of the US iron and steel industry, 1907-30', *Review of Economics and Statistics*, 67, 429-37.

Yamawaki, H. (1991) 'The effects of business conditions on net entry: evidence from Japan', in Geroski, P. and Schwalbach, J. (eds), *Entry and Market Contestability: An International Comparison*, Oxford: Basil Blackwell.

Yip, G. (1982a) *Barriers to Entry: A Corporate-Strategy Perspective*, Lexington, MA: Lexington Books.

Yip, G. (1982b) 'Gateways to entry', *Harvard Business Review*, 60, 85-92.

Index

302

Index